MW00680106

Kaca L Penna

# Levels of Analysis in Psychology

# Levels of Analysis in Psychology

A Companion Reader for Use with
the IB Psychology Course

Jennie Brooks Jamison, M.Ed.
St. Petersburg High School IB Program, Florida

**Worth Publishers**
**New York**

*Senior Publisher:* Catherine Woods
*Acquisitions Editor:* Erik Gilg
*Marketing Manager:* Cindy Weiss
*Development Editor:* Valerie Raymond
*Associate Managing Editor:* Tracey Kuehn
*Project Editor:* Jenny Chiu
*Cover Designer:* Kevin Kall
*Text Designer:* Lee Ann McKevitt
*Production Manager:* Barbara Anne Seixas
*Composition:* Northeastern Graphic, Inc.
*Printing and Binding:* Victor Graphics

"International Baccalaureate" is a registered trademark of the International Baccalaureate Organization (IB). The material in this text has been developed independently of the IB, which was not involved in the production of this text and in no way endorses it.

Library of Congress Control Number: 2009928468

ISBN-13: 978-1-4292-3813-7
ISBN-10: 1-4292-3813-5

Printed in the United States of America

First Printing

Worth Publishers
41 Madison Avenue
New York, NY 10010
www.worthpublishers.com

# About the Author

Jennie Brooks Jamison, M.Ed., has been teaching International Baccalaureate (IB) psychology since 1986 at St. Petersburg High School in Florida. Jennie leads workshops for IB psychology and is an experienced examiner for the internal assessment project and external exams. Jennie's first book, *Research Methods in Psychology for High School Students,* was published in 2006. Jennie lives in St. Petersburg, Florida with her husband and three cats.

# Contents

# Preface

"I am not a test score!" How many times have I heard this complaint about the educational system's focus on standardized testing? I agree with Jerome Bruner (1977) that there is far too much emphasis on achievement testing than on the intellectual atmosphere of the classroom. Education is most relevant when it prepares students *for the future.* It is far more beneficial for students to have an understanding of a subject than it is for them to see the material simply as facts. *Drawing defensible relationships between ideas* is a critical skill for organizing large amounts of information. Facts come and go, but thinking is always applicable. Investments in thinking are not easily demonstrated on objective tests. This is why I support the IB program; the test is about thinking. The *process* of learning *is* the IB test preparation.

Psychology is maturing and the IB psychology syllabus reflects its advancements. It is no longer useful to think of human behavior in terms of compartmentalized perspectives. Nature *versus* nurture is now the interaction between nature *and* nurture. The IB psychology syllabus has a future-oriented framework. Its integrative level of analysis approach provides a more complex but realistic view of human behavior. New research will fit right into the framework, and the framework is unlikely to go out of style. Although people believe new advancements in a subject will simplify explanations, in fact, it is the other way around. Advancements in research show more complexity.

The IB psychology course is more concept driven rather than topic/fact driven. Even when topics are specified, the learning outcomes ask primarily for high-level processing.

Teachers have a great deal of freedom to select the material they wish to teach. The trick to teaching the IB psychology course is to sample a range of topics without littering the table with too many topics. Students tend to manage large amounts of unrelated facts by compartmentalizing the information. They easily get lost in the vast amount of facts available. Can we select a small number of topics and demonstrate how the required concepts are related to each other?

Introductory texts are useful for explaining basic concepts, and provide wonderful diagrams and pictures. However, the purpose of an introductory text is to introduce students to a broad range of material. IB psychology is not an introductory course, and students must go beyond the basics. The purpose of this book is to help students make meaning of the IB psychology syllabus.

I had two main challenges in writing this book. One was to break down important ideas without losing their complexity. The other was to thread a small number of topics through the required concepts.

The small number of topics in this book is a model for threading ideas through the levels of analysis. I teach more topics in my course, but I use the same approach.

## Note to the student

1. This book supplements an introductory psychology text with up-to-date, in-depth information relevant to the IB syllabus. My goal is to prepare you to earn top marks on the exam. It is hard to find a lot of in-depth information all in one book.

2. This book follows the IB syllabus headings, called "learning outcomes," for Paper 1 and the abnormal psychology option. I created a few extra headings to provide context for the learning outcomes, and contribute to the cross-cultural focus of the book.

3. All questions on the IB exams come from the learning outcomes. Each learning outcome contains a "command term," and each term is defined in the syllabus guide. The command terms reflect different levels of Benjamin Bloom's taxonomy.

4. IB test questions will contain command terms *at or below* the level stated in the learning outcome. The syllabus contains all of the command terms in the order of their depth. You should be prepared to respond to questions at the highest level stated in the learning outcomes.

## Note to the teacher

I plan on teaching the IB psychology course from learning outcome to learning outcome. I changed the order of some learning outcomes, so that some fundamental aspects of each level of analysis come first and support the other learning outcomes.

I added a few headings of my own for depth and transition, and to create an international perspective. The chapter on behaviorism is my own invention; it will help you find the right place for classical and operant conditioning in a course taking a level of analysis approach.

The discussion of each learning outcome takes an integrative approach, and the material from each learning outcome includes supporting material from other levels of analysis. The discussions show students how to start and follow through with an argument about the topics and thread the arguments through all parts of the course related to Papers 1 and 2. Frequently, more than one study relevant to each learning outcome is detailed so students have some choices.

Notes to the teacher are included throughout the book to direct you to important films, activities, or ideas to keep in mind as you teach.

Last, I selected many articles that are free on the Internet, so you could read the original papers. The References at the end of this book includes the source of these articles. Every time I read something I like, I look up the article title on the reference page and Google it. Oftentimes, the article is free.

# Acknowledgments

This book would not have been possible without the help of many people. I thank my husband John Jamison for doing a lot of extra housework and being patient during the writing process. Erik Gilg and Cindy Weiss from Worth Publishers were willing to take a chance on a new idea. Valerie Raymond, my development editor, made a huge contribution with her suggestions as I edited the draft. Francine Almash, my copyeditor, was extremely helpful to me in polishing the final draft of the book. I am extremely grateful to Hank Davis, IB psychology teacher and workshop leader, for his comments and support throughout the project. Hank and Mario Nogare, another IB psychology teacher and workshop leader, reviewed a draft for Worth and made valuable comments. And as in my first book, John Brooks, my father and statistics instructor at Virginia Commonwealth University, contributed to my statistical knowledge. Last, I am indebted to Martin Tarter, my teacher at Virginia Commonwealth University and career-long mentor. He is the one who pounded into my head the advantages of designing curriculum centered on drawing relationships between ideas and spending "time at the starting gate."

The following researchers were generous enough to send me articles that I had difficulty obtaining. They made it possible for me to include the up-to-date information that I wanted to use. They are Nigel Blackwell, Susan Bookheimer, Cynthia Bulik, Avshalom Caspi, Larry Christensen, Robert Cialdini, Roger Giner-Sorolla, Rachel Hull, Hyeonjeong Jeong, James Jones, Donald Price, Laura Southgate, Deborah Stipek, Yohtaro Takano, and Qi Wang.

# 1 Introduction

What can I give you to take home each day from a psychology class that will help you successfully navigate through a more and more complex world? How can I use psychology to give you personal strength and hope for the future? Can I challenge you to think about the development of your own thinking?

Psychology is where you learn how to live and the information should give you a sense of control over your future. Psychology applies to all aspects of our lives, such as raising children, taking care of mental and physical health, understanding friends and family, getting the edge as an athlete, considering the best way to teach, avoiding blunders from misunderstanding other cultures, and succeeding in careers such as medicine, law, and business.

Making meaning of human behavior is not easy. Many things contribute to any one behavior. Do not be fooled by popular media that makes it *appear* as if human behavior or answers to life's difficult problems are simple.

This book is a companion to an introductory text. Introductory texts give basic information on topics such as neurotransmitters, schemas, eyewitness testimony, and conformity. Introductory texts would be far too large for you to carry if an author included fully developed discussions on each psychological concept and related it to all the other ideas.

I do not define the same words that are in a traditional introductory text. Instead, I talk *about* the topics in more depth and organize the book around IB learning outcomes.

I use **culture** as an organizing principle to unite the material. There are two reasons for this. One is the scope of the program. This is a lot of material to cover and students need a way of organizing everything. Culture mediates all behavior, even gene expression, and is a framework that will survive into the future of psychology. Another is that we are learning more and more about how psychological concepts unfold within cultures and must answer the question, to what extent do psychological concepts apply to everyone? Under the umbrella of culture, I thread four topics and some important concepts through the Paper 1 and abnormal psychology learning outcomes. The four topics are **language**, mental illness (featuring **depression**, **anorexia**, and related material on **stress** and health), **aggression**, and **education**. Important concepts include **neuroplasticity**, **schema**, and **social learning**. Much of the material discussed under the Paper 1 learning outcomes is also relevant for the abnormal, health, and developmental psychology options. **Gender** pops up regularly; it does not need a separate heading.

This book is divided into two parts. Part one examines three levels of analysis: biological, cognitive, and sociocultural. The levels work together to produce complex behavior. Individual researchers tend to specialize in one level of analysis, but modern psychologists recognize that the three work together. Part two takes a level of analysis approach to the abnormal psychology option—an option that is very popular with students.

I use two **bidirectional** models (defined in section 3.4) as our point of departure for examining how the levels of analysis work together. A level of analysis approach assumes bidirectional thinking. All current psychology is bidirectional.

A level of analysis approach is different from a perspectives approach. In the past, psychology was thought of as a series of competing perspectives, such as behavioral, humanistic, biological, cognitive, and psychodynamic. Categories of perspectives even changed over time. An earlier IB psychology syllabus defined the perspectives as behavioral, humanistic, psychodynamic, and cognitive. A later IB syllabus omitted psychodynamic as a perspective and included biological. Many texts still use perspectives but are moving to a level of analysis approach. Currently, perspectives have merged into a more complex view of human behavior where all the levels contribute something to explanations. Any **reductionism** perceived in these levels of analysis is really an attempt by theorists to pull apart and examine one aspect of behavior. Steven Pinker (2002) divides reductionism into two categories, **good reductionism**, also called hierarchical reductionism, and **bad reductionism**. Good reductionists specialize in one level of analysis but do not have the same goals as the bad reductionists, also known as destructive reductionists. Pinker defines bad reductionism as theories "trying to explain a phenomenon in terms of its smallest or simplest constituents" (pp. 69–70). Pinker writes that bad reductionists hope that a breakthrough will revolutionize an entire field. Good reductionists investigate one aspect, or level of analysis, of a behavior, but do not attempt to replace existing explanations from other levels of analysis. Humans are always cognitively processing information, the brain is always active during cognitive processing, and culture mediates the entire process. Good reductionists join with others to produce richer accounts of behavior. Bad reductionists are now part of psychology's history.

You may be less certain about *why* humans behave the way they do after reading this book. But you should have a greater understanding of the *complexities* of human behavior, why it is difficult to provide concrete explanations, and how to offer some *tentative* explanations. It is a more realistic goal. Sorry, there is no simple way to analyze others.

An introductory text is background reading for my book; I build on the material while following the IB syllabus learning outcomes. In addition, there are places where I provide more details about important topics. Examples are Bandura's social learning theory, Triandis' ideas on individualism and collectivism, and an introduction to Traditional Chinese Medicine (TCM) with its applications to abnormal and health psychology.

In no way does this book try to cover all existing research on the four topic areas or abnormal psychology. The examples just illustrate the type of research available on the topics and add more depth.

The IB program is *supposed* to be a challenging intellectual experience. However, IB psychology does not need to be overwhelming. The trick is to have some good organizing principles. The IB program should push you beyond what you would do on your own. The IB program gives teachers a format to make students, in Vygotskian terms, a head taller than they are in normal life.

# Ideas That Organize Facts

This is a very short chapter. What is the best way to remember a large number of concepts for the IB exam? A small group of ideas organize everything. Try and relate all of the material to these organizing ideas. Facts related to meaningful ideas are easier to remember. Eventually you should say, "I keep seeing the same thing over and over." Once you can say this it means you are drawing defensible relationships between ideas.

The theme of this book is *humans living together in cultures*. The theme is certainly appropriate for a program promoting internationalism. Influential researchers such as Harry Triandis and Susan Fiske, both reviewed in Chapter 5, make it clear that cultural considerations have changed modern psychology.

**1.** All behavior must be understood in terms of **culture**. Cultural values affect behavior to a great extent. All cultures have **schemas** for thinking about behavior and these schemas are often **reifications**. Reifying means to turn abstract ideas into real things. Definitions of abnormal behavior are often reifications. (Section 4.4 includes a discussion of schemas about abnormal behavior and reifying.) Ideas that benefit a group become valued and, therefore, real for that group, even if those ideas are not actually real. Your own values are culturally determined. Sometimes we do not think about how our culture influences our actions; our behavior is too familiar. Humans need schemas; schemas are innate and assist in cognitive processing. But cultural values determine what goes into schemas.

**2.** Human behavior is adaptive, meaning that we are constantly changing to fit the circumstances. Practices that serve a group well become culture. Culture is then socially transmitted to children through **language**. **Social learning theory** is applied at all levels of analysis, and since it is required, go ahead and thread it throughout the program.

**3.** Humans are social beings. Most of our time is spent thinking about other's thinking and making meaning out of the social world. A large body of research shows that humans evolved a **social intelligence** to make sense of social relationships. The human mind is set up to think about other's thoughts, called "mindreading" (the **theory of mind**), which is explained, along with social intelligence, in section 3.5. Language is essential to mindreading and is a good cognitive process to thread through the course.

**4.** Psychology has moved away from bad **reductionism** to more complex **bidirectional** models of human behavior. Bidirectional means that biology and the environment influence each other in a reciprocal (give and take or complementary) relationship. **Neuroplasticity**, or brain changes in response to the environment, is critical to understanding modern bidirectional thinking.

**5.** I have two generalizations about genetics that are helpful to understanding behavior within a level of analysis framework.

    **a.** Genes cannot affect behavior unless they are expressed. There is complex interplay between genes, other genes, and the sociocultural environment.

    **b.** The brain is a product of its environmental history over the lifespan.

## Why I Promote Studying Modern Research

*Modern research is where you are going to see the levels of analysis.* A level of analysis approach implies integration. This is what I expect from psychology as a maturing discipline. Older theories and research are often compartmentalized, unrelated, and contradictory.

Because modern research is integrated, it is possible to *thread* a small number of topics through the entire syllabus. A smaller number of organizing concepts relate the topics elegantly.

This does not mean to throw out everything from the past. Some older research is still relevant to modern psychology and fits in with modern ideas. One example is Bandura's Bobo experiments (section 5.15). You only need to know *why* the Bobo experiments are still relevant, which is the kind of thing I address in this book. Sometimes a study appears dated due to the time period the research was conducted. One example is Michael Cole's research on the Kpelle in Africa about cognitive skills (section 4.7)—more than 40 years later, Cole's findings are still relevant. But while some historical studies are still valid, others are outdated or have been greatly modified.

## Relating My Organizing Ideas to the Critical-Thinking Framework in the IB Syllabus

The IB syllabus *does not demand* that students study modern psychology. However, it *does* say that the different parts of the syllabus should *complement* each other. Modern research draws more relationships between syllabus headings. While the IB syllabus consists of distinct headings, the topics are actually quite intertwined and are united under culture.

The IB syllabus contains a section reminding students to use a critical-thinking framework. My organizing principles and approach in the book emphasize this framework. The guide directs us to avoid oversimplification and reductionism, tolerate uncertainty, keep a cross-cultural focus, and evaluate research methods.

This is a whole lot for teenagers to do.

Adolescent minds are still developing. Sometimes students need help drawing relationships and seeing how ideas are integrated. I often point out how concepts thread through the topics. In addition, I frequently remind students that a study is useful for other headings.

# 3 The Biological Level of Analysis

## 3.1 Introduction to the Biological Level of Analysis

The first lesson of a class is the most important; I need you to buy into studying some pretty complex topics and stick with them over the entire course. I call the first lesson the "time at the starting gate." This is when I spend some time cultivating an interest in the levels of analysis.

When I mention biology to students there is usually a lot of cringing around the room. Biology is so often associated with memorizing facts about the brain or conducting dissections. My approach is different; we want to look at the people part of biology. Knowing about a section of the brain or a gene is most relevant when it relates to living in our social world. I feel compelled to start with the biological level of analysis if only to get rid of misconceptions about genetic determinism; the idea that "genes cause behavior" in a direct way. Helping you realize how much control we have over what happens to us is a primary goal of my class. The material in the course is not just about preparing for an exam. It is a way to think about the world and how you want to live your lives. In addition, biological concepts are the building blocks of behavior, which I locate at the base of my general bidirectional model (see section 3.4).

Two topics that my students find fascinating are autism and the teenage brain, so following a very short section on the principles that define the biological level of analysis, I included a section on these topics. After that we'll look at some basics on genetics and then move onto the other headings from the IB syllabus.

## 3.2 Outline Principles That Define the Biological Level of Analysis

I start each of the three chapters in part one with basic principles for you to keep in mind as you read. The syllabus guide mandates that students be able to explain how these principles are demonstrated in theory and research.

Current psychologists investigating the biological level of analysis assume that certain principles are true before they start their work. These assumptions cannot be *proven* true, but are believed to underline theory and research in biological psychology. Here are a few that are useful for a modern integrated level of analysis approach to psychology:

1. Biological psychologists reject the idea that the mind exists independently of the physical brain. This means that any time you are thinking, the brain is doing something important in the background that becomes fundamental to behavior.

2. Genes are an important basis of behavior but are not the entire story. The expression of genes depends on their interaction with environmental factors and other genes. Behavior is the result of a **bidirectional** process, though biological psychologists emphasize inherited factors and **evolution** in their research. Again, bidirectional means that biology and the environment influence each other in a reciprocal relationship. It is accepted that sociocultural and cognitive factors shape the brain.

5

3. Animal models establish a base from which to consider human behavior. While researchers cannot make a direct generalization from animal research to human behavior, animal research is useful for the exploration of human behavior. Animal research increases the **method triangulation**, meaning that studies using different research methods show the same thing, behind claims about human behavior, especially when it is unethical to experiment on humans.

Principle #1 works in the background of all psychological concepts. All modern biological studies illustrate principle #2. This is an advantage of taking a modern approach; theory and research are easily related and unified. While my book does not highlight animal research, principle #3, I have an example of a mouse **knockout** (see section 3.4) study, meaning that mice are engineered to lack the expression of a gene; in this case the nNos gene is "knocked out" to study its link to aggression. I include animal research where they give context or support to human studies.

## 3.3 The Time at the Starting Gate: Getting Interested in the Levels of Analysis by Studying Autism and the Teenage Brain

David Matsumoto (2008) and Michael Tomasello (2004) make it clear that *humans evolved to live in cultures; cultures that required the evolution of complex biologically based language and cognitive abilities for development.* Human culture is always evolving and is very different from the world of animals. I use the words biology, cognitive, and culture all in one sentence but note that culture gets the top position. Take everything you study back to this opening sentence. All complex human behavior takes place within all three levels of analysis. When a group of people do not function in all three levels, it is an opportunity to investigate why all three levels of analysis are important. The study of autism is one such opportunity.

### What is autism?

#### Note to the teacher

My course starts with two films. One is *The Impact of Disorders and Trauma on the Social Brain*. The other is *Rage for Order: Autism*. Both are available from Films for the Humanities and Sciences. The films introduce some people with autism so you can see what their lives are like. In addition, we can learn a great deal about the purpose of human culture.

Autism is a disorder organized around severe deficiencies in social interaction and communication. For example, people with autism are not very interested in relationships with other humans (DSM-IV-TR, 2000). Many autistics never develop language. Even high functioning autistics have delays in language development and have trouble decoding the intentions of others in social relationships. Autistic persons have limited and rigid interests, such as extensive detailed knowledge of a specific topic. Their impairment is obviously outside of normal functioning.

### The case of Temple Grandin

Temple Grandin provides a useful example. She is a high functioning autistic; do not think that most autistics are like her. Temple is an associate professor at Colorado State University with a specialty in cattle management. Temple's language development was delayed until between ages 3 and 4, which is actually early for many autistics. It was very frustrating for

Temple and she could not communicate with words. Instead she screamed or made noises. Temple developed a squeeze machine to help her manage her anxieties and later this machine was adapted to help calm animals in slaughter houses. Temple was lucky that someone recognized her talents and helped her develop a life around a career.

Temple refers to other humans as ISPs, or interesting sociological phenomena (Grandin, 1999). She openly admits that autistic people are socially inept. Other humans are too complicated and Temple avoids complex social relationships. Temple believes it is more productive to help autistics organize their lives around a career rather than try to improve their social skills. Temple did not even realize that humans communicated emotions through their eyes until she read Simon Baron-Cohen's book about mindblindness. Baron-Cohen's book is discussed in section 3.5 about the evolution of social intelligence.

Temple has a clear rule system with four categories to guide her social behavior. The first is "really bad things," such as murder. The second is "courtesy rules" such as table manners. The third is "illegal but not bad" such as illegal parking, though Temple says taking a handicapped parking space is especially a problem because it also infringes on courtesy rules. The last is "sins of the system," such as going to jail for using illegal drugs. Anytime Temple faces a social situation, these four categories guide her behavior. Temple is celibate because the rules about social relationships are so complex and emotional that she fears that she might commit a sin of the system. Temple thinks jobs are so important for autistic people that they should never jeopardize them by committing a sin of the system in a social relationship with a colleague. Temple says that autistic people have to learn sets of rules and follow them exactly. Navigating social relationships is hard, but if an autistic person wants to date and marry, they should do it outside of work with someone who shares career interests. Autistic people rarely marry and have children. An autistic person would have trouble transmitting culture to the next generation. In fact, autistics need the assistance of other people who are concerned about their welfare to give them cues about how to behave in a world they have trouble understanding.

Temple thinks in sets of pictures similar to a series of Internet pages stored in her long-term memory. Temple scrolls through these "Web pages" for clues relating to her rigid categories before deciding what to do. Temple says she can pass simple "theory of mind tests" (see section 3.5) that require someone to view a situation as another might. But Temple has trouble passing complex mindreading tests. In addition, she has trouble thinking "on her feet" when faced with new social situations where there is no available "Web page." By age 4, most children consistently pass mindreading tests and use information for social purposes. Many autistics cannot pass mindreading tests at all.

The typical person does not create rigid categories that fit every social situation. People receive and process cues from individuals, the group, the situation, and the larger cultural expectations before deciding what to do. They respond one way in a specific context and then differently in another, unlike people with autism. I recommend getting to know Temple by reading her article in class.

Autistic people really exist outside of the human cultural context. Autistics are intelligent and are capable of learning detailed physical information but lack the symbolic mental representations needed to process other's social behavior (Pinker, 2002). For example, an autistic may know detailed information about electrical equipment or the weather, but the information is not used to navigate through human social relationships. Rather, it is recited.

The social learning process in autistics is damaged. Attempts at social learning in autistics do not meet the demands of human culture. For example, many autistics imitate in odd ways, such as echoing another's speech instead of trying to make sense of it (Pinker, 2002). The poor social functioning in autistics is caused by damage to the social brain. This damage often starts early in fetal development. An essential feature of our evolved human culture is that we think about what others are thinking, and we adjust behavior accordingly to what we think others are thinking (Matsumoto, 2008). For example, when meeting someone new, you automatically start evaluating the other person. Are they nice or smart? Do they seem to like you? In addition, you manage impressions about yourself for the benefit of the other person's same judgments about you. We instinctively read other's intentions when we meet up with someone in a social situation and make appropriate changes as needed. We do not scroll through a series of pictures in our minds before deciding what to do; we automatically behave in give and take social relationships that are tied to language. Think of all the social negotiations that go on with a simple task such as manufacturing clothing on a large scale. If humans could not work together, each individual would make their own clothing, including growing and weaving.

## The teenage brain: The brain needs the sociocultural environment to develop

Studying autistics is an opportunity to realize how important the social context is to development and what happens when the brain is not equipped to enter human culture. Another example of the importance of the cultural environment relates directly to the **adolescent brain** and adolescent behavior. Why is it that adolescents sometimes come into conflict with adults? The answer may lie in the brain.

Some states have laws forbidding adolescents from driving with other adolescents in the car for the first year after they receive their license. Why is this? Research shows that teens are more likely to make poor decisions in everyday life, even though cognitive tests show they are as smart as adults (Steinberg, 2008). The different rate of maturation of emotional and cognitive functions is the reason. The arousal of the social/emotional system matures quickly starting at puberty. Cognitive skills mature later. Steinberg said that teen decisions are often analogous to starting the engine before a skilled driver is behind the wheel. The results of research on the developing adolescent prefrontal cortex have shaped laws about teen driving.

### Note to the teacher

> I show the *Frontline* film "Inside the Teenage Brain," available from www.pbs.org along with this material.

There are a few brain parts in tact at birth. The **amygdala** is one, which makes it likely that it is important for survival. One thing the amygdala is responsible for is the fear response, without which we might not live very long. However, most of the brain is immature at birth and develops within a social/cultural context. One example is **language** development. We come equipped with the ability to learn language but the actual language we need must be acquired. Another example is the **prefrontal cortex**. The prefrontal cortex has a major growth spurt during adolescence. Excess neurons die off as the brain is refined. It makes sense that the brain waits this long to mature. If you were born with a mature brain it would be more difficult to learn. Every time you learn something, new neurons are created in the brain. Since most of human behavior must be transmitted through the culture, children need their brains to adapt. If you play musical instrument, these neurons are emphasized. If you play a sport, other neurons are emphasized. If you use drugs or are under continual stress, then neuron damage can occur.

Scientists used to think that the human brain was generally developed by age 5. We know now that this is not true. The undeveloped frontal cortex may be a good explanation for why teenagers sometimes have poor self-control, make bad decisions, and engage in risk-taking behavior (Sabbagh, 2006). Sabbagh reports an experiment by Beatriz Luna where **fMRI** scans were used to compare adult and adolescent brains while completing a task. Participants were told to either focus on the flashing lights generated from a computer or to try and avoid looking at the lights. Teenagers used far more of their prefrontal cortex than the adults did. It appears this small task was much harder for the teens. Adults used large portions of their prefrontal cortexes only during far more complicated activities. Other research by Deborah Yurgelun-Todd (*Frontline,* 1999) suggests that teens use their brains differently than adults. Teens may rely on the limbic system more to make decisions than adults. An fMRI scan examined the brains of adults and teenagers as they identified emotions from photographs of adult faces. The teens used their limbic systems to try and guess the emotions differently from the adults. The teens were less able than the adults to identify the emotions and emotional parts of the limbic system. However, there is some contradictory research suggesting that there may be situations when adolescents use their brains the same way that adults do. The topic needs more research.

I want to end this section with an important generalization—*the brain is a product of its environmental history over the lifespan.* The teen brain needs a healthy environment to mature properly. The brains of autistic persons develop more slowly and differently, but still respond to the environment.

Scientists are beginning to understand how everything comes together. However, the more we learn about the human brain and cognitive abilities developing in a cultural context, the more complex the picture becomes. Any new knowledge leads to more questions. This is the reality of knowing. The rest of this chapter explores how the brain transforms into the mind within a cultural context.

## 3.4 To What Extent Does Genetic Inheritance Influence Behavior? Bidirectional Thinking: Genes, Behavior, and Important Models

### To what extent does genetic inheritance influence behavior?

Genes are important but do not exist in a vacuum.

It is common for people to blame their personality, their ADHD, their depression, or their health problems on their genes. I think that popular media is responsible for creating the widely held misconception that genes directly cause behavior. *We must become better consumers of media.* Complex human behavior is not caused by a single gene. Genetic determinism is *no longer accepted.* We must give the old phrase "nature versus nurture" a proper burial. Modern psychologists study the interplay between nature *and* nurture.

Knowing that genes do not directly determine complex behavior gives us hope that we can make effective changes in our lives and helps us understand that life events shape behavior. In an article aptly titled, "My genes made me do it," Stanton Peele and Richard De-Grandpre (1995) explain that "Americans are increasingly likely to attribute their own—and others'—behavior to innate biological causes" (p. 1). Peele and DeGrandpre suggest that demands for clear causes of behavior rest on incorrect assumptions about genes and how they influence behavior. "The quest for genetic explanations of why we do what we do more accurately reflects the desire for hard certainties about frightening societal problems than the true complexities of human affairs" (p. 1). This article is worth reading and is available free at the Stanton Peele Addiction Web site, www.peele.net/lib/genes.html.

Then how do we answer the question, "To what extent do genes influence behavior?" The answer is a little tricky. Genes are the building blocks of behavior and influence behavior to some extent, but they are not the entire story. The answer is that genes *contribute* to complex behavior rather than determine it. It may be helpful to think about genes this way—*genes cannot affect behavior unless they are expressed*. We are even learning more about how to *prevent* the expression of genes for behaviors we do not want.

While modern psychologists know that genes do not determine complex behavior, what we *do* know about genetic contributions is getting stronger. The study of **epigenetics**, **gene-environment correlations**, and **cultural neuroscience** are revolutionizing our understanding of genetics.

## Note to the student and teacher

> Epigenetics, gene-environment correlations, and cultural neuroscience are where you are going to see the levels of analysis in genetics research.

**Epigenetics**, meaning "beyond genetics," studies how factors such as parenting and stress affect the expression of genes (Higgins, 2008). Psychologists are finding out that positive parenting, stress reduction, dietary changes, exercise, psychotherapy, or medication may prevent gene expression for unwanted behaviors such as depression. Armed with knowledge from epigenetic studies, psychologists can help people become more resilient to mental and physical health problems.

**Gene-environment correlation** is a research method useful for studying how genetic differences between people shape the way they respond to their environment (Caspi et al., 2003). Gene-environment interaction is a popular buzzword in modern psychology, but it is one thing to say that environmental factors interact with genes and quite another to actually show the relationship in a study. Gene-environment correlation studies can now show the interaction. One example is research on depression and 5-HTT, the serotonin transporter gene. Some people are genetically predisposed to be more reactive to life stressors and this increases their risk of depression. In the past, psychologists could not always demonstrate genetic contributions because of limitations in research methodology (Caspi et al., 2003). Now scientists can study people with specific life histories and compare them to people with other life histories to test the importance of genes as they interact with particular environments. While some people carry more risk for depression or aggression, awareness can reduce the risk. The results of gene-environment correlation studies help shape **resilience** theories.

**Cultural neuroscientists** are investigating how cultural differences in genetics are correlated with cognitions and emotions (Chiao & Ambady, 2007). Chiao and Ambady point out that about 70 percent of genes are expressed in the brain. This means that cultural differences in cognition and emotion are possibly linked to genetic influences on neurotransmission. In addition, differences in cultural experiences affect the acquisition and maturation of neural pathways related to cognitions and emotions.

So genes are *part* of the total picture.

My next task is to introduce some concepts that will help you understand how genes really affect complex behavior. If genes cannot affect behavior unless they are expressed, then how do specific genes turn into complex behavior?

## An introduction to behavioral and molecular genetics

**Behavioral genetics** and **molecular genetics** offer different approaches to studying genes and behavior.

**Twin studies** and **adoptions studies** are behavioral genetics methods. Both methods uncover if there is *some* genetic contribution to behavior but neither method reveals anything about specific genes. For example, twin studies suggest that genes account for about 50 percent of schizophrenia. This leaves a lot of room for environmental factors, such as stress. Twin and adoption studies are designed to *control* for environmental influences so they are not very helpful in telling us about specific environmental influences.

*The future of genetic research lies with molecular genetics studies.* Gene-environment correlation studies are already showing which genes vary across culture. In addition, it is expected that future cross-cultural genetic research will reveal more about why cultural differences exist in neural processing during cognitive tasks.

Avshalom Caspi and Terrie Moffitt (2006) write that there has been a recent shift away from using twin and adoption study methods toward **molecular genetics**. Molecular genetic studies identify specific genes related to behavior. Gene-environment interaction research is gaining momentum. There are three approaches to studying specific genes.

One approach uses **linkage studies** and **association studies** (both defined in section 3.12) to find a direct linear relationship between a gene and a behavior. The linear approach assumes that genes directly cause behavior, an idea that came from single-gene Mendelian studies. While some pieces of useful evidence come from linkage and association studies, replications have been difficult to achieve.

A second approach searches for **endophenotypes**. This method does not look directly at how a gene affects a specific behavior. Instead, the research targets an inherited intermediate factor, such as hormones or neurotransmitters that are *related* to a behavior such as depression or aggression. It is assumed that the genetics of endophenotypes are easier to study than those of the actual disorder. These studies do not give us direct access to knowledge about a specific gene linked to a behavior, just one that may be related. For example, relatives of schizophrenics have problems with visual tracking that are similar to those found in the schizophrenics (Walker & Tessner, 2008). The mechanisms behind the visual tracking problems *may* have a genetic basis that is passed through families and are correlated with schizophrenia.

The third and newest approach looks for **gene-environment correlations** (Caspi & Moffitt, 2006). This approach differs from the other two in that it includes environmental factors in genetic studies; they are set up to examine bidirectional relationships that allow scientists to see the effects of genes. The approach answers a big question about behavior, "How does an environmental factor, external to the person, get inside the nervous system and alter its elements to generate the symptoms of a disordered mind?" (p. 1).

## Gene-environment research is one way scientists are opening links between genes, the brain, and culture

The primary organizing idea of this book is that all behavior must be understood in terms of a person's culture. This leads to the term **cultural neuroscience**. Joan Chiao and Nalini Ambady (2007) write that cultural neuroscientists study the relationships between the brain, genes, the mind, and cultural practices. *Culture cannot be ignored by modern neuroscientists.* Chiao and Ambady write that a growing body of evidence is showing how cultural practices affect biology in a bidirectional way; "biological factors may lead to cultural variation at the neural and genetic levels, and cultural factors may lead to variation in brain structure and function, as well as gene expression" (p. 238). While most human genes are conserved, meaning they have stayed the same over time, studies such as those investigating 5-HTT, the serotonin transporter gene, show that there are variations in the frequency of genes across different cultural groups. This is support for the idea that humans come into the world with a set of potentialities that unfold within one's culture.

## Culture, cognitive processing, the brain, and genes

Now neuroscientists have the ability to explain cultural differences in cognitive processing at the neural and genetic level (Chiao & Ambady, 2007). There is a vast amount of modern research showing cross-cultural differences in cognitive processing. Chiao & Ambady give some good examples such as those from Boroditsky, Masuda, and Nisbett. In 2001, Boroditsky reported that people speaking English refer to time as horizontal, while people speaking Mandarin refer to time as vertical. Also in 2001, Masuda and Nisbett found that persons from Eastern cultures attend to the context of a picture, while Westerners attend to specific objects. Language, emotions, memory, the theory of mind, and spatial reasoning are other behaviors with cultural differences. Scientists know that the environment affects neural processing and now cultural neuroscientists have the chance to explain these differences in cognitive processing.

Future cultural neuroscience research will likely provide more evidence about which behaviors are universal, **etics**, and which vary across culture, **emics**. For example, in section 4.10 I discuss how biological and cognitive factors interact in emotion. Paul Ekman's cross-cultural research revealed that certain emotions are universal to humans (2003). Cultural neuroscience research now backs up Ekman's conclusions. Brain research shows that cultural differences can exist at the biological level even when a behavior is similar across cultures (Chiao & Ambady, 2007). For example, Japanese persons living in Japan and Japanese persons living in the U.S. can accurately identify the emotions in both Japanese and European Americans faces. However, fMRI research showed that they recruited different neural networks to complete the task. Research supporting Ekman exists now at the biological level of analysis; universal emotions probably evolved to increase human survival. On the other hand, we will find that some behavior differs across cultures and also differs biologically. In these circumstances, the social learning of cultural values will be more influential in explaining the behavior.

In addition to cultural differences at the biological level for cognitive tasks, there are cultural variations in genes related to depression. I will explore an example of cultural variations in 5-HTT later in this section when I discuss gene-environment interaction and depression.

New methodologies have allowed the field of cultural neuroscience to flourish (Chiao & Ambady, 2007). Many advances have occurred in designing cross-culturally sensitive ways to collect data, such as questionnaires that are **back translated** to control for language differences in participants. Cultural neuroscientists also use new neuroimaging technology, such as **fMRI**, to see the brain at work. Further, genetic research now allows scientists to search for gene variations and then design studies investigating their effects on neural or cognitive processes.

In addition to cultural differences in cognitive processing and genes, it is understood today that many environmental factors affect the expression and course of mental disorders such as depression, antisocial behavior, and schizophrenia (Caspi & Moffitt, 2006). These factors include maternal stress during pregnancy, birth complications, stressful life events, parental maltreatment and neglect toward the child, exposure to toxins, family conflicts and violence, the death of a parent, and head injury. Other mental disorders, such as autism, probably do not have as many environmental influences but since the concordance rates between twins is not 100 percent, something from the environment is placing stress on the brain.

## The important aspects of gene expression are aspects we might be able to control

You may have studied genes in a biology class. Often biology classes focus on simple Mendelian inheritance, or single-gene behavior processes, to teach the basics. Complex human behavior involves a great deal more. Complex behavior is either **oligogenic**, meaning there are a few genes involved in a behavior, or **polygenic**, meaning there is a large number of genes involved in a behavior (Carey, 2003). The complex behaviors psychologists think about are most likely polygenic. The fact that most human behavior is polygenetic makes it pretty complex to study. Each gene involved contributes something and it is hard to pull it all apart.

We do not directly inherit genes. Rather we inherit **DNA** strands that come on **chromosomes** (Carey, 2003). Chromosomes contain many genes. DNA is a spiral ladder of **nucleotide** chains that are pairs of the chemicals adenine, thymine, guanine, and cytosine (letters A, T, G, and C) that come in varying sequences (Lahey, 2008). The genetic code is carried in the sequences of nucleotides. **Genes** *are portions of DNA sequences that code for protein synthesis; this is how we get behavior.* DNA strands are very long and must be coiled up tightly to fit into cells; DNA strands are coiled around **histones**. Histones are important to know about because they must be uncoiled for a gene to express and affect behavior. Epigenetic research is starting to understand how the coils become unraveled (Higgins, E., 2008).

Most human DNA is the same. Human diversity is partly due to the fact that some genes are different from one another, either in multiple versions or in a single variation (Lahey, 2008). When a stretch of DNA comes in multiple versions, it is called a **polymorphism**. **Single nucleotide polymorphisms** (SNPs) are chains of DNA that differ in just one letter. An **allele** is a variation of a gene and can be either an SNP or a polymorphism. Alleles can increase the risk of disorders, such as 2 short alleles for 5-HTT, increasing the risk of depression.

Why should we care about these technicalities? We need to carry the idea all the way to the end—the behavior. Genes do not affect behavior unless they become templates, or master patterns, for proteins (Higgins, E, 2008). There are two ways that DNA turns into proteins, **transcription** and **translation**. These processes are the ones we really want to understand because *this is where we have some control*. Perhaps we can learn to be more effective parents, choose better diets, limit exposure to chemicals, and reduce stress.

The phrase **gene transcription** means that the genetic code is transferred from DNA to intermediate molecules of mRNA, or messenger RNA (Lahey, 2008). Messenger RNA codes for amino acids that determine which proteins appear in the cells. These proteins make up the structure of behavior; they are translated, meaning the message on the mRNA is read so the end product of protein synthesis can occur. Even though all cells contain the same genes, different cells use the genes differently (Higgins, E., 2008). This is why neural cells differ from, for example, liver cells.

Two kinds of cells relevant to psychology are those that make up neurons and endocrine glands. Much of our behavior is related to **neurotransmitters** at the **synapses** between neurons or from **hormones** produced by the endocrine system.

Epigenetic research is showing how specific environmental experiences affect the transcription process and gene-environment correlation studies demonstrate how genes make one more reactive to certain environments. The presence of **cortisol** (stress hormone) appears important.

Epigenetic factors, such as the stress from parental maltreatment, can make the histones unravel. It is thought that groups of molecules called methyl groups that attach to DNA interfere with gene expression (Higgins, E., 2008). In contrast, acetyl groups of molecules assist in the unraveling of the DNA coils. Higgins gives an example of research done by Eric Nestler in 2006 about **depression**. A growth factor protein, brain-derived neurotropic factors (BDNF), is low in the blood of depressed women. Treatment with antidepressants, exercise, and electroconvulsive therapy (ECT) raise BDNF levels. Nestler wanted to know more about BNDF and he found that **bullied** mice have greater amounts of methyl groups on histones near the BDNF gene than in normal mice. The antidepressant imipramine added acetyl groups, and the mice were less anxious.

Gene-environment correlations, several of which are reviewed in this section, attempt to show a meaningful relationship between genes and stressful life situations. We are starting to find useful gene-environment correlations for behaviors such as depression and **aggression**.

## Three ways that genes and the environment become correlated

Genes and the environment are *correlated* in three ways. These are passive, active, and evocative correlations (Lahey, 2008). Different studies try and control factors that isolate a particular type of gene-interaction. For example, section 7.10 includes a discussion of passive, active and evocative gene-environment correlations for eating disorders.

These specific types of gene-environment correlations help psychologists understand just what it is about the environment that interacts with genes. Armed with this knowledge, we might be able to help people become resilient to mental illness.

Let's start with **passive gene-environment correlation** and a behavior such as aggression in children. Parents contribute genes and provide an environment for the child. A passive correlation means the child's aggressive behavior is not dependent on anything the child does, but rather, it is the result of having inherited both genes and an aggressive environment from one or both parents. The MAOA gene study, which follows later in this section, is an example of passive gene-environment interaction.

In **active gene-environment correlation**, a child may select certain environments, implying that a child's behavior is important to the correlation. For example, children select peer groups that may enhance aggressive delinquent behavior.

In **evocative gene-environment correlation**, the actions of a child are also important for the gene-environment interaction. A child with a particular temperament might help create their own environment by encouraging abusive behavior from already hostile or rejecting parents.

## Why it is challenging to study genetic contributions to behavior

Genetics is different from many other sciences because it spans multiple layers, or levels of analysis (American Psychological Association, 2000). But while epigenetics and gene-environment interaction are more recent approaches to understanding the role of genes in behavior, *even current technology is limited*.

We cannot *directly* study genes and how they combine with other genes and the environment the way you might wish. Scientists instead rely on statistical models using correlations to analyze data about the behavioral effects of genes (American Psychological Association, 2000). Most human makeup is similar, making it difficult for psychologists to account for why individual behavior differs. It is correct to say that correlations are "statistical relationships" and not the cause-and-effect results from experiments. Some of these relationships are *strong and useful* to psychologists trying to help others. Scientists use the correlation method because they have to but perhaps in the future scientists will be able to directly study genes.

Our knowledge of genetics is fairly new. Discoveries in the 1950s and 1960s found that, "genes are contained in DNA molecules, that the genetic code is transcribed into RNA and then translated into a protein, and that this process is often regulated by environmental stimuli" (American Psychological Association, 2000, p. 380). This is an example of what we mean by the bidirectional process.

Most examples about genetic influences come from researching abnormal behavior. It is much easier to find suspicious genes for abnormal behaviors; scientists can use linkage and association studies when they are first trying to identify suspected genes. Genes for common behaviors, such as educational differences between males and females or the self-serving bias, are far more difficult to study accurately.

## Three option areas that require knowledge of gene expression

Abnormal, health, and developmental psychology are closely related. Gene-environment correlation studies and epigenetic research are important components for a bidirectional view of abnormal and health psychology. **Stress** hormones are important. In addition, epigenetic research sheds some light on factors contributing to addiction and obesity, topics required for the health option. Good **parenting** is emphasized in both gene-environment correlations and epigenetic research; it inoculates children against reactivity to stress, increasing **resilience**. The developmental psychology option requires knowledge of resilience.

## Two useful models for all three levels of analysis: The general bidirectional model and the Walker-Tessner model for psychiatric outcome

A level of analysis approach is a modern way of viewing the complex relationship between genes, the brain, and the environment. In fact, *all current psychologists studying behavior from any level of analysis take a bidirectional approach*. Two visual models for bidirectional thinking keep us organized.

A **model** is a framework for seeing an entire process that is represented as a flow chart. **Theories**, on the other hand, are individual explanations for behavior that fit within models. Many theories can fit into the same model. I ask my students to draw the models on their tests as appropriate.

The first is a **general bidirectional model** that explains a wide range of complex human behavior. The model shows how everything relates.

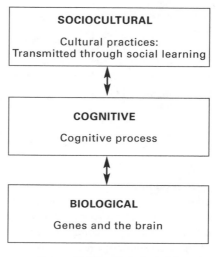

**General bidirectional model**

Each level influences the others and there are not always clear distinctions between the layers. Culture is at the top because humans adapted to live in cultures. Psychologists eventually hope to take any behavior and show how all the different layers work *together. We can never be reductionist and say that one layer explains everything.* There is a reciprocal relationship between all of these layers.

More and more topics in modern psychology have research spanning all three levels of analysis. One example of three levels of analysis is the study of the **self-serving bias**, where one study investigates the self-serving bias cross-culturally, revealing something about cultural effects on the mind and its effects on social behavior, and is immediately followed by an fMRI study on the neural mechanisms of the self-serving bias. We can assume that genes are involved in the self-serving bias in some way, but we do not know the specifics of the genetic contribution.

We have the most complete picture of a behavior when studies span all three levels and include genetics, which we are able to do with depression and language.

Abnormal behaviors such as aggression and mental disorders are popular topics with students. The second model, the **Walker–Tessner model for psychiatric outcome**, is a specific way of visualizing all of the factors that contribute to *abnormal* behavior. I was lucky to hear Elaine Walker (2001) speak on the topic of gene-environment interaction and its influences on psychiatric behavior. She used this model in her presentation and I have used it ever since. This model emerged in 1997 from thinking about advances in the study of schizophrenia (Walker & Tessner, 2008). The model applies to any abnormal behavior and is flexible enough to allow research on the causes of different abnormalities to emphasize different parts of the model.

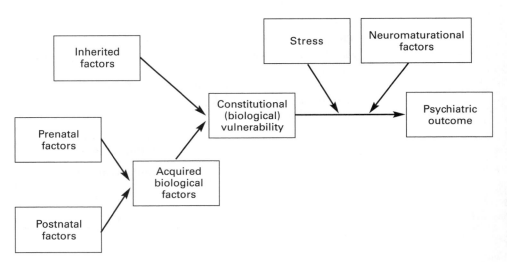

**The Walker-Tessner model for psychiatric outcome**

A good introductory text points out that behavior is the result of genes interacting with other genes and the environment. This is the basis for a levels of analysis approach. The entire bidirectional framework works on the assumption of **neuroplasticity**, an important concept for modern psychology and a good selection for the IB syllabus heading about the effects of the environment on physiological processes. Neuroplasticity means that the brain can change in response to the environment and to genes.

## Tolerate uncertainty: It is the reality of life

It might be hard to untangle the influence of genes and the environment. Which comes first? We may not be able to tell. Adrian Raine (2002) writes that many social factors are biological in nature, such as birth complications, and many biological factors have social aspects, such as genetic contributions to poor parenting. It maybe difficult to isolate which part of the model is primarily responsible for causing a behavior. It is a chicken or the egg question. Perhaps it is better to look for *contributing factors* to behavior rather than *causes*.

A level of analysis framework is fundamental to examining the total effect of all factors contributing to behavior.

There are no easy answers to problems and no simple explanations for behavior. Current explanations are more complex, but more interesting and realistic.

## Examples of how both bidirectional models work

Go ahead and assume that the general bidirectional model explains all complex behavior so any topic in the book can be used as an example.

To help you fully understand the Walker–Tessner model, I first need to define the terms on the model. The word *biological* is too general. Biology is inherited, acquired, or both. In reality, every behavior ends up biological and affects the brain, even if it originates in the environment.

Two examples of "inherited biological factors" are genes and energy (Qi or chi) in Traditional Chinese Medicine (TCM) (see section 5.10).

"Acquired biological factors" are everything else on the model.

"Prenatal factors" are things that happen to the fetus before birth. Prenatal factors include maternal viral infections, stress, and drug use. For example, stress is a key factor for many physical and mental health problems. The fetal nervous system needs some cortisol to develop. But cortisol can pass through the placenta and affect the developing brain. Heightened and chronic cortisol levels contributes to many problems, including changes in neurotransmitter development and functioning, alterations in the structure of the hippocampus, and inference with HPA axis so it cannot function normally when one is exposed to stress after birth (Walker, 2001).

"Postnatal factors" are things that happen to the developing brain from birth throughout one's early years, such as birth complications, maltreatment and other stress, and diet. Here is another example about stress and cortisol levels. Cortisol levels are associated with personality and cognitive performance (Walker, 2001). An external locus of control is correlated with higher cortisol levels. In addition, high cortisol levels are negatively correlated with poor performance on memory tests.

"Constitutional factors" are the total liability (risk level) that one's physiological system has for sensitivity to future difficulties. The early years are the most vulnerable time for the developing brain. These constitutional vulnerabilities are a combination of inherited factors and all the pre- and postnatal factors. A person's constitution is their brain makeup; there are changes to the brain for some people that make them more sensitive to life stress. Reactivity to stress may be set early in life, and then may in turn affect our personality, how our brain processes cognitive tasks, and our vulnerability to mental disorder. Long-term effects of stress are *genomic;* they alter gene expression through the **transcription** process (Walker, 2001). Cells such as neurons have receptors for stress and sex hormones. "The receptors are transcription factors, in that they contribute to differences in the gene expression of different types of cells" (p. 202). So even if someone has a genetic predisposition for mental illness, an environment without stress means that the genes are not affected.

"Neuromaturational factors" are changes in sex and adrenal hormones. Estrogen and testosterone can bind to receptors and these receptors act on the transcription process (Walker, 2001). During adolescence, baseline levels of cortisol also increase. Between changes in sex and stress hormones, adolescence is a primary time for gene expression, making adolescents vulnerable to mood, anxiety, and schizophrenic disorders.

"Stress" refers to general life stressors, which are both good and bad. Leaving for college, going to camp for the first time, and getting married are good stressors. Bad stressors are things such as serious family and school problems. Both good and bad stressors activate the HPA axis. This is why psychologists developing resilience theories are concerned about preventing early damage to the HPA axis.

The boxes on the Walker-Tessner model represent factors that increase one's risk of developing a disorder. A **risk model** is a good approach for considering how each factor contributes to a behavior. I borrowed the idea from Ben Lahey (2008). If there are no risk factors, or constitutional liabilities, then a person goes through life pretty normally. If there is one risk factor, for example, a genetic predisposition, then the risk increases for a mental disorder. Add another risk factor, such as maltreatment, and the risk rises. People with constitutional vulnerabilities have more risk factors than people without constitutional vulnerabilities; they have a greater risk that life stress and neuromaturational factors will affect the expression of genes. *A risk model approach is a particularly useful tool for sorting through all of the contributing factors to mental disorder.*

Any abnormal behavior can be put through the Walker-Tessner model. However, different parts of the model are emphasized in different disorders. In addition, researchers place emphasis on different aspects of this model in their theories. For example, Albert Bandura downplays the role of genetics in aggression and depression, though he recognizes that there are genetic predispositions for both. Other researchers, such as Avshalom Caspi, examine how specific genes increase the risk for depression and antisocial behavior, though they recognize that the genes work within an environmental context.

## Note to the teacher

Next are some ideas for class research and discussion about depression, antisocial behavior, autism, and the different components of the Walker-Tessner model. The model is useful for studying all mental illnesses, including eating disorders and anxiety disorders.

## Inherited factors

1. Depression. The interaction between the serotonin transporter gene and life stress is one example. Stress hormones are known epigenetic factors. Qi, a Chinese medicinal term for energy, is an inherited factor.

2. Antisocial behavior. The MAOA gene and how it regulates the effects of child abuse on neurotransmitters is an example. Research on the MAOA gene is reviewed in this section.

3. Autism. It is possible that 100 genes or more are associated with autism. One example is that genes may compromise the immune system and make some children more vulnerable to certain environmental influences such as vaccines. This is controversial and a great topic for class discussion. Autism may have fewer environmental factors than other disorders but the concordance rate for twins is not 100 percent, so there are some environmental factors.

## Prenatal factors

1. Depression. Maternal stress and diet are prenatal factors.
2. Antisocial behavior. Maternal stress is a prenatal factor.
3. Autism. Exposure to drugs, viral infections, and environmental toxins are prenatal factors.

## Postnatal factors

1. Depression. Diet, anything that heightens stress such as maltreatment and the neighborhood you live in, exercise, cognitive style, and self-efficacy are examples.
2. Antisocial behavior. Stress, the neighborhood you live in, peer groups, and self-efficacy are examples.
3. Autism. Diet, vaccines, and the overuse of antibiotics are examples. For example, while controversial, I suggest that you examine the work of Steven Edelson and Sherri Tenpenny. Cultural schemas have a way of predisposing us to look at particular evidence. Their views are worth considering.

## Constitutional factors

All four disorders involve changes in the structure of neurotransmitters and other brain parts, such as the hippocampus.

## Neuromaturational factors

Sex and adrenal hormones change during adolescence and can trigger the transcription process of genes that might otherwise remain silent. Neuromaturational factors are not important for autism, as it is a developmental disorder that is expressed by the time a child is about 30 months of age.

## Life stressors

Life stressors are many things and are involved in the onset of depression and antisocial behavior. However, getting a bad grade on a test is probably not enough of a stressor for you to develop a mental disorder. Stress is a factor primarily if a person experiences many stressful events and if the stress is prolonged.

Now that some basics have been introduced, let's look at how these ideas are studied by psychologists.

# Genes and aggression: An example of genetic research on animals

Genetic research on **aggression** is conducted on a variety of animal species, including rhesus monkeys, mice, rats, fish, birds, and crustaceans. Animal studies serve as models for human studies. Invasive techniques not allowed on humans are allowed on animals provided that the scientific benefit to humans is great. Ethically, animals must be treated with great care in the labs, their pain must be minimized, and if necessary, they must be humanely euthanized at the end of the study.

Stephen Maxson and Andrew Canastar (2006) report that approximately 36 genes in mice are related to aggression. Lab experiments use two strategies for observing the effects of genetics where **knockout mice** (genetically engineered to lack the expression of a gene) are compared to wild-type (WT) mice, both before and after WT mice are given a drug that suppresses a substance derived from a gene engineered out in the knockouts. One strategy is called the resident-intruder test, where an intruder is placed into a resident's cage. The neutral cage test is the other strategy where both mice are placed in an unfamiliar cage.

One example of such research is an experiment on mice to test the connection between genes and aggression. Silvana Chiavegatto and colleagues (2006), write that one genetic contribution studied in mice is **nitric oxide** (NO). NO is an endogenously manufactured (meaning that it is produced within the body) gaseous free radical and affects the immune system, neurons, neuroendocrine function, and behavior. Aggression is one effect.

Knockout mice were bred for experiments to lack the nNOS gene, hindering NOS production in neurons. The small *n* in nNOS means that this NO is found in neural tissues. NOS means NO synthase, an enzyme.

Students and mice caretakers initially noticed that nNOS mice displayed more than the typical male mouse aggression. When the resident-intruder test compared nNOS knockouts to WT mice, the knockouts initiated about 90 percent of the aggression and showed little submissive behavior.

Were differences in aggression between nNOS knockouts and WT mice because of the nNOS gene? It cannot be assumed. The nNOS knockouts were compared to WT mice given a drug that suppressed nNOS activity. Mice given the drug were similarly aggressive as the nNOS knockouts and less aggression than WT controls not given the drug. Thus, there is evidence that NO is a variable in aggression.

**Hormones** are another factor contributing to mouse aggression. **Testosterone** appears necessary for the increased aggression in male mice. Castrated nNOS knockouts and WT mice both showed less aggression. Hormone replacement increased aggression to normal levels in the nNOS mice.

Researchers noted a **gender difference**. The nNOS knockout females never showed inappropriate aggression. WT mice without the drug suppression displayed aggression only in relation to maternal behavior, and the nNOS knockout females were very docile in their presence. Researchers found that NO is released in the PVN (paraventricular nucleus) of the hypothalamus during maternal aggression. Males and non-lactating females did not show this change in the hypothalamus.

Hormones, therefore, have opposite but important effects on NO and aggressive behavior.

The story does not end here. NO is also associated with **serotonin** (detailed in section 3.8 and referred to frequently throughout this book). Serotonin is a key **neurotransmitter** related to aggression. Male knockout mice were more aggressive and their attacks were more violent and quick than the attack behavior in WT mice. It is thought that 5-HTT genes (the serotonin transporter gene) are either directly related to aggression or indirectly through other molecules that use the serotonin paths in the brain. *One indirect way that serotonin effects aggression may be related to NO.* The nNOS knockouts showed decreased serotonin metabolism in several brain regions such as the hypothalamus and cortex as compared to WT mice. This decreased metabolism resulted in an increase of serotonin. It is believed that drugs can reduce the levels of serotonin in the brain and thus reduce aggression. Drugs used in WT mice to increase serotonin levels resulted in increased aggression. There are two other NO synthesis pathways in the brain other than neural, so different synthesis pathways affect aggression differently. Studying NO in relation to serotonin strengthens the argument that NO is related to aggression.

Stress is an important ingredient. In addition to interacting with serotonin, NO may interact with the **HPA axis**, increasing its complex role in aggression. Although there is little research on the topic, scientists notice that nNOS knockouts have higher rates of **corticosterone**, the most important stress hormone in mice, than WT mice. Studies where mice are given NOS inhibitor injections ease the ACTH release in the pituitary gland.

The authors conclude that serotonin is probably the most important neurotransmitter associated with aggression and that NO strongly interacts with serotonin. NO also appears important to HPA activation, and stress is an important factor in aggression.

## Note to the teacher

Research on humans suggests that NO is important for the relaxation response. If you teach the health option, the article, "Association between oxygen consumption and nitric oxide production during the relaxation response" by Jeffrey Dusek and colleagues (2006), will help students evaluate the effects of stress reduction practices. I found the article using Google Scholar. Here is a chance to draw a possible relationship between stress management and research on aggression.

## Genes, environment, and aggression: Related studies show how researchers build on each other's work

Next are three studies showing how researchers *build on each other's work*. There are many contributing factors to **aggression** and more pieces of the puzzle are fitting together.

Numerous twin, adoption, and molecular genetic studies show genetic contributions to aggression. It is however, a more challenging task to figure out *how genes interact with social factors* (Raine, 2002). The newer study results are of great importance to both refining future investigations on genes and aggression and in designing prevention programs reducing risk (Caspi et al., 2002).

Genetic effects may not be easily identified in broad samples; we must study genes in relation to the specific contexts where they have a greater risk for expression. Ultimately, the goal is to find the underlying processes that make the interactions work (Raine, 2002). For example, what specific aspects of home environments trigger "maltreatment"? What is the likelihood that the personality of a child influences how they are treated? Is it possible that there is some kind of shared heritability between parent and child that results in maltreatment? As the research is association (uses correlations), how do we know the actual pathway to the final behavior?

Two studies showing how genes affecting **serotonin** affect behavior *in relation to specific environments*.

In the first study, Avshalom Caspi and colleagues (2002) studied the MAOA gene, located on the X chromosome. The MAOA gene "encodes the MAOA enzyme, which metabolizes neurotransmitters such as norepinephrine, serotonin, and dopamine (DA), rendering them inactive" (p. 851). How do we know this? Knockout mice lacking the MAOA gene have lower levels of all three neurotransmitters and higher rates of aggression. Rare cases of naturally occurring human "knockouts" lacking the MAOA gene also show increased aggression. At the same time, studies show that early life maltreatment is linked to increased rates of aggression. Early life stress interferes with the normal production and function of neurotransmitters throughout the lifespan, predisposing maltreated persons to a heightened sensitivity for stressful events.

Caspi and colleagues aimed to study the two variables (genes and the environment) together. They hypothesized that the MAOA gene regulated the effect of child abuse on neurotransmitters. Would the MAOA gene and an abusive environment predict higher rates of antisocial behavior?

The sample consisted of 1037 members of the Dunedin Multidisciplinary Health and Development Study in New Zealand who are genotyped for a polymorphism for the transporter of the MAOA, *which affects gene expression*. The sample is 52 percent male and all were studied 10 times between ages 3 and 26, a longitudinal study. The Dunedin sample is representative of the general population rather than coming from the often-used nonrepresentative clinical samples. The groups had the same MAOA variation, but clear differences in environmental maltreatment. Three types of maltreatment were identified and labeled severe, probable, or no maltreatment, representing 8, 28, and 64 percent of the sample respectively.

Correlations were made between the following four measures and antisocial behavior: (1) DSM-IV criteria measured if a participant had a conduct disorder, (2) police records showed violent crime convictions, (3) psychological assessments at age 26 examined personality dispositions toward aggression, and (4) informants, defined as persons knowing the participant well, gave valuable information for part of the profiles.

Results showed that MAOA gene variations were not important on their own. However, a gene X environment interaction test showed that the two together were important.

Researchers found important correlations between all four of the measures for antisocial behavior. Males with low MAOA activity had higher rates of conduct disorder diagnoses, committed higher rates of violent crime, had personality profiles predisposing them to violence, and had higher rates of antisocial personality disorder as noted in informant reports. The group with no maltreatment had the lowest levels in all four measures. The authors concluded that 85 percent of the maltreated males showed some form of antisocial behavior over time.

Of course this study needed replication. Over the next four years, childhood maltreatment in males was studied numerous times. Four studies replicated the results of this study, while others failed to find similar results (Sjoberg et al., 2008). One of the failed replications found similar but non-significant results. The other failed replication used a nonrepresentative clinical sample, so its comparability to the original is questionable.

Julia Kim-Cohen and colleagues (2006) conducted one of the successful replications. The sample was 975 7-year-old Caucasian boys from the Environmental Risk Longitudinal Twin Study in England and Wales. This is a representative sample where all the study mothers represented mothers between the ages of 15–48 giving birth to twin boys between 1994 and 1995.

The authors placed controls on the study to ensure that the study was really measuring a **passive gene-environment correlation**, where parents provide a poor living environment *and* a genetic predisposition to developing the antisocial behavior. Remember that the original Caspi study in 2002 examined the possibility that antisocial behavior was predicted by the interaction between a gene and maltreatment. The researchers had to make sure that a third variable did not account for the correlations, controlling for an **evocative gene-environment correlation**, where the genetic makeup of a child makes the child behave in such a way as to bring on abuse from others or simply having a mother that was antisocial.

DNA samples were taken from the boys at ages 5 and 7. They were characterized as having either high or low MAOA activity. A **gender** consideration comes up in this study. Girls are not comparable to boys on MAOA activity because they have two copies of the X chromosome. Girls cannot be categorized as simply low or high MAOA activity as it is unknown whether MAOA activity comes from one or both copies of the MAOA gene. In addition, previous research on females and gene-environment interaction has provided mixed results.

After DNA testing, each twin was rated separately for level of maltreatment through a standardized interview with the mothers. An example question is, "Did you worry that you or someone else may have harmed or hurt (child's name)?" Boys were rated as being exposed to physical abuse or not exposed to physical abuse. The group "exposed to physical abuse" was created from two measures, the boys whose mothers directly reported abuse and the boys suspected of being abused whose parents scored in the top 5 percent distribution of an intimate partner violence scale. The boy's mental health was further measured in several ways that included a Child Behavior Checklist, a Teacher Report Form, and DSM-IV criteria for ADHD. Examples of behaviors from the antisocial scale of the Child Behavior Checklist are "physically attacks people" or "lying or cheating."

Significant correlations were found, showing that "the effect of physical abuse exposure was significantly weaker among boys with high MAOA activity than among boys with low MAOA activity" (Kim-Cohen, 2006, p. 907). In addition to their own findings, the authors pooled together the results of five other studies that showed the same thing; correlations between poor family environments and antisocial behavior were strongest in boys with low MAOA activity. Boys with low MAOA activity also showed more mental health problems in general. Specifically, Kim-Cohen and colleagues contribute to the risk model by showing that these correlations are important even early in life. The authors concluded that these neural changes took place early in life. Prevention programs then have the best chance for success in early childhood, before the brain matures.

The authors believe that one of the strengths of their research is that it combines their findings from those of five other studies; they claim **observer triangulation**, meaning that more than one researcher has found the same thing. However, the homogeneity of the sample is a limitation and the study should be replicated using non-Caucasian boys. In addition, cause and effect cannot be known from the correlations. Last, the authors see this work as a point of departure for studying the effects of MAOA activity on the brain, not the full answer.

A third study by Richard Sjoberg and colleagues (2008) builds on the MAOA research by investigating the role of **hormones** in the process. Sjoberg and colleagues investigated the contributions of both testosterone *and* MAOA activity on antisocial behavior. Testosterone interacts with the MAOA promoter to influence gene transcription. If true, it is one more piece to the puzzle.

The authors believe that one explanation for **gender differences** in aggression is sex hormones. MAOA activity and testosterone may have an interactive effect. Perhaps testosterone has a direct effect on the MAOA gene. *Genes have receptors for both glucocorticoids and sex hormones.* Testosterone and glucocortoids compete for the same receptors, so it is one possible reason that high testosterone levels might be a critical factor in aggression.

Participants were 95 Finnish male alcoholics with criminal records who were incarcerated for at least the first month of the study (they were drug and alcohol free) and 45 healthy controls.

Testosterone levels were measured from cerebrospinal samples. In addition, the presence of psychiatric disorders was measured through a structured clinical interview using DSM-III criteria. A self-report questionnaire, the Brown-Goodwin Lifetime Aggression, measured aggressive behavior, containing questions on physical and verbal aggression and disciplinary actions for antisocial behavior. No one in the control group had psychiatric disorders. Eighty-two percent of the criminal group was alcohol dependent and 48 percent had antisocial personality disorder. Last, all participants were genotyped and grouped into either high or low MAOA activity.

Three independent variables were tested. Testosterone level, high or low MAOA activity, and the interaction of the two were correlated with scores on the Brown-Goodwin scale.

Results showed several interesting things. High testosterone levels were not significantly correlated with aggression scales on the Brown-Goodwin and MAOA activity level did not predict antisocial behavior. However, the interaction between the two was important. The authors found that "higher levels of testosterone were associated with increased Brown-Goodwin scores among individuals with the low activity MAOA genotype but not among individuals with the genotype conferring higher levels of MAOA transcription" (Sjoberg et al., 2008, p. 428).

The authors gave two possible explanations for their results. One was that **testosterone** had a direct effect on the MAOA gene. The other was that monoamine transmitters, such as dopamine and **serotonin**, were modulated by both testosterone and the MAOA gene. Genes are an important factor and the influence of testosterone may depend on MAOA activity level. Hormone interaction with genes in females is harder to study because only about 9 percent of females have the genotype for low MAOA activity.

Strengths of this study include having a uniform, well-controlled sample. However, a limitation is that the sample was nonrepresentative, as participants were recruited from advertisements. Another limitation is that cause and effect cannot be inferred from a correlation study.

Researchers investigating genetics and aggression believe that genetic contributions are best seen in relation to social factors that heighten their effect. Otherwise, genetic effects on behavior might go unnoticed.

## Genes, environment, and depression: A study on gene-environment interaction

One important **polymorphism** discovered by Avshalom Caspi and colleagues (2003) in a gene X environment correlation study may explain how genes contribute to **depression**. The 5-HTT gene, the serotonin transporter gene, appears to *heighten one's reactivity to stress*. But the gene alone is not a reliable predictor of depression.

Caspi and colleagues (2003) investigated the relationship between genetic type, having one short **allele** (s/l heterozygotes), two short alleles (s/s homozygotes) or two long alleles (l/l homozygotes) of 5-HTT, with responses on questionnaires about stressful life events and having depression symptoms.

Everyone experiences stressors. Why do some people respond with depression? Let's use our **risk model**. Persons with large amounts of life stress have an increased risk for depression. As the amount of stressful events rises, the risk increases. For people with two short alleles, the risk is even greater. The risk for depression goes down if a person has two long alleles, even in the presence of stress. Possessing two long alleles is correlated with **resilience** to depression.

Genetic vulnerability for reacting to stress is related to a polymorphism in the promoter region of 5-HTT (Caspi et al., 2003) Promoters are near the genes they regulate and assist in the transcription process. According to the **monoamine–deficiency hypothesis**, serotonin transporter system is important because low levels of the neurotransmitter serotonin are correlated to depression, (though this is not the only theory explaining depression). How do people get lower levels of serotonin? The transcription process of genes is not efficient if the transporter system is malfunctioning.

5-HTT is *not a direct cause* of depression, but "moderates the serotonergic response to stress" (Caspi et al., 2003, p. 387). This study builds on earlier animal and human experiments.

In previous lab experiments, mice with either one or two short alleles for 5-HTT were compared to control mice with two long alleles. Mice with the short alleles had more fearful responses to stress and secreted more stress hormone than those with two long alleles. Groups of mice with any of the alleles showed no differences in fearful reactions when exposed to a non–stress condition.

Similarly, lab experiments showed that rhesus monkeys with the short allele raised under stressful conditions had a decrease in the amount of serotonin in their spinal fluid as compared to monkeys with the short allele raised under normal living conditions.

Last, human experiments using brain imaging technology support animal experiments. Researchers documented greater neuron activity in the amygdala in response to fearful stimuli among people with one or two of the short allele than in people with the long allele.

Study participants were 847 Caucasians from New Zealand, all 26 years old. Gender was controlled by using an approximately equal number of males and females. Subjects were placed into three groups based on whether they had one short allele, two short alleles, or two copies of the long allele.

Participants filled out a life history survey, consisting of questions about life events related to areas such as employment, health, and relationships. No difference was found in the amount of stressors experienced by participants in the three groups.

The researchers measured depression levels between ages 25 and 26 using the Diagnostic Interview Schedule. Major depression was defined as meeting DSM-IV requirements. Seventeen percent of the total subjects qualified for a major depression diagnosis. Gender differences in the depressed subjects, 58% females and 42% males, were the same as reported for this age group in other U.S. research. To control for the possibility that participants lied on the Diagnostic Interview Schedule, researchers gathered "informant" data from a questionnaire mailed to a person selected by the study participant.

Data were analyzed with correlations between depression symptoms and genotype, stress events, and the interaction between the two. Researchers correlated having a short allele with greater self-reports of depression. The authors controlled for depression symptoms that occurred before the reported stressful events between ages 21 and 26, and found that subjects with a short allele had increased depression between ages 21 and 26. Caspi and colleagues further correlated having a short allele with a new diagnosis of depression between ages 21 and 26 in subjects without a previous diagnosis.

Correlations do not show cause and effect but this study is part of a larger body of research on stress, genes, and depression. Resilience to stress is of current interest to psychologists because it is the part that we can control. Reports of low stress environments predicted lower rates of depression regardless of genotype.

**Culture** affects who has the different 5-HTT risk alleles. Research that has been replicated several times shows that 70–80% of a Japanese sample has the s/s or the s/l alleles (Chiao & Ambady, 2007). In comparison, 40–45% of Caucasian samples from Western Europe and the United States have the s/s allele and 55–60% have the l/l allele. This is a significant difference. Future research may reveal the extent to which the genetic frequency differences account for differences between cross-cultural samples on cognitive and affective measures. Why is there a difference in emotional functioning? Right now we are not really sure. The differences might be explained by evolutionary factors, such as genetic drift, meaning that chance factors caused certain alleles to survive over time, or adaptation to the environment or protective cultural practices.

Let's now move into a discussion of why it is important to understand the impact of stressful events on depression. Stress hormones affect physiology in a number of ways and Robert Sapolsky (2004) sums up these effects. Along with helping us answer IB questions about genes, Sapolsky's comments are relevant for questions about hormones, neurotransmitters, and both the abnormal psychology and health psychology options.

## Depression: Stress hormones, neurotransmitters, and genes

### Note to the teacher

> I highly recommend the National Geographic film, *Stress: Portrait of a Killer* (2008). It features Robert Sapolsky. The film is available from www.amazon.com.

The World Health Organization predicts that depression will be the number one health problem in the future, so increasing rates of depressive symptoms are a global concern.

Why are depression rates increasing? Sapolsky believes that **stress** is a good organizing principle for considering the problem; stress ties together many **depression** theories.

What we know about stress and depression makes sense, though the subject is complicated and needs a great deal of further research.

Sapolsky writes that **glucocorticoids** (stress hormones) are secreted any time we experience the *fight-or-flight syndrome*, which is important if you almost step out in front of a car or have to run from a predator. But most human stress is not about almost stepping in front of cars or running from predators. Rather, the *expectation* of stressful situations may be more relevant for understanding human and some animal stress.

While humans have some real emergencies and difficult life situations to manage, many human stressors are *imagined stress*. Imagined stressors are social and psychological in nature; we spend a lot of time anticipating events. Unfortunately, both real and imagined stress affects physiology the same way, so people who frequently worry about imagined stressors have their fight-or-flight system constantly activated, just as if they were constantly running from a predator.

Textbooks document the cascade of events that happen in the **HPA axis** when stress is experienced. The end result is that a constantly activated HPA axis can weaken the immune system, impair memory, shrink the hippocampus, and increase the risk of depression. Sapolsky presents a convincing argument that neurotransmitters, genes, and the hippocampus respond under the *umbrella of stress* to create depression in some people.

Depressed people have higher levels of glucocorticoids (**cortisol** is the most important one for humans). While an activated HPA axis helps to make sure you jump out of the way of an oncoming car, there should be a mechanism in everyone to reestablish normal levels of stress hormone once you are safe. This deactivation system appears deficient in depressed persons, possibly related to genes such as the 5-HTT.

People with depression have malfunctioning **neurotransmitter** systems. Sapolsky says that chronic high levels of stress hormones can alter the structure and function of serotonin, dopamine, and norepinephrine. For example, stress affects the release and breakdown of serotonin and it depletes the amount of dopamine in our pleasure centers.

It is currently unclear how many neurotransmitters malfunction when someone has depression, but three that are interesting to researchers are serotonin, norepinephrine, and dopamine. Serotonin is getting the most attention, but some newer drugs also regulate norepinephrine. Sapolsky says that researchers argue about which neurotransmitters are most important and they also argue about whether depression is caused by too much or too little of them. Since people respond differently to different antidepressant drugs, it is likely that numerous neurotransmitters are associated with the beginning of different types of depression. To further complicate the situation a neurotransmitter associated with pain called substance P may be involved with some cases of depression. A drug that interferes with substance P to relieve pain can also act as an antidepressant. Substance P is discussed further in section 7.13.

In addition, many people with depression have a smaller **hippocampus**. The hippocampus is part of the limbic system, which is responsible for things such as emotion regulation and some memory functions. The cortex is layered above the limbic system. The cortex in people with major depression tells the limbic system that life is threatening. A part of the cortex called the anterior cingulate cortex (ACC) plays a role. The ACC is related to emotion and lights up when subjects are asked in experiments to look at pictures of people and focus on either the people's emotions or whether the pictures are of an indoor or outdoor environment. The ACC activates only when people think about the emotions in pictures. The prefrontal cortex (PFC), a very human brain part, is right in front of the ACC. Sapolsky cites research showing that the PFC is very responsive to emotion and it seems to be **localized** for either positive or negative moods. In scanning studies, the left side of the PFC lights up in response to positive moods and the right side lights up in response to negative moods. Depressed people have decreased left PFC functioning and heightened right PFC functioning. Thus, the hippocampus is bombarded with stress hormones. Cells in the hippocampus have receptors for stress hormones and long-term exposure to stress means that glucocorticoids can bind to cells and change them, possible permanently (Walker, 2001). Declarative **memory**, which is the most damaged type of memory in depressed people, is related to the hippocampus.

Finally, high stress levels affect genes. According to Sapolsky, "people who are undergoing a lot of life stressors are more likely than average to succumb to a major depression, and people sunk in their first major depression are more likely than average to have undergone recent and significant stress" (pp. 291–292). Glucocorticoids even "regulate how much 5-HTT is made from a gene" (p. 307). As we have already learned from Caspi's gene-environment correlation study of 5-HTT, stress interacts with genes to increase one's risk of depression.

It seems that neurotransmitters, stress hormones, and genes are related in a complex way that we are just beginning to understand.

Humans are thinking beings and social creatures. This makes us interesting and complex, but our thinking and social expectations are also large factors in creating imagined stressors. **Negative cognitive style** and **low perceived efficacy** are two mechanisms for signaling the release of large doses of stress hormones in the brain, thus triggering the HPA axis.

Sapolsky highlights the need to reduce stress and he recommends, for example, meditation. Lifestyle changes are hard so I give students a grade for sticking with the challenge. We practice tai chi and take the food and sleep challenge (a copy is in the appendix).

Next, let's look at another factor that complicates the interplay between stressful events and behavior, gender differences in experiencing stress.

## Depression: Gender, stress hormones, and genes

Why do women have higher rates of depression? Susan Nolan-Hoeksema thinks that women experience more stressors and experience stress differently than men. Just as Sapolsky described above, a constantly activated HPA axis damages our physiology, including an increased risk of gene expression.

Nolan-Hoeksema (2004) takes an integrated approach to explaining why females are twice as likely as males to experience depression. Stress is a major component of her argument.

Females have more social stressors than males, making them more vulnerable to depression. Two particular life events are correlated with higher rates of depression. First, women experience more childhood sexual assault, which is more important to developing depression than assault in adulthood because of the vulnerability of the developing brain. In addition, women tend to have lower social status than men and often do not have as large a say in decision making.

The only *consistent* research result about self-concept relates to interpersonal orientation. Females are more concerned with their relationships with others than males. Females tend to place less emphasis on their own needs and are more vulnerable to depression when relationships are in trouble or end. Sandra Bem provides experimental evidence for the existence of a gender **schema** that may play a role in what female's value. Please see section 4.4 on schemas for Bem's research

To complicate the situation, females tend to ruminate, meaning to think over, more than males about problems. Rumination further increases the risk for depression.

Females may also be more biologically reactive to stress. One interesting theory that needs more research is that sex hormones affect the stress system. Sex hormones have not been shown to directly affect mood. But as females experience more social stressors, they are prone to more disturbances in the HPA axis, which may affect gene expression.

## Language: A summary of a genetic research study

The KE family gave scientists a chance to study the genetics of **language** (Haesler, 2007). For several generations, members of the KE family showed difficulties producing grammar, speaking clear, understandable sentences, and keeping chronological facts in order. They were normal in all other ways.

Members of the KE family with language difficulties had a mutation on chromosome 7 that probably contributed to the problem. With luck, an unrelated person turned up with the same defect on chromosome 7. This boy kept researchers from a time-consuming process of using trial and error to sift through all of the genes on the chromosome to look for a specific suspect gene. A gene called FOXP2 on chromosome 7 was identified as the problem for the KE family.

Ever since this discovery researchers have been considering what FOXP2 contributes to language.

The following research results are *tentative but promising*.

It appears that mutations in FOXP2 interfere with normal brain development (Haesler, 2007). FOXP2 is important in early fetal development so it impacts other genes. It acts as a transcription factor, meaning that it affects whether or not other genes are correctly read and transformed into their appropriate functions.

Numerous brain parts can be affected. These include differences in the volumes of the cerebellum and basal ganglia. **Wernicke's** and **Broca's areas** are also affected. Because the FOXP2 gene is active from early development is hard to know what the direct and indirect effects of it might be. It may have something to do with the general wiring of the brain. Thus, FOXP2 is probably indirectly related to language, but important, meaning that the gene does not have "language" directly written on it.

The work of Sonja Vernes and colleagues (2008) provides some clues about the indirect effects of FOXP2 on the developing brain. They located 184 families with specific language impairment and performed genomic screening for the regions surrounding FOXP2. One gene in particular, CNTNAP2, was identified as a problem. CNTNAP2 is a gene that encodes neurxin, proteins concentrated at synapses that help hold neurons together. It appears that "FOXP2 binds to and dramatically downregulates CNTNAP2" (p. 2337). Downregulation means that a cell, in response to external stimuli, decreases the number of its receptors. The cell is then less sensitive and is not able to function properly. Neurxin is expressed in the human cortex and probably contributes to normal language capabilities. The authors are intrigued that "this same region coincides with one associated with language delays in children with **autism**" (p. 2337).

The discovery that many animals also have the FOXP2 gene has given us another vehicle for research. Although most animal communication is fully innate, there are some species of songbirds that have a social learning component to their songs. The process is somewhat similar, though not as complex, as the social learning process between children and adults. For example, sparrows have an early period called a subsong that is similar to the babbling of babies. The subsong represents the first attempt of the bird to learn the full song of the species.

In an animal study, the amount of FOXP2 was reduced in zebra finches to the point where it resembled the amount that was similar to the deficiency in affected humans. These birds had trouble learning their songs. Researchers concluded from this study that FOXP2 was not only related to early development but must also have something to do with the continuing role of the brain in language after birth.

## 3.5 Examine One Evolutionary Explanation of Behavior

### The evolutionary basis for human culture

How often you think about what someone else is thinking? Thinking about other's thoughts probably takes up the majority of your time. It is extremely useful to know something about your parent, teacher, or friend's thoughts *before* you say or do something.

Nicholas Humphrey writes (in Baron-Cohen, 1995) that it was an *evolutionary breakthrough* for humans to develop the ability to reliably guess what another, especially a possible rival, was thinking. If we are going to study humans living together in cultures, then it is important to know something about the evolution of "mindreading," which is not to be confused with psychic abilities. Mindreading, or having a **theory of mind** (TOM), evolved as part of human **social intelligence**, defined as "the ability to process information about the behavior of others and to react adaptively" (Baron-Cohen, 1995, p. 13).

Many other aspects of studying humans, such as a child's cognitive development or making attributions, are tied in some way to the TOM.

David Premack first used the term "theory of mind" when he studied the extent to which chimpanzees had language. Michael Gazzaniga and colleagues (2002) define TOM as "the ability to represent and infer unobservable mental states such as desires, intention, and beliefs from the self and others" (p. 676). The most current thinking about the TOM in animals is that chimpanzees have *some* aspects of it (Call & Tomasello, 2008). Chimpanzees have knowledge and perception of others and can understand some intentions. However, chimpanzees fail at "false belief" tests, where they have to understand that someone else has beliefs that are different from theirs; that another can believe something different. So chimpanzees have not evolved all aspects of the fully developed human TOM. Human children master false belief problems consistently by age 4. People with **autism** have trouble with false belief tests. Without a fully developed TOM, they have trouble with social relationships.

The TOM is brain based. Rebecca Saxe and Anna Wexler (2005) found **fMRI** evidence that the right temporo-parietal junction (RTJP) is active when humans decode the intentions of others. What makes the RTJP special? It was recruited specifically when study participants made **attributions** of other's mental states. RTJP activity was the most active in conditions where participants had to make sense of incongruent information about others. This finding shows that the brain has a specific function devoted to the TOM and is probably a fundamental aspect of human social cognition. It makes sense that the brain evolved a special mechanism to facilitate social cognition. *As one entire section of the sociocultural level of analysis is about social cognition, you should know something about the biological basis of it.*

This introduction to the TOM leads into a discussion of modern **evolutionary psychology** (EP) and the evolution of social intelligence.

So much of what humans do is directed at being social. As stated at the beginning of this book, *humans evolved to live in cultures.* We evolved complex cognitive abilities to be social and our social lives take place within cultures.

I selected EP because it is one attempt to try and explain the evolution of our complex cognitive abilities, such as language. If we are going to study human behavior then we need to get some insight into the question, why do humans have complex cognitive abilities? The assumptions of EP are outlined below but understand that they are almost impossible to verify. Currently there are competing evolutionary theories about language and we may never know which one is the best explanation because of the difficulties of conducting research.

## Assumptions of evolutionary psychology and how culture solved adaptation problems

Introductory texts explain the basics of **natural selection** and evolutionary psychology and point out some common misconceptions. Defining principle #2 for the biological level of analysis includes the evolutionary basis of behavior. For the IB exam, it is appropriate to use natural selection and modern evolutionary psychology as evolutionary explanations of behavior. You must understand natural selection because natural selection explains the evolution of many other topics that IB students study, such as emotions and cognitive abilities. Just remember that humans *do not decide to evolve.* This is the primary misconception that students have about evolution.

*EP is one of the theories that explain the cognitive processes that define us as humans.* Examples of theorists taking an evolutionary perspective are Simon Baron-Cohen, Steven Pinker, and Leda Cosmides.

Modern evolutionary psychologists explain cognitive processes with an evolutionary framework and do not believe that all behavior comes from genes (Gazzaniga et al., 2008). EP "aims to account for the functioning of specific cognitive mechanisms and processes in humans" (Baron-Cohen, 1995, p. 11). The general purpose of evolution is to make sure that genes spread and survive. Humans meet this goal by *adapting* to the environment. Individuals reproducing more than others spread more genes around. Evolution does not have a goal to improve an organism; survival of genes is the main goal. Over time, the evolution of adaptive mental processes in humans increases the fitness of the group.

"The mind is a set of information-processing machines that were designed by natural selection to solve adaptive problems faced by our hunter-gatherer ancestors" (Cosmides & Tooby, 1997, p. 1). Evolutionary psychologists reject the notion that the mind is a blank slate that is filled with information from an outside source (Cosmides & Tooby, 1997). Instead, humans evolved different modalities in the brain for the different adaptive problems faced (Baron-Cohen, 1995) Evolutionary psychologists see the human mind as a "collection of reasoning and regulatory circuits that are functionally specialized and, frequently, domain-specific (Cosmides & Tooby, 1997, p. 3).

Cosmides and Tooby outline EP's assumptions.

1. The brain is a system with circuits to *generate* behavior that best fits with one's environment.

2. Natural selection designed these circuits to solve problems faced by our ancestors. These circuits are not designed to solve *any* problem, just *adaptive* problems. How do Cosmides and Tooby define adaptive problems? They are problems that keep coming up in evolutionary history. Solutions to these problems must affect *reproduction* in some way, which is the basis of natural selection. **Language** is an example of a good solution to evolutionary problems related to communication and raising children.

3. Most problems that must be solved require very complicated brain circuitry. People are not conscious of all the brain's workings. You are only consciously aware of the end products, such as a sentence you speak, and not everything the brain goes through to construct a sentence. Try not to oversimplify the mind's workings based on conscious experience.

4. "Different neural circuits are specialized for solving different adaptive problems" (p. 8). For example, babies come into the world with evolved circuits that allow them to pay attention to faces. Even 10-minute-old babies pay attention to faces. Babies have innate hypotheses about a number of things in their world, such as objects, the TOM, and physical causality. Life is difficult for those missing these hypotheses.

5. Natural selection took a long time to design brain circuitry, so our modern minds are similar to ancient minds. Our minds did not evolve in modern societies. Rather, our brain lived most of its evolutionary existence in hunter-gatherer societies. For about 10 million years, natural selection shaped the brain with neural circuitry that solved adaptive problems.

Think of the many problems humans encountered in their environments, such as creating social groups so people could live and work together successfully, attracting mates, raising children, navigating territory, and meeting safety needs (Matsumoto & Juang, 2008). These needs are biologically based and have social consequences. **Culture** *offered a solution, a way to survive.* "Culture is a solution to the problem of individual's adaptations to their contexts to address their social motives and biological needs" (p. 8).

An evolutionary point of view still allows for individual differences (Baron-Cohen, 1995). There are just some evolutionary universals that we all need to survive as humans. Through natural selection humans have evolved mental apparatus to solve problems. *Transmitting practices to the next generation was probably the greatest adaptive problem for humans.* A brain-based language was an excellent solution.

The view that culture is a solution to biological adaptation fits well into the general bidirectional model where culture mediates mind, brain, and genes and there is a give-and-take relationship between all four levels.

## Why is it hard to support an evolution theory explaining human cognitive abilities?

While EPs believe that environmental challenges such as raising children and communicating pushed humans to adapt by developing cognitive skills such as language, can we actually correlate the existence of cognitive abilities with these environmental challenges?

David Buller (2009) writes that it is impossible. This is why there are several competing theories about why language evolved and there is currently no way to support one over another.

Tolerate uncertainty. I want to stay focused on the traits that make us human, and while it is impossible to know why we evolved these traits, Matsumoto, Simon Baron-Cohen and Patricia Kuhl give some good reasons to consider the merits of EP.

According to Buller, in order to correlate the environmental demands with an evolved trait, the trait must be compared in different species that have a common ancestor. If the different species have different traits, perhaps some environmental factors might have prompted the different adaptations can be correlated with the trait. Our closest relative, the chimpanzee, does not have a complex language system or sophisticated cognitive processes. However, the common relative we shared with them is extinct, so it is impossible to know if they evolved differently from the common ancestor.

Next, let's look at some evidence to show that the EP explanation is plausible.

## The evolution of social intelligence

The evolution of the human brain required a social environment (Baron-Cohen, 1995). Psychologists generally agree that the social intelligence was a primary adaptive problem that drove the human brain's evolution.

Social behavior is very complex; recall what Temple says about trying to manage her life. The most adaptive way to manage social behavior was a mechanism that allowed humans to decode the intentions of others, the TOM. Baron-Cohen has an interesting idea about the development of human mindreading that has some research support.

Mindreading is universal; people in all cultures have a TOM. Humans are born with innate *skills* that form the basis of mindreading, consistent with EP assumption #1. There are at least four of these assumptions, the **intentionality detector** (ID), the **eye-direction detector** (ED), the **shared-attention mechanism** (SAM), and Alan Leslie's **theory-of-mind mechanism** (TOMM) (Baron-Cohen, 1995). Each becomes available to children at specific times in development. All four are assumed to be evolutionarily advantageous to humans and fit with EP assumption #4. We are not conscious of these processes; the mechanisms probably require large amounts of neural circuitry, as EP assumption #3 suggests.

The ID and EDD are phase 1, from approximately birth to 9 months (Baron-Cohen, 1995). The ID helps infants read any motion or sound signal that is related to their needs. The EDD relates to the visual system. It helps infants to recognize someone's eyes and know if these eyes are looking at them, giving babies the ability to understanding other's perceptions. Experiments support the existence of EDD in 3-year-olds. Baron-Cohen cites a study that he conducted in 1992. Children were shown two sets of photographs. Each set showed a face looking at them and one looking away. One of the pictures in each pair only showed the eyes looking at the child, with the entire face slightly turned. The other photograph in the pair showed both the nose and eyes aimed at the child. Regardless of which cue the children received, they knew which photograph was facing them instead of turned away. Others replicated this study on infants, giving the EDD **observer triangulation**. Animals also have the ability to know if something else is looking at them. In order to survive, animals must know if a predator is watching them.

The SAM is phase 2, from about 9-18 months. SAM shows children the relationship between three important things—an agent, the self, and an object/other agent. For example, "Mom sees (and I see) the flower." Mom is the agent seeing an object, the flower, and the "I" is the child's self. This is an amazing skill and is required for high-level social interaction where the baby infers that they are sharing a perception with another, seeing the same thing. The EDD, the visual system, is frequently used by SAM. SAM requires perceptual information to work correctly and, for example, if someone says, "Look at that flower," we use our visual system to attend to the correct object. In addition, SAM can get perceptual input from the needs identified by the ID.

Baron-Cohen (1995) believes that the full TOM might need what Alan Leslie defined as the theory of mind mechanism (TOMM). While the ID, EDD, and SAM are building blocks to the TOM, there are still mental states that young babies do not understand. These include guessing, pretending, imagining, deceiving, and understanding false beliefs. The TOMM helps children understand that there are many mental states and that they can relate to each other. Baron-Cohen gives the following example. "The statement 'Snow White *thought* the woman selling apples was a kind person' can be true, while 'Snow White *thought* her wicked stepmother was a kind person' may be false" (p. 53), even if they are the same person. Snow White is a complicated story and children have to *develop* the ability to understand it.

## Note to the teacher

Collecting children's **narratives**, a type of story, at different ages is a fun class project. I notice that 3-year-old children struggle with sentences such as those about Snow White. Children understand these complicated stories by 4 or 5, when they consistently pass TOM tests. The material on narratives in section 4.5 is necessary for the project. Get permission from the parent and then record stories from children at various ages. Next, transcribe the stories and share them in class. Perhaps the class can conduct a content analysis on the stories, looking for themes showing different stages of development.

There is probably a complex relationship between language and the TOM; *they may have helped each other develop* (Baron-Cohen, 1995). Here is another reason to study **autism**. Autistic persons have difficulty with language and typically lack a TOM. In an interview cited by Gazzaniga and colleagues (2002), Baron-Cohen says that autism research should be situated in an evolutionary context. "A theory of mind was so central to human social behavior, that in all likelihood it had evolved to support social behavior- and its impairment in autistics might just be the strand of neurological evidence to allow this evolutionary question to be tractable (easy to work with)" (p. 674).

It makes sense that the TOM and language have an evolutionary basis, though they do *not arrive intact in a baby.* Instead, natural selection gave us the *ability to learn* (Pinker, 1994). This fits in with EP assumption #1. All species, even amoeba and bacteria, can learn (Pinker, 1994). "Learning is an option, like camouflage or horns, that nature gives organisms as needed— when some aspect of the organism's environmental niche is so unpredictable that anticipation of its contingencies cannot be wired in" (p. 243). Pinker says that the ability to learn language is a good example of natural selection at work. Children come into the world with specific skills that allow them to learn the language they need to learn in their cultures. I know that many students learn about Noam Chomsky's (1981) **nativist theory of universal grammar**. But Chomsky did not situate language in evolution theory. Chomsky's view that universal grammar is accounted for by natural physical laws is not well supported. Studies do not support the idea that children have an innate understanding of grammar as Chomsky suggested (Kuhl, 2000). Rather, we evolved the ability to *learn* language.

The TOM may be related to **mirror neurons**, discussed in section 5.15. The first mirror neurons were discovered in monkeys and while monkey mirror neurons are not related to language, they fire in the equivalent of **Broca's area** (Gazzaniga, et al., 2002*). Mirror neurons may have evolved to help with mindreading.* Section 5.15 includes a recent study showing that mirror neurons appear linked to human intentions. In addition, new research shows that mirror neurons do not fire correctly in autistic persons (Ramachandran, no date).

## How do evolutionary-based behaviors become cultural practices?

The **cultural acquisition device** (CAD) may be the answer. Melvin Konner (2007) writes that the cultural acquisition device (CAD) is a set of biologically-based universal behaviors that allow us to *generate* (as said in EP assumption #1) *cultural behavior out of innate skills.* Each culture evolves distinctly from the CAD.

1. The first category is **reactive processes**, and includes **classical conditioning** and habituation. The ID and EDD are examples of reactive processes. These are basic functions from which a child's **enculturation** grows.

2. The second is **facilitative processes**, or our **social learning** and includes imitation, instruction, and collaboration. Instruction means to have **scaffolds** teach the practices of a culture, where more experienced adults assist children in learning skills necessary for survival in their culture. Collaboration means that members of a culture co-construct **schemas** for what things mean to them.

3. The third is **emotional enculturation**, such as **attachment** and emotion management. Emotion management means that cultures have rituals for emotional displays that define the goals of a group and these rituals provide comfort for individuals. I want to draw another relationship here to Ekman's (2003) research on emotion. While Ekman did not start out his research agreeing with Darwin, he discovered that there were universal emotions. Ekman's work is reviewed in section 4.10.

4. The fourth category is **symbolic processes**, such as **narrative** construction. Narratives are the stories of cultures and are fundamental to the cognitive construction of human experience.

## Patricia Kuhl: The evolution of skills required for language

The evidence on language acquisition does not support either **B. F. Skinner** (who believed that language was acquired through operant conditioning) or **Noam Chomsky's** views (Kuhl, 2000). Children are not blank slates and one's innate ability to learn language has nothing to do with operant learning. In addition, children do not have innate grammar that activates and grows upon hearing language.

Kuhl's position fits in with the evolutionary view that babies come into the world with evolved skills that helped them *learn* their culture's language. Babies are innate language learners, but not in the way Chomsky claimed. "What is innate regarding language is not a universal grammar and phonetics, but innate learning biases and strategies that place constraints on perception and learning" (p. 11856). Babies infer the rules of the language used by their cultures from early perceptual abilities. "Language is innately discoverable" (p. 11856). This process is made possible by the concept **neuroplasticity**; the brain is very plastic for language in early life. Some of the same basic built-in biases are shared with animals to help them survive.

Kuhl identifies six components of the innate learning process.

**1.** *Infants have an innate ability to perceive the basic units of speech.* Young babies are really "children of the world," as Kuhl put it. They can hear and respond to the phonemes, or the sounds of speech that are different from others, of *all* languages. Categorical perception experiments showed that babies discriminated the differences between sounds from all languages, whereas adults discriminated sounds based on the language they spoke. Animals also have categorical perception; they are able to tell when a sound changes. *A general auditory processing mechanism probably evolved for this ability that was not specific to speech.* Infants do not understand the meaning of the sounds; they just have an innate ability to discriminate between them.

**2.** A child's language development is not selectionist. Older theories suggested that as children develop, they lose the ability to hear sounds that are not relevant to the primary language of their culture; the culture's language was selected. This was a "use it or lose it" theory; the selectionist theory was subtractive. Janet Werker's experiments are documented in some of the films shown in high schools. Werker's research was originally interpreted as supporting the selectionist position. However, the next group of studies showed that listeners did not ever completely lose the ability to detect sounds from other languages. These studies found that adults could discriminate the sounds of other languages under certain conditions, such as extensive training. While these studies did not specifically show that the subtractive theory was incorrect, they prompted new research on babies that did. The new research showed that infants were engaged in an entirely different kind of language learning that was not subtractive. (Werker's original studies are available free on the Internet at http://infantstudies.psych.ubc.ca/vitae_pub.html.)

**3.** What are babies doing that is different? They use learning strategies that map language rules. These strategies actually change the child's perceptual abilities. It is a reason why many people find it harder to learn a second language after age 6. However, a child's perceptual abilities have to change so they can learn their culture's language, and become "children of culture." It is a 3-step process. First, babies must detect patterns in language. Patterns must be identified both in phonemes and in the stresses and intonations relevant to their culture's language. By 9 months, babies can detect the legal pattern of sounds for their culture's language. For example, the sound combination "zw" and "vl" is legal in Dutch but not in English. By 9 months, babies learning English pay attention to English longer and Dutch babies pay attention to Dutch longer. Kuhl says that the babies do not know what words mean, but have a "perceptual sleeve" that words will fit into as they develop. It is the perception abilities that are getting a fine-tuning. Second, studies using artificial words show that infants are now able to group together sounds that are typically linked. Kuhl described it as the gestalt theory of the "common fate," where groups of sounds that are linked are perceived as units. Third, "language experience warps perception" (p. 11853). The Native Language Magnet Model explains this process. As a child's perception becomes fine-tuned, one sound becomes a prototype, meaning the sound is an example of other sounds that are similar. Prototype sounds act as magnets for other related sounds. While animals have basic abilities to perceive sound differences outlined in #1, they do not have sound magnets. Babies are getting close to actually producing speech at this time. For example, research on Japanese and English speakers shows differences in perceiving the r–l sounds. Japanese speakers hear them as one sound and English speakers hear them as two sounds. Experience hearing language contours one's perceptions of sound and this is universal; the language of one's culture shapes the brain.

**4.** Children next learn to become native speakers of their culture's language. Children imitate the perceived vocal patterns they hear other's produce and hear their own production. Interestingly, a similar study that links mirror neurons, motor imitation, social learning theory, and language is reviewed in section 5.15.

**5.** Motherese, or parentese, a universal way of talking to babies, is beneficial. Motherese helps babies discriminate speech sounds. Studies examining women from the United States, Russia, and Sweden show that infant-directed language from all three groups exaggerates the sounds that babies must learn to perceive. In addition to exaggerating sounds, infant-directed language assists babies in learning to form categories by repeat words in stereotyped sentences, such as "See the _____," and "Where is the _____?" that highlight ways to use new words. Infant-directed language is done unconsciously and helps babies map out the sounds and rules of language.

**6.** Is there a **critical period** for language development? Yes, but it is related to one's language *experience* rather than some older views that it is just a time period. The new view is a **neural commitment view**. This means that the ability to learn language later in life may be constrained by the initial mapping involved in learning one's native language. Studies in learning a second language support the neural commitment view. It is easiest to learn a second language when both are heard during the time when innate perceptual abilities are tuning into the sounds of language and then acting as magnets for other related sounds. Otherwise, it is harder to hear all of the necessary sounds. In addition, research on training others to learn a second language shows that the best training strategies are similar to motherese. These involve exaggerated speech sounds and large amounts of listening experience.

### Let's not forget about memes: They may explain some rapidly changing cultural phenomenon

Evolution can take place quite rapidly. Jeffrey Fagan and colleagues (2007) write that some human social behaviors may evolve through **memes**, *cultural software* that "is expressed in **language**, behavior, and **normative** expectations or behavioral **scripts**" (p. 691). Richard Dawkins (2006) invented the term memes in his book, *The Selfish Gene*. Susan Blakemore (2000) says that similar to genes, memes are a form of information that rapidly replicates through imitation. Any time you tell a story, sing a song, send a chain letter, or demonstrate a skill, even if you slightly change any of it a little, you are passing memes on to the next person.

I can draw a relationship between memes and **aggression**. New York saw a dramatic increase in the rise of homicides starting in 1985, followed by a dramatic decline a decade later (Fagan et al., 2007). These rapidly changing rates were different from rates in other places, making New York, in a sense, its own culture. Sometimes behaviors spread so rapidly that they are called **social contagions** that are similar to flu epidemics. Social contagions arise from "the mutual influence of individuals within social networks who turn to each other for cues and behavioral tools that reflect the contingencies of specific situations" (p. 689).

Memes are ideas that socially evolve in a way similar to genetic evolution; memes just change more rapidly then genes. Memes function like genes, meeting all the requirements of Darwinian evolution—replication, variation, and selection (Blakemore, 2000). Memes are the fittest ideas, ones that are rapidly copied through imitation, and ones that arise out of close proximity between people in social networks (Fagan et al., 2007). Memes sometimes even violate more typical social **norms** that evolved through the CAD. Beliefs are slow to change and although general cultural values are constantly changing, it is unlikely that they change quite this rapidly. Memes spread through *social synapses*. Psychologists know that **synapses** are modified by social situations, influencing the overall **neural network**.

Memes might help explain certain types of aggression, such as unexplainable acts of mass suicides or gross cruelty that is not part of an individual's typical personality. My students say that the Internet is constantly spreading memes. One unfortunate example is pictures and vicious gossip about someone, which may fuel **bullying**. Bullying is part of the Human Relationships option and memes may be an important concept. As technology becomes more sophisticated, memes have more and faster ways to spread.

## 3.6 Explain the Functions of Hormones in Human Behavior

**Hormones** are a *contributing* factor to behavior. Both bidirectional models have a place for hormones. No modern psychologist suggests that hormones are the *only* factor explaining human behavior, though some emphasize their impact.

### The importance of cortisol, estrogen, and testosterone

Two types of hormones are most useful for our discussion of behavior. One is the stress hormone **cortisol**, the most important of the glucocorticoids. Second are the sex hormones **estrogen** and **testosterone**. Both types are **steroid hormones** and are powerful influences on behavior.

Steroid hormones are produced from cholesterol by the adrenal cortex and the gonads, two of the endocrine glands.

There are two important things to keep in mine. First, both of these steroid hormones can influence the transcription process of genes. Second, hormones contribute to the differences between males and females on some cognitive tasks.

## Aggression, depression, and gender differences in cognitive abilities: Examples of how hormones affect behavior

Four previous studies in the book, reviewed in section 3.4, relate to the influence of hormones on behavior. Two are about **aggression**. These are Chaivegatto's study on hormones, genes, neurotransmitters and the effect on aggression in mice and Sjoberg's study on testosterone, genes, neurotransmitters, and human aggression in section. The other two are about **depression**. These are Caspi's study on hormones, genes, serotonin and the effect on depression and Sapolsky's view on stress hormones, genes, and depression. All four are reviewed in section 3.4 and can be used for exam questions on genetics, for questions about hormones and behavior, and for questions about neurotransmission and behavior. This is a chance to triple dip!

In this section, I raise the question, "To what extent do sex hormones explain **gender differences** in mathematics and verbal skills"? This material can also be used for section 3.10, "The interaction between cognition and physiology in terms of behavior."

## Note to the teacher

I highly recommend the film on spatial abilities from the series *The War of the Sexes,* available from the Films for the Humanities and Sciences.

Before students learn about gender and cognitive differences, I let them take some spatial rotation and verbal memory tests. One spatial test is available from www.encarta. msn.com/media_461547595/mental_rotation_test.html. Doreen Kimura's book, *Sex and Cognition* (1999) includes many spatial and verbal tests, along with reviews of study results. The students like to compare their answers and discuss why any gender differences exist.

## Some context for thinking about the role of male and female hormones in cognitive abilities

How might you answer the question "Why aren't more women in science"?

Many researchers have tackled the question but as of yet, none of the controversies are settled. While it is agreed that hormones make *some* contribution, some think they are more influential than others. Doreen Kimura emphasizes the role of hormones while Diane Halpern and colleagues take the middle position that hormones have some importance. In contrast, Deborah Stipek believes that **stereotypes** are the primary factor. The study by Herbert and Stipek (2005) reviewed in section 5.13 is a good contrast to the research on hormones.

One problem in answering the question is that studies isolating any one factor contributing to cognitive differences between males and females and the resulting career choices are extremely difficult to design. Another problem is that *most of the connections made between individual factors and cognitive abilities are correlations.* This includes the opinions of Kimura, Halpern, and Stipek.

My goal is to sort through some of issues involved in correlating hormones and gender differences in cognitive tasks.

Here are the facts. Females get better grades than males in school, test better than males on achievement tests, and have enrolled in undergraduate sciences majors increasingly over recent years (Kimura, 2007). In addition, females far outperform males on tests that include writing samples (Halpern et al., 2007). At the same time, men score consistently better than women on mathematical aptitude tests that use problems not rehearsed in school, enroll in science graduate programs far more than females, and dominate scientific fields such as physics, engineering, and architecture (Kimura, 2007).

Gender differences do not exist in broad mathematical or verbal abilities and are not evident in general intelligence testing (Kimura, 2007). Rather, there are some very specific performance differences. Kimura writes that hormones organize male and female brains differently in a *general* way so it is unlikely that researchers will find *one* specific brain part that accounts for the differences.

Kimura (2007) examined 50 years of research into the gender differences and found some consistent trends.

1. Prenatal and developmental sex hormones are important factors for spatial ability.
2. These differences appear early in life before social factors influence behavior.
3. The difference exists across **culture**.
4. The differences do not change when females receive extensive training as adults.
5. The performance has not changed over time for the highest levels of mathematical reasoning.
6. Animals show the same sex differences in spatial performance.

What are the specific performance differences? Kimura divides them into large and small differences.

Here are the large differences.

1. Males perform better on some spatial tasks, particularly mental rotation, mechanical reasoning, and throwing accuracy.
2. Females perform better on tasks of verbal memory and object location memory.

Here are the smaller differences.

1. Males are favored on mathematical reasoning and spatial visualization tasks.
2. Females perform better on verbal fluency and perceptual speed tasks.

Kimura is concerned that psychologists automatically conclude that the differences are explainable by social influences. But since data are primarily analyzed with correlations, Kimura thinks it could easily be the other way around, and innate differences could be the greatest contributing factor to performance. Kimura interprets the research differently than many others. Bidirectional thinking allows researchers to place emphasis on one factor contributing to a behavior as long as the others are not completely ignored. Do you think Kimura has a point? Your class should decide if her explanation represents good or bad **reductionism**.

Kimura outlined the results from Camilla Benbow's 1988 SMPY (studies of mathematically precocious youth, including males and females). Even within this elite group, males still outperformed females on the above-mentioned tasks at the rate of about 10:1. The females in the SMPY study were also more likely not to select career fields that emphasized specialized mathematical skills.

The performance differences between males and females are *robust,* meaning that differences show up over large populations each time the research is conducted.

David Lubinski and Camilla Benbow (2007) and Halpern and colleagues (2007) also notice that males are over-represented at both ends of the cognitive abilities scale and find fewer performance differences in the middle range of the science and math achievement test distributions. The largest differences are at the highest and lowest of the math and science ranges, with males at both ends. Males outnumber females on developmental disorders such as retardation and learning disabilities *and* on the highest functioning tasks associated with science, technology, engineering, and mathematics. These observations hold true across multiple samples.

Lubinski and Benbow write that individual *interests* complicate interpretations about cognitive abilities. Studies typically focus on what people are good at in school and how interests influence skills. How can we understand the relative contribution of any one factor? Females talented in math may pursue verbal related careers because they perform *even better* on verbal tests than they do on spatial tests. Talent does not ensure that someone will choose a career in a particular field. Interest is an important variable. Surveys repeatedly show that females are more interested in working with people and males are more interested in things.

This preference difference was also seen in the study, where mathematically talented girls choose to become physicians more frequently and the males choose to become engineers and physical scientists. In addition, females report on surveys that they wish to work 40 hours per week or less, preferring to make time for families. Work preferences could have something to do with career choices and how far a career will develop.

It is difficult to know how much preferences are shaped by innate factors and social learning.

## How do we investigate whether hormones play a significant role in cognitive abilities?

There are four steps to figuring out the answer to this question. First, research must show the performance differences. Next, it must be established that there are brain differences between males and females that might account for the differences. Then it must be established that these brain differences served an evolutionary need. Finally, it must be shown that hormones affected the evolved brain differences in some way.

This is a lot to do.

## Two studies by Kimura on gender differences in spatial and verbal abilities

The studies by Kimura show that gender differences in performance are real. The two films from *The War of the Sexes* series review studies from other researchers who also favor biological explanations.

### Study #1: Gender differences in mathematics performance

Modern research takes **cognitive mapping** far beyond Tolman's rats. Kimura (1999, 2002) describes a cognitive mapping experiment on human males and females that she conducted in 1993. Kimura asked if significant gender differences appear when study participants learn new routes. This is quasi-experiment where males and females are compared and an independent variable is not manipulated. First, researchers traced a route with a stylus, a tracing pen that left no lines on the map. Participants then traced the routes from memory while the researchers corrected and counted mistakes until the subjects completed the task two times without errors. Results showed that males had fewer errors, took fewer trials to complete the task, and completed the task in less time. These findings are similar to other research showing that males have better mapping skills than females, increasing the **observer triangulation** for gender and cognitive mapping research.

Kimura then correlated the results of the mapping experiment with male and female performance on an imaginational rotation task. Better scores on the rotation task were correlated with better mapping performance. Kimura considered this important evidence for her argument. General intelligence is not correlated with mapping skills. So the correlation between mapping skills and mental rotation implies that there is a distinct skill that accounts for these specific tasks. Kimura thinks that the male advantage for mental rotation tasks had an evolutionary basis. As we continue thinking about cognitive differences, it appears that the hormone argument is closely tied with evolution.

### Study #2: Gender differences in verbal task performance

Kimura and Paul Clarke (2002) ran a quasi-experiment testing the hypothesis that females have better verbal memory than males. Verbal memory differences are *not* related to overall verbal ability, which is associated with general intelligence. Forty-four females and 41 men participated in three experimental conditions. The tasks in all three conditions tested various types of verbal memory skills using the same 16 words, such as elephant and freedom. The first condition required participants to recall as many nouns as they could from the list of 16. This list was shown three times to subjects in varying order. In the second condition, the 16 words were paired together in an unrelated way. Participants heard 10 pairs of unrelated words three times in varying order and recalled as many as possible. In the third condition, the 16 words were grouped in pairs containing an abstract and a concrete word. After participating in one of three experimental conditions, all subjects took a general vocabulary test. Results showed that females outperformed males on all three conditions. Since there is no significant gender difference on general vocabulary, the experimental differences are not explainable by overall verbal ability. Verbal memory appears to be a distinctive skill that may have evolutionary roots, just like mental rotation.

## Some brain research that might explain mathematics and verbal differences

Kimura's position is that *hormones organize male and female brains in a general way* so it is unlikely that the brain is **localized** for cognitive abilities. It makes sense that multiple brain processes must come together to produce verbal and mathematical reasoning.

Reuben Gur and Raquel Gur (2007) examined a large group of studies and identified gender differences in four areas of brain anatomy and physiology that *might* contribute to gender differences in cognitive abilities.

1. differences in **gray matter** and **white matter**
2. differences in the **corpus callosum**
3. differences in cerebral blood flow and cerebral glucose metabolism
4. differences in the neurotransmitter **dopamine**

Gray and white matter makes up our brain tissue. Structural MRI shows that males have higher percentages of white matter and females have higher percentages of gray matter. These differences are localized to some extent. Males have a higher proportion of their gray matter in the left hemisphere and there is no localization difference for female's gray matter. Even though this localization difference exists, females still have an overall larger volume of gray matter in the brain. What does the gray and white matter difference mean? It is hard to know because so few studies examine the question. Gur and Gur correlated cognitive performance with gray and white matter in their own sample. Results showed that females scored higher on verbal tasks and males scored higher on spatial tasks. This is a correlation study, so it is unknown if gray and white matter cause the cognitive differences. Gur and Gur noted a difference in *developmental* periods of gray and white matter growth that may explain cognitive differences. Gray matter development in the frontal cortex and the occipital region peaks earlier in females. White matter increases in both males and females from ages 4 to 22 but at a higher rate for males. The longer development time in males is correlated with spatial performance.

A small amount of imaging studies suggests that the corpus callosum is larger in females. The corpus callosum is a bundle of fibers connecting the left and right hemispheres that facilitates hemispheric communication. There is evidence that the splenium, the back section of the corpus callosum, is larger in females. Could the larger corpus callosum and splenium give females an advantage in verbal abilities? The splenium may have something to do with greater hemispheric communication that translates into greater verbal abilities. Males have a larger midsection of the corpus callosum, called the genu. The genu is used in motor coordination in men and may have been related to better spatial abilities. Watch making a sweeping generalization here because there is really no consensus on these findings; there are no clear standards for measuring the corpus callosum.

Women have higher rates of resting cerebral blood flow than men. Females have higher activation in both hemispheres when completing language tests than males. Female brains work harder when completing spatial tasks than male brains, calling additional brain regions to help solve tasks. On the other hand, resting metabolic glucose rates are equal in males and females. Male brains use higher glucose metabolism in all basal ganglia areas and the cerebellum, both of which help control movement. Females have higher glucose metabolism in the cingulate gyrus, which is part of the limbic system and is correlated with better language task performance.

Correlation studies show that females have greater amounts of dopamine available in the caudate nucleus and that they also perform better on verbal tasks than males.

Is it reasonable to conclude that these brain differences are at least partially responsible for gender differences in cognitive abilities?

Halpern and colleagues (2007) believe that only tentative conclusions are possible from the limited evidence available on brain differences and cognitive abilities. Few large-scale studies exist on the topic. Halpern's group does make some hypotheses about brain localization and cognitive tasks that need future verification. One hypothesis is that female brains have better communication between the hemispheres, helping girls excel more at tasks requiring bilateral activation. For example, it is predicted that girls should have the advantage at tasks where they use language to integrate spatial information. Kimura also suggested that females had an advantage in spatial skills requiring language. Conversely, males should excel in tasks requiring lateralized activation.

The next step is to ask how these brain differences might be related to hormones. Questions about the relationship between brain differences and hormones are closely tied to evolution.

## Evolution's contribution to explanations of gender differences in cognitive abilities

To what extent did evolutionary solutions to the problems humans faced create the brain differences between males and females, and to what extent did hormones influence brain evolution?

Halpern and colleagues (2007) believe that evolution is a *contributing* factor to the observed gender differences in cognitive skills, one piece of the puzzle. In addition, hormones probably *contributed* to the evolution of the brain differences.

We must think bidirectionally. While Kimura is not alone in identifying the robust gender differences in spatial and verbal behavior, her emphasis on hormones as a primary explanation is not shared. Halpern's group examined the evidence and found that as a single explanation, hormones were not sufficient, though they played a role. Too many things interfered with identifying hormones as the fundamental cause of cognitive differences. Halpern cites difficulties in conducting research, limitations of correlations, confounding variables, and alternative explanations. In addition, Halpern's team points out that since experience changes the brain (**neuroplasticity**) "causal statements about brain differences and success in math and science are circular" (p. 1). Biological factors are important, but they combine with other factors such as culture, family, school experience, and training.

Here are the conclusions that Halpern and colleagues drew about the evolution of the human brain, the role of hormones in shaping it, and the potential impact of evolution and hormones on cognitive abilities:

1. All evolved traits were adaptations to solve problems. As the mathematics and sciences are recent human activities, it is unlikely that evolution is a *direct* cause of the differences in cognitive skills. Rather, evolution probably had an *indirect* impact, where brain differences between males and females built on other adaptive solutions to the problems humans faced.

2. Darwin proposed that natural selection accounted for the evolution of gender differences. These differences come from mate selection. Males *competed* with other males for the best female mates and at the same time females made *choices* to select best mates. Traits that helped individuals compete and choose were selected and passed on to the next generation.

3. Here is where hormones are important. Traits to help competing and choosing were influenced by pre and postnatal exposure to **androgens**. Androgens are the hormones responsible for masculine traits. Testosterone is the primary androgen. It is believed that the level of androgens in a person influences their general brain organization and this general brain organization may affect cognitive abilities. One example is the male advantage in spatial skills. To compete successfully for mates, males developed brains that helped them to navigate over large distances and fight off rivals. The male advantage in mental rotation skills was directed at navigational skills. The male advantage in throwing accuracy and tracking movement in 3-D space may be leftover from the need to create weapons such as spears.

4. Halpern and colleagues write that if hormones are valid explanations of differences in cognitive skills, correlations should be obvious between the expression of the traits (better spatial skills) and exposure to androgens.

One way to study the correlation between spatial skills and androgens is to study females with **congenital adrenal hyperplasia (CAH)**. CAH females are prenatally exposed to abnormally high levels of androgens. Females with CAH show masculine play behavior and this is sometimes offered as evidence for the role of hormones. But Halpern and colleagues argue that too many variables confound the interpretation of these cases over time. The cases are unreliable evidence as the girls *develop*. For example, CAH females often are treated with drugs as soon as they are diagnosed. In addition, parents exaggerate the demands for the girls to take on a feminine role that counteracts the effects of the androgens. These cases are inconclusive.

Even if studies identify gender differences in developmental tasks, the tasks are hard to correlate with evolved competition/choice behaviors and exposure to hormones. It is not hard to document gender differences in performance that emerge in school but it is hard to link them directly to evolved behaviors of competition/choice and hormone exposure. Alternative explanations for any correlation are social and cultural factors, such as Herbert and Stipek's (2005) study about stereotyping and cognitive differences. It is well known that *culture has a greater effect on slow developing species,* such as humans. Biology has more of a direct influence on animal development.

## Conclusions about the claim that hormones explain gender differences in mathematics and verbal performance

The idea that hormones *contribute* to gender differences in cognitive abilities, but do not account for all of the differences, fits neatly into modern bidirectional thinking. Halpern and colleagues point out that many psychologists have taken a *middle position* on the role of hormones in verbal and spatial task differences. They believe that hormones are important, but emphasize adaptations to the social and cultural context. Science and math skills are relatively new for humans, so the demands of modern society play an important role for a complete explanation.

## 3.7 Discuss Two Effects of the Environment on Physiological Processes

The concept **neuroplasticity** is necessary for understanding how the brain adapts to the environment. Neuroplasticity refers to "the brain's ability to reorganize itself in response to the environment throughout the lifespan. Neuroplasticity allows neurons in the brain to compensate for injury or disease and to adjust their activities in response to new situations or changes in their environment" (www.medterms.com).

## Note to the teacher

*Scientific American Frontiers* has a video titled "Changing Your Mind" that examines research on neuroplasticity. The entire film series from *Scientific American Mind,* hosted by Alan Alda, is very popular with students. This particular film includes an interesting experiment about neuroplasticity and changes to the visual cortex after blindness. The study is by Alvaro Pascual-Leone. The film is available from www.pbs.org.

Neuroplasticity is an abstract topic so I find it helpful to use this film to introduce students to neuroplasticity before I discuss Brian Kolb's ideas.

## Introduction to neuroplasticity

**Bidirectional** thinking *assumes* neuroplasticity. Experiences are powerful modifiers of the brain; the brain is constantly changing. A few of the experiences that affect neuroplasticity are stimulating environments, sex hormones, diet, genetics, and stress (Kolb, Gibb & Robinson, 2004). We have control over many of these factors. Human brains are highly plastic because a child's brain is immature at birth and must develop within the **cultural** context.

Neuroplasticity research overlaps the topics of neurotransmitters, neural networks, localization, hormones, and genes. It is one of the concepts that unite a large number of modern psychology topics.

Any general psychology text discusses neurons, synapses, glia and dendrites. All are necessary to understand neuroplasticity.

The assumption underlying neuroplasticity is that *as behavior changes there must also be a corresponding change in the neural circuitry that produces behavior* (Kolb, Gibb, & Robinson, 2004). When new neurons are created in response to experience, it is called **neurogenesis**. Plasticity and neurogenesis occur *over the entire lifespan,* though the brain is most plastic early in development. Research on neurogenesis is new and it is unclear if the changes are permanent, though the research appears promising. Anyone studying memory and learning should be interested neurogenesis and the hippocampus.

## Research on stimulating environments and how they affect the brain

Early research on neuroplasticity asked if stimulating environments affected the growth of neurons in rats (Kolb, 1999). It does.

One experiment performed by Brian Kolb and colleagues compared rats placed in enriched environments for three months beginning at weaning or as young adults with those of similar ages raised in standard cages. Rats housed in enriched environments at both ages showed better performance on a variety of behavioral tasks than the control rats living in standard cages. Both age groups housed in enriched environments showed a large increase in the length of dendrites in cortical pyramidal neurons. In addition, rats of different ages showed different brain changes. In comparison to control rats, the older rats had an increase in neuron spine density and the younger rats had a decrease in neuron spine density. It is unclear why there are age related brain changes in addition to the general ones. The list of brain areas where plasticity and neurogenesis occur is growing.

In another experiment pregnant rat mothers were housed in enriched environments and compared to control rats. Their babies had increases in synaptic space on cortical neurons as adults. It is possible that hormonal changes in the mother were passed onto the babies through the placenta and these **hormones** gave messages to genes (Kolb, Gibb, & Robinson, 2004).

## Tolerate uncertainty: Ethical and methodological challenges in studying neuroplasticity

Rats, mice, and primates are subjects in experiments where scientists compare specific brain damage to normal brains under varying conditions. We cannot damage human brains in the lab. Kolb (1999) warns that we should not assume that human brains are plastic in exactly the same way as rat brains. However, some generalizations from rat experiments probably apply to humans.

Elizabeth Gould and Charles Gross (2002) show in experiments that plasticity and neurogenesis occurs in adult primate brains; the evidence is not limited to lower cognitive animals. Neurogenesis is now generally accepted and may advance research for humans with a wide range of difficulties, such as depression and Alzheimer's. However, the research is still new with some methodological challenges to resolve.

Brian Kolb and colleagues (2004) write that measuring neuroplasticity in the lab is challenging. It involves deciding if synaptic changes have occurred between neurons. As the human brain contains roughly 100 billion neurons and each neuron makes about several thousand synapses, it is not easy to study. Scanning the brain for changes takes too much time. A better measuring technique is a method that stains a random subset of neurons so that cell bodies and dendritic trees are visible. This staining technique has only been done on animals in experiments manipulating a specific variable, such as an enriched environment, specific damage, or a mineral supplement. Researchers can estimate the number of synapses on the dendritic surface at a given time. The amount of space available for synapses on dendritic surfaces is known, so it is assumed that increases or decreases in the dendritic surface reflect changes in synapses.

The substance BrdU is one way to stain (mark) new neurons (Gould & Gross, 2002). BrdU is used because it is absorbed by cells undergoing DNA synthesis. Researchers use stereological methods to count the new neurons, a technique by which 3-dimensional material is estimated from viewing 2-dimensional planes. Research using BrdU marking shows that neurons grow even in higher species, such as in the prefrontal cortexes of monkeys. Gould and Gross estimate that about 270,000 new cells are produced in the dendrate gryus of rats each month. Imagine how many new cells might grow in an adolescent's maturing prefrontal cortex. We can measure some positive adaptive changes to the existing human brain structures right now in lab settings, such as how tactile systems in the blind are given space on the original visual cortex. Conversely, animal experiments show that exposure to stress decreases neurogenesis.

Studying plasticity and neurogenesis in labs *does not prove anything.* In fact, there are some frustrating limitations to this research. For example, BrdU is toxic and researchers must monitor the dosage. Because it enters cells during protein synthesis, BrdU has the potential to cause mutations. Ethical guidelines allow animals to be put at more risk than humans if the research is of great scientific value to humans. But how can we validate neurogenesis and plasticity in humans? Is there a safe level for humans in research or are we limited to inferring brain changes from animal experiments? Another concern is that lab conditions might keep new neurons from surviving as long as they would in a natural environment. It is possible that lab studies have underestimated the amount of neuron growth in animals.

The brain imaging studies on neuroplasticity in humans just identify general brain activity. Human neurons are not marked with BrdU in any of the neuroplasticity studies in this book.

## Etiologies of depression and neuroplasticity

Section 7.9 includes a study by Small and Vorgan (2008) suggesting that technology use alters neural circuitry. Small and Vorgan introduce us to the iBrain.

## Depression treatment and neuroplasticity

Section 7.14 includes a study by Goldapple and colleagues (2004) suggesting that both cognitive therapy (CT) and drug treatments alter the brain. Here is a chance to use the same study for this section and for treatments of mental illness.

## Bilingualism, localization, and neuroplasticity

Section 3.9 on **localization** of brain function reviews two studies demonstrating how the brain adapts to environmental demands. One is an experiment by Carreiras and colleagues (2005) on shepherds who use a whistling language in the Canary Islands. The other is a meta-analysis by Hull and Vaid (2006) showing that bilinguals who learned their second language on or before age 6 had more bilateralism than bilinguals who learned their second language after age 6 or monolinguals.

## Stress and the brain

Stress affects neurotransmitters and can even shrink the **hippocampus**. Studying modern abnormal psychology and health psychology requires that you understand the bidirectional relationship between stress and the brain. See Sapolsky's comments on stress, depression, and the brain in section 3.4. Stress affects the brain at all points on Walker's bidirectional model.

## Some concluding general ideas about neuroplasticity

Kolb (1999) makes some good generalizations about neuroplasticity.

1. Neuroplasticity occurs throughout the lifespan, though the brain is most plastic early in life.

2. "Cortical plasticity functions to reorganize the cortical structure that is defined by a basic genetic template" (p. 32). Kolb says the genetic blueprint does not code for specific destinations of new neurons, but gives general instructions, allowing for novel connections or modifying existing neural circuits.

3. Behavior changes occur *after* neuroplasticity changes.

4. The brain can reorganize itself after injury. The brain spontaneously reorganizes itself right after injury so this is the best time for treatment.

## 3.8 Explain Effects of Neurotransmission on Human Behavior

**Neurotransmitters** affect everything you do and everything you do affects neurotransmitters. Genes and hormones affect neurotransmitters, which then affect behavior. In addition, learning, psychotherapy, stress, and even the food you eat affect neurotransmitters.

This section focuses on the dietary affects on neurotransmitters, which then affects mood. Diet, meaning what you eat rather than a weight loss plan, is something you can control. We cannot control the genes we inherit. But since genes cannot affect behavior unless they are expressed, perhaps lifestyles changes can reduce the risk of problems associated with neurotransmitter imbalances.

Higgins (2008) writes that doctors may one day include dietary changes as a way to reduce **epigenetic factors** that increase the risk of mental illness.

### Food and mood

Why do so many people fail to eat properly? There are hundreds of reasons, such as busy schedules and lack of good information. The food/sleep challenge project (see Appendix) is a way to experiment with healthier diets. I do it together with my class to build a support system. Diet affects most aspects of the Walker-Tessner bidirectional model of psychiatric outcome. The building blocks of normal neurotransmitter functioning start prenatally. Improper manufacture and functioning of neurotransmitters is a constitutional vulnerability. Continued poor diet negatively affects one's ability to cope with life stressors. Life stressors in turn contribute to increases of stress hormones and a greater risk of mental and physical health problems.

**Culture** has a lot to do with what foods are available. I am not suggesting that all high school students eat poorly. But unfortunately, many students "eat on the run." As a consequence, in cultures where fast food is plentiful and affordable, we may be seeing many consequences of diets deficient in the essential amino acids such as the **tryptophan** needed to manufacture the neurotransmitter **serotonin**.

The saying "you are what you eat" is true. Food impacts how neurotransmitters function in the brain, which then affects behavior. Approximately 70 neurotransmitters regulate nerve functioning and contribute to normal mood, memory, and sleep patterns (Somer, 1999). Incorrect amounts of a wide range of neurotransmitters and hormones interfere with the communication between neurons that increases the risk of mental illness such as depression.

Serotonin is currently a popular neurotransmitter with researchers and the media, one highlighted in many studies reviewed in this book. Serotonin is linked to a large range of behaviors seen by clinicians, including **depression**, **antisocial behavior**, **autism**, **anxiety**, **addictions**, and **eating disorders** (Manuck, Kaplan, & Lotrich, 2006).

Serotonin is a **monoamine**, part of a group of neurotransmitters that includes dopamine and norepinephrine. Each monoamine is synthesized from a single amino acid. Serotonin is synthesized from the essential amino acid tryptophan. Elizabeth Somer (1999) writes that our bodies do not produce tryptophan; we must get it from foods such as milk, meat, vegetables, and fruit. "No other neurotransmitter is as strongly linked to your diet as serotonin" (p. 14). Serotonin is synthesized both in neurons in the central nervous system and in cells located in the gut. Contrary to popular belief, most serotonin is not located in the brain. Rather, serotonin is carried to the brain after it is synthesized in the gut (Manuck, Kaplan, & Lotrich, 2006). The lesson here is that a proper diet can go a long way to helping you maintain proper levels of brain serotonin. Low levels of serotonin are linked to depression. As people have different sensitivities to foods and drugs treatments, and react differently to therapy, treatment must be individualized. Health care practitioners must find the right dietary treatment for each patient (Somer, 1999).

Besides providing essential amino acids, food provides other nutrients vital for proper neurotransmitter functioning. B vitamins, vitamin C, selenium, and magnesium help the body produce neurotransmitters that protect it from damage (Somer, 1999). Consuming too many fats or carbohydrates outside of balanced meals contributes to depression by making neurotransmitters either over or under active. A lack of some nutrients, such as protein and zinc, can potentially cause irreversible damage to the nervous system, effecting mental function and personality. Many food additives interfere with normal neurotransmitter functioning, stopping their manufacture or blocking their release.

Diets should be balanced. Diets too high in protein or in simple carbohydrates cause imbalances in both blood sugar levels and neurotransmitters that affect mood (Somer, 1999). Diets high in simple carbohydrates, especially refined sugar, are the greatest problem for many persons. The tendency is to either skip breakfast or eat something high in sugar content, such as a donut and fruit juice, a soda, or coffee loaded with sugar and caffeine.

Sugar is a good source of energy, so why does it cause low mood and energy (Somer, 1999)? There are two kinds of carbohydrates. Simple carbohydrates, such as refined sugar, convert more quickly to a rise in blood sugar, whereas complex carbohydrates, such as beans, enter the bloodstream at a slower rate. "Sugar rapidly enters the bloodstream, causing a dramatic rise in blood sugar. To counteract this rise, the pancreas releases the hormone insulin, which shuttles excess sugar from the blood into the cells. Consequently, blood sugars drop, often to lower levels than before the snack" (p. 108). At the same time, foods high in sugar and caffeine raise serotonin levels in the brain, which can slow people down. A vicious cycle begins, where someone has low energy and mood, and uses sugar and caffeine to raise energy and mood. Unfortunately, the highs associated with sugar and caffeine drop dramatically after a short time and the person reaches again for the same foods. Meals and snacks balanced for fats, proteins, and carbohydrates do not cause this cycle; in fact, eating a mixture of carbohydrates and proteins create stabilized blood-sugar levels for about 3-4 hours at a time (Somers, 1999).

People with depression tend to prefer and crave sweet carbohydrate and fat-rich foods that rapidly raise and then lower blood sugar (Christensen, 2001). Christensen (2007) proposes an integrative model about the development and maintenance of distress that may explain these preferences and cravings. Negative mood starts the process of food cravings because foods high in sugar and caffeine reward the brain with a good feeling. The person selects the foods most likely to give quick relief to low mood and energy. The positive effects of sugary and caffeine laden food is temporary; low mood and energy result. A vicious cycle then exists where a person self-medicates their low mood and energy with food preferences that end with the same or lower mood and energy.

## Research on food, neurotransmitters, and depression

Depressed people may benefit from diets low in sugar and caffeine. Better diet can stabilize neurotransmitters that in turn stabilize mood. Larry Christensen & Ross Burrows (1990) conducted an experiment testing this idea. Twenty participants were recruited from newspaper advertisements and university referrals. Several assessment scales, including the Beck Depression Inventory (BDI), were used to select participants meeting DSM-III-R depression criteria. Participants rated the severity of symptoms such as levels of sadness, guilt, and self-blame. After screening for depression symptoms, researchers selected *only those whose depression was related to diet with the Christensen Dietary Distress Inventory (CDDI)*. The CDDI contains questions such as "What is the most frequent cause of your depression when you experience it"? Participants were also administered questionnaires measuring their level of expectancy for the outcome of their participation. Subjects were randomly assigned to groups, 10 in each, and dietary changes were made for three weeks. The experimental group eliminated added sucrose and caffeine. The control group eliminated red meat and artificial sweeteners. Participants kept records of the foods they ate over the course of the study and received sample food plans to help guide their choices. Saliva tests measuring caffeine content were used for a baseline measurement of caffeine in the body and then throughout the study to assess faithfulness to the plan. Participants returned once a week for a short interview and a saliva test.

The food records and saliva tests showed that participants followed their diets over three weeks with only minor lapses. Those removing sucrose and caffeine from their diets had significantly fewer depression symptoms than those from the control group at the end of three weeks. The benefits were maintained after three months. The authors concluded that dietary changes were successful for most but not all of the study participants.

The results are not generalizable to *all* depressed patients. Participants in this study were selected because it was believed that diet was contributing to their depression; *they were not a random sample of depressed patients.* This study took place over an extended period of time. It is not fully controlled, though rigorous measures were taken to encourage participants to stay on their assigned diets.

More research is necessary on depression and food. While research suggests that certain foods are problematic for depressed persons, there are still individual differences in sensitivities. It is difficult to identify food sensitivities and attempts to measure them using psychometric tests are crude (Christensen, 2001). In addition, dietary changes take a lot of time and motivation.

Theories explaining the relationship between depression and diet are incomplete (Christensen, 2007). Though cravings are an important research variable, operationally defining cravings is difficult. Different definitions are used in research and cravings vary by age and **gender**. Women have more cravings for refined sugar and fat-rich foods. More research is needed on the biology of cravings, the role of food cues in cravings, and the resulting mood and energy.

## Concluding remarks on food and depression

Diet is *one* factor that increases the risk of depression. By highlighting the diet material in this section, I am not downplaying any other contributing factors.

I want my students to consider their diet, and not just because food relates to mood. Food choice is essential to overall good health. After the food challenge, students report *less stress*. Eating a balanced breakfast is the most important aspect of the food challenge; it is easier to stay awake in morning classes. In addition, many parents notice more stable mood in their teenagers. There are even cases where an entire family does the food and sleep challenge together, reporting that the family "gets along better now."

## Other examples of neurotransmission affecting behavior

Section 3.4 contains several studies on neurotransmission, depression, and aggression. These studies may be used for questions about neurotransmission.

## 3.9 Explain One Study Related to Localization of Function in the Brain

### An introduction to localization

The brain is localized for some specific functions but modern research shows that it is not as localized as once believed. **Neuroplasticity** allows the brain to adapt. Recent research shows that the right brain plays more of a supportive role in language than originally thought from studying people with abnormal brains. In addition, the environment even has some influence on localization in development. **Language** is the focus of my discussion for two reasons. First, a great amount of localization research concerns language. Second, I want to stay focused on some important neuroscience behind the cognitive process that is fundamental to human **culture**—language.

**Broca** and **Wernicke** are researchers frequently cited on exams. However, psychologists have learned a tremendous amount about localization and language since then. Recent research has modified the early **classic localizationist view**. If you plan on using these early cases on the exam, please consult a critique of them by Michael Gazzaniga and colleagues (2008). A full analysis of historical cases requires students to know their limitations.

**Split-brain cases** are also frequently cited on the IB exams. Gazzaniga warns that split-brain patients had abnormal brains even before their operations. These cases suffer from population validity problems, meaning that the results do not generalize well to persons with normal brains.

Modern localization research is an opportunity to relate research to current concepts that unite modern psychology, such as neuroplasticity, bidirectional thinking, and the influence of culture on brain development. In addition, my examples about the whistling language and bilingual speakers are about people with *normal* brains. Without research on normal people, students have an incomplete picture how the brain functions.

Jerome Kagan (2007) writes that the urge to find a single cause for behavior contributes to the attractiveness of localization theories. Some sensory functions are localized to specific neural regions. But complex abstract human cognitive processing is possible only with the coordination of many smaller brain regions. "The error in the argument for localization is the assumption that if a select area of the brain is reliably activated by an event or task, then the psychological process being engaged by the event is probably localized in the same area" (p. 362). For example, damage to a specific part of the brain may make a person unable to comprehend language but it does not mean that language comprehension is localized in the damaged area. The specific damage is just disruption in one part of the total process. Language comprehension requires "an intact basal membrane, an auditory nerve, several brain stem nuclei, a thalamus, parts of the frontal lobe," *and* **Wernicke's area** (p. 363). Damage to Wernicke's area is not sufficient to explain language comprehension problems.

Popular culture has contributed to the common **reductionist** view of localization. Left-brain/right-brain explanations for behavior are oversimplified and part of popular culture (Kalat, 2007). The modern research on localization does not support a *strict* division. You may have taken a test to see if you are left- or right-brained. Persons typically claim that they are "right-brained," for example, simply on the basis of performing poorly on a logic test or well on a creativity test. But without a brain scan it is impossible to know if you are primarily "right-brained."

## Modern research on localization: The whistling language

Manuel Carreiras and colleagues (2005) write that shepherds in the Canary Islands use a whistled language called *Silbo Gomero* to communicate with other shepherds over long distances. Silbo is a rare "language" that is endangered in our modern world. Silbo whistlers provided a chance to study how the brain adapts to environmental demands. The authors conclude "that areas of the brain normally associated with spoken-language function are also activated in proficient whistlers, but not in controls, when they are listening to Silbo Gomero" (p. 31).

This is a quasi-experiment, where groups consist of those proficient at using Silbo and controls that are not.

Silbo reduces the total range of the Spanish language phonemes, the sounds that are different from each other, to two, along with four consonants. Silbo "words" change Spanish words into whistles that range from low to high pitch and differ in melody. Silbo whistlers use *context* to figure out the *meaning* of the whistles. *The demands of the environment shaped the way the shepherds communicated in their culture and their brains adapted.*

The left temporal and inferior frontal lobes of the brain are not limited to the processing of spoken language as one might think; they are also activated when deaf persons process visual sign language and when people process nonlinguistic acoustic symbols.

The aim of the study was to see if the whistled language was also processed in the left temporal and inferior frontal lobes and to see if the brains of Silbo users differed from the brains of non-Silbo users.

Silbadores, users of Silbo, and nonusers had their brains scanned with **fMRI** while completing two tasks. The first task was a baseline scan. Both groups listened passively to Silbo and Spanish sentences that were compared to digitally reversed Silbo sentences. In the second task both groups paid attention to Silbo and Spanish sentences that were mixed with silent periods.

The results showed that the brains of proficient Silbo whistlers in both tasks used parts of the left hemisphere associated with speech production. In addition, the brain scans of Silbo users showed an activation of the right-hemisphere superior-midtemporal region when using both Spanish and Silbo. It is interesting that the right hemisphere is involved to some degree. This is something that is found in other research on bilinguals.

Carreiras and colleagues conclude, "Silbo modulates cortical activity in the Silbadores and not in the controls" (p. 31). How are the brain changes in Silbo users explained? Silbo uses pitch and melody that are distinct from spoken language. But at the same time, the sounds are a way to communicate. Even if the whistled sounds are unusual, the left hemisphere responds to them *because* they are used as a language.

## Modern research on localization: Bilingualism

I am frequently asked if the brains of bilingual persons are different from the brains of monolingual persons. The answer is yes. Acquiring a second language early in life affects brain localization.

**Neuroplasticity** explains the differences. Acquiring two languages on or before age 6 stimulates more and different neural pathways than in children who speak just one language and in people who acquire a second language after age 6 (Hull & Vaid, 2006).

This study is a **meta-analysis**. I give details on meta-analysis research at the end of the section, but generally, a meta-analysis looks for themes in a large body of studies on the same topic that use different designs. Little differences in study design make comparisons confusing without meta-analysis research.

Rachel Hull and Jyotsna Vaid examined 23 studies on a total of 1234 normal monolingual and bilingual participants. All of the studies tested monolinguals and bilinguals speaking the same languages. A primary aim of the meta-analysis was to see if and under what conditions second language experience affected brain development.

Unanswered questions from previous studies on bilinguals led Hull and Vaid to believe that the right hemisphere was important. First, studies suggested that while the left hemisphere was dominant for language processing, the right hemisphere supported the process more than was typically believed. The idea that the right brain was not important in language processing was based on studies using monolingual participants or on studies of damaged brains. Second, case studies on language loss and recovery in bilingual aphasics led researchers to believe that multiple languages might be localized in different brain areas. Third, the age that someone acquires a second language and their level of proficiency might affect the pattern of left hemisphere dominance.

Hull and Vaid identified four hypotheses to explain possible right hemisphere involvement.

One is the **second language hypothesis**, suggesting that bilinguals use more of the right brain.

The second is the **balanced bilingual hypothesis**, suggesting that proficient bilinguals are more right-brain lateralized than monolinguals.

The third is the **age of second language hypothesis**, suggesting that the closer in time two languages are acquired, the more similar the brain localization.

The fourth is the **stage of second language hypothesis** suggesting that the early stages of learning a second language depends largely on contextual cues, which are localized in the right hemisphere. The left hemisphere becomes dominant as the person becomes more proficient with the second language and it is processed in a way similar to the first.

Would results of the meta-analysis support any of the four? Hull and Vaid included these three variables in their study.

1. *Experience.* Participants were either monolinguals or bilinguals.
2. *Proficiency.* Brain differences between proficient and non-proficient bilinguals were examined.
3. The *age* of acquiring the second language; either early, on or before age 6, or late, after age 6, was examined.

Some of the important findings of the meta-analysis are listed below. *Early experience appears the key variable.*

1. Monolinguals and bilinguals who acquired their second language after age 6 showed the most left hemisphere dominance. This was the most striking finding and supports the age of second language hypothesis.
2. Early bilinguals were bilateral. This supports the second language hypothesis.
3. There were no significant hemispheric localization differences between the proficient and non-proficient bilinguals. This means that the balanced bilingual hypothesis and the stage of second language hypothesis were not supported by this meta-analysis.

Hull and Vaid wonder if "the privileged early left hemisphere growth so often observed in monolinguals is a *consequence* rather than an antecedent of housing only one language system, and that the right hemisphere could similarly undergo rapid early growth when multiple languages must be accommodated" (p. 459). Their view contrasts theories suggesting that the brain evolved left hemisphere localization. Gazzaniga and colleagues (2008) believe that there may have been an evolutionary advantage to being able to access language quickly. It would take longer to access language if it were bilateralized. But Hull and Vaid feel that traditional theories suggesting that language is localized in the left brain are based on studying monolinguals and the brains of abnormal patients. Hull and Vaid are speculating and more evidence is needed. However, Hull and Vaid feel that bilingualism is insufficient as an explanation for bilateralism, since late bilinguals are more left hemisphere dominant. *The most important variable for bilateralism appears to be early development, when the brain is most plastic.*

The left hemisphere was not totally dominant in *all* of the language experiments that Hull and Vaid reviewed. Research on aphasics with left hemisphere damage has influenced psychologists to believe that language is strongly left hemispheric dominant. However, the right hemisphere appears to play an important supporting role in monolingual language processing. For example, the experiments reviewed that gathered data through visual hemifield testing, where written words were randomly presented to either the left or right visual field, showed important right hemisphere involvement. Hull and Vaid feel that more research needs to clarify their findings but there is some evidence out there that left hemispheric dominance even in monolinguals is not absolute.

*We have come a long way since Broca's and Wernicke's cases in our understanding of brain localization.*

## What is a meta-analysis?

Meta-analyses make sense of a wide range of studies on a topic (Coolican, 2004). Let's say that you want to study gender and behavior. There are hundreds of studies investigating the topic. After conducting a literature search you may decide that it is impossible to make useful generalizations about gender and behavior. This is because the studies are *not fully comparable.* They use a variety of samples, tasks, and designs. At best, generalizations that are made in texts are usually based on a very selective number of studies. How can psychologists make clearer statements about the entire body of research on a topic? This is where a meta-analysis is helpful.

Meta-analysis is fairly new. It organizes hundreds of studies in such a way to make them comparable. Researchers conducting meta-analyses create new data by sorting studies into categories. The new study, the meta-analysis, uses the data in such a way that an individual study becomes similar to an individual's response in a single study. Researchers statistically analyze the effect sizes of the studies in the meta-analysis to draw conclusions. Researchers cannot assume that significant differences between groups or conditions mean that the IV is a *strong* cause of the change in the DV. Calculating the size of the effect tells the researchers something about the strength. There is a way of figuring effect size and you do not need to know it. Just know that meta-analysis studies compare the effect across a wide range of studies to create the best generalizations.

## 3.10 Examine One Interaction between Cognition and Physiology in Terms of Behavior

Studies using normal participants relate to student's everyday life. The results of studies obtained from abnormal brains are hard to generalize to the everyday lives of normal people. Mathematics performance is the behavior I selected for this section.

Two studies investigate the interaction between biology, cognition, and the affects on mathematics performance. First is the material from section 3.6 on hormones and cognitive abilities.

The second study, outlined in this section, clearly illustrates the general **bidirectional** model where culture mediates the mind and the brain and then affects behavior.

## Culture, the brain, and differences in mathematics performance

Jessica Cantlon and Elizabeth Brannon (2006) write that Chinese speakers generally perform better than English speakers on mathematics tasks. How do we account for these differences? One factor is social; the Chinese educational system has a more rigorous mathematics curriculum. However, recent research links the brain, cognition, culture, and behavior. *It appears that the language we speak influences how the brain processes some mathematics tasks.*

Mathematics performance is the behavior. **Language** is the cognitive process. Brain activity in **Wernicke's area** and **Broca's area** or in the premotor activation (PMA) is the physiology. Culture and language mediate the brain structures used in mathematical tasks, but *only the mathematical tasks that are language-dependent* (Cantlon & Brannon, 2006).

Yiyuan Tang and colleagues (2006) conducted the original quasi-experiment on the topic. Participants were 12 native Chinese speakers, with an average age of 23.8, and 12 native English speakers with an average age of 26.8. All participants lived in China, were right-handed, and in good health. Many cross-cultural experiments are quasi-experiments where subjects are not randomly assigned to groups.

Four mathematical conditions were tested. One task was symbol judgment. The task required participants to decide if the orientation of one of three symbols was similar to two others. The symbols were either sitting upright or were in italics. The second task was number judgment, the same as with the symbols, except that Arabic digits were used. The third task was addition. Participants decided if a third digit was equal to the sum of two others. The last task was about comparisons. Was the third digit larger than the largest one of the first two in a series of three Arabic digits? **Functional MRI** (fMRI) recorded brain activity as participants pushed a button saying "Yes" or "No" for each task.

The scans showed a significant difference in brain activity between the two groups on all but the first task. Wernicke's and Broca's areas were more active in native English speakers. PMA activity was stronger in native Chinese speakers.

What does the difference mean? It appears that some aspects of culture may influence the way people process numbers (Cantlon and Brannon, 2006). Writing systems vary across cultures. The Chinese writing system is logographic, where an entire word is represented in a symbol, and the English writing system is alphabetic. Chinese symbols are visually complex. Brain differences are noticed between English and Chinese readers and these differences may affect other tasks, such as the ones used in Tang's study. Another cultural difference is that some Chinese children still figure mathematical calculations with an abacus. "By age 11, masterful abacus users can add together five three-digit numbers in about three seconds" (Cantlon and Brannon, 2006). Abacus practice enhances visuospatial skills. Children skilled with the abacus use visuospatial processing when they see Arabic numbers. Last, the Chinese language has fewer words representing numbers that may give native Chinese speakers the advantage in working memory.

Tang's research shows brain differences during language-dependent mathematical tasks. Future research needs to test *why* we see the differences.

Tang's sample is small and limited to a specific age range. Further research should replicate this study in other cultural groups and in different ages.

## 3.11 Discuss the Use of Brain Imaging Technologies in Investigating the Relationship between Biological Factors and Behavior

Introductory texts explain a wide range of neuroimaging technologies. Neuroimaging technology provides *correlations* between brain activity and behavior and do not explain why differences exist. Neuroimaging technology is frequently used in modern experiments to identify brain differences between groups while they perform cognitive tasks.

As **fMRI** scanning has a high status in modern psychological literature, it is the focus of my discussion.

Michael Gazzaniga and colleagues (2008) view fMRI as revolutionizing neuroimaging. Scientists can now watch the working brain.

David Dobbs (2005) writes that fMRI is used in a wide range of studies, such as comparing the brains of teenagers and adults or normal and abnormal brains. In addition, psychologists make some pretty strong claims about memory, emotion, and consumer preferences based on fMRI.

While an exciting advance, we must get some perspective. Functional MRI is not perfect. In fact, it has many critics. Functional MRI is a method with advantages and disadvantages, just like any other research method. I expect to see many future refinements in fMRI scanning.

### Advantages of using an fMRI scan

1. One advantage is a practical concern (Gazzaniga et al., 2008). Most hospitals already had MRI scanners, and they were easily converted to fMRI. Fewer hospitals use **PET** scanners, perhaps in part because a large group of trained professionals are needed to run them.

2. Functional MRI scans have methodological advantages (Gazzaniga et al., 2008). PET images have a spatial resolution of 6 to 9 cubic millimeters and fMRI scans have higher spatial resolutions of 2 to 3 cubic millimeters (Dobbs, 2005). As we get stronger magnets, fMRI spatial resolutions are becoming even more refined (Gazzaniga et al., 2008).

3. Functional MRI does not require the use of radioactive injections (Gazzaniga et al., 2008). They are safer. As the same individual can be repeatedly tested, scientists now have a complete analysis on an individual. In contrast, subjects in PET scan studies can only have 12 to 16 radioactive injections. So studies using PET scans use computers to *average* data gathered from a smaller number of scans from more participants. These averages are then superimposed on what is supposed to look like an average brain.

4. Localizing brain activity during a task is easier with fMRI (Gazzaniga et al., 2008). Data can be collected all in one session. Localizing brain function is not as precise when PET images are averaged. In addition, subjects receiving PET scans must also have an MRI for scientists to localize function and it is hard to line up the results of PET and MRI scans.

5. The temporal resolution, or the time it takes to complete measurements, is faster with fMRI scans (Gazzaniga et al., 2008). It takes about an hour for a PET scan to complete a picture of the brain. It takes an fMRI scan only 1 to 2 minutes to scan most of the brain (Dobbs, 2005). In addition, it is possible with fMRI to isolate the BOLD (blood-oxygen-level-dependent) effect for specific time periods, called **event-related fMRI** (Gazzaniga et al., 2008). Blood releases oxygen to active neurons faster than to inactive neurons. This is how fMRI sees which neural regions are used. Event-related fMRI allows researchers to randomly administer control and experimental conditions. This is because even-related fMRI scans permit the BOLD response to be timed to detect neural activity in response to single events. As it is hard to see metabolic changes to single events, researchers then average a number of scans to make sure that no background interference confounds, or interferes with, the readings. Now researchers are more certain that participants are paying attention to the specific tasks assigned to them in conditions. Psychologists even have the ability to combine data any way they wish if they use event-related fMRI.

## Limitations of using an fMRI scan

1. We must consider the ethical issues that come with gathering data as fMRI becomes more popular. Section 3.13 addresses **neuroethics**.

2. There is concern over fMRI accuracy (Dobbs, 2005). Functional MRI measures blood flow changes during cognitive tasks. In addition, it gives correlations between cognitive tasks and brain activity, not statements about causation (Gazzaniga et al., 2008).

   a. Susan Bookheimer (2002) writes that blood flow is an indirect way to view neuron activity. Blood flow in the brain is fairly slow; starting about two seconds after neural activity starts and hits the highest point between five and seven seconds. Thus, the image is recorded more slowly than actual neural activity.

   b. One accuracy criticism is that fMRI scans collect data in voxels, a combination of volume and pixels (Dobbs, 2005). Each voxel contains thousands of neurons, so for the image to light up, thousands or even millions of neurons must light up in order for the scan to perceive them—as if "an entire stadium had to shout to be heard" (p. 2).

   c. In addition, some neurons that are important to a cognitive task may not draw as much blood as other neurons or may use little blood because they are more efficient (Dobbs, 2005). In both cases, the scan might not detect important neuron activity.

   d. Researchers must make inferences about the pictures they receive from fMRI scans (Dobbs, 2005). These inferences come from selecting and adjusting algorithms to process data. There is always room for error in these selections.

   e. Great skill is needed to design experiments using fMRI (Bookheimer, 2002). The activity seen on the scans representing neural activity is not exact. Small design flaws can easily confound the aims of the study. For example, there might be subtle differences in difficulty of two experimental tasks. Skilled researchers must be aware of and control for the smallest interferences. In addition, studies using fMRI are not exact and great skill is needed to interpret the results.

3. There is concern that fMRI is not as legitimate, or as justifiable, as we might like to think (Dobbs, 2005).

   a. For example, fMRI scans may make it look like brain activity is more **localized** than it is in reality (Dobbs, 2005). Does fMRI scanning have the potential to become a modern version of phrenology? Perhaps, but few credible psychologists believe that the brain is set up for a strict localization. Functional MRI is new and responsible researchers realize that it is an early version of future scanning technology. In fact, neuroimaging has the ability to correct **stereotypes** about brain localization. For example, in section 3.9, a meta-analysis on localization and language by Rachel Hull and Jyotsna Vaid (2006) shows that across 23 studies comparing monolinguals and bilinguals, the right hemisphere plays more of a supporting role in language than early studies on brain damaged patients led psychologists to believe. There are other fMRI studies on language that show the same thing. Section 4.9 contains a review of fMRI studies by Bookheimer (2002) showing that the right hemisphere supports several aspects of language processing.

    **b.** Many fMRI scans use univariate, meaning one variable, algorithms to process data, which makes it seem that the brain is more localized than it is in reality (Dobbs, 2005). If a scientist uses univariate algorithms, then it is hard to see how, for example, one voxel relates to other voxels. Scientists using univariate processing see all of the voxels involved, but not in a way that shows their relationships. Multivariate processing that looks at many variables at one time is complex and still limited. Dobbs says it is similar to listening to a string quartet and hearing only the one sound produced rather than how each instrument complements and responds to the others. Multivariate algorithms use is growing and should become part of fMRI's future.

**4.** As a result of accuracy and legitimacy problems, there is a lot of room for error. Sometimes fMRI images are over interpreted. Dobbs (2005) gives two examples that show how enticing fMRI images are for professionals, the media, and the public.

    **a.** Researchers claimed to have located the physical markers for ADHD in a group of 30 studies. In reality, these studies had design flaws. The researchers did not control for the fact that the participants were taking Ritalin, which could have caused the physical changes in the brain. The sample confounded the results. It is hard to find children with ADHD in the U.S. who are not taking medication. Even those not taking medication are usually doing something else to reduce the symptoms. Dietary or other lifestyle changes affect the brain.

    **b.** Even the adolescent brain versus the adult brain experiment reported in my introduction could be an over interpretation of fMRI images. Yurgelun-Todd's (1999) research appears in the popular *Frontline* video "Inside the teenage brain." The video makes the results sound firm. However, there is another fMRI study suggesting that adolescent brains work the same as adults in some situations, such as when they see color photos of adolescent faces rather than black-and-white photos of adult faces. Is it possible that adolescents have to be interested to pay attention to experimental conditions? The lesson is that studies need triangulation before they are accepted. *Frontline* did not report whether Yurgelun-Todd's study was part of a larger body of research. In fact, her comments may have been edited. *Frontline* is a popular media show, even if it is a pretty good one. I find that many educational films fail to address strengths and limitations of research; these discussions do not play well on television. Again, we must be better consumers of media.

## An example of fMRI research: Conformity and the brain

Many studies reviewed in this book use fMRI. This example is useful for evaluating **conformity** research in section 5. 17. Bern's experiment illustrates how the biological and sociocultural levels of analysis interact.

    Gregory Berns and colleagues (2005) write that many replications exist on the Solomon Asch experiment. But without scanning evidence, the mechanisms of conformity remain a mystery. It is still unclear whether conformity is a decision-making process, meaning individuals conform even though they know the group is incorrect, or if the group actually modifies an individual's perception. This is the first experiment to investigate specific brain mechanisms of conformity. The hypothesis was, "if social conformity resulted from conscious decision making, this would be associated with functional changes in prefrontal cortex, whereas if social conformity was more perceptually based, then activity changes would be seen in occipital and parietal regions" (p. 1). Thirty-three normal, right-handed participants were tested, 14 males and 19 females with an average age of 26. Deception was used in the study. Participants did not know that two male and two female actors were hired to give wrong answers.

The procedures offered a large amount of control. First, each participant was shown into a waiting room. Every time a new participant entered the waiting room, the actors also arrived, but in a haphazard way so they looked like participants showing up for the experiment. To promote group cohesiveness and ensure that the participants could do the task on their own, participants and confederates practiced the task 20 times on computers together. Pictures were taken of both the participants and the confederates so that when inside the fMRI scanner, participants could match the responses with the correct person.

The task was to decide if pairs of abstract 3-dimensional figures were the same, meaning they could be rotated to fit together, or different, meaning they could not be rotated to fit together. The angles varied from 100 to 180 degrees. The angles were rotated randomly and counterbalanced. Whether the angle pairs were correct or incorrect was varied. Participants were told that others would know their answers.

Each participant was placed in an fMRI scanner. The angle pairs were shown on a computer screen with the pictures of the other group members lined up on one side. A box beside each picture flashing the answer was provided for each trial.

The first phase of the experiment consisted of 48 trials, where participants were shown varying pairs of angles and the group's answers. The 48 trials were split into three categories. The first was baseline answers, where participants were shown angle pairs but there were X marks beside each picture of the group. The second group of trials was the correct group responses, where the actors were assigned to give the correct answers. The third group of trials was the incorrect responses, where the actors were assigned to give incorrect responses. Interspersed in these three conditions (baseline, correct, and incorrect), researchers used six split-decision trials to ensure that the experiment seemed believable.

A second phase of the experiment consisted of the same trials with a computer. Computer answers were set up identical to those of the actors and were counterbalanced randomly within the trials. To ensure that the computer was not automatically judged as more competent, participants were told that the computer would judge the angles pairs based on a simple algorithm.

Conformity was operationally defined as going along with incorrect information, either from the computer or the group.

Results showed that participants judged the accuracy of the group and the computer to be about equal, 65.1% and 61.2%. In addition, participants conformed to incorrect information from both sources, though slightly more to the social pressure of the group. Baseline error rates averaged 13.8% and increased to 41% for the social pressure of the group's incorrect answers.

On the debriefing questionnaire, participants rated the computer and the group as almost equally reliable.

Next, fMRI scans were examined. Baseline trials, where the participant made their own choices, showed activity in a network of brain regions that included parts of the **frontal cortex**, the **occipital cortex**, and the **parietal cortex**. These same brain regions were affected during social conformity but not when subjects conformed to the computer's answers. *The brain is doing something different when conformity to a social group or conforming to computer answers.* In addition, when acting independently, defined as giving correct answers when the group answers incorrectly, the right **amygdala** and **right caudate nucleus** are activated. The brain is also doing different things when socially conforming or acting independently.

Bern and colleagues concluded that *social conformity related more to perception than decision-making.* In addition, the authors reported that consistent with other research on perception, they found that changes in **visual cortex** regions occurred when participants *started* to conform. Changes in the visual cortex appear related to perception more than decision-making.

The authors write that inconsistencies exist in replications of the Asch study, so it is important that their results are replicated. The authors realize that a group of peers might create a **social desirability** problem, so conformity might occur more often than normal. The authors recommend that further research examine the appeal of the group members to participants to see how this affects the brain and social conformity.

## 3.12 Discuss How and Why Particular Research Methods Are Used at the Biological Level of Analysis: Studying Genes, the Brain, and Behavior

This section covers research methods that best fit the goals of biological research and/or ethical requirements: experiments, postmortem studies, neuroimaging technology, and correlation studies.

Research conducted at each of the levels of analysis should have **method triangulation** on the same topic from the other two levels of analysis. This means that, for example, research on the biology of language should complement language research from the other two levels of analysis. A number of the newer studies on biology are in the field of **cultural neuroscience**.

Always pay attention to *sampling* when you read a study. Samples are often limited. It is usually impossible to get good representative samples. Frequently scientists wait for opportunities to collect data on people with certain injuries or genetic histories. *Sampling limits the interpretation of research in all levels of analysis.* Samples are most useful when they are tightly controlled and reflect a clearly defined **target population**, the population to which researchers wish to generalize their results.

### Research methods for the biological level of analysis

**1. Experiments** on humans and animals. Psychologists like using experiments when possible. *Ethics determines whether a biological experiment can be run on humans.* Examples of human experiments are the fMRI experiment on conformity (section 3.11) and the quasi-experiment on language, culture, and mathematics (section 3.10). But there are limits to using humans in biological experiments and animals are subjects in two types of biological research: 1) where the manipulated conditions are potentially harmful for humans; 2) when researchers alter the animal brain or gene expression and compare the behavior of the altered animals to that of normal animals. One example is an experiment (in section 3.4) that tests differences between normal wild mice and mice genetically engineered so that they lack the expression of the nNOS gene (called the **knockout mice**). The American Psychological Association (2002) states that animals may be used in research where the conditions are potentially harmful to humans and where the results have great benefit for humans. The animals must be treated with respect and if they cannot be restored to normal functioning after the study, the animals must be humanely euthanized. Experiments are the only method showing cause and effect, but suffer from poor ecological and population validity unless they have **triangulation** with other findings.

**2. Case studies.** Case studies are often times used at the biological level of analysis when scientists want to follow the case of a human with a particular type of damage or when the topic is a new field of study. A case of naturally occurring abnormalities such as H. M.'s amnesia is frequently cited in introductory texts. Case studies are a way to interpret data collected in a number of ways. The use of case studies by biological scientists helps them describe data collected over time, particularly on people with unusual circumstances. Descriptive case studies often follow the detailed history of one person with a particular kind of damage that researchers cannot create in the lab on humans. It is by chance that scientists have the opportunity to study these cases. Detailed cases of a single person have much to offer science, even if the cases have limitations (Goodwin, 1998). While case studies suffer from poor external validity and are hard to replicate, *similar* cases can lead scientists to find patterns that prompt future research. Case studies "provide insights into behavior that cannot occur in larger studies that collect limited amounts of data per subject" (p. 396). Case studies might be the *only* way some phenomena are studied. In addition, case studies help with falsification. Case studies might raise questions about strong claims that point researchers in new directions. For example, the Freudian explanation that Capgras Syndrome (where a person thinks their family members are imposters) was a severe Oedipal Complex was accepted for many years. New cases provided data that this might not be so. Neurologist V. S. Ramachandran (1998) investigated Capgras patients and discovered that the syndrome was better explained by temporary brain damage from accidents. Ramachandran writes that, "in neurology, most of the major discoveries that have withstood the test of time were, in fact, based initially on single-case studies and demonstrations" (p. xiii). Initial case findings are confirmed through other methods. Ramachandran believes there is no need for tension between researchers using either experimental or nonexperimental methods.

**3. Postmortem studies.** Robert Sternberg (2006) writes that postmortem studies allow researchers to directly study brain tissue. Postmortem studies are often **case studies**. Sometimes postmortem cases are **longitudinal**, meaning that researchers collect data at specific points over a long period of time and analyze data with correlations (defined later in this section). An example of a postmortem study is Paul Broca's case of Tan, a man named for the one sound he could make. Broca documented Tan's case while he was alive and dissected his brain after death. Cause and effect cannot be easily determined from postmortem studies. Their main advantage is pinpointing specific brain locations for further study.

**4. Neuroimaging technologies** such as PET and fMRI provide hard evidence about what the brain is doing. Brain scanning technology can be used in experiments. While a significant difference might be seen between the scans of the two groups, imaging technology does not reveal why the brain differences are there.

**5. Correlation.** Correlations are used to analyze data in biological studies for two reasons. First, ethics might prevent a scientist from conducting an experiment. Second, a correlation may be the only way to study a topic. For example, genetic research uses correlation because we cannot directly study genes. Correlations are non-experimental and show *relationships;* not causes and effects. Hugh Coolican (2004) writes that the term *correlation study* is confusing. First, correlation is a statistic rather than a method and is used in two ways. One, correlations show differences between preexisting groups; there is no random assignment to groups. For example, biological psychologists collect data for many twin studies with questionnaires and analyze the data with correlations. Identical and fraternal twins are the comparison groups. The answers to the questionnaire are correlated with being an identical or fraternal twin. Second, correlations are a way to study the *relationship* between an independent variable (IV) and a dependent variable (DV). These studies do not predict that the

IV causes the change in the DV the way an experiment does. One example is the Caspi study on 5HTT, the serotonin transporter gene (section 3.4).

John Brooks (personal communication, May, 2007) warns that there is a tendency to *over-interpret* the meaning of correlations. Correlation studies measure how straight a line is when results are plotted on a graph. For a correlation to really have much meaning it should be strong, at least .80. I see the term "significant" correlation used frequently and have wondered what it meant. Brooks clarified that significance has a particular meaning in experiments, which is the probability that the IV caused the change in the DV. The term significance is used rather loosely at times outside of experiments, so check the *strength* of the correlation rather than check for the word "significant." The term "significance" when referring to correlation studies is different than what "significance" means in experiments. For example, when experimental data are analyzed with a *t*-test it is tested directly against a level of significance, something that is not available to correlation measurements. Square a correlation coefficient to get the percentage that is actually accounted for in the relationships found. So, a correlation coefficient of .80 has only 64 percent of the relationship accounted for and 36 percent unaccounted for. This leaves a great deal of room for error, plus other variables can contribute to the behavior, as studies of relationship are uncontrolled.

## Specific methods for genetic research that use correlations to analyze data

Because **genetic research** is frequently misunderstood, all of the following examples discuss strengths and limitations of the methods used to investigate genetic explanations of behavior. Twin and adoption studies are behavioral genetics methods. Linkage, association, and gene–environment interaction studies are molecular genetic studies. All genetic research has a specific goal in mind and is appropriate for that goal. These studies use **questionnaires** to gather much of the data, so each individual method *also* is subject to strengths and limitations of questionnaires. Questionnaires should have both **reliability** and **validity**, but it must also be remembered that many questionnaires are **self-reports** and subject to memory distortion and social desirability.

The choice of which genetic method to use depends on what you want to know.

**1. Twin studies.** Twin studies tell researchers if genes are likely contributors to behavior but never identify a specific suspect gene. Twin studies assume that environments are the same, that "environmental factors do not make [monozygotic] MZ twins more similar than they make [dizygotic] DZ twins similar" (Carey, 2003, p. 298). The incidence of the investigated behavior in one twin is examined against the incidence that the behavior also exists in the other twin. Comparisons are then made between MZ twins, DZ twins, non-twin siblings, and the incidence in the general population. If the correlation is highest in MZ twins and then goes down according to the amount of genetic similarity, it is assumed that genes contribute something to the behavior. The greatest weakness of twin studies is that twins rarely share the exact same environment. In fact, twins are often regarded differently, with one treated as the first-born (Toman, 1976).

**2. Adoption studies.** Adoption studies also tell researchers if genes are likely contributors to behavior but never identify a specific suspect gene. Adoption studies assume that any "shared genes are the only reason adopted children show similarity with their biological relatives" (Carey, 2003, p. 301). If an adopted child resembles the adopted parent, it should be because of the environment. Carey says that one issue critical to adoption method validity is "selective placement." This means that the selection of adoptive families may make them too similar to the biological parents on variables that influence behavior. Religion is a popular selection variable. Religion might influence a behavior commonly measured in adoption studies on alcoholism. Critical design elements could limit the interpretation of adoption study results. Adoption studies can take a long time to conduct. After an adoption, the child is followed as he or she grows up. The researchers want to know if the child develops the same behavior as the biological parent.

**3. Linkage studies.** A linkage study might be the first attempt to locate a specific gene that contributes to behavior. Linkage studies find "the approximate location of a gene for a trait" (Carey, 2003, p. 181). A linkage study cannot ever tell you which gene causes a behavior. Rather, linkage studies select a trait that has a known location on a chromosome. The trait with the known location becomes the "marker." The marker does not *cause* the behavior under investigation; it just helps investigators make predictions about a genetic variation that may contribute to behavior. For example, if people with alcoholism also have the marker trait for Tourette's syndrome, then the gene variations involved in Tourette's syndrome are predicted to be influential in contributing to alcoholism. No one is saying that Tourette's syndrome causes alcoholism. Many traits, such as blood type, are used as markers.

**4. Association studies.** Association studies often follow a successful linkage study. Association studies also point scientists in the direction of possible genes contributing to behavior. Association studies test actual genes that may be implicated in a behavior (Carey, 2003). Association studies are population-based or family-based. Population-based studies compare people with a particular trait to a control group from the general population. ADHD research is an example. Ritalin alters dopamine receptors in the brain and preliminary data implicates the D4 receptor for dopamine on the DRD4 gene as a potential problem. Both groups are genotyped to see if they have the suspicious alleles. An association exists if a greater percentage of people with ADHD have the suspicious alleles than people from the general population. The greatest weakness of population-based studies is *nonequivalence of ethnicity,* as traits are not evenly dispersed through a population. Imagine trying to find a match for someone who is half French, one-quarter Irish, and one-quarter German! This sounds pretty hard, so researchers often turn to family-based studies. In family-based studies, the person with ADHD is tested against a sibling without ADHD. Both the person with ADHD and the sibling are genotyped for the suspect allele. Of course you have to have a brother or sister without ADHD who is old enough so that researchers know that the person is unlikely to develop ADHD! Complicated, yes, but this is what really happens.

**5. Gene-environment correlations.** See section 3.4.

## 3.13 Discuss Ethical Considerations Related to Research Studies at the Biological Level of Analysis and Discuss Ethical Considerations in Research into Genetic Influences on Behavior: Neuroethics and the Ethics of Genetic Research

Many ethical concerns arise from neuroscience and genetic research. There are no exact answers to these questions, rather, points of view are either well defended or poorly defended.

### Part 1: Neuroethics

The word "**Neuroethics**" was first used in 2003 to describe how discoveries about the brain affect everyday life situations (Gazzaniga et al., 2008). The Web site http://neuroethics.upenn.edu/ is a valuable source for identifying questions about neuroethics and thinking through the concerns. Neuroethics includes a wide range of topics from "clinical neuroscience (neurology, psychiatry, and psychopharmacology) and basic neuroscience (cognitive neuroscience and affective neuroscience)" (p. 1). Neuroethical concerns include "problems with advances in functional imaging, brain implants, brain-machine interface, and psychopharmacology, as well as by our growing understanding of the neural bases of behavior, personality, consciousness, and states of spiritual transcendence" (p. 1).

Neuroethics are organized into two broad categories; problems relating to *what we can do* and problems relating to *what we can know* (Farah, 2008). Here are sample questions from each area.

## What we can do

1. Functional MRI allows scientists to see the structure of the brain as it completes tasks. How should we use this information? How accurate are the scans? Are there potential problems with court evidence, such as jury perceptions of the credibility of evidence? Do the scans invade one's privacy?

2. Businesses are developing lie-detection tests using fMRI. In addition, business is using fMRI to convince people that their brains are different when using different products, called **neuromarketing**. The fMRI study on Coke and Pepsi preferences by Samuel McClure and colleagues (2004) has been the object of some discussion. The fMRI scans found that different parts of the brain were activated depending on whether the sodas were labeled or not. Do the scans show any differences that are actually useful to consumers?

3. If drugs are developed to help people with specific cognitive dysfunctions, should healthy people also have the right to use the drugs to enhance cognitive abilities? Should healthy people take, for example, SSRI drugs (an antidepressant, such as Prozac) to change or enhance their personalities? Where do we draw a line between treatment and enhancement?

## What we know

1. To what extent should we use information about the brain to change society? Should we make laws that restrict adolescent behavior based on fMRI scans showing brain differences between teen and adult brains during cognitive tasks? Should employers and insurance companies have access to a person's biological information? Should there be there any restrictions on their use of this information?

2. To what extent should people be held responsible for their behavior? This question is also relevant for the ethics of genetic research. For example, neuroimaging technology shows brain differences in persons with antisocial personality disorder. In addition, scientists are learning more about the environments in which genes related to aggression are most likely to be expressed. So should criminals be held responsible for their antisocial behavior? Watch taking an extreme position on this topic. Genes and bad experiences negatively affect the brain but drugs, diet, acupuncture, and psychotherapy treatments positively affect the brain.

3. **Cultural neuroscience** studies the biological basis of culture; people sharing similar meaning systems (Chiao & Ambady, 2007). Unscrupulous persons could take this information, distort it, and use it to discriminate. Cultural neuroscience is not about race; many races live together in cultural groups. These concerns are also relevant for questions about the ethics of genetic research.

4. To what extent will biological knowledge conflict with a religious belief in a soul?

5. What impact might biological knowledge have on ideas on defining life and death? For example, this question impacts our judgments about people with severe brain damage.

## Part 2: Ethics of genetic research

The Web site http://genomics.energy.gov is a valuable source for identifying questions about the ethics of genetic research and thinking through concerns about the availability of genetic information. Click on the section about the Human Genome Project. Most of my headings and questions mirror those used on this Web site.

### Fairness in how genetic information is used

To what extent should insurance companies, employers, courts, schools, adoption agencies, and the military, for example, have access to someone's personal genetic information? If you think any of these groups should have access to the information to some degree, should there be limitations on how the information is used?

### Privacy and confidentiality

Who owns and controls genetic information?

### The stigmatization and psychological consequences that are caused by an individual's genetic differences

How might knowing about someone's personal genetic information affect the individual and how that person is perceived and treated by others? How might genetic information affect minority group members?

### Reproduction

What kinds of decisions might parents make for their children if they had access to genetic information? Should there be limits to parental decision-making based on genetic information? What should be involved in the genetic counseling parents receive? Is fetal genetic testing reliable and useful? Does the use of reproductive technology have a larger societal impact?

### Clinical concerns about educating health professionals, patients, and the public about genetic testing, including scientific limitations and social risks

How can we best prepare health care professionals for genetic technologies? How can we best prepare the public to make informed choices? As a larger societal issue, how should current scientific and social risks be balanced with long-term benefits of genetic technologies?

### Uncertainties that come with testing people for potential genetic susceptibilities for complex problems, such as heart disease and mental illness that are linked to multiple genes and gene-environment interactions

Should we allow testing even when there are no known treatments? Should parents be allowed to have their children tested for mental and physical health problems that do not typically begin until adulthood? What should parents have the right to do with this information? Should other groups, such as schools and the police, have access to this information? To what extent can health care professionals interpret this information accurately and reliably?

### The conceptual and philosophical implications about free will and determinism, the impact of your answer on human responsibility, and ideas about health and disease

To what extent are genes responsible for our behavior? To what extent are people responsible for their behavior? For example, how might your answer affect attitudes toward criminals? How do we define acceptable diversity?

# 4 The Cognitive Level of Analysis

## 4.1 A Brief Introduction to Cognitive Psychology

Current cognitive psychologists recognize that the mind has a biological basis and develops within a cultural context. How did the cognitive level of analysis evolve to this current view?

Psychology is a young science. It was only in the later half of the 19th century that psychology identified itself as distinct from philosophy and physiology. Many early psychologists had medical backgrounds and an interest in philosophy. Scientific psychology arose when experimental methods used in physiology were applied to philosophical problems about human conscious experience. Psychology as a science has its roots in Germany, probably because of Germany's strong university emphasis on research. Scientific psychology spread through Europe and the United States (Goodwin, 1999).

Many early psychologists were cognitive psychologists. Wilhelm Wundt (1832–1920) studied sensation, perception, and attention. Hermann Ebbinghaus (1850–1909) studied memory. J. Ridley Stroop published his famous Stroop experiment in 1935. However, cognitive psychology was not promoted as a primary way of thinking in the United States during this early time. Americans were more fascinated with figures such as John Watson.

Watson proposed that introspection was not appropriate for the scientific study of behavior. Watson thought everyone should be a behaviorist. By the 1930s, behaviorism was the focus of American psychology and it remained the primary focus for decades. Not everyone agreed with Watson, choosing instead to study cognitive processes. Gestalt theorists argued with behaviorists during the 1930s and 1940s, and Europeans Lev Vygotsky, Jean Piaget, and Frederick Bartlett were busy studying cognitive processing. However, their impact on American psychology did not gain steam until the 1960s.

Behaviorism was an American passion, fueled by Watson and then by B. F. Skinner's personality. George Miller (2003) writes that by the 1950s it was clear that behaviorism could not explain complex behavior. Researchers such as Miller and Jerome Bruner offered relevant cognitive explanations of complex human behavior level even during the time of behaviorism's domination in the United States. Psychologists now focused on human "mental life" and combined the best research from varying disciplines, including anthropology, linguistics, and neuroscience with psychology.

Miller recalls the date, September 11, 1956, the second day of the Symposium on Information Theory held at the Massachusetts Institute of Technology, when it was clear that there was support for a change in thinking; it was the beginning of the cognitive revolution dates. Several papers were presented that day by such figures as Noam Chomsky, who spoke on nativist language theory.

For many, Skinner's radical behaviorism went too far when he wrote *Verbal Behavior* in 1957. Skinner claimed that language was really a behavior; a chain of verbal behaviors reinforced through verbal operants and maintained by the sociocultural environment. Skinner was open to attack. Chomsky wrote an article criticizing the basic premises of verbal behavior principles, claiming that the creative use of language was unexplainable and untestable through Skinnerian principles (Sternberg, 2006).

Jerome Bruner (1990) clearly sums up what happened to traditional learning theories. Two forces led to its demise, the **cognitive revolution** and **transactionalism**. "The cognitive revolution simply absorbed the concept of learning into the broader concept of the acquisition of knowledge" (p. 105). Transactionalism started later than the cognitive revolution and is still rearranging psychology. "It was the view that human action could not be fully or properly accounted for from the inside out—by reference only to intrapsychic dispositions, traits, learning capacities, motives, or whatever. Action required for its explication that it be *situated,* that it be conceived of as continuous with a cultural world" (p. 105). Bruner's view stands the test of time; it spans all three levels of analysis and is important for the future of psychology.

## 4.2 Outline Principles That Define the Cognitive Level of Analysis

Here are some useful principles for cognitive psychology. The most current cognitive processing theories have been tested cross-culturally.

1. Cognitive psychologists assume that there is an important biological basis for all human cognitive processing and its resultant behavior but focus research on how the brain translates into mind.

2. Mental processing in the mind can be studied scientifically. Theories of cognitive processing are studied through various methods.

3. Behavior change is explained as a result of cognitive processing that goes on in the mind. The steps of cognitive processing are as follows:
   a. Information is acquired from the world.
   b. The information is stored.
   c. Stored information is represented in the mind.
   d. Internal representations direct behavior.

I want to make a case for studying **language** as a cognitive process.

1. *Language is the most fundamental of all the cognitive processes* and is responsible for the development and use of the other human cognitive processes, such as memory and perception.

2. Language is the vehicle of **cultural** transmission and **social learning** (personal communication with Hank Davis, June, 2008).

3. Language separates humans and animals. Animal models are not very useful for studying sophisticated human cognitive processing. Animal studies primarily show the limitations of animal "language" and "thinking." Animal "thinking" is limited to the world of objects. Human thinking involves objects but is mainly about the symbolic representation of objects; language is required. All other cognitive processes are removed from objects *because* of language.

4. Language is probably the most important of the sophisticated cognitive processes that humans evolved so that we *could* live together in cultures. It is part of the evolution of social intelligence (see section 3.5).

## Note to the teacher

Language is an easy cognitive process to thread through the program. Language and cognition is abstract, so I start with two films that help students see why language is fundamental to human culture. One is "The Ragin' Cajun" from Oliver Sacks' film series *The Mind Traveler* about Usher Syndrome, available from Films for the Humanities and Sciences. Persons with Usher Syndrome are born deaf and use American Sign Language as their first language. By middle age, they are also blind and must learn tactile signing. Sacks follows Danny Delcambre and his friends as they confront the challenges. The second is *Monkey in the Mirror*, which reviews research about primate intelligence, communication, and mindreading (see section 3.5). Even though primates have many skills, the film shows their limitations. The film is available from www.pbs.org.

I teach other cognitive processes but only after I teach language and *situate* cognitive processing in a cultural context.

## 4.3 Discuss How and Why Particular Research Methods Are Used at the Cognitive Level of Analysis, Including Ethical Concerns

### Research methods for the cognitive level of analysis

This section covers research methods that best fit the goals of cognitive psychologists: experiments, correlation studies, naturalistic observation, interviews, questionnaires, case studies, psychobiological research, and computer simulations. Again, research at any one level of analysis, in this case cognitive, needs to have **method triangulation** with the other two levels of analysis. As with research in the biological level of analysis, many newer studies on cognitive processing also focus on **culture**.

**1. Experiments**, mainly using humans, including lab, quasi-, and field experiments. Experiments are the only method showing cause and effect, so they are very useful. Lab experiments clarify theoretical rather than real-life applications and are *supposed to be artificial*. The material in section 4.5 on Jerome Bruner and language includes two lab experiments on **narratives** and development. A single experiment lacks **ecological validity**, meaning it cannot be generalized outside of the study conditions. Other studies investigating the same topic using different methods should have similar findings. *If an experiment fits in with a larger body of research, its lack of ecological validity is not a problem.* **Quasi-experiments** are frequently used when researchers cannot randomly assign participants to conditions. Cross-cultural research and studies comparing males and females often uses quasi-experimental designs. Participants are placed in groups according to their culture or gender. Quasi-experiments do not have the same control as lab experiments but are required in many cases. The cross-cultural study on own-race bias (ORB) and eyewitness memory in section 4.8 is an example of a **field experiment**. Field studies test experimental conditions in the natural environment. Field studies do not have as much control as lab experiments but are more ecologically valid. However, sometimes it is necessary to study a cognitive process in its natural environment to provide **method triangulation** with other research.

**2. Correlation studies.** Sometimes cognitive psychologists use correlation to show a relationship between two variables. For example, correlation was used in addition to the field experiment data in the ORB study on eyewitness memory in section 4.8. Researchers use correlation studies when it is unethical or difficult to create conditions in a lab.

**3. Naturalistic observation.** Michael Cole's study on the Kpelle in Africa in section 4.7 and Bruner's observation of Emily's language development in section 4.5 are examples of naturalistic observations. Naturalistic observations have high ecological validity and give researchers the chance to view people in the richness of real settings. This information may not be available through experiments. However, observation studies lack control.

**4. Interviews**, including **verbal protocols**, and **self-reports**. Interviews allow researchers to gather highly detailed information that is impossible to collect in experiments. However, researchers must be well trained. Weaknesses of interviews are that they are time consuming and if the researcher is not well trained, the information may be contaminated with **experimenter bias**. Another weakness is that the process of gathering data may interfere with the cognitive processing (Sternberg, 2006). One technique for interviewing cross-cultural samples is the **narrative interview**. These interviews allow participants to "tell their story" and this information is useful for designing culturally valid experiments. Michael Cole, reviewed in section 4.7, used narrative interviews.

**5. Questionnaires.** Many cognitive studies, particularly interview studies, use questionnaires. One example is the cross-cultural study on flashbulb memories in section 4.11. It is assumed that all questionnaires used in studies are **reliable** and **valid**. Questionnaires are a cost-effective way of gathering data from large groups of people. The reliability of **self-reports** is a limitation.

**6. Case studies.** The case studies use information gathered from a wide range of sources, such as interviews, and observations. Often, cognitive psychologists rely on psychobiological case studies to examine brain deficits on cognitive processing. Case studies allow researchers to gather detailed data about individuals that might not be otherwise available. However, cases are not representative of a larger group, meaning that **population validity** is limited. Section 4.10 includes a case study about emotions and the brain.

**7. Psychobiological research.** Cognitive processing is often studied in combination with biological research. Section 4.10 contains an fMRI study on the interaction of biology and cognition in emotion. In addition, **postmortem studies** using neuroimages of human brains are used whenever possible. Psychobiological research provides "hard" evidence of what happens in the brain during cognitive processing. But this hard evidence cannot answer questions about why the brain functions the way it does. In addition, psychobiological information gathered from abnormal brains does not provide a full explanation of cognitive processing. However, one main purpose of psychobiological research is to get ideas for future research from studying brain deficits, either naturally occurring or from lab animals.

**8. Computer simulations.** Computer simulations are used by cognitive psychologists but *they say nothing about how cognitions are situated within a cultural context*. Processes in computer simulations and in studies using artificial intelligence are not necessarily the same processes a human brain uses. Bruner rejected the view that human cognitive processing was similar to a computer. Memory models are sometimes studied through computer models. It is limiting to see human cognitive processing as simply analogous to a computer model of information processing.

## Ethics of cognitive research

Ethical considerations are always present in research. Here are some things to consider about research conducted at the cognitive level of analysis.

1. Sometimes humans cannot be studied. This is not usually the case but sometimes animals are used to examine how a specific brain deficit relates to the ability to process information. These animal studies allow researchers to create brain deficits in a con-

trolled setting. Human brains cannot be deliberately damaged, but the animal studies must be compared to case studies of humans with naturally occurring deficits.

2. Some neuroimaging technology exposes humans to harmful substances and may be used for unintended purposes.

3. Deception is sometimes used in human experiments. To use deception, the scientific benefits of a study must be such that it outweighs the rights of participants to be informed.

4. Researchers should make every reasonable effort to protect participants from harm. If someone is going to be exposed to harm, the informed consent form should outline the risks associated with the study in advance. Studies documenting cognitive deficits caused by sleep deprivation in labs are examples of this issue.

5. In general, informed consent forms are critical components of research at the cognitive level of analysis. All participants should be debriefed about the exact nature of the study as soon as possible after their participation.

6. Observation studies do not need the consent of participants as long as the researcher does not alter the natural environment in any way and the identity of anyone observed remains anonymous.

## 4.4 Evaluate Schema Theory with Reference to Research Studies

### Schemas and culture

**Schemas** are organizational frameworks in the mind. Humans are born with basic survival behaviors that are the basis of schemas, such as bonding, though most schemas develop within one's cultural context. Schemas categorize objects, events, and human practices in meaningful ways. Cultural schemas are part of the **Cultural Acquisition Device** (CAD); schemas are so important that they are built into us. Cultures are not just there to filter perceptions; cultures actively build schemas about expected behavior (Konner, 2007). Konner gives an example from the highlands of New Guinea. Common practice is to give all goods and services to one respected man who is trusted to distribute them fairly. Attitudes about handling all goods and services reflect this practice.

Introductory texts give general definitions of schemas and experimental evidence that humans use schemas to organize experience.

Frederick Bartlett and Jean Piaget are familiar names associated with schema. However, we have schemas for everything we do and schema is a fundamental part of modern psychology.

Schemas span all levels of analysis. Schemas are biologically based. The brain is set up to categorize and these categories change as a child interacts with others. Culture determines the contents of schemas. Schemas influence the mind; they are fundamental to human cognitive processing.

Two applications of schema theory are developed in this section. One application of schema theory relates to studying mental illness. A second application is the use of **scripts** in children's narratives. Scripts are schemas about events in time (Gray, 2007).

### Schemas and mental illness

Genetic determinism is no longer accepted as an explanation for mental illness. **Cultural schemas** offer a better framework. All cultures have schemas about abnormal behavior. While there are some universal aspects to schemas, the details usually vary.

Richard Castillo (1997) writes that cognitive schemas are created in cultural groups based on how the group thinks about and experiences behaviors. These cognitive schemas **reify** a belief into something real for the group. Reifying "occurs when people are collectively projecting onto an object a level of reality the object does not actually possess" (p. 19). The way a behavior is thought of in a cultural group is real to them, even if it does not exist in reality. The brain adapts to these cultural schemas and the group treats a set of behaviors as real mental illnesses. Reification is the concept that gives us an international perspective on all behavior; it influence how societies come to label anything as important, such as intelligence or achievement testing. Do not assume that others outside of your culture share your schemas.

How do schemas form about mental illness? Castillo writes that a specific behavior is noticed by a cultural group and is interpreted as a mental illness within a cultural definition. **Neuroplasticity** accounts for how schemas grow and change. Neuronal circuitry is changed in the brain during learning and memory. Castillo believes cultural schemas serve three important purposes. Schemas are *representational,* serving important symbolic functions for a group. Schemas are *constructive,* consisting of a social agreement about what is important to a society that is communicated through stories. Last, schemas are *directive,* telling people what is important to do.

This is why it is sometimes hard to diagnose **depression** outside of Western cultures. In the United States, a specific set of behaviors is considered "major depression." This diagnosis is based on how **stress** is generally expressed in the United States. It may be ethnocentric to say, "This is how someone experiences depression in another culture." **Etics** and **emics** help us understand why. Stress is an etic, something common to all cultures. However, different experiences in expressing stress are emics. For example, the word depression means something different to the Pakistani. An interview study about the emics of depression in Pakistani ethnic groups living in the United Kingdom is reviewed in the section 5.5. In China, stress is more often experienced in bodily symptoms. While the CCMD (Chinese Classification of Mental Disorders) has a category called "depressive episode," the diagnosis is not used as frequently as it is in the West. Often, Chinese people rely on Traditional Chinese Medicine (TCM) (see section 5.10) for explanations and treatment or combine Chinese psychiatry with TCM. TCM makes no distinctions between physical and mental health. Current Chinese psychiatry is a combination of Western medicine and traditional beliefs that shape the way depression is expressed. Somatic (bodily) symptoms have far more meaning in Chinese cultural schemas. Castillo points out that the depressive symptoms experienced in the West are not as important to Chinese cultural schemas, and little attention is paid to them.

In addition, cultural schemas about distress are closely tied to the **dimensions of culture**, discussed in section 5.6. For example, Castillo writes that the Micronesians are a collectivist group. They express stress in relation to the loss of important personal relationships. In the schemas of Micronesians, the emotion called *lalomweiu* may be the closest thing to the U.S. schema for depression, but is thought of in collectivist way, the "loneliness and sadness caused by the loss of a loved one" (p. 205).

## Gender schemas and depression

**Gender schemas** are relevant for studying depression. Women are diagnosed with depression far more than men. Depressive symptoms may be related to cultural schemas about how females are expected to express distress. Sandra Bem (1998) says that children need cognitive consistency. Schemas are natural, and children create self categorizations in terms of what cultures value. Once a child constructs a gender schema, this representation serves as a reference point for what is valued about being male or female. Bem does not believe that gender has to be a category; it is not naturally more perceptible for children than other attributes. Anything used as a category for schemas, such as a caste system in some cultures, is only relevant if given functional significance for the group. Bem promotes raising children free of gender schemas.

Gender schema processing is studied experimentally. One experiment examined 48 male and 48 female participants who were designated as sex typed or non-sex typed through the Bem Sex Role Inventory. Participants viewed 61 randomly ordered words at 3-second intervals, including animal names, proper names, and clothing. Some of the words were feminine and some were masculine. After the word presentation, participants wrote down as many words as they could recall. As hypothesized, both males and females recalled equal numbers of words, but the order in which the words were recalled differed according to who was designated as sex typed or non-sex typed. For example, a sex-typed participant recalling a feminine word then went on to recall a series of feminine words in clusters. The non-sex-typed participants used different clustering. The findings support the notion that sex-typed people are more likely to create categories based around gender. How might this experiment relate to depression? According to Bem, "sex typing results, in part, from the assimilation of the self-concept itself to the gender schema. As children learn the contents of their society's gender schema, they learn which attributes are to be linked with their own sex, and hence, with themselves" (p. 265). Gender schemas may be related to how women experience stress.

Even cognitive therapists think about depression in terms of schemas. Depressed schemas are negative automatic thoughts that are hard to change (Engler, 2003). Aaron Beck's cognitive therapy addresses these negative automatic thoughts. Depressive schemas develop early in life from experiences within cultures.

## Note to the teacher

Mental illness is my main example of schema because of the popularity of the abnormal psychology option. Sandra Bem's (1998) experiment is relevant to section 7.11 about gender and mental illness.

## Schemas, scripts, and language

**Scripts** are schemas about events in time rather than schemas for objects, such as the script for what happens at a birthday party (Gray, 2007). Scripts are sometimes studied through the **narratives** that make up much of the **language** exchanges between parents and children. Narratives are stories of what is supposed to happen and are tied to cultural expectations. In section 4.5, Bruner describes an experiment by Joan Lucariello about birthday party narratives. What happens at birthday parties is just one example of the many scripts that govern human lives. **Memory** schemas are called upon to define expected behavior. Memory schemas are created through narratives.

## 4.5 Evaluate Two Models or Theories of One Cognitive Process: Lev Vygotsky and Jerome Bruner on Language

### Some good reasons for selecting Vygotsky and Bruner

My brother John once told me that his 3-year-old daughter was a math genius. His observation was based on Lauren's ability to count to 50. I asked if I could interview her. We were having supper and Lauren was sitting in her high chair. I asked Lauren what she did that day. Here is our exchange:

"I am getting married."

"Who are you marrying?"

"Dustin," (A boy from her daycare.)

"Does Dustin have a job?"

"Yes."

"What is his job?"

"It is his job to get spanked."

"How much does that pay?"

"About 40 cents."

"Is that a lot of money?"

"Yes."

"What can you buy with 40 cents?"

"Oh, a house."

John could not stop laughing. Lauren was not a math genius, at least in the way he thought. In fact, she did not know what it meant to have 40 of something. But what fascinated me is that Lauren was trying to figure out what it *meant* to have a job or get married, things she heard adults regularly discuss. Lauren was preparing to live in her culture and she was doing this primarily through storytelling. Many of Lauren's stories were starting to meet the requirements of **narratives**, a special kind of story that helps her understand what to do in her **culture**.

Children's stories are funny. Television hosts Bill Cosby and Art Linkletter were good at drawing out amusing stories from children. But children's "talk" is quite significant to their development. Peggy Miller and colleagues (2007) write that young children tell very simple stories, but these stories are important for a child's moral and emotional development.

Miller and colleagues stress that *culture is transmitted to children through repeated interactions with family members that are mediated by narratives and other communication.* Narratives assist children in learning about a culture's **norms**; the content of narratives is specialized for the demands of individual cultures.

A large body of research shows that narratives define who we are as people *throughout the lifespan.* Parents narrate to children before they can produce speech, much of the interaction between parents and children contains narratives, most children's "talk" is narrative, and narrations are still important in later life.

Language, cognitive development, and narratives span all three levels of analysis. Language has a biological basis. Vygotsky and Bruner argue that language is primarily responsible for cognitive development. Narratives are part of the biologically based **Cultural Acquisition Device** (CAD) (Konner, 2007) and are **etics**, "a universal tool of meaning making" (Miller et al., 2007, p. 596). Vygotsky and Bruner argue that language is a fundamental cognitive process, so the cognitive level of analysis is covered, with narratives a particularly significant part of language. Last, narratives are specialized for cultural needs.

Everyone seems to teach **Jean Piaget**. He thought cognitive abilities were dependent on brain maturation. Piaget's theories on cognitive development and language are not as current as Vygotsky's and Bruner's, even if texts still refer to him. Vygotsky and Bruner turned Piaget's explanation completely around and claimed that maturation took place as a result of cognitive skills, particularly language. Culture is built into both Vygotsky's and Bruner's theories, which is one reason they are relevant cognitive processing explanations today. Both are better frameworks for psychology's future. Piaget did not construct his theory in a cultural context. Most applications of Piaget's work are modifications. Both Vygotsky and Bruner criticize Piaget. Most of Piaget's theoretical limitations stem from observing small culturally bound samples. Piaget is best remembered for describing the problems of children's logic use but is weaker in explaining *development.*

Some texts now include Vygotsky and Bruner. Language as a cognitive process dominates human cultural life and these two theorists have the most defensible explanations.

I start this section with Vygotsky, as he built a framework for thinking about the importance of language to a child's development. Then, I review Bruner's language theories, including a thorough discussion of narratives and development. Last, I review a study on narratives, culture, and understandings of the self.

## Lev Vygotsky: Language and cognitive development

### Note to the teacher

> The film *Play: A Vygotskian Approach* helps students understand the zone of proximal development (ZPD) and the importance of play in development. The film is available from www.davidsonfilmstore.com/Play.htm.

It is too bad that Vygotsky died in 1934 at the age of 34. While no one is without critics, Vygotsky's theories still have current support.

Vygotsky's work was suppressed by the Soviets and it took a long time for it to be translated into English. Vygotsky's work re-emerged in the 1970s and 1980s in the West. Vygotsky was a contemporary and critic of Jean Piaget and claimed that he offered a limited explanation of development.

Vygotsky examines the process by which elementary thought, which is recall in children, becomes internalized abstract thought. He considers language the most important cognitive process in humans. Vygotsky shows how other cognitive processes such as memory, attention, problem solving, and perception, are dependent on language. Vygotsky's theory is *interactionist*, meaning that a child develops with the help of parents, teachers, competent older children, and play. The interactions with others take place within a child's cultural context. Make sure to interpret the term *context* the way Vygotsky meant it. Michael Cole (2003) is an authority on Vygotsky and defines context as "the social situation of development is a relational construct in which characteristics of the child combine with the structure of social interactions to create the starting point for a new cycle of developmental changes which will result in a new, and higher, level of development" (pp. 7–8).

Vygotsky's theories fit neatly into the general **bidirectional** model where culture interacts with the mind, the brain, and genes. His research methods are "pilot studies," uncontrolled demonstrations that he called experiments in his writings. Many others have tested Vygotsky's theories using both experimental and nonexperimental methods.

In *Thought and Language* (1934), Vygotsky rejected the idea that animals had language. Human thought is clearly tied to language and animal thought is not tied to their communications. Animal abilities are limited without the technical aid of language.

Vygotsky writes that language and thought begin as separate functions in early development. Sometime during the second year, language and thought follow separate paths. There are prelinguistic and pre-thought behaviors in the actions of babies. When thought and language meet as the child develops, thought becomes verbal and speech rational. At this point a child moves rapidly into symbolic thought—far beyond animal development.

Vygotsky criticizes Piaget's emphasis on **egocentric speech** (when it appeared that children talked to themselves) in young children as a sign of their maturational level. In a pilot study, Vygotsky repeated Piagetian tasks but made them more difficult to show that Piaget was incorrect. When the tasks were hard, "egocentric" speech almost doubled in children. In the same tasks without obstacles, the "egocentric" speech occurred less frequently. If Piaget was correct, then the level of egocentric speech should remain constant. Jerome Bruner agreed, finding that **narration** increases when children solve novel problems. The self talk really facilitates problem solving and plays a large role in development.

Vygotsky's demonstrations led him to theorize that egocentric speech was actually an intermediate phase leading to inner (abstract) speech. Vygotsky calls egocentric speech **externalized speech** and claims that it is socially motivated. Notice how children talk out loud when playing or doing a task. It is as if they *have* to say it out loud. Older children and adults sometimes talk out loud, but it is done less often and primarily during a difficult task or a novel situation. The use of externalized speech simply represents a time in a child's development when thought and speech are still unifying.

Language development is responsible for a child's general cognitive development. This means that a child's ability to think abstractly and use all of the other cognitive processes depends on language. Vygotsky (1978) writes that all development depends on the social environment, and especially what happens within the **zone of proximal development (ZPD)**.

Vygotsky distinguishes between development and learning. Learning refers to task acquisition. Development deals more with the overall level of functioning that a child exhibits. Learning should be paired with a child's developmental level; learning awakens the developmental process.

The ZPD arises from the theory of development. Vygotsky defines the ZPD as "the difference between the actual developmental level as determined by independent problem solving and the level of potential development as determined through problem solving under adult guidance or in collaboration with more capable peers" (p. 86). The ZPD creates the environment where external processing in children becomes internalized symbolic thought. Think of the ZPD this way. On their own, children can only achieve so much. This is the actual developmental level. But with the help of an adult or more capable peer, a child rises to the top of their developmental zone. Tutoring raises a child to the upper limits of his or her capabilities. Teachers are important in the ZPD process; they bring students up to the top of their zone of development. My job as a teacher is to break down material so that it brings students to the top of their ZPD. Each new accomplishment raises the next ZPD.

**Play** is an important ZPD. In play, children act more maturely than they do in normal life. During play the immediate perceptual field does not constrain behavior. Something new and abstract happens when a child enters an imaginary world. *Meaning* is more important than rote action in play. What goes unnoticed in real life become explicitly acknowledged rules for behavior. Vygotsky studied two sisters in one of his pilot demonstrations. He asked these real life sisters to play being sisters. In real life, the "sister" behaviors go unnoticed. In play, both are concerned with showing their "sisterhood." The girls are explicit about the rules associated with being sisters, such as who the leader is, how they dress, and how they treat each other differently than others. In the sister game, the girls understood more about their sibling relationship as opposed to other relationships. *Real play is socially and culturally motivated and contributes to development.* Children use language in play to make sense of the world.

*Animals are not building blocks for humans.* The key difference is that human thought is tied to language. Vygotsky (1934) writes that Wolfgang Kohler's ape studies only show animals performing actions. Sultan the ape needed all the objects in view in order to use them. Animals only perform actions to complete tasks. Children in similar situations act *and* speak, and do so increasingly and persistently when a task becomes more difficult. When children are faced with complicated problems, action, speech, and perception are aimed at the same task. Animal problem solving lacks this unity.

Vygotsky demonstrated the unity of action, speech, and perception by giving children a task so complicated that they could not use tools to solve it. No adults were available to help. Children had to use *thought*. Children's externalized speech increased dramatically as they worked on the task.

Vygotsky makes similar distinctions between animal perception, attention, memory, and problem solving and human abilities.

Animal problem solving is completely determined by perception. Animals are unable to modify their perceptual field. Humans can change their perceptual field at will. If I ask you to think about something happening in another country, you easily shift your perception. It was once thought that human perception was simply a continuation of animal perception. This idea comes from early experiments on 2-year-old children showing that they described different elements of problems separately. Vygotsky changed the parameters of the early studies to allow children without full command of language to pantomime their answers. Children pantomiming their answers understood more than early studies showed. Young children could see the picture as a whole when language was removed. It is only later, when language is more developed, that children can use it to describe entire problems. Vygotsky shows that humans have a unique perceptual ability to see the world as a whole, with meaning as well as form.

Vygotsky claims that human attention works in a similar way. Humans direct their attention in a dynamic way to different perceptual fields with the aid of language.

There is modern evidence supporting Vygotsky's distinctions between human and animal abilities. For example, recent research supports Vygotsky's view that attention works differently in animals and humans.

This evidence relates to the **evolution** of human **social intelligence** (section 3.5). Henrike Moll and Michael Tomasello (2007) write that social competition drove chimpanzee evolution. In contrast, humans evolved uniquely because of social cooperation. There is research supporting the "Vygotskian intelligence hypothesis." Animals do communicate, however, the nature of their communication is different from that of humans. Researchers make clear distinctions between chimp-to-chimp cooperative communication, chimp-to-human cooperative communication, and human-to-human cooperative communication. Think about human communication, even something as simple as pointing to a rainbow and saying, "Look at that beautiful rainbow." Children even hear stories about a pot of gold at the end of a rainbow. The stories require shared attention, where the parent points out the rainbow and the child looks. The parent and child talk about its beauty and they admire it together. Chimpanzees do not do this. Moll and Tomasello say that chimps communicate, and even gesture to other chimps, such as in initialing play, but never have been observed to *point out* something to another chimp. They lack the (abstract) shared attention. However, chimp abilities are greater once they interact with humans. Chimps use humans as tools and point to objects they want. But the chimp's understanding of pointing is missing something: the shared attention that humans routinely use early in life (this concept was introduced in section 3.5). Human cooperative communication is on an entirely different level. Even 14-month-old babies have an understanding of abstract pointing gestures. In studies where an adult infers (by pointing) that they prefer one of several containers, the babies make the correct selection. This behavior is the beginning of the human theory of mind (TOM). Human infants can communicate cooperatively "to simply share interest in things and inform others of things" (p. 7).

Vygotsky writes that when a child acquires verbal skills, memory is freed from recall and becomes a synthesis of past and present that is directed at purposeful goals. Children with language skills construct memory and this construction is socially and culturally motivated.

Vygotsky used simple examples of tying a knot or marking one's place so as not to forget. These are artificial symbolic behaviors that we call symbols of human culture and they increase with age.

As you learn about cognitive processes other than language, think about how important language is to them.

## Jerome Bruner: Language and cognitive development

Bruner theorized that Noam Chomsky's **language acquisition device (LAD)** was incomplete as a model of how children actually used language. Chomsky downplayed the role of parenting and culture, suggesting that an innate LAD explained how children in all cultures acquired language. Another limitation of Chomsky's theory is that it is too **reductionist**. Bruner introduced the concept **language acquisition support system** (LASS) as a more fruitful theory explaining how children move from innate **prelinguistic skills** to *making meaning* within the cultural context of a child's daily life. Human development has a biological basis, but the interaction between a caregiver and child *activates* this biology.

Research on Bruner's theories has method, observer, time (the research takes place in more than one time period), and space (cross-cultural) **triangulation** and spans all three levels of analysis. Experimental evidence exists for the theory, but over time Bruner has become an advocate for the use of nonexperimental methods. The natural setting, though uncontrolled, is the only place where one sees the real interactions between adult and child.

The LASS implies that parents are **scaffolds**, meaning supportive frameworks, for child development. Scaffold is very similar to Vygotsky's ZPD. **Culture**, **intersubjectivity** and **intentions** are important concepts for understanding the LASS.

Bruner (1996) situates language and development in a cultural context. Bruner believes that human minds evolved in the context of a symbolic culture shared by others. Language makes understanding the rules of one's culture possible. "Culture, then, though itself man-made, both forms and makes possible the workings of a distinctively human mind. On this view, learning and thinking are always dependent upon the utilization of cultural resources" (p. 4).

Intersubjectivity and intentions go together. **Intersubjectivity** means that there is interplay between adults and children long before children have actual language. It is a natural "dance," a reciprocal relationship, where one has an **intention** to connect to the other and decode what the other person intends to convey (a TOM). This all takes place at a symbolic level. Intersubjective experiences are part of daily human relationships throughout the lifespan. Intentions are uniquely human and probably have a biological base, as it appears that babies come into the world with innate **schemas** to figure out the intentions of others. Babies have prelinguistic behaviors that can be seen in **play** such as "itsy bitsy spider" and "peek-a-boo."

Animals do not have the ability to read sophisticated intentions from others. Of course, a mother cat teaches her kittens how to use a litter box, but this teaching is innately wired into cat behavior. It is not a cognitive intention coming from a sophisticated brain that is considering all the possibilities for a child. No cat mother considers raising one from the litter to be a cat president! Animals do not have the brainpower or language to even consider this idea. In contrast, *human scaffolds spend their time making the world manageable for children.*

Bruner thinks that **cognitive development** is largely dependent on language. Development unfolds in three phases. The first is the **enactive** phase. Babies have **skills** that enable them to manipulate objects. These skills are functionally the equivalent of language and develop from an innate set of action patterns hardwired into the brain at birth. Examples of these building blocks are grasping, sucking, and looking. Babies quickly move into the second **ikonic** phase. The ikonic phase takes place from about 2 to 5 years of age, when children learn actual language but still think in images rather than in symbols. The third phase is called **symbolic**, where the child now internalizes symbolic abstractions and has full command of language. Children of 6 to 7 years of age should have symbolic thought.

The outcome of development depends on the way that children are instructed. For example, language develops in a sociocultural context where performance feedback is important. An observation study shows this process (Bruner, 1983). A mother and baby played peek-a-boo to demonstrate the **intersubjective** experience between the mother and child. The mother initiates the game and the baby responds with babbling and eye contact in place of language at the appropriate times when language is used by the adult. This type of interaction helps the baby learn how to do things with words. As you might guess, **play** is important to the entire intersubjective experience between adults and babies. Development moves rapidly during play; children use imagination to create problem-solving strategies without real-world consequences.

Bruner (1990) writes that children need the help of caregivers to develop language far more than Chomsky believed. Making meaning is far more important to developing cognitive processes than information. "The acquisition of a first language is very context sensitive, by which is meant that it progresses far better when the child already grasps in some prelinguistic way the significance of what is being talked about or of the situation in which the talk is occurring" (p. 71). Once a child in the enactive phase masters the general give and take of relationships, he or she is ready to use language.

**Narratives** are the format children use to master language and show they understand the ways of their culture. Narratives, or particular types of stories, are the most frequently used type of human communication. "All narrative environments are specialized for cultural needs" (p. 84). Susan Engel (1995) describes the mechanisms of narratives. One difference between animals and humans is the use of narration. Animals live in one world, that of objects. Humans live in a double world; humans know objects but also have a second level of inner cognitive experience, where we try to understand life. Stories create a child's sense of self and are where children integrate affect, cognition, and action. Not all stories are narratives. Engel outlines Bruner's criteria for identifying narratives from other types of talk.

A narrative:
1. must have a sequence.
2. must have a plot that conveys meaning.
3. must have a high point, a tension that meets some kind of resolution.
4. remains a narrative whether it is true or untrue.
5. makes distinctions between the usual and the unusual.
6. directs attention to personal and subjective experience. (pp. 70–71)

## Note to the teacher

Here is a great activity. Students obtain signed consent from parents to record stories from children between ages 2 and 7. Make sure the children also want to participate. Students have to participate a great deal in the narratives of young children, but by the time they are 7, children should be able to narrate on their own. Transcribe the stories and look for evidence of narratives. Developmental differences in the stories and changes from ikonic to symbolic thought are clear. Students can write their results as case studies and even use a content analysis, where themes about developmental level and characteristics of narratives are identified.

People narrate frequently; narratives make up most human "talk." Think about it. If you call a friend on the telephone it is probably not to announce that you are going to the post office to buy stamps. Telephone calls are about the interesting and/or unusual things that happen, such as difficult homework assignments or problems with a friend.

Research shows that children narrate more when they must make sense out of something unusual. Bruner (1990) describes an experiment by Joan Lucariello with 4- and 5-year-olds. Lucariello wanted to see what kinds of things started narratives. Children were divided into two groups. Children heard either a story about typical events at a birthday party or about a visit from a child's cousin who had come to play. Some of the stories violated accepted **norms**, such as the birthday girl pouring water over the candles instead of blowing them out or that she was unhappy that day. Lucariello then asked the children questions about the stories. Lucariello found that the unusual stories sparked a large amount of narration as the children tried to make sense of them. For example, one child tried to explain the unhappy birthday girl by suggesting that she did not have the right dress to wear. When directly asked questions about why things went as usual in the regular stories, the children had little to say and even shrugged as if it were unclear why the researcher was asking the question. Even a slightly unusual story about the cousin coming over to play received four times more elaboration in narratives than the regular story. *Children talk more about why things are different than why they are normal.*

Engel (1995) describes another narrative experiment performed by Christine Todd that shows a similar finding. Two groups of pre-school children participated in either high or low emotion events. Children recalled the high emotion events more vividly and frequently afterward.

Bruner (1990) describes an observation study that gives these two experiments **method triangulation**. Emily's bedtime stories were observed and recorded from ages 18 to 36 months. A baby brother was born in the family during this time, not only replacing Emily as the center of attention but also taking her room. Emily made great strides in language development during this time as she made sense of these events. Bruner noted an increase in Emily's use of terms such as "and then" and "because" to explain events. In addition, Emily moved from simple statements of Sunday morning breakfasts such as "Daddy did make some cornbread for Emmy have" (p. 91) to social **scripts** that had explanatory value, such as "Tomorrow when we wake up from bed, first me and Daddy and Mommy, you, eat breakfast eat breakfast; like we usually do, and then we're going to play, and then soon as Daddy comes, Carl's going to come over and play awhile" (p. 93). By age 3, Emily could integrate the correct sequence of events with accepted behavior. Emily was figuring out what happens in human culture.

## A study building on narratives and cultural variations in behavior

Many new studies are investigating narratives. One example is a correlation study by Qi Wang (2007) that pulls together all of the following concepts: **language**, **intersubjective** experiences and reading the **intentions** of others, **narratives**, **memory**, the **independent self** seen more in **individualist** cultures versus the **interdependent self** seen more in **collectivist** cultures, the effects of **parenting** and **culture** on **cognitive development**, and contributions to a child's **identity**. This is again the value of modern research; it unites many concepts necessary to thread topics through the IB program.

Wang studied the narrative exchanges between mothers and children in three groups, European Americans, Chinese living in China, and first-generation Chinese living in the United

States. Wang collected data on the level of elaborations mothers used during narrative exchanges and the effect of elaboration level on the child's personal (autobiographical) memories. In addition, Wang correlated high or low elaboration by a mother with a child's construal, or understanding, of the self.

A large body of research shows that narratives help children learn what is expected of them. Three general findings pointed Wang to the study's aims.

First, parents are either high elaborators or low elaborators during narrative exchanges. Both high and low elaborators are acting as **scaffolds** to give children feedback about **norms**. High-elaborative parents embellish stories with lots of feedback for children; it is a co-construction of a child's autobiographical stories. Low-elaborative parents engage children in repetitive conversations, asking and repeating precise questions in an attempt to get specific answers from their children. Children with high-elaborative parents have greater memories for past personal experiences. However, these conclusions came primarily from studies using white, middle-class, Western samples. Would Wang find the same thing cross-culturally?

Second, an initial round of studies examined narrative elaboration cross-culturally. European American mothers engaged in more high-elaborative narrative exchanges, and Korean, Japanese, and Chinese mothers used more low elaboration. But these data are from cross-sectional studies; data are collected at one point in time. Wang saw it as a weakness. Would she get the same findings in a longitudinal study?

Third, related research about the self showed that sharing narrative pasts was important for parenting and socialization. Parent-child reminiscing in narratives is a universal behavior, but the *purposes* and *forms* of the exchanges vary by culture, reflecting different socialization goals. Many students are familiar with the research on the independent self and interdependent self from Markus and Kitayama in 1991. Wang believes that narrative exchanges between parents and children play a large role in the cultural construal of the self; the stories are important in constructing one's identity. European American parents use the narrative exchanges to help children construct elaborate and logical personal stories. Perhaps the goal is to build unique individual identities, an independent self. In contrast, Asian parents use a more directive narrative exchange style. Perhaps the shared memories are used to define hierarchical relationships between parents and children that emphasize social conformity, an interdependent self. Wang could not draw any specific relationship between narrative style and independent/interdependent self without gathering specific research about the parental beliefs of the self. This was another goal of the study.

The sample consisted of 189 mother and female child pairs. Fifty-eight pairs lived in Beijing, China. The other groups lived in New York. Sixty pairs were first-generation Chinese immigrants and 71 pairs were European Americans. All of the children were from middle-class families and most of the parents had college educations.

Data were collected at three points in time, when the children were 3, 3.5, and 4 years old.

Two native female researchers collected data in both locations. Both researchers were bilingual so that participants could talk in the language they used the most. All materials were written in Chinese and English. All questionnaires were **back translated** to control for consistency in meaning.

Three pieces of data were collected, two questionnaires and the narrative exchanges. Mothers filled out both questionnaires. One was the Child Development Inventory that asked about the children's language production and comprehension. The other was the Self-Construal Scale that assessed the mother's self beliefs, if they had an independent self or an interdependent self. Last, researchers videotaped two narratives between mother and child. The stories concerned any two different one-time events from the last two months that the mother selected, such as a trip to the zoo. The mothers were told to select one story with positive emotional content and one with negative emotional content for the child. The stories could be as long as the mothers wished. Wang counterbalanced the narrating of positive and negative stories to make sure that the results were not caused by a child's hearing either positive or negative emotional content in a story first.

Two general findings emerged. One was that that European American mothers used high elaboration more than the other mothers and that European American children recalled more autobiographical memories. A correlation was found between hearing high-elaboration stories and reporting more past memories. Second, a correlation was found between a mother's value orientation toward an interdependent or independent self and their level of elaboration in the narrative exchanges.

Wang concluded that her findings on high and low elaboration in narratives helped explain cultural differences in self-construal. In addition, Wang's study is another piece of evidence showing that intersubjective experiences between parents and children are reciprocal. Children play an active role in narrating. In turn, the intersubjective experience assists children in understanding expected social roles that "unfold in a larger cultural context" (Wang, 2007, p. 469).

## Comparisons between Vygotsky and Bruner

1. Vygotsky and Bruner both have **domain-general theories**, where one underlying process accounts for all developmental changes (Jarvis, Russell, & Gorman, 2004). Language is the primary vehicle for the development of other cognitive abilities, such as memory and perception. In addition, general cognitive development is accounted for in both theories.

2. Vygotsky and Bruner believe that language develops within a **cultural** context. Culture is built in to the theories. Both believe that children use language to make meaning out of their social world.

3. Vygotsky and Bruner both have **continuous developmental theories**. Development does not stop at specific points, as it does in discontinuous (stage) theories. Stage theories are largely historical.

4. Vygotsky and Bruner reject the idea that animals have language. Both say that Kohler's research shows only the actions of animals, not sophisticated cognitive processing. Human cognitive processing is removed from action.

5. Vygotsky and Bruner believe that human babies have prelinguistic skills that develop into full human language.

6. Both Vygotsky and Bruner criticize Piaget. One criticism concerns Piaget's concept of **egocentric speech**. In addition, both have evidence that development occurs more quickly than Piaget believed. Children are better at figuring out the conservation task if it is more manageable.

7. Vygotsky and Bruner recognize the importance of **play** as a child's "work." Play is where children use language to develop.

## Contrasts between Vygotsky and Bruner (including contrasts with Piaget)

1. Vygotsky and Bruner used different research methods. Vygotsky used uncontrolled pilot studies. Bruner initially used experiments in his theories, but moved toward less experimental methods as his career matured. Both make similar points about language, but there are differences in their investigative methods. Bruner worked in more modern times and his research methods reflect it.

2. Bruner is more explicit about the actual biological contributions to language. Bruner's LASS incorporates innate prelinguistic skills in babies. While Vygotsky thought there were biological predispositions to behavior, his Marxist orientation led him to focus on the social context, believing that children's language and development was socially and culturally motivated. In addition, we knew less about biological predispositions during Vygotsky's life. Bruner's concepts of intentions and intersubjectivity have a clear biological basis. Bruner's ideas on language and cognitive development fit directly into the current psychology's framework where people decode other's intentions.

3. For students interested in Piaget, the contrasts between Vygotsky/Bruner and Piaget lie in three main areas. One relates to a domain-general approach. Piaget also had a domain-general theory. But his assumption that brain maturation is fundamental to cognitive development is turned completely around by Vygotsky/Bruner. Second, Vygotsky thought that language was the vehicle by which development occurred. Piaget thought language reflected brain maturation. Third is Piaget's concept of egocentric speech, with which Vygotsky/Bruner disagreed. In addition to these three contrasts, Piaget's methods of research were limited. Piaget primarily observed his three children and some Swiss school children. He did not examine enough children to validate his claims. I am not suggesting that everything Vygotsky said is true today, but Piaget's primary assumptions about development are faulty.

## How to use the language material in the developmental psychology option

In addition to being applicable to this heading, Vygotsky and Bruner's theories on language and development are also relevant for parts of the developmental psychology option. Vygotsky and Bruner's theories apply to the heading "evaluate theories of cognitive development." In addition, the concept "narratives" is helpful in several ways. First, it is part of Bruner's theory of language and cognitive development. Second, it helps with the section titled "General Framework," specifically as sociocultural and cognitive factors that influence human development, including relevant psychological research and the section titled "Cognitive Development." Third, parenting and culture are two social/environmental factors that affect cognitive development.

## 4.6 Explain How Biological Factors May Affect One Cognitive Process

### A good night's sleep might improve your school performance

**Sleep** is a topic dear to the hearts of teenagers. Teens love sleep but do not seem to get enough of it. Mary Carskadon and others find that sleep is linked to the cognitive skills necessary for high school achievement. Students may think that they can perform well without adequate sleep, but is this true?

The biological effects of sleep deprivation on cognitive processing and its resultant effects on educational performance are a consequence of living in rapidly changing cultures.

Carskadon (Frontline, 1999) reports that adolescents need 9¼ hours of sleep each night for optimal performance, challenging what students think they need. Surveys show that teens average about 7½ hours of sleep each night, with about a quarter of teenagers getting 6½ hours or less. The effects of sleep deprivation are numerous, including dangerous driving, **depression**, parent-child quarrels, increased sensitivity to **stress**, and impaired cognitive skills.

Sleep deprivation is a general societal problem that affects everyone. A rapidly changing society has made so many things available to teens at night when they should be sleeping, such as the Internet, cell phones, and jobs. In addition, many U.S. school districts with small budgets save money by using buses in shifts. First, the buses service high schools, then middle schools, and then elementary schools. One result is very early high school start times for adolescents. Some school districts have switched to later school start times and report increased student attention and higher grades.

Adolescents face other obstacles to getting proper sleep. Hormonal changes beginning at puberty push teen circadian rhythms forward at night (Harvard Mental Health Letter, July, 2005). Many sleep-deprived adolescents use the weekends to catch up on sleep. It may seem like a good strategy but it further exasperates the problem during the school week. For example, if the brain gets signals that nighttime is from 2 a.m. until 1 p.m. the next day on Friday and Saturday, it is hard to reset the sleep cycle on Sunday night.

Amy Wolfson and Mary Carskadon (1998) report sleep habits and grades from the Sleep Habits Survey using 3120 high school students in Rhode Island. This survey was a self-report from the teenagers and is uncontrolled, counting on participant honesty. Between ages 13 and 19, the amount of sleep decreased by as much as 50 minutes each night. Adolescents describing themselves as struggling academically reported sleeping an average of 25 minutes less each night than those reporting good grades. In addition, students with bad grades reported that they go to bed later on weekend nights than those with good grades.

Experiments conducted in sleep labs show that sleep deprivation negatively affects many cognitive tasks, such as memory, verbal abilities, and attention. For those insisting that 8 or more hours of sleep are unnecessary or packing schedules so full that adequate sleep is impossible, the evidence is not in your favor.

One experiment by Genevieve Forest and Roger Godbout (2004) shows that even one night of sleep deprivation impairs immediate and delayed recall of stories more than the recall of those not sleep deprived. An additional experiment had subjects memorize a spatial map of a library. A week later participants were tested to see if they remembered the map. Those getting adequate sleep performed significantly better than those with impaired sleep. In one other experiment, A. C. Randazzo and colleagues (1998) randomly assigned 16 children aged 10 to 14 to either receive 11 hours or 5 hours of sleep for one night. Participants getting 11 hours of sleep showed significantly greater performance on tests of verbal creativity, verbal fluency, and verbal flexibility than those getting 5 hours of sleep.

Since these experiments are conducted in sleep labs, it is important to consider the effects of the sleep lab on performance (Forest & Godbout, 2004). Participants are not sleeping in their own beds and often are outfitted with technology showing sleep stages in the brain.

While the research shows that sleep is important, there are still many unanswered questions about the relationship between sleep and cognition. Recent research is investigating whether sleep is necessary for *all* cognitive tasks or just certain ones and if developmental level is important.

## A study connecting sleep, memory, and learning

Ines Wilhelm and colleagues (2008) conducted a quasi-field experiment to see if both **declarative memory** and **procedural memory** require sleep and if one's developmental level is also a factor. Declarative memories are factual memories. There are two kinds of declarative memories. One is episodic, memories of personal experiences and the past. The other is semantic memory, the meaning of words and their use. Procedural memories are the things you know how to do. A large number of the cognitive tasks necessary for successful school performance are related to declarative memory. In addition, the authors thought that the role of developmental sleep in memory consolidation was unexplored.

Fifteen healthy children with a mean age of 7.5 and 15 healthy adults with a mean age of 26.5 were tested in both a sleep and a wake condition that took place one week apart. This experiment took place in the participant's home to reduce problems related to collecting data in sleep labs. Collecting data in a natural setting increases the **method triangulation** of studies conducted in sleep labs. The sleep and wake conditions were balanced to control for order effects. In order to prevent confounding variables from interfering with the study results, detailed observations were collected by parents about their children's moods, motivation level, and tiredness.

Children in the sleep condition started learning both tasks at 8:00 p.m. and the adults started learning at 10:00 p.m. after they were outfitted for polysomnographic readings. A polysomnogram takes a variety of readings, such as EEG and eye movement (EOG). Testing took place an hour after waking, with an average of 11 hours between learning and testing.

For both children and adults in the daytime awake condition, learning took place one hour after waking. Testing occurred 11 hours after learning. In between, all participants kept a regular routine.

Declarative memory was tested using word-pair associative learning and a two-dimensional location test. The children had 20 pairs of words and the adults had 40 pairs. The object location task was similar to a game of concentration using 15 card pairs. Procedural memory was tested through a finger sequence tapping task.

The results for adult participants were similar to those from other experiments. Adults performed better on both declarative and procedural tasks after sleep than they did in the daytime awake condition. In contrast, children's performance depended on the type of memory task. Children performed better on the declarative memory task after sleep and performed better on the procedural memory task in the daytime awake condition.

Since declarative memory tasks make up much of what children do in school, proper sleep is vital. Declarative memories are related to **hippocampus** activity, which helps with new memory formation and is part of a system that helps consolidate declarative memories. It appears that some offline learning is necessary to consolidate declarative memories.

The authors speculated about why the children performed the procedural memory task better in the daytime wake condition. One explanation is that children learn procedural memories easier during waking states. Another explanation is that the children approached the procedural task differently than the adults did. The children took longer to learn the finger tapping than the adults and spoke out loud during the task. It is possible that the children relied on hippocampal-related skills while learning the finger tapping that interfered with recall after sleeping. Future research should clarify the developmental differences found in this study. Wilhelm and colleagues recognize that their findings do not rule out the possibility that sleep would benefit procedural memory in the long term.

What can we do to get more sleep? If students do not get enough sleep, even the best teaching methods may not be effective.

## Note to the teacher

I address sleep problems through the "food and sleep challenge." The details are in the Appendix. The sleep challenge is a month-long project. It is a partnership between students, parents, and teachers. After the sleep challenge, students report more alertness at school, better recall for class work (not as much need to restudy!), less reactivity to stressful situations, and better mood.

## 4.7 Discuss How Social or Cultural Factors Affect One Cognitive Process

Of the two studies in this section, Michael Cole's (1996) research on the Kpelle and Vai in Africa is an example of the effects of **culture** on **intelligence** and **memory** and the neighborhood study by Tama Leventhal and Jeanne Brooks-Gunn (2004) is an example of the effects of **social factors** on **verbal abilities** and intelligence.

The material in this section is also useful for the developmental psychology option. The option includes a learning outcome on how social and environmental variables affect cognitive development. Cole demonstrated that both culture and schooling affect cognitive development. Living in a poor neighborhood affects many aspects of child development.

### Why are Michael Cole's studies important?

In the 1960s and 1970s, Michael Cole and colleagues conducted a series of experiments investigating two areas of cognitive functioning (Cole, 1996). One set of studies examined how the Kpelle and Vai in Africa performed on memory and intelligence tasks. The other set of studies examined the effects of schooling on cognitive processing. Cole tells a great story about the challenges involved in gathering credible data. The process was full of twists and turns, unexpected findings, and challenges to traditional research models. Getting past stereotypes was a major research design challenge. As Cole says, it is hard to conduct cross-cultural research when we are immersed in it.

### Michael Cole: Culture and memory research

In 1971 Cole and colleagues tested Frederick Bartlett's idea that nonliterate African tribal people used rote recall on memory tasks for which they had no emotional connection. Experiments using free recall tasks in the United States were a popular memory research format. When given free recall tasks for familiar objects, U.S. subjects clustered the items into categories. Educated American adults used the clustering strategy increasingly with numerous trials. Small children do not perform well at clustering, even with numerous trials.

When Kpelle farmers in Africa took the same type of free recall test, they selected items representing familiar categories. However, there was no clear pattern of organization in how these subjects recalled the items. This finding was contrary to the popular **stereotype** that nonliterate persons had tremendous memories. Even practice did not improve the Kpelle's memory. Cole did not want to simply report that Kpelle farmers had poor memories. Instead he set out to make the research *culturally relevant.*

Cole designed a series of experiments to make the free recall experiment culturally relevant. Before running the studies, Cole first had to figure out how to present the objects to the Kpelle so that they *could* recall them.

How did Cole make the experimental tasks culturally relevant? Most importantly the tasks had to represent something significant to the Kpelle. Otherwise, how could they recall the items? The decision was made to try narratives as the context for the free recall task. Remember that Bruner (section 4.5) uses narratives to study how people make meaning of their cultures. **Narrative interviews** *are useful cross-cultural research tools.*

Free recall items were planted within two different stories that made sense to the Kpelle about the bridewealth for a chief's daughter. In one story, different suitors offered clothes, food, tools, or utensils. In the second story, a man kidnapped the girl who drops the same items along the way, but in no specific order by category.

Results showed that how the items were embedded into the stories affected the way in which they were recalled. Participants hearing the first story clustered the items. Those hearing the second story recalled the items according to the order they were presented in the story.

One lesson to learn here is that *researchers cannot simply use the same task to test cognitive processing across cultures.*

## Michael Cole: The effect of schooling on cognition

Developmental psychology and cross-cultural research flourished in the 1960s (Cole, 1996). After World War II a great deal of thought was given to improving education in countries with low economic development. It was thought that giving children access to *formal education* would take them beyond their communities. This is in contrast to the idea of *fundamental education,* where children learn community traditions. Cole and colleagues studied the impact of formal education on cognitive development in Africa.

During the 1960s many African nations included more formal education in their school systems. However, the nature of this education was based on Western schooling. What were the results? African students showed low performance. In 1963 Cole joined a project to study students in Liberia, particularly in areas populated by the Kpelle.

Kpelle students had much more difficulty learning mathematics than students in the United States. Cole aimed to show how making the material *culturally relevant* to the lives of the Kpelle students might improve mathematics performance. When Cole observed classes, he noticed that students were required to use rote memorization.

Cole was told that three things explained the poor performance. First, the children had perceptual problems that kept them from identifying geometrical shapes. Second, the children could not classify. Third, children used rote recall instead of thinking to try and come up with answers. When teachers used examples to teach in class and used similar items on tests, the students complained that these items were not covered in class.

Cole did not believe these claims.

Were Liberian students less capable than students from the United States? In order to avoid such a gross generalization, Cole had to think creatively. He noted, for example, that the Kpelle showed high skill levels when trading in the marketplace. If people performed poorly in Western traditional schooling tasks but performed well in settings important to their culture, then a new research strategy was needed.

Ethnographies led to the construction of culturally relevant experimental tasks to test Kpelle mathematical skills. Cole "needed to examine the circumstances in which Kpelle people encountered something recognizable to us as mathematics" (Cole, 1996, p. 74). Kpelle everyday activities were studied along with how Kpelle adults transmitted this knowledge to their children. *Here was an instance where nonexperimental research of everyday life helped define relevant experimental research,* increasing the **method triangulation** of cross-cultural research on schooling.

One complaint about Kpelle students was that they could not measure, so an obvious place to study Kpelle measurement was in the marketplace. Kpelle people measure rice in the marketplace differently than what is done in U.S. supermarkets. The Kpelle measured rice in several ways, such as *kopi,* a tin can measuring one dry pint, a *boke* or bucket, *tins* or tin cans, and bags. The relationship between these measurements was based on the common metric of the cup, but not as exact as standards in the United States. How these measurements were used in the marketplace also varied according to whether someone was buying or selling. Buying rice involved a kopi with the bottom pounded down to increase the volume and selling rice involved kopi that had a flat bottom to decrease the volume.

An experiment using Kpelle measurement was constructed. Participants were American and Kpelle adults and school children. "Each subject was presented with four mixing bowls of equal size holding different amounts of rice (1½, 3, 4½, and 6 kopi), shown the tin to be used as the unit of measurement, and asked to estimate the number of tin cans (kopi) of rice in each bowl" (Cole, 1996, p. 76).

The results showed that the Kpelle could indeed measure; in fact the adults were very accurate. American adults overestimated the amounts of rice, up to 100% for the 6-can measurement. Both American and Kpelle children made estimating mistakes.

Cole's experiment is an example of how making experimental tasks culturally relevant shows that people from all cultures have skills related to what is relevant to everyday practice.

John Gay and Michael Cole (1967) write that formal schooling *does* impact Kpelle development. But cultural *values* explain their behavior. Before the introduction of formal schooling, Kpelle education was based on tribal tradition with several fundamental values. First, learning was practical, such as how to build a house. Since **individualism** was downplayed, an individual's superior house-building skills were frowned upon. Maintenance of the group was demanded, so Kpelle answers to questions reflected the knowledge of elders. Second, children did not have to give reasons for answers, something valued in the West. Preserving the culture was primary, so simply performing a task was enough. Rarely did individuals justify actions if they maintained the culture. Third, a lot of education was *nonverbal*. Children learned through observation that was highly relevant but without the verbal link between the teacher's actions and the child's understanding of them. **Conformity** was expected. When Kpelle children entered formal school, they spent time learning English. Often there were no equivalent words in Kpelle that helped solve traditional Western tests of memory and measurement.

It is helpful to think about how **language** explains the challenges Kpelle faced when schooling changed from fundamental (learning traditions) to formal schooling. For example, Western formal school performance for measurement tasks requires knowledge of words such as "half" and "set." This seems obvious to someone in the United States. But Kpelle words for half mean one of two things. It could mean an indeterminate part of a whole or else be a meaningless symbol used in school. This is why Kpelle children called 1/10 "half." The task was outside of their cultural context. Kpelle have different ways of classifying sets according to their use in everyday life. There are numerous distinct words for countable objects rather than just using the general term "set." Some things, such as water or rice, are not thought of in countable sets at all.

In addition, Gay and Cole found that children might learn a skill in school, but did not show the "skill" in adult life. Did development stop after about age 10? Of course not. As the Kpelle got older, they learned to do things that matched the values needed to survive in their culture that "interfered" with the schooling. Remember that Kpelle were expected to behave in such a way as to preserve the culture. Instead of coming up with efficient answers to problems, Kpelle adults thought of clever exaggerations that left the problem unanswered. It does not always make sense to a Western researcher, but the successful Kpelle is the one who comes up with an unanswerable solution; they do not have to be right. The right answers were known through cultural practices that maintained traditions.

Cole and his colleagues replicated the findings of the Kpelle experiments with Maya and Mestizo subjects in the Yucatan Peninsula in the 1970s (Cole, 1996). The patterns were the same as those found with the Kpelle.

## Social factors: Neighborhood effects on cognitive abilities and school performance

Tama Leventhal and Jeanne Brooks-Gunn (2004) write that neighborhoods are important. Research on the effects of neighborhoods on **cognitive abilities** is new but promising. In addition to cognitive abilities and education, neighborhood factors affect mental health and aggression.

Studying the *contexts* of development is gaining momentum. Today more children are growing up in poor families and live in poor urban settings. What effect does growing up in a poor neighborhood have on cognitive abilities and school performance?

Correlation studies, field experiments, and quasi-experiments are methods used to study the psychological effects of neighborhoods. Socioeconomic status (SES) is the variable most often studied. High SES is defined by a neighborhood's income level and the percentage of professionals and college-educated persons in the neighborhood. Low SES is defined by the percentage of poor households, the percentage of homes headed by females, the percentage of households where an adult is unemployed and/or on public assistance, and ethnicity.

Correlation studies in the United States and Canada using longitudinal and cross-sectional data have similar findings. Living in an affluent neighborhood is positively correlated with good **verbal ability**, **IQ scores**, and school performance for pre-school and school-age children. In addition, prosperous neighborhoods are positively correlated with high adolescent school performance, particularly for males. On the other hand, living among low SES neighbors is positively correlated with poor mental health and more delinquency. It is challenging to design these studies and researchers must control all factors that interfere with neighborhood effects, such as genetics, age, race, and educational level.

Families are randomly assigned to live in certain places in field experiments, thus controlling for the confounding variables in correlation studies. One quasi-experiment is Chicago's Gautreaux Program, where people living in public housing use vouchers to move out of poor neighborhoods. Random assignments for the moves are based on available housing. After 10 years, children living in higher SES neighborhoods performed better academically than children living in poor neighborhoods.

Another field experiment randomly assigned 4600 families to move out of public housing in five U.S. cities. After several years, children who moved out of poor neighborhoods performed better academically and had better physical and mental health. Field experiments are uncontrolled. It is impossible to control for all factors that might influence outcomes.

At this time researchers only have theories about how high SES neighborhoods contribute to cognitive abilities. The **norms and collective efficacy theory** suggests that neighborhoods are institutional structures that have specific social expectations for children. So far, changes made after moving to more affluent neighborhoods are positive.

The changes in children participating in field experiments are greater than the changes made in correlation studies. The effects of the changes in the correlation studies are moderate, probably because neighborhood changes initiated by poor families tend to be less dramatic than those initiated by researchers.

Research on neighborhood effects has a promising future, but must account for the underlying processes involved in different neighborhood settings. Since SES is largely determined from census reports, research models in the future need new definitions of neighborhoods, such as ones based on crime models from statistics or interviews with non-study participants about their opinions of their neighborhood. The results of neighborhood studies may help guide future public policy.

# 4.8 To What Extent Is One Cognitive Process Reliable?

## The consequences of faulty eyewitness memory

James Newsome and Calvin C. Johnson both served long jail sentences for crimes they did not commit (Wrightsman et al., 2002). Eyewitnesses identified Newsome as the person who shot and killed a Chicago grocer, even though the fingerprints of a known killer out on parole at the time that did not match Newsome's fingerprints were left at the crime scene. Later the real killer was identified and Newsome released. Johnson had a similar experience. He spent 16 years in prison for a rape he did not commit. The victim selected Johnson from a photographic lineup two weeks after the attack and the jury convicted him, even though forensic tests were presented at the trial showing that Johnson was not the right suspect. Johnson was released after DNA testing showed he could not be responsible. Faulty witness memory was responsible for injustices.

Jurors value eyewitnesses, even though research shows that eyewitness memories are unreliable. In addition, jurors place great value on the expressed confidence level of eyewitnesses.

Elizabeth Loftus is a leading figure in studying **eyewitness testimony**. Her experiments demonstrate that memory is easily distorted with even the simple change of a word during questioning. Loftus' experiments are background knowledge for this section and they are reviewed in introductory texts. Her studies raise the question, should eyewitness testimony be used as evidence?

## Culture and eyewitness testimony

A study on **culture** and eyewitness testimony adds another variable to the dilemma.

Daniel Wright and colleagues (2001) write that **Own-Race Bias** (ORB) affects eyewitness memory. ORB means that people are best at remembering faces from people of their own race. This field experiment increases the **method triangulation** of lab experiment and case-study evidence suggesting that eyewitness memory is unreliable.

Participants were 201 black and white persons at shopping centers in Cape Town, South Africa, and Bristol, England. Males and females between the ages of 10 and 50 were approached by four confederates, one black and one white, at each location. The confederates asked one of four set questions, such as "Excuse me, do you have the time?" Three minutes later a researcher debriefed each participant about the nature of the study and asked if they agreed to participate further. All agreed.

The witnesses completed three tasks for the study. First, they identified photographs in a modified sequential line-up where all of the photographs were shown at once. Second, participants selected a photograph of the suspect in a forced-choice line-up from the entire group. Third, participants rated their confidence level in photograph selections on a Likert scale from 1 to 7.

Photographs of the confederates wearing different clothing from those worn when at the shopping center were mixed in with nine filler photographs in the line-ups.

Results confirmed that ORB affects eyewitness memory. Thirty percent of the witnesses correctly selected the confederate in the sequential line-up, and they were more likely to do this if the witness and the confederate were of the same race. Sixty-three percent of the witnesses selected the confederate in the forced-choice line-up, and again, they were more likely to do so when the confederate was of the same race. There were significant differences between the identifications made between the own-race conditions and different-race conditions. Unfortunately, between 40% and 70% of the identifications were incorrect in both line-ups. In addition, a correlation was found between high confidence levels and selecting someone of the same race.

How can the results of eyewitness memory studies help jurors? It is hard to know. Jurors believe that eyewitness memories are accurate. Jurors might have difficulties processing technical study results. A better tactic might be to simply warn jurors about ORB.

Theories explaining ORB vary. One is a contact theory. People may be more likely to recall faces from their own race because they are experts at examining these faces. We know that when people have more contact with others, ORB lessens. *Perhaps a positive consequence of living in a global society is a lessening of ORB.*

This field experiment tested a more varied sample than lab experiments that typically use college students. In addition, field experiments are more ecologically valid than lab experiments. The authors realize that the study has limitations. It is impossible to control all variables that might influence a field study's outcome. Only one kind of situation was tested, a simple question from a stranger. Ethics prevent researchers from staging situations more similar to those eyewitnesses typically experience. Finally, the study used deception, but each participant was debriefed within three minutes of participation and the conditions of the study were nonthreatening.

## Stress hormones, the brain, and memory

Are there clues from studying the biology of **memory** that explain why eyewitness memory is unreliable? Robert Sapolsky (2004) believes that **stress hormones** can damage memory consolidation.

This information is also useful for section 4.11 about **flashbulb memories**, since crime witnesses often have flashbulb memories of the experience. In addition, knowledge about stress hormones are needed for the abnormal and health psychology options.

It would be unethical to expose participants to the severe stressors that occur during real eyewitness experiences, so information about the brain and eyewitness memory comes from related research.

Sapolsky (2004) explains, "Short-term stressors of mild to moderate severity enhance cognition, while major or prolonged stressors are disruptive" (p. 204).

Two important brain sites related to memory are the **cortex** and the **hippocampus**. Sapolsky uses a computer analogy to explain their functions. The cortex is the hard drive, where memories are stored. The hippocampus is a keyboard, which allows you to input and access memories in the hard drive.

Memories are stored in **neural networks**, meaning patterns of excitation of many neurons, within the cortex and hippocampus. To learn and store a memory, "strengthening" of some neural networks must occur. Here is another application for the concept **neuroplasticity**. The brain changes any time you learn something new. Strengthening of neural networks occur when **neurotransmitters** cross the **synapses** between neurons. **Glutamate** is probably the most excitatory of all the neurotransmitters and is the one used more than others in the cortex and the hippocampus. For most neural communications, it only takes a small amount of excitation for a little bit of neural network strengthening to occur. But glutamate works differently. A little bit is not enough. But when a large amount of glutamate is released, the excitation, or strengthening process really takes off, and learning occurs.

If this is how learning occurs, what happens when stress hormones are added?

Sapolsky says that people are most likely to remember things that have *emotional* significance, such as the flashbulb memories from witnessing a crime. When emotions are involved, so are stress hormones.

During a stressful situation, the sympathetic nervous system activates and pours epinephrine and norepinephrine into one's bloodstream. When the sympathetic nervous system activates it also signals the hippocampus into a more alert state, heightening memory consolidation. In addition, the sympathetic nervous system stimulates memory by increasing the amount of glucose in the bloodstream, which increases the amount of blood going to the brain. So during a mild to moderate stressor, cognition is enhanced. For example, this is why you can easily recall the events from your favorite band's concert.

But what happens to memories after a really shocking event? Why are these memories often unreliable?

Too many **glucocorticoids** damage the neural network strengthening process. The hippocampus has two different receptors for glucocorticoids, a high-affinity receptor and a low-affinity receptor (Sapolsky, 2004). Glucocorticoids are better at attaching to high-affinity receptors and will do this first; these receptors enhance the learning process. So when stress is mild to moderate, these receptors are filled first. But if a large amount of glucocorticoids flood the brain at once, they also find their way to the low-affinity receptors, which decrease learning. In addition, during great stressors, the **amygdala**, part of the emotional brain, sends messages that activate the hippocampus and further contributes to damaged memories. If this is not enough, large amounts of glucocorticoids weaken neural networks and interfere with **neurogenesis**.

Let's connect this information to abnormal psychology. Elaine Walker (2001) writes that the hippocampus can shrink in size after prolonged stress. It becomes a circular reaction, where stress damages the hippocampus, which then causes someone to be more reactive to stress, which then further damages the hippocampus. The hippocampus is not just about consolidating memories, it is also important for emotional stability. Prolonged stressors damage memory consolidation and emotional stability, a process that also increases the risk of mental illnesses.

Of course we cannot control being in the wrong place at the wrong time and do not plan on being at a convenience store when someone threatens others with a weapon. But at least you know what happens to the brain in these situations.

## 4.9 Discuss the Use of Technology in Investigating Cognitive Processes

Both the experiment on the whistling language and the meta-analysis on monolinguals and bilinguals in section 3.9 are part of a larger body of **fMRI** research on **language** as a cognitive process. This purpose of this section is to place the two studies within the larger context of modern language studies using brain-imaging technology and to summarize fMRI research on bilinguals and trilinguals.

Susan Bookheimer (2002) reviewed a group of language and brain imaging studies for the *Annual Review of Neuroscience*. Her findings support the studies suggesting that the right hemisphere plays an important role in language processing.

In addition, Hyeonjeong Jeong and colleagues (2007) found that L1 (native language) and L2 (second language) brain activation depends on how close the syntactic structure of the second language is to one's native language in **trilinguals**. This study is important because it examines brain activity in cross-cultural samples and in people speaking more than two languages.

### How have fMRI studies changed theories about language and the brain?

Bookheimer (2002) supports Jerome Kagan's (2007) position (introduced in section 3.9) that *many historical ideas about language and the brain have been modified*. For 150 years, much of the research driving our understanding of how the brain processes language was based on studies of abnormal brains. Cases of brain damaged patients led scientists to believe in a "large-module conceptualization of functional organization, an approach in which rather widespread territories of cortex is deemed responsible for broad categories of function"

(Bookheimer, 2002, p. 151). **Broca's area** and **Wernicke's area** were thought to be two primary modules in language processing. It was believed, for example, that the deficits of patients with Broca's aphasia were evidence that Broca's area was responsible for a wide variety of language processes. But similar to Kagan's comments that language comprehension involves more than just Wernicke's area, a vast number of neural circuits would be required for Broca's area to simultaneously account for all of the processing attributed to it. The large module view does not make sense.

Over the years, some cases disputed Broca's conclusions. In addition, the cases did not help scientists create a comprehensive theory about how the brain processed language. This is because patient symptoms varied and scientists were not always clear about the exact location of their lesions. But with the introduction of neuroimaging technology, scientists were finally able to see all of the lesion variability in aphasic patients.

The invention of functional neuroimaging, including fMRI, has made it possible for scientists to understand how the brain processes language. *Together these studies challenge the large module approach.* Here is a summary of those challenges.

**1.** *Language processing takes place in smaller clusters of interconnected modules.* Each small module has a unique function. Studies examining semantic processing, syntax, and phonology found separate subsystems of the interior frontal gyrus (IFG) that are responsible for these functions. For example, the anterior IFG (Broadman's area 47) plays a role in aspects of semantic processing. The anterior IFG serves as an executive over a number of other related tasks, such as semantic working memory.

**2.** *The language processing areas of the brain, including Broca's area (part of the IFG), are not limited to language functions.* Instead, these modules serve more general purposes that give rise to both language and non-language functions. For example, Bookheimer (2002) reports a 1999 study by Iacoboni and colleagues showing activation in Broca's area during motor imitation. Imitation is important for developing language, so motor imitation and language are related. It may be that Broca's area is also related to **mirror neurons**. A discussion of mirror neurons is in section 5.16, but what is important to note here is that Broca's area may house a number of abilities. Patricia Kuhl (2000) highlights motor imitation and language in the discussion of language acquisition in section 3.5. It is also known that persons with **autism** have trouble with imitation. Bookheimer reports that the left parietal lobe and pars opercularis of the left IFG are activated during motor imitation.

**3.** *The right hemisphere (RH) makes a substantial contribution to language, particularly in making meaning and situating language in context.* The two localization studies reviewed in section 3.9 also support a larger role for the right hemisphere. Bookheimer organizes the studies on the RH's role in language into four groups. The four groups are linguistic context studies, reasoning and logic studies, cohesion and repair studies, and prosody studies (meaning research on the patterns of spoken language that includes stress and changes in pitch).

    **a. Linguistic context studies.** One example is from Kircher and colleagues (2001). Kircher modified the traditional study format of word or verb generation so that subjects had to use the context of an entire sentence to fill in a blank word, such as "These days the weather is rather _____." Compared to subjects who chose an answer from two pre-selected words, those generating a word showed activity in the right temporal lobe, generally comparable to Wernicke's area. Along with similar research, it appears that the right hemisphere gets involved when the context of a sentence is important. It seems the right hemisphere helps people make sense of things.

    **b. Reasoning and logic studies.** Bookheimer reviewed an example study from Caplan and Dapretto in 2001. They hypothesized that the left hemisphere was active during logic tests but that the right hemisphere joined in to help make sense of the entire context of an activity. Caplan and Dapretto asked study participants to judge if two answers to a question made sense. In the first condition, fMRI recorded brain activity when subjects judged whether the responses were on or off topic from the original question. For example, the question "Do you believe in angels?" had two responses, "Yes, I have my own special angel" (on topic) and "Yeah, I like to go to camp" (off topic). In the second condition, fMRI recorded brain activity when subjects judged whether the two responses to a question were logical. For example, the question "Do you like to have fun?" had two responses, "Yes, because it makes me happy" (logical) and "No, because it makes me happy" (illogical). The left hemisphere was dominant in the logic task, specifically in Broadman's areas 44/45 and 22. The on- or off-topic task activated similar areas in the right hemisphere. Bookheimer concludes that the left and right hemisphere play a role in making sense of a conversation but in unique ways. Again, the right hemisphere is important for understanding context.

c. **Cohesion and repair studies.** Some neuroimaging studies have examined what the brain is doing when a study participant responds to words or phrases that do not go together. The brain responds differently depending on whether the incorrect words or phrases are semantic or syntax irregularities. Bookheimer reported a 2000 study by Meyer and colleagues on repair, meaning that subjects were instructed to fix the inconsistencies in the sentences. Participants in two conditions listened to sentences and decided if they were grammatically correct. In one condition, subjects were also asked to silently fix the incorrect sentences. Brain activation when judging whether the sentences were grammatical occurred bilaterally in anterior, middle, and posterior temporal portions of the superior temporal gyrus. When some of subjects silently repaired the sentences, there was an additional increase in activity in the right middle temporal gyrus and the right frontal lobe. Once again, context demands required more right hemisphere involvement.

d. **Prosody studies.** Bookheimer reports a study from 2000 by Buchanan and colleagues that looked at brain activity in participants while they listened to sets of four rhyming words that differed in the beginning sound. One group, the verbal condition, monitored the words for differences in sound alone. In the other group, the prosody condition, participants monitored the words for one of two emotional states, such as anger. Those in the prosody condition showed greater activation in the right IFG (which occurred primarily in Broca's area 45) and right inferior parietal regions. In contrast, members of the verbal condition showed left hemisphere activity in the anterior IFG and the posterior temporal cortex. Both conditions showed activation in the bilateral temporal cortex when compared to a resting baseline condition. Other prosody studies have similar findings.

## Cultural research on the brain and language processing: Korean trilinguals

Rachel Hull and Jyotsna Vaid (2006) found that the *age* when one learns a second language is an important factor in cortical organization. In addition, Hull and Vaid (2006), Manual Carreiras and colleagues (2005), and Susan Bookheimer (2002) show that the *right hemisphere* plays an important role in language processing.

A correlation study using **fMRI** on Korean **trilinguals** by Hyeonjeong Jeong and colleagues (2007) builds on what we know about how the brain processes language. Jeong and colleagues were the first to ask whether the *similarity* of a second language to one's native language made a difference in cortical organization during sentence processing.

Japanese is similar to Korean, while English is very different from both Korean and Japanese. These were good languages to test the following hypotheses.

1. Brain activity in native Korean speakers while performing sentence-processing tasks in both Korean and Japanese would be similar because of the syntax similarities in the languages.

2. Brain activation in native Korean speakers while performing sentence processing both in Korean and English would be different because of the syntax differences in the languages.

Thirty native Korean speakers, 13 males and 17 females, equally proficient in both English and Japanese, participated in the study. All subjects lived in Japan at the time of the study (average length of 17 months), but did not live outside of Korea before age 10. All participants acquired both L2s primarily in a classroom setting, though currently living in Japan gave them some everyday experience with Japanese. Some of the participants had visited or lived for short periods of time in English-speaking countries.

All participants learned the L2s after adolescence. Research suggests that the early learning of L2 relies on the same brain regions that L1 uses. What happens in the brain when both L2 languages are learned after age six?

Short simple sentences were constructed by the researchers using basic vocabulary from beginner texts. One example of an English sentence is "John met the teacher at school." Participants listened to the sentences through headphones and had two seconds to press one of two buttons to show that they either understood the sentence or did not. Blocks of data were collected. Each block consisted of five trials of the task that were compared to four trials of a baseline condition where participants pressed the buttons after a white noise stimulus. Each block consisted of sentences in each language, counterbalanced to control for order effects. These blocks were repeated eight times while the fMRI recorded brain activity.

Here are the results:

1. The bilateral superior temporal cortex was activated during tasks in all three languages.

2. The pars triangularis of the left IFG was activated during all L2 processing.

3. The right cerebellum, the pars opercularis of the left IFG, and the posteriomedial part of the superior frontal gyrus were activated for only the English task.

4. Greater brain activation was found in the pars opercularis of the left IFG, the right cerebellum, and the right superior temporal cortex during the English task. There was no difference in the activation of these same areas between the Japanese and Korean tasks.

The authors made three conclusions from the results. All three conclusions are explained by syntax similarities and differences in L1 and L2.

1. Brian activity during sentence processing was different between the Japanese and English languages.

2. Brain activity during English sentence processing was different from brain activity during Korean sentence processing.

3. Brain activity during Japanese sentence processing was similar to that of Korean sentence processing.

The authors reasoned, "Linguistic similarities between L1 and L2 are reflected in cortical activation during second language processing" (Jeong et al., 2007, p. 198). Native Korean speakers used more complex processing of English than they did of Japanese.

Are there alternative explanations for these results? Even though participants first learned both L2s in classroom setting, all participants were immersed in Japanese culture and language at the time of the study. Was the L2 *learning situation* a factor that explained the results? The authors felt that it was not. If greater everyday exposure to Japanese accounted for the lesser amount of brain activity during the Japanese task than the English task, then the authors would expect to see a negative correlation between the time spent in Japan and brain activation during the Japanese task. In fact, no correlation was found between the time spent in Japan and brain activation during the Japanese task.

This is a correlation study so there is no evidence that characteristics of L1 and L2 cause the brain activity.

## 4.10 To What Extent Do Cognitive and Biological Factors Interact in Emotion?

### Managing relationships: The importance of emotions

Most of our time is spent thinking about and managing relationships with others. Emotions play a large role in thinking about and managing relationships; emotions are primarily about dealing with other humans (Ekman, 2003).

Cognitive and biological factors interact in emotion to a great extent and **culture** influences the process.

This section highlights research on the basic emotions that make up the human **facial affect program** along with research about **fear** (one of the basic emotions) connecting the brain, cognitions, and emotions. The discussion spans all three levels of analysis.

First, I outline David Matsumoto and Linda Juang's general model of emotions to show you that emotions influence behavior on many levels and I also relate studying emotions to understanding others. Next, I explain how culture influences the interaction between the brain, cognitions, and emotions. Then, I ask, "How did Paul Ekman discover the facial affect program (that the basic emotions were universal)?" I end with Elizabeth Phelps' study about fear that relates the brain, cognitions, and emotions to **social learning theory** and **language**.

### Emotions influence behavior in many ways

Matsumoto and Juang (2008) identified five levels in their general model of emotions. These levels interact to produce the human experience of emotion.

1. Expressions, such as those on the face and in gestures
2. Subjective experiences, such as feelings
3. Biological reactions, such as heart rate
4. Cognitions, such as attributions, memories, and perceptions
5. Motor behavior, such as running away or hitting

Emotions are fundamental to humans when decoding the **intentions** of others. You might take the ability to infer the meanings of other's facial expressions for granted. The typical human automatically reads another's facial expressions. The skill is essential to **social cognition** and is part of **social intelligence** (introduced in section 3.5). Persons with **autism** illustrate what happens when the brain is damaged and this social skill is absent. These cases help show that emotions are biologically based.

Michael Gazzaniga and colleagues (2008) write that autistic persons have trouble labeling emotions from facial expressions. In studies where they are presented with a series of facial expressions, autistics categorize the photographs by something unrelated to the faces, such as type of clothing. Humans must be able to read the emotions of other's faces in order to decode their intentions and participate in human culture. This is another reason why studying autistics is so important; we are learning so much about human emotions from them.

But while emotions have a biological basis, cultural rules about displaying and perceiving the meaning of emotions defines the human experience.

## Why we should take a cultural point of view on emotions

Ekman (2003) writes that all humans have an innate facial affect program that decodes and responds to emotional triggers, mainly from other faces, and particularly from the eyes. Matsumoto and Juang (2008) add that emotions are products of both the facial affect program *and* **cultural display rules**. Here is how it works. An emotional stimulus sends out two messages. One message is sent to the universal facial affect program. This innate program contains all of the basic emotion themes and the resulting facial patterns stored in them. A second message is sent to the part of the brain that houses cultural information (that is socially learned) about which emotions are appropriate to display in which contexts. These display rules tell individuals to, for example, exaggerate, mask, or neutralize an emotion. Display rules are different in **individualist** and **collectivist** cultures. The facial affect program dictates what emotions are displayed unless a cultural display rule tells the person to modify the emotion. *Cultural display rules account for variations in emotions even though we all have a facial affect program.*

## Ekman's cross-cultural research showing that basic emotions are universal

Ekman is famous for discovering that everyone has a set of basic emotions that are distinct and recognizable on the face. The basic emotions are happiness, anger, disgust, surprise, fear, contempt, and sadness. They are universal and make up an innate facial affect program for responding to emotional triggers.

Ekman (2003) was not originally interested in human emotional expressions. His first interest was hand movements. But many of life's important turning points are serendipitous, and Ekman was in the right place at the right time to receive a grant to study emotions.

In the beginning, Ekman did not believe that emotions were universal. Prominent anthropologists at the time, such as Margaret Mead, believed that emotions were socially acquired. Ekman started with this same idea, well aware that Charles Darwin believed the opposite, that emotions were universal. Ekman originally speculated that Darwin was wrong.

Ekman's first study examined five cultures, Chile, Argentina, Brazil, Japan, and the United States. Participants were shown photographs and asked to identify the emotion. Results showed that there was a great deal of consistency, enough for Ekman to start believing that emotions were universally expressed. Ekman realized that he needed more evidence; his initial findings went against the prevailing view.

Next, Ekman studied Japanese display rules. When alone, the Japanese and Americans showed the same emotions. In public, only certain emotions were displayed. It appeared that culture played a role in emotions. Context was the key; universal emotions existed but were only displayed at certain times.

To further validate his beliefs that emotions were universal, Ekman decided to study a group that was socially isolated from other cultures and the media. Ekman needed evidence to challenge the explanation that his previous study participants had simply learned social cues from the media and exposure to other cultures.

Ekman went to Papua New Guinea to study an isolated group called the Fore. Another researcher had already filmed the Fore and Ekman analyzed the film, becoming more convinced that emotions were universal. To make sure that his research controlled for the possibility of getting cues about emotion from the social context, Ekman edited the existing films so the facial expression could be seen but nothing else.

Gathering data in Papua New Guinea in the 1960s was quite a challenge. Conditions were harsh and language barriers required the help of translators. The Fore had no written language, so Ekman could not directly ask subjects what emotion they saw in the film and he could not ask them to select a word from a list. "Instead, I asked them to make up a story about each facial expression, 'Tell me what is happening now, what happened before to make this person show this expression, and what is going to happen next'" (Ekman, 2003, p. 7). Ekman got his data, but it took a long time for subjects to convey their stories. As Ekman worked through translators, it took a long time for the Fore to get their ideas across to him. Participants received incentives to participate, such as cigarettes or soap, so he had many volunteers. Results showed a large amount of similarity in the content of the stories, but Ekman was unclear how to show that the stories corresponded with specific emotions. He suspected that data from the Fore was evidence for his universal emotions theory.

Back in the United States, Ekman learned a new strategy for gathering data from research participants who could not read. He returned to New Guinea in 1968. Ekman read stories to subjects and asked them to select one of three pictures that most accurately described the emotion in the story. To control for experimenter bias and demand characteristics, Ekman showed only one picture at a time. In addition, each picture was coded a certain way so the researcher did not have immediate access to its true label. "The results were clear-cut for happiness, anger, disgust, and sadness. Fear and surprise were not distinguished from each other. . . . . .But fear and surprise were distinguished from anger, disgust and sadness" (Ekman, 2003, p.10). There were no gender differences in the responses. Ekman noted that fear and surprise were always distinguished in literate cultures. He was not sure how to account for this difference.

In a different experiment, Ekman had a translator read a story to nine Fore volunteers. Subjects were asked to make a face that represented what happened in the story. The faces were videotaped. Even Americans correctly identified the videotaped emotions.

Ekman presented his findings in 1969 but many of his colleagues were still unconvinced; they truly believed that behavior was attributed to nurture rather than nature. Behaviorism's influence in the United States was impacting the acceptance of new research about the biological basis of behavior. It took a number of years for psychologists to accept that emotions were universal and what varied by culture was the display. Some psychologists challenged Ekman, claiming that it was impossible to know that emotions were universal because not every culture was studied. Ekman felt this challenge was unjustified. No one would be able to publish any research if every culture had to be tested.

After these early studies, Ekman's research focus switched to the physiology of facial expressions. In 1978 he published the **facial action coding system** that is widely used in emotion research. This coding system "measures each muscular movement in each expression" (Ekman, 2003, p. 14) and has even been used to detect lying.

## Buddhism offers insights to Ekman about emotion, cognition, and the brain

Recently, Ekman met with the Dalai Lama and other social scientists and to discuss Buddhist views on the nature of happiness and destructive emotions and the relationship between these views and psychology. Paul Ekman and colleagues (2005) write that Buddhist views of emotional life reveal a great deal about *the interactions between biology, cognitions, and emotions.*

The languages of Buddhism have no exact word that means happiness. Instead, Buddhists use the term **sukha**, which means an enduring trait, "a flourishing that arises from mental balance and insight into the nature of reality" (Ekman et al., 2005, p. 60). Buddhist meditation focuses on cultivating sukha, which is not analogous to the fleeting Western feeling of happiness that is usually associated with the acquisition of some material or personal goal. It is interesting that in the West, we have made few attempts at teaching people to cultivate enduring states. To put it in Western terms, Buddhists believe that through sustained practice one can change the underlying personality and make the change last.

During sukha, Buddhists see things *as they really are;* thinking is not distorted by notions about *how things should be.* Achieving sukha takes work and time.

It is interesting that the languages of Buddhism, such as Tibetan, lack a word for emotion. Buddhists do not need a word for emotion; in Buddhism, *emotions relate to cognitions that are inseparable from physiology.* In Western psychology, emotion is viewed as distinct, something that should be studied separately from other processes. However, the brain circuits for emotion and cognition are intertwined. The way the brain is set up fits in well with the Buddhist view. "Every region in the brain that has been identified with some aspect of emotion has also been tied up with aspects of cognition" (Ekman et al., 2005, p. 59).

The Buddhist view is consistent with the fact that emotion has no specific **localization** in the brain.

Ekman and colleagues also considered destructive emotions. Practicing sukha helps individuals come to terms with how they experience destructive emotions and how these emotions impact the self and others. Sukha practice assumes that people can learn to judge their own mental states.

## Biological factors: Evolution and important brain activity

Ekman (2003) writes that natural selection shaped innate responses to emotional triggers. Ekman called these innate responses *themes.* These themes are part of a biological blueprint for emotional responses. For example, if someone interferes with what you want to do, it triggers the anger theme. Loss triggers the sadness theme. In human evolutionary history these themes were selected and passed on to children because they helped individuals compete for food and mates.

**Emotion themes** are the result of evolutionary learning. Ekman assumes that part of human genetic hard wiring is the "desire to pursue goals, the capacity to threaten and attack, and the ability to learn from success in removing obstacles" (Ekman, 2003, p. 25). While people can learn variations of the basic emotion themes from their cultures, such as display rules, the basic themes are not acquired from the social environment.

Ekman originally thought that human emotions were the product of the social environment; humans could learn and unlearn emotion. But his research showed that this was incorrect. The basic emotion themes are pancultural; responding to emotion triggers is so important for survival that biology primes the ability. If humans learned emotion from the social context, then why are the facial expressions of children blind from birth the same as those with normal sight? In addition, how could the social environment account for the different facial muscles used in facial expression or the fact that emotions such as anger, fear, and sadness come with different heart rates, blood flow, and skin temperature?

Ekman makes a good argument that emotions evolved. But what do psychologists know about brain activity when emotions are experienced? And how is brain activity during emotions related to cognitions?

## Studying fears, the brain, emotions, and cognition

Michael Gazzaniga and colleagues (2008) write that modern researchers study emotions and cognitions together. The brain activity for emotions and cognitions are *intertwined*. The amygdala, the orbitofrontal cortex, and the insula have been identified as important for emotion.

My example is about the role of the **amygdala** and **fears**. The amygdala is important for some emotions, such as fear, but not all emotions. And it appears that the amygdala does not work alone in all fear learning. The **insula** also gets involved for *socially learned* fears.

A good place to start investigating the role of the amygdala is to find someone with damage to it.

Case studies such as S. M. shed light on the brain activity associated with Ekman's basic emotions. At age 20, S. M. was diagnosed with Urbach–Wiethe disease, which caused her amygdala to deteriorate (Gazzaniga, Ivry, & Mangun, 2008). The damage was bilateral and specific only to the amygdala.

S. M. tested in the normal ranges on general intelligence and cognitive tests. The problem showed up when S. M. tried to identify emotions from faces. While S. M. identified all of the other emotions correctly, she could not identify fear. S. M. knew that some emotion was displayed in these faces, but she could not identify the emotion as fear. In addition, S. M. could not draw a fearful face. Researchers were puzzled because S. M. could describe situations about fear, so she had the ability to think about it.

What did researchers learn from S. M.'s case? One, the amygdala is important for emotion. Second, since S. M.'s deficits were specific to fear, the amygdala was not the only brain part active in emotions.

Actually, three types of research show that the amygdala is important for fears. These are case studies, such as S.M., animal studies on conditioned fears, and human studies on conditioned fears. But most human fears are *socially learned* rather than conditioned. So the next round of research needed to see the brain in action during modeled fear.

Elizabeth Phelps and colleagues (2001) conducted an experiment that clarified the amygdala's role in **modeled fears** in normal participants.

It was already known that the amygdala was active during the learning of conditioned fears. Phelps and colleagues asked if the amygdala was also involved in fears that were not really experienced. They reasoned that the social learning of a potential threat takes place through **language**, creating mental representations of fear that correspond with brain activity.

Phelps used the example of fearing dogs. One way to learn a fear of dogs is through direct experience; a dog bites you. Another way is through the beliefs of others. You might be *told* that a neighborhood dog was mean. "The dog is associated with an imagined and anticipated aversive event, resulting in cognitive representation of the aversive properties of the dog" (p. 437).

Phelps examined amygdala activity using **fMRI** in 12 participants (six male and six female) as they completed an "instructed fear task" (p. 437). Each participant had an electrode strapped to their wrist as well as to their second and fourth fingers. The electrodes attached to the fingers measured skin conductance response (SCR). While no one really received a shock, participants were told they would receive between one and three mild shocks to the wrist at some time during the threat condition.

The study used three conditions. The blue square was the threat condition, the yellow square was the safe condition, and the third was a rest condition where the word "rest" appeared on the screen. Each condition appeared on the screen for 18 seconds. The blue and yellow squares contained digits in the middle that counted down the time. Participants anticipated a shock during the time that the blue square was shown.

Results showed several interesting things. First, there was a significant increase in SCR in the threat condition over SCR in the other conditions. No difference was found in SCR between the safe and rest conditions. The researchers also collected data on the experiences of participants during each of the three conditions at the end of the study. Participants reported that they felt more anxious during the threat condition.

Next, the authors correlated amygdala activity with each condition. The amygdala was more active during the threat condition than in the other conditions.

A difference in the type of amygdala activity was found in this experiment from amygdala activity in conditioning studies. In conditioned fear studies, the right amygdala was active. In contrast, the left amygdala was active during modeled fear. So while the amygdala is active in both types of learning, it is localized according to the type of learning. The authors suggest that the localization difference is seen because of the nature of the learning; modeled fears require the person to interpret the situation. When a threat is learned through language, "the subjects must generate a mental representation of the aversive event because it does not exist in the immediate environment" (p. 440). The reason that modeled fear is represented differently in the brain than conditioned fear is because of the *cognitive nature of the modeled fear.*

In addition to the amygdala, the insular cortex plays a role in modeled fear. Phelps and colleagues conclude that the insula is important because of the cognitive nature of modeled fears. The anticipation of fear may require that information be relayed to the amygdala via the insula.

The conclusions of the study were made from 12 participants. Replication is needed.

## 4.11 Evaluate One Theory of How Emotion May Affect One Cognitive Process

### Flashbulb memories fit in with the theme of humans living together in cultures

I recall when I heard about the September 11th attacks. I was teaching an IB psychology class when another teacher came in the room and said to turn on the television. We were confronted with planes crashing into the World Trade Center. At first I was in shock—it just did not seem real. It took a little while to piece together the news, as the reporters were speculating about it, but then the news took on a terrible reality. Just typing this brings back the sadness and the sound of the total silence of my students (very unusual!).

If you can also recall the September 11th attacks, or recall the assassination of a world leader, or recall hearing the news about the death of a loved one, or if you have survived a natural disaster, or witnessed a crime, you might have flashbulb memories about the event.

**Flashbulb memories** make up a lot of important storytelling that goes on within **cultures** so we must know if they are reliable. Flashbulb (FB) memories give us a chance to *situate* **memory** within the sociocultural context. FB memories are related to **language** with the concept of **narratives**, the special type of story that aids meaning making. Finkenauer and colleagues (1997) believe that "individual memory contents become social through interpersonal communication" (p. 192).

FB memory research spans all three levels of analysis. It is a cognitive process, the brain is active, and culture acts as a mediator.

This material is also relevant for section 4.8 on **eyewitness testimony**. Eyewitnesses often have flashbulb memories.

## What are flashbulb memories?

Catrin Finkenauer and colleagues (1997) write that FB memories are "distinctly vivid, precise, concrete, long-lasting memories of the personal circumstances surrounding people's discovery of shocking events" (p. 191). Robert Sternberg (2006) adds that FB memories are memories "of an event that are so powerful that the person remembers the event as vividly as if it were indelibly (permanently) preserved on a film" (p. 219).

FB memories are different from memories about the actual event. Rather, FB memories bring out very clear personal memories of the *context* in which someone hears the news. This context is called the "reception context" and may be more important than the news of the real event. Time affects the forgetting curve for FB memories less than it does with other memories.

## The first theory about flashbulb memories: The photographic theory

The idea that vivid memories are hard to forget has been around for a long time. The concept of flashbulb memories dates back to 1899 when F. W. Colegrove asked people to recall where they were when Lincoln was shot (Colegrove, 1899).

Roger Brown and James Kulik coined the term "flashbulb memory" in their 1977 study. Brown and Kulik asked 40 white and 40 black Americans to fill out a questionnaire asking for their memories about the death or failed assassinations of nine historical figures, including JFK and Martin Luther King, and the shocking death of a personal acquaintance. In addition, data on consequentiality (level of personal relevance) and rehearsal (such as talking about the event or hearing about it in the media) was collected.

Brown and Kulik hypothesized that black Americans would have greater FB memories for the leaders most associated with civil rights, which was believed to be of higher consequence. The hypothesis was confirmed. Consequentiality scores for personal shock were higher than those of historical figures among both white and black Americans with one exception. Among Black Americans, consequentiality scores for Martin Luther King's assassination were higher than the shocking death of a personal acquaintance. Brown and Kulik concluded that Martin Luther King had great survival significance for black Americans.

Brown and Kulik created the first theory about flashbulb memories, called the **photographic theory of flashbulb memories**, and explained it within a biological and evolutionary context. They thought that FB memories were strong because they elicited a "Now Print!" neurophysiological mechanism. Brown and Kulik wrote that surprise, consequentiality, and rehearsal strategies were important to registering FB memories in the brain. If the news is a shock and is of great consequence to the individual, then it likely compels frequent rehearsal. The event is "on a person's mind" and is the subject of conversations. But Brown and Kulik figured that rehearsals were probably not simple reproductions of the event. Rather they were constructions and a "verbal narrative is likely to be created" (p. 58).

Brown and Kulik reasoned that FB memories must have evolved early in our species. Without mass media, a person only had his or her individual memories. Important events were "printed" neurologically and stored in the mind. Anything apart from the ordinary that is of consequence to survival must be stored and easily accessed. For example, while presidential assassinations were not on the minds of early humans, a predator invading one's territory was important. The event itself needed storing so the individual could keep their expectations of similar events easily accessible. But details of the person's whereabouts along with the level of consequence were also crucial for knowing what similar situations to avoid. "The 'Now Print!' mechanism must have evolved because of the selection value of permanently retaining biologically crucial but unexpected events" (p. 63). Brown and Kulik write that in modern times, culture has taken over the role of recording important events; humans do not need to retain them. However, we still automatically register startling events and seem attracted to them.

Since Brown and Kulik's photographic theory, many studies have supported the existence of FB memories and two newer theories have emerged to explain the creation and maintenance of them. These are Martin Conway's "Comprehensive Model" and Finkenauer's "Emotional-Integrative Model."

According to Olivier Luminet (personal communication, January 2009), *the Emotional-Integrative Model is the most current and supported of the FB memory theories.*

## Finkenauer's Emotional-Integrative Model of flashbulb memories

Finkenauer and colleagues' (1998) **Emotional-Integrative Model of flashbulb memories** distinguishes between the different components of emotions, something missing from the other two theories. Finkenauer writes that the Brown and Kulik model has some support but no study examines all of the required components at one time. Brown and Kulik thought that novelty directly led to subjective emotion but this idea was never tested. Finkenauer also writes that Martin Conway's theory adds a person's prior knowledge to Brown and Kulik's theory but is limited because it assigns emotions a marginal role in the creation and maintenance of FB memories. Conway did not consider the role of novelty.

Finkenauer and colleagues believe that emotions are not simply subjective feelings or states or arousal. They are more complex and involve information processing, response, and regulatory components. Each component is important to creating a FB memory.

What happens when you have an emotion? First, a cognitive appraisal is made of the situation. The person assesses the importance of the event to their survival, well-being, and goals. Second, an individual's personal characteristics influence the cognitive appraisal. These include previous experiences and attitudes. Third, factors such as the novelty of the situation and whether it is consistent with a person's values are assessed. Fourth, if the event is personally relevant, the person "prepares to respond adaptively to this environmental challenge" (p. 12). The person is now in a state of readiness, which involves cognitive (such as narrowing of attention) and physiological changes (perhaps a motor response). Last, the person experiences a subjective emotion.

Experiencing intense subjective emotions compels a person to socially share their views and learn about other's views. Rehearsing the event through narratives and media stories adds to the vividness of the memories. *The more intense the emotion, the more it is socially shared.*

The Emotional-Integrative Model distinguished between the different components of emotions. There are five parts to this theory. The key to the theory is that it contains both *direct* and *indirect pathways* from the actual event to FB memories.

1. An appraisal of novelty leads to surprise, which *directly* affects the FB memory.

2. If one appraises the event as novel and the event also has personal significance, a person experiences an intense subjective emotion. The subjective emotions affect FB memories in two ways. First, the subjective emotions, in addition to surprise, contribute *directly* to the FB memory. Second, the emotions trigger rehearsal, the next step.

3. The intensity of one's emotional state and the FB memory trigger rehearsal of the event. Rehearsal takes place through narrating and listening to media accounts. Rehearsal has an *indirect* but important affect on the FB memory.

4. The entire process is mediated by previously existing person characteristics, such as knowledge of the event, attitudes, and values.

5. The end product is the FB memory of the event.

Finkenauer and colleagues tested the Emotional-Integrative Model against the other two theories after King Baudouin of Belgium unexpectedly died of a heart attack in 1993. The king's death had a great impact on the Belgian people because he was successful at unifying a country that was divided by culture and language. Participants were 394 French-speaking Belgians. Data was collected through a questionnaire seven to eight months after the death. The questionnaire asked about the different factors thought to contribute to FB memories, such as where and what a person was doing when the news arrived, memory of the event, rehearsal of the event, subjective emotions, surprise level, novelty level, importance level, and level of sympathy.

The researchers supported the Emotional-Integrative Model over the others. Brown and Kulik's model was not supported because there was no evidence that importance and subjective emotions directly determined the FB memory. Conway's theory was not supported because the reaction to the event (surprise and subjective emotion) did not directly determine the FB memory.

## A cross-cultural study on flashbulb memories

The Emotional-Integrative Model was tested on a Western European sample, and while it is the most current and supported FB memory theory, cross-cultural studies are starting to expand existing theories about FB memories. Group membership appears to be one variable that affects both the direct and indirect pathways for memories and is the subject of the following study.

Antonietta Curci and Olivier Luminet (2006) ran a quasi-experiment on flashbulb and event memories about the September 11th attacks with participants from five different countries. The results of the study support some aspects of the Emotional-Integrative Model, but adding culture (defined as group membership for this study) raises some questions about the direct and indirect pathways (from the event to the actual FB memory) in the model. Revised theories may spring from cross-cultural research.

The study had three aims. The first was to show that people really had flashbulb memories of the attacks. The second was to show that the strength of both flashbulb (the circumstances when the person hears of the event) and event (the details of the actual event) memories varied cross-culturally. The third was to show how time and a person's culture affected the variables related to creating and maintaining flashbulb memories, such as emotions, surprise, importance, rumination, social sharing, and media coverage.

Curci and Luminet used a *test-retest design,* typical of flashbulb memory research, where participants are tested right after the event and then after a longer period of time. Data for this study was first collected an average of 21 days after the attacks and then again 524 days later.

The sample consisted of 985 participants representing six countries, the United States, Belgium, Italy, the Netherlands, Japan, and Romania. The average age was 30, approximately 70% were females, and 45% were students.

The authors had several hypotheses. U.S. participants were expected to have the greatest flashbulb memory consistency and event memory. Dutch, Italian, and Belgian participants were also expected to have high levels of flashbulb memory consistency and event consistency. The Japanese and Romanian participants were expected to have the lowest levels of flashbulb memories and event consistencies. Curci and Luminet reasoned that participants from Japan had different cultural rules about social sharing that would affect reporting memories. The Romanians had the least access to mass media and the authors wondered how this would affect rehearsal.

Data were collected with questionnaires using Likert scales for 10 different categories, such as flashbulb memory attributes, event memory, rumination, social sharing, novelty, importance to the person, and watching media reports. Here are some examples of question topics: The section on flashbulb memory attributes asked about the time of day of the attacks, where participants were when hearing of the attacks and how they received the knowledge (from family, friends, or media news), and ongoing activities throughout the day. Event memory questions asked about, for example, the number of hijacked planes, the airlines, and the number of persons on the planes. Importance was measured through questions about the significance of the event personally, for their country, and internationally.

Results included the following:

1. As expected, U.S. participants had the highest level of flashbulb memory attributes and were more accurate for event memory. As expected, the Dutch and Italians had the next highest level of flashbulb memory attributes and accuracy of events. Contrary to predictions, Belgian participants had flashbulb memory scores below the mean. The first aim is supported.

2. The findings were contrary to the second aim. As flashbulb memories consist not only of detailed memories but are assumed to be stable over time, it was interesting and contrary to predictions that there was no difference in memory consistency among the cultural groups. The participants reported that the attacks were of varying levels of importance but the flashbulb memories appear stable over time, even for persons living in different cultures.

3. The third aim was supported. American and European participants scored higher on most variables affecting flashbulb memories than Romanian and Japanese participants. The Romanians did not report rehearsing the event over and over through media stories. The Japanese reported the fewest emotional variables. It can be assumed that culture affects social sharing.

To what extent do these results support the Emotional-Integrative Model? The key to the model is the existence of both *direct* and *indirect pathways* between the actual event and the FB and event memories that occur after it.

All participants in the study had consistent FB memories of the September 11th attacks over time. However, the results of this study show that the *direct and indirect pathways appear to work a little differently across culture.* Curci and Luminet found that both direct and indirect pathways were involved in the memories of U.S. and Western European participants, supporting the model for Western samples. But differences occurred in the Romanian and Japanese samples. The indirect pathway had the least effect on the memories of Romanian participants (they had limited access to media). The direct pathways had the least effect on the memories of Japanese participants (remember they reported the fewest emotional variables). Japan is a **collectivist** culture and the public sharing of emotional events is not as accepted.

Curci and Luminet did not divide up the groups according to whether a country was individualist or collectivist. So any interpretations about individualism/collectivism and flashbulb memory are speculative, even if the argument makes sense. One idea for future cross-cultural research is to correlate Curci and Luminet's findings with individualism and collectivism.

Qi Wang and Cagla Aydin (2009) write that we are just beginning to understand how culture affects FB memories. Wang and Aydin's recommendations for future research include but are not limited to the following topics:

1. Information transmission varies by culture and it may impact an individual's reception context for events, which affects what is socially shared.

2. Three mechanisms of FB memories appear to be **etics**; importance, the experience of intense emotion, and post-event social sharing. However, **emics** affects each mechanism. For example, people living in cultures that value a person's individuality and self-expression report more intense emotions, more reflection, and more social sharing about FB memories than people in cultures that do not value individuality and self-expression.

3. FB memories play an important role in defining an individual's self and identity and are a vehicle for placing the self within the larger context of historical events. We must take into account the different ways that people view the self across cultures. Independent and interdependent self-construals affect memory. For example, individuals with an independent self seem to have more access to long-term memories and have more vivid emotions about these memories. The vivid emotional experiences and the individual nature of the memories reinforce a sense of autonomy. So far, there are no published studies that include data about self-construal. Perhaps individuals with an interdependent self-construal will recall more in relation to others present when receiving the news. In addition, might individuals in cultures with clearly defined social hierarchies conform more to the expressed memories of those in an authority position?

## Not everyone agrees that flashbulb memories are reliable

Ulric Neisser and Nicole Harsch (2000) write that "Memories become flashbulbs primarily through the significance that is attached to them *afterwards*" (p. 70). The term "benchmark" is a better description of the memories than the term "flashbulb memory." The problems of eyewitness memory are the same as those of FB memories; these memories are often wrong in the first place or are easily altered over time. Neisser believes that pondering the events, talking about them over and over with others (narrating), and hearing media reports are responsible for the vividness of the memories.

Neisser and Harsch were concerned about how FB memory study results were interpreted by researchers. They conducted a study about memories of the Challenger crash that call into question the reliability of FB memories. Participants filled out a questionnaire about their recollections of the Challenger crash within 24 hours of the crash and then again three years later. Neisser and Harsch found more discrepancies than expected as well as high confidence levels that the memories were correct. Interviews were conducted with some of the participants to clarify the results. Of interest to the researchers was the surprise and disbelief that some participants showed about the discrepancies between their two sets of data. Neisser expected that the interviews would revive correct original memories but this did not happen.

## The brain and flashbulb memories

Patrick Davidson and colleagues (2005) conducted one of the few experiments available about the brain and flashbulb memories. Their study suggests that the **frontal lobes** are important for FB memories.

Using a test-retest and a quasi-experimental design, patients with medial temporal lobe/diencephalic (MTL/D) damage and patients with frontal lobe (FL) damage were compared to healthy controls on their memory for both event (details of the attacks) memories and source—"when, where, and/or from whom they learned information" (p. 916)—memories for the September 11th terrorist attacks.

Davidson and colleagues had 2 hypotheses. First, patients with MTL/D damage would have the most impairment for event memories, more than those with FL damage. Second, MTL/D-damaged patients would have reliable source memories when they also had reliable event memories, but were uncertain if the FL-damaged patients would have source memory impairment.

Forty-five participants made up the three groups, 14 with MTL/D damage, 13 with FL damage, and 18 healthy controls.

Data were collected with a FB memory questionnaire, administered in an interview, with questions about both event and source memories. The first set of data was collected between three and 30 days after the attacks. The second set of data was collected six months later.

Results included the following:

1. Long-term memory impairment was found only in MTL/D-damaged patients. This is consistent with earlier research. Long-term event memories were just as reliable in FL-damaged patients as they were in normal controls.

2. MTL/D-damaged patients, even though they retained fewer long-term event memories, retained slightly more source memories than FL-damaged patients.

3. FL-damaged patients were inconsistent in their ability to recall source information. However, FL damage varied considerably in participants, so possibly the greater the damage, the more likely the person was to recall fewer source memories.

The authors wondered if specific subregions of the FL would give scientists more information about the brain and source FB memories. In addition, there may be certain conditions under which persons with FL and MTL/D damage have source and event memory impairment. Both are good areas for future research.

related to
social
*cluding four* 
chological con
torched rev
I include son
topics. These are
and Traditional
Many of my
material to one

## Outline
## Level of A

Carol Tavris and
ciocultural persp
people and by th
ently" (p. 350,
Four principl
the next and une
(2007) conclud
cial network

1. Susan B. the
   and explain
   the dy

2. H
   ity
   (Fiske

3. The imp
   survival or

4. "From the
   we would b
   help us su
   derstand
   Fisk
   bering
   core mot
   show t
   Fisk
   tural data re
   vated to be
   For exam
   mole comp

# 5 The Sociocultural Level of Analysis

## Introduction to the Sociocultural Level of Analysis

There are two purposes for this introduction. One is to show why culture is a good way to organize the sociocultural level of analysis. I selected Harry Triandis's ideas to help you understand the important role that cultural research played in expanding social psychology.

The other is to show why an integrated approach using the general bidirectional model is critical to interpreting social psychology research. I selected Susan Fiske and Shelley Taylor's ideas to help you understand that social psychology is now integrated with the other levels of analysis. "Mind" is the second level of the general bidirectional model and social cognition goes here. While the IB syllabus uses the phrases "sociocultural cognition" and "social norms" to categorize social psychology concepts, the concepts in both categories illustrate what goes on in the minds of humans as they maneuver through the social world.

First, let's look at why culture is a good organizing principle. The next three sections outline my argument.

### Culture is useful in organizing the material as long as you avoid reductionism

The sociocultural level of analysis unites social learning theory and social psychology with cultural psychology. My approach combines all three areas under the umbrella of culture. It fits right into the general bidirectional model, where culture is on the top.

This approach organizes the large amount of sociocultural material *and* integrates it with the other levels of analysis. Otherwise, it is too easy to get lost in the details of all the material and end up compartmentalizing facts. It makes sense; culture mediates all social practices, so culture is an umbrella over social psychology and social learning theory, as well as all of the biological and cognitive material.

For example, there are classic studies in social psychology, such as Asch's conformity experiments (conformity is addressed in sections 5.17 and 5.18), and in social learning theory, such as the Bobo experiments (section 5.15). However, *modern psychology has evolved toward situating social, cognitive, and biological factors into a cultural context.* Asch and Bandura already demonstrated how conformity and social learning work in the lab; more recent studies show how culture mediates conformity and social learning so the theories apply to everyone.

Just be careful to avoid **sociocultural reductionism** (Tavris & Wade, 2001). Just as I cautioned earlier in the book against saying "My genes made me do it," never say "My culture made me do it." There are no such things as "culture genes" that make culture responsible for behavior (Tavris & Wade, 2001). Humans evolved to live in cultures, so it is more useful to think of behavior as it *unfolds* in cultures.

## Social learning theory and culture

**Social learning theory** is already generally classified under culture. Social learning theory investigates how a culture transmits information to children. Bandura's early writings are full of cultural material. His classic lab experiments, such as the Bobo studies, verify critical social learning concepts. However, the modern approach is that the Bobo studies should fit in with research conducted in the natural setting demonstrating how the concepts work cross-culturally. Social learning theory must be studied in its cultural context to be correct. Section 5.15 contains a detailed account of culture and social learning.

## Cross-cultural studies make social psychology concepts relevant for everyone

Different from the development of social learning theory, social psychology concepts were not originally conceived with culture in mind. However, *cross-cultural studies make social psychology concepts relevant for everyone*. I address these issues throughout my discussions of the social psychology material. Harry Triandis (1999) writes that one important goal of cultural psychology is to clarify the limitations of social psychology; most of the key constructs of social psychology, such as the self, conformity, intelligence, and well-being, are culture bound. Social psychology concepts differ in *meaning* in **individualist** and **collectivist** cultures.

Social psychology is limited in several ways without cross-cultural research.

One limitation is that many social psychology experiments are designed for participants to make judgments around *consistency* and *decontextualized* judgments (Triandis, 1999). Consistency and decontextualized thinking are attributes of individualist cultures. For example, ratings in experiments about the intelligence of others differ by culture. Those in individualist cultures are likely to classify someone as intelligent or unintelligent without reference to context. On the other hand, persons from collectivist cultures are likely to consider specific contexts when classifying others as intelligent or unintelligent, such as "that person is intelligent in the marketplace." The concept of intelligence is culture bound without research on thinking, context, and culture. The original social identity theory (SIT) is another example. SIT was formed specifically around people making decontextualized judgments and was culture bound. Section 5.14 includes cross-cultural research on context and SIT.

Second, experiments gathering data without sensitivity to context may place demand characteristics onto participants (Triandis, 1999).

Third, the entire framework for many social psychology experiments was conceived within the cultural expectations of individualist cultures and the subjective experience of Western researchers (Triandis, 1999). Theories created in the West typically do not take into account that individuals from collectivist cultures consider the context of the larger social group before they behave. For example, when studying **depression**, well-being in the West is primarily viewed as having more positive than negative emotions, while in the East, well-being can represent a social condition. Another example is **attributions**. In the West, the causes of behavior are mainly related to personal attributions and dispositions, while in the East, they are mainly related with duties, roles, and situations.

Now let's look at why an integrated bidirectional approach is necessary for understanding social psychology.

## Culture, context, and bidirectional thinking in social psychology

Susan Fiske & Shelley Taylor (2008) emphasize the importance of using a **bidirectional** approach to studying social psychology; it pulls together cognition, biology, and culture. *Social cognition has neural foundations and is embedded in culture.* In addition, social cognition is about *making meaning and sense of others.* This ties the sociocultural level of analysis to the theme of this book about humans living together in cultures.

First, cognition is at the center of how we make sense of our social world: Humans are social thinkers (Fiske & Taylor, 2008). Social psychology research models evolved through five views of humans. Each view had limitations that prompted new research models. Each new model incorporated the best of the earlier ones and also made advancements. As we start the 21st century, a current research model viewing human social thinkers as **activated actors** is driving research where "social environments rapidly cue perceivers' social concepts" (p. 13). The activated actor approach uses a **dual processing model**, where processing social cues falls along a continuum from **automatic/unconscious** processing to **controlled/conscious** processing. We move between these two modes to meet the **core needs** of belonging, understanding, controlling, self-enhancement, and trusting. These core needs are outlined under section 5.2. Behavior that satisfies **social norms** *can be* the result of controlled conscious processing, but is *probably most often* fairly automatic. The ways we attribute, stereotype, identify with in-groups, comply with requests, and conform are primarily automatic responses. The social psychology research in this chapter supports the "activated actor" approach. Advanced technology allows psychologists to study just how fast we process these cues. We quickly *attend* to people as stimuli (much of which comes from *reading faces,* (something people with **autism** have trouble doing), encode to **memory** factors that are *salient* (features that stand out as the most important or striking), and then automatically behave. Controlled conscious processing also explains behavior. The distinction between automatic and controlled social thinking can be important. For example, most **stereotypes** are the result of automatic thinking and may not be avoidable. In contrast, people may be more responsible for the deliberate prejudice and discrimination that are potential consequences of controlled conscious stereotyping.

Newer social psychology research investigates people as activated actors. In addition to learning classic social psychology studies, *I advise you to learn something current that ties social psychology concepts to neural foundations and the cultural context.*

Second, social cognitions cannot be studied outside of current neuroscience (Fiske & Taylor, 2008). People's cognitions about other people are different from cognitions about objects. People have **intentions** to influence and control their social world, and at the same time, others have intentions to do the same thing. Social cognitions are really mutual cognitions that we hold with others. Neuroscience, specifically with the popularity of **fMRI**, now allows scientists to see patterns in the neural activity that takes place during social cognition. For example, three areas of the brain have emerged as patterns: the medial prefrontal cortex (mPFC), the superior temporal sulcus (STC), and the fusiform gyrus (FFA). The mPFC activates during general social cognition, the STC activates when making judgments, and the FFA activates for faces and objects associated with a person's area of expertise, such as cars for a car mechanic. All of this neural activity is oriented toward social interaction and may be related to reward circuits in the brain, making sure that we are motivated to socially interact with others. In addition, it is hypothesized that the brain during social interaction is the *default resting state,* and other types of behavior, such as interacting with general objects, are a departure from this default resting state. This is more evidence that humans are primed to live in social worlds.

This leads to the cultural aspect of social cognition. Our brain is always doing something during social cognition, which is probably most of the time. "Our brains are predisposed to pick up our cultures as they socialize us" (Fiske & Taylor, 2008, p. 20). Research can establish the neural correlates of social cognition to see just how sensitive the brain is to social cues that come from our cultures. This new research is changing the future direction of psychology. "*New cultural comparisons have been forcing social cognitive researchers to reexamine the entire basis of our field*" (p. 20).

### How I organize the sociocultural level of analysis

I begin Chapter 5 with general principles, research methods, and a discussion of ethics. Because I use culture to organize social psychology and social learning, the learning outcomes related to culture are addressed before the learning outcomes about social psychology and social learning theory. *It is essential that you understand how cross-cultural research is conducted, including how psychologists use the dimensions of culture.* This reason is that the majority of psychological concepts, even those not originally conceived in a cultural context, are either being studied cross-culturally or will be soon.

I include some headings that are necessary for an international perspective on popular topics. These are in-depth discussions of Harry Triandis, Geert Hofstede, Edward T. Hall, and Traditional Chinese Medicine (for the abnormal and health psychology options).

Many of my research examples illustrate cultural research. The other examples link the material to one of the four main topics, which are also embedded in cultural psychology.

## 5.2 Outline Principles That Define the Sociocultural Level of Analysis

Carol Tavris and Carol Wade (2001) write, "The basic assumption of researchers in the sociocultural perspective is that as human beings we are constantly being influenced by other people and by the requirements of society, even when we believe we are acting independently" (p. 359). **Culture** mediates the entire process.

Four principles build on Tavris and Wade's general assumption. Each principle leads to the next and unites all social behavior under the banner of culture. Alan Fiske and Susan Fiske (2007) conclude, "Culture is what organisms acquire by interacting in a community or social network" (p. 283).

1. Susan Fiske (2004) claims, "Social psychology is the scientific attempt to understand and explain how the thoughts, feelings, and behaviors of individuals are influenced by the actual, imagined, or implied presence of other human beings" (p. 4).

2. Human behavior is explained by the social **situation** more than individual personality. Situations play a greater role in human behavior than most people want to believe (Fiske, 2004).

3. The importance of the social situation **evolved** as the most important adaptation for survival over time within cultures (Fiske, 2004).

4. "From the idea that we need other people for our basic survival, it follows that over time we would have developed some **core motives** that interact with the social situation, to help us survive in groups" (Fiske, 2004, p. 14). The five core motives are **belonging, understanding, controlling, enhancing the self**, and **trusting** (Fiske, 2004, Fiske & Fiske, 2007). Fiske & Taylor (2008) use the mnemonic **BUC(k)ET** as a way of remembering the core motives. Any conclusions drawn about the universality, or **etics**, of these core motives should be viewed within the context of cross-cultural research that also show the **emics**, or specific cultural practices related to the motive. Triandis (1999) and Fiske & Taylor (2008) write that self-enhancement is culture bound without cross-cultural data to show how it applies to everyone. In addition, people in all cultures are motivated to belong but the need to belong differs according to culture (Fiske & Fiske, 2007). For example, cultural self-theories explain that persons from collectivist countries place more emphasis on relations with others to promote harmony and belonging. On the

other hand, persons from individualist countries are more independent and create harmony and belonging through autonomy. One example in this book about culture's affects on belonging is in section 5.14 about social identity.

## 5.3 Discuss How and Why Particular Research Methods Are Used at the Sociocultural Level of Analysis, Including Ethical Concerns

### Research methods for the sociocultural level of analysis

The sociocultural level of analysis groups together three areas of research, cultural psychology, social psychology, and social learning theory. Methods used in all three areas overlap to a great extent, *but cultural research has extra complexities.* Social interaction occurs within a cultural context, so a current and future theme for research is to figure out how culture mediates social psychology and social learning.

This section covers the key sociocultural research methods and the extra complexities found in cultural research. Note that social learning theory is studied primarily with lab experiments or questionnaires that are analyzed with correlations.

Currently, a common way to study culture and behavior is through a **dimension of culture** category, particularly the individualism/collectivism dimension. Numerous research examples in this book collect data using a dimension of culture.

Again, the best studies are part of a larger body of research where the results of many studies offer **triangulation** between the levels of analysis.

**1. Experiments**, including lab, quasi-, and field experiments. Experiments are the only method showing cause and effect, so they are very useful. Lab experiments clarify theory and are *supposed to be artificial.* See Bandura's comments about the value of lab experiments in section 5.15. Lab experiments randomly assign participants to conditions and tightly control all variables influencing an independent variable. Matsuda's conformity experiment in section 5.18 and Bandura's Bobo experiments in section 5.15 are lab experiments. Matsuda can claim, within a predicted margin of error, that it was the type of group that caused the conformity. However, random assignment is not always possible or an intention of the researcher. Cross-cultural experiments are frequently **quasi**-experiments. Experiment variables frequently emerge from **ethnographies** in cultural psychology, such as in Michael Cole's research on the Kpelle (section 4.7).

**2. Surveys** and **questionnaires** are frequently used in **correlation** studies. The purpose is not to manipulate variables, but rather to collect information and relate it to a selected variable. For example, James Jones collected data on time orientation through questionnaires and then analyzed the results with correlations (section 5.9). Jones could not ethically manipulate a person's time orientation and he did not want to; rather, he wanted to see the relationship between time orientation and behavior.

**3. Naturalistic observations**. The purpose of observation research is to view participants in natural settings. The observations in cultural psychology are **ethnographies**, observations of cultural group practices. Ethnographic methods are borrowed from anthropology. Ethnographies gather rich detailed knowledge about behavior through observations, **interviews** and small **focus groups** (Triandis, 2007). The typical process involves Western researchers approaching a village with a general idea about universal behavior, an **etic**. Because of language barriers, an **informant**, or local person assisting the researcher, helps the researcher understand local practices. Typical ways of gathering data, such as through questionnaires, were not always useful. Cole's research shows why questionnaires generated in the West are not always appropriate for non-Western participants. Most observations in cultural psychology are **nomothetic** (Hank Davis, personal communication, December 2007). An outside observer, usually an observer-participant rather than a participant observer, conducts nomothetic studies. They are **qualitative** studies and participants represent the larger group of like individuals. Albert Bandura writes that naturalistic observations should compliment lab experiments. Section 5.15 includes observation research on aggression from non-Western cultures that compliment the Bobo experiments.

   **4. Interviews.** Interviews are used both as a primary way to gather data and in ethnographies. However, it cannot be assumed that having interviewers with the same cultural background and language as the participants will produce data consistent with Western expectations about getting individual opinions. Section 5.5 includes an interview study about etics/emics and mental illness that illustrates the problem.

   **5.** A small amount of cultural research is **idiographic**. Idiographic studies are **case studies** of individuals that represent the larger group (Hank Davis, personal communication, December 2007).

   **6.** Cross-cultural research has specific complexities in addition to the typical method considerations. Dov Cohen (2007) divides these complexities into four themes, organized with the acronym **COSI**. *COSI stands for causality, operationalism, sampling, and interpretation.*

   **a. Causality.** Much of the cultural research is correlation, ethnography, or uncontrolled field and quasi-experiments. Even if people want to infer cause, it is unlikely that an underlying dimension, such as **individualism**, *caused* changes in behavior. Instead, differences are correlated, observed, or confounded by variables not controlled outside of lab settings. There are many aspects of individualism and **collectivism**, such as **tightness** and **looseness**, which make cross-cultural research more complex at the individual level. Triandis' account of these complexities is in section 5.7. The dimensions of culture are artificial categories that were invented for studying behavior differences. In addition, so many of the experiments just compare one person to another. As we know that the **situation** has powerful effects on behavior, perhaps studies should collect data about the person plus the situation, and even the person plus the situation plus cultural interactions plus a cultural dimension. These designs are more complex but more realistic. For example, section 5.18 reviews conformity studies that show how someone in a particular situation might conform. Even within cultures that have a tendency toward collectivism, individuals conform according to specific contexts. It is incorrect to assume that people from a collectivist country conform more than people from a individualist country.

   **b. Operationalism.** All operational definitions and methodologies must be the same when comparing cultures or the study will have no meaning (Matsumoto, 2008). One potential problem is **language**. *Concerns over language are taken seriously because language is probably the most salient (significant) variable in cross-cultural research.* For example, even if the word depression exists in many cultures, does it have the same meaning? Language must be equivalent in all instruments used to collect data. **Back translation** is the most effective technique for ensuring equivalence. Second, researchers sometimes define culture as nations. Hofstede's analysis of the IBM survey operationalized cultures as nations. In reality, culture is far more complex than a nation. Third, researchers must consider **emic** and **etic** aspects of cultures. Etic approaches to research assume that categories of universal behaviors (such as individualism) are beneficial to researchers. Etics often guide initial cultural studies.

However, instruments used to collect data should be designed so that researchers *can* collect culture specific (emic) data (Triandis, 1994). Sometimes questionnaires are modified so that emic features are measured. Fourth, researchers should compare their results with studies gathering data through other methods (Cohen, 2007).

c. **Sampling.** Are the samples really comparable? Researchers must control for all variables that might confound the comparisons, such as educational and socioeconomic levels. How do we even adequately define these confounds? For example, socioeconomic status and income level may have little meaning to a Buddhist who does not value possessions. In addition, **random sampling** is rarely used in cross-cultural studies. Generalization of results is limited because of sampling.

d. **Interpretation.** One problem is the **cultural attribution fallacy**, meaning that researchers claim that a difference is explainable because of culture when there is no evidence for the claim (Matsumoto, 2008). For example, if an experiment examines conformity in Japanese and American students, the researcher cannot claim that the differences are because of individualism or collectivism *unless the experiment explicitly collects data on individualism and collectivism.* Even if these data are collected, there are many individual levels of variations of individualism and collectivism. A second problem is **stereotyping**. How do we describe patterns seen in research? To what extent can we really say that all members of a culture are like the study results? A third problem arises when **social desirability response bias** alters self-reports in interviews and surveys. There are two types of biases, self-deceptive enhancement (viewing the self positively) and impression management (Matsumoto, 2008). For example, American students make more self-deceptive enhancements and Koreans are more likely to manage impressions. Interpretations must take the social desirability response into consideration.

## Ethics of sociocultural research

1. Social psychology research often involves deception.

2. Informed consent is desired, but if using deception, informed consent might negatively influence study outcomes. One solution is warning participants that they might be misled. Generally it is expected that participants are informed about all aspects of the study. If this is not possible, participants should be informed about all tasks they must complete for the study. Dispensing with informed consent is complicated.

3. Participants must be debriefed at the end of their participation in the study or as soon as possible after the study.

4. Social learning researchers investigating **self-efficacy** must be careful not to lower someone's self-efficacy in experiments. As one example, social learning experiments on snake phobics use people with pre-existing low self-efficacy and raise everyone's self-efficacy by the end of the study.

Some ethical situations are specific to cultural research (Hank Davis, personal communication, December 2007).

1. Research, writing, and films should be presented in such a way as to be bearable and intelligible to the people under study.

2. Do researchers have the responsibility to give something back, to offer something relevant to native peoples regarding their own society?

3. What is the point of coming and living with people, becoming part of their lives, and then simply leaving them? The researcher's presence automatically impacts the culture.

4. How long does a cultural study last? Until the grant money runs out?

5. Informed consent. Early research did not always get informed consent. Today it is expected, but there are specific issues related to informed consent for cultural research. One is making sure everything is properly translated. Modern researchers still must be concerned about offending members of cultural groups. Many of the informants and research participants in Mead's New Guinea studies are now reading about themselves as university-level students and finding her comments objectionable.

6. In addition to Hank Davis' ideas about informed consent and cultural research, the concept of *risk* is viewed differently across culture (Triandis, 1994). Researchers should discuss their plans with colleagues. If a procedure in a study seems risk-free to one culture but not to another, find another method.

## 5.4 Define the Terms "Culture" and "Cultural Norms"

### A definition of culture

I use David Matsumoto and Linda Juang's (2008) definition of **culture**. Culture is "a unique meaning and information system, shared by a group and transmitted across generations, that allows the group to meet basic needs of survival, pursue happiness and well-being, and derive meaning from life" (p. 12). This definition helps develop the theme of this book; humans evolved to participate in culture and this participation required the evolution of complex cognitive abilities rooted in language.

Next, I discuss some details on how culture is shared and transmitted.

### Linking culture and language

Karl Heider (2003) writes that human culture is learned and shared. Culture is not genetically inherited. For example, language ability is innate, but we learn the specific language we speak. Babies adopted from birth by parents from a different culture do not spontaneously make the sounds of their biological parents. Instead, they make the sounds of the language they hear each day. "Language is the most obviously shared pattern of behavior" (p.3). Language is the cognitive process by which we establish meaning and most human activity takes place at the symbolic level.

In order to share cultural practices, there must be some way of communicating and making meaning with children (Heider, 2003). This communication in humans is done primarily through language in a process of **enculturation**. Enculturation refers to the how children go about learning the practices of a culture.

In order to enter human culture, children must learn language and cultural practices from other humans. As Bruner writes, **narratives** are the primary way that children learn about their culture. Because *enculturation takes place primarily through narratives,* it is unlikely that children can enter human culture without other humans.

### Note to the teacher

You may want to cover the few studies that exist on feral and abused children that point to this conclusion in your class. I know students are fascinated with cases such as Genie and feral children, but we must give these cases some context. Perhaps children can *survive* without other humans if, for example, they are taken care of by dogs, but they do not develop language and understand human culture without other humans. The *Nova* film "The Secret of the Wild Child" includes a segment where Bruce Perry discusses what really happens to these children's language capabilities.

There are well-developed theories and extensive research support for the idea that *children learn through other humans through symbolic language*. Bruner, Vygotsky, Tomasello, and Matsumoto all give good reasons why we should believe this idea. Think about it for a minute. What do you do each day and what do you talk about? You might go to school, a job, play on a team sport, or go on a vacation. Animals do not do any of these unless humans involve them for a human purpose. What do you talk about? Most human talk is not about objects. Human language and thinking is symbolic and largely removed from objects. Animals live only in the world of objects. It is unlikely that you get together with friends and talk about a table or postage stamps. Even so, these objects have symbolic meaning for humans, such as the meaning given to a treasured antique table. Your talk is primarily through narratives, where you *make meaning* about something. You might talk about the difficulty of a test or share some new gossip. Even in the age of technology where it seems there is more useless information, most communication is about making meaning. I doubt you call your friends to announce that you are going to the post office to buy stamps. Instead, your telephone discussions are about making sense of what happens. However, the meaning of what happens varies between cultures and is the subject of cultural research.

Human children have plenty of time to acquire culture. Of all the living species out there, human children are dependent on adults for the longest amount of time (Heider, 2003). While animals come into the world with genetically programmed behaviors, human babies come into the world with a large amount of genetically programmed *potentials* that have to be shaped by culture. Human babies are *unfinished* at birth. As James Kalat (2007) puts it, babies should come into the world with the instructions "some assembly required!"

Human culture is distinct from the communications in animal social groups (Matsumoto & Juang, 2008). Human cultures are complex, are differentiated (can be modified or changed), and institutionalized (Matsumoto, 2008). Matsumoto further says that humans have grammatical language, a theory of others' minds, a need to enhance the self, complex social relationships, mathematics, art, sports, hobbies, schools, space exploration, and organized war. Humans play varying roles, such as parent, brother, coworker, and soccer goalie. **Norms** for each role vary and are communicated to children as they are enculturated. Future generations benefit from our improvements and continue them. Consider all that goes into food production. We may take it for granted, but only humans working together with other humans can mechanize food production, send food to all parts of the world, and sell it in stores. Animals do not have the symbolic thinking and language required to have complex, differentiated, and institutionalized lives. If you celebrate your dog's birthday, it is because you want it; the dog has no conception of a birthday. Dogs do not create doggie designer clothing, decide between buying organic or nonorganic food, or get together to design better housing or educational systems.

One goal for the future is educating students so they respect other cultures (Matsumoto, 2008). Teaching about ethnocentrism and cultural relativism is a key component to respecting others.

## Ethnocentrism and cultural relativism

The concepts of **ethnocentrism** and **cultural relativism** remind us that other cultures make *meaning* in different ways. (Hank Davis, personal communication, December 2007). Both concepts are important for studying design and interpretation, as well as everyday life situations.

If we fail to recognize the role of the processes of enculturation, we increase the risk of becoming ethnocentric (Hank Davis, personal communication, December 2007). Ethnocentric people treat their own culture as if it was the model by which all cultures should be judged. The reason I selected the depression study for the heading of etics/emics (section 5.5) is because it reminds us to be careful about assuming that a word's definition is similar from one culture to another. The study illustrates the problem of assuming that depression means the same thing across cultures.

Cultural relativism is the principle that helps minimize ethnocentrism. Cultural relativism does not mean to accept everything or think that all cultural practices are correct. We do not want to become *extremists* about cultural relativism (Tavris & Wade, 2001). It just means that others *can* be right and judgment must be made without ethnocentrism.

The relativist view of cultural research can sometimes conflict with psychology's history of studying universals. However, more and more psychological research tries to find out how culture mediates common human characteristics.

Ethnocentrism and cultural relativism represent extremes of a continuum; neither are useful positions.

## Social and cultural norms

The concepts **social norm** and **cultural norm** appear frequently in psychology literature. *A norm is expected behavior. Cultural norms are the rules of a cultural group.*

Harry Triandis (1994) uses the term **subjective culture** to describe how people view the man-made aspects of their culture. Everyone creates categories, but what goes into those categories varies tremendously between cultures. Norms arose out of survival needs and pertain to both ecological (natural) factors, such as geographical features, and subjective culture. Norms often serve to control behavior. There are many types of norms, such as *folkways,* where a subgroup has a particular way of doing things, such as how they bring goods to the market, *mores,* an accepted set of behaviors, such as how a wedding should be conducted, *taboos,* or what should be avoided, and *laws,* which are created and enforced by governments. In addition to these, *roles* are a special kind of norm that deals with how people should act in a social situation. For example, there are gender and parental roles.

Children learn about cultural norms from parents, peers, and institutions (Triandis, 2002). "Elements of culture are shared standard operating procedures, unstated assumptions, tools, norms, values, habits about sampling the environment, and the like" (p. 136). Norms come from the *cognitive processing* that depends on how a group samples information from the vast amounts around them. These samplings of information are the psychological process studied by psychologists. How a group samples information shows where the group generally fits on different **dimensions of culture**. For example, people in individualist cultures are more likely to view the self as independent and evaluate the self in terms of personal performance. People from collectivist cultures view the self in terms of relationships with others and evaluate the self in terms of creating harmonious relationships with others. These samplings affect a wide range of behavior. For example, social learning theorists examine how the different views of the self in individualist and collectivist cultures affect depression. These different views are norms about the self that are created when cultural groups sample different aspects of the world. Section 5.15 includes a study on **social learning theory** and depression. Section 5.14 investigates norms and **social identity theory**.

## 5.5 Using One or More Examples, Explain "Emics" and "Etics"

**Etics** and **emics** are abstract concepts that are useful to researchers. *Etics are universal behaviors and emics are culture-specific behaviors.* Researchers often approach a cross-cultural study with an etic description of a concept in mind, such as a Western view of depression. The behaviors defining the category "major depression" are useful to the researcher but may be different from emic descriptions of "depression" within another culture. If paying attention, researchers quickly realize that the original etic description really does not apply and must collect data on the emic description to avoid **ethnocentrism**. Emic descriptions may include the word "depression" but can be used quite differently.

Both Paul Ekman (section 4.10) and Michael Cole (section 4.7) were highly sensitive to distinctions between etic and emic descriptions, and this is one reason why their work is still so valuable.

Let's start with a study that shows why it is important to take emic descriptions of a concept into account, and then we'll look at John Berry's comments on using emics and etics properly in research.

The goal is to use the principles of emics and etics to benefit others.

## An interview study about etics/emics and depression

What are the differences between the **emics** of depression and the Western **etics** used to evaluate and treat depression in ethnic populations living within Western cultures?

Rashda Tabassum and colleagues (2000) conducted an interview study to answer this question. They compared emic definitions of depressive symptoms from Pakistanis living in the United Kingdom with the existing predominant etic descriptions used by Western psychiatrists treating them. The study explored women's mental health needs and clarified inconsistencies about the frequency of mental disorder, attitudes toward mental disorder, and **attributions** contributing to attitudes about mental illness. There was concern that Western etics dominated how data was collected in the past and dictated how Pakistanis were viewed as either mentally healthy or unhealthy.

First- and second-generation Pakistani women were participants. All lived in a poor U.K. urban setting. It was hard to get a sample. The interviews were all conducted in family groups because males typically would not allow females to meet with the researchers alone. Twenty-two males born in Pakistan, 29 first-generation women, and 23 second-generation women participated. Interviews took place in participant's homes in English, Urdu, Punjabi, or a combination of the languages. Only seven families allowed the researchers to record the interviews, creating transcription difficulties. When recording was not possible, researchers took detailed notes and categorized responses immediately after the interview. The interviews contained 21 questions. Topics included the perception of causes for mental disorder, help-seeking behavior, family perception and reaction to mental disorder, and the community status of people with mental disorder. The researchers experienced some difficulties translating the questions because Western symptoms did not always directly translate and the Pakistani culture had some different ways of conceptualizing mental disorder.

Data were reported as percentages.

Results showed an emic description of mental disorder centering on *physical* symptoms. The participants were fairly knowledgeable about Western etic mental health models. However, 63% viewed *aggression as a main symptom* of abnormality. Pakistani culture is **collectivist** and emphasizes politeness in social behavior, so aggressive displays are viewed as abnormal, more important than anxious or depressed symptoms. However, many of the other identified causes of mental disorder were similar to those from Western models, with 63% emphasizing **stress** as a primary factor. Recall that stress is an etic, though there are emic features of how the Pakistani display stress.

Some participants used the terms "anxiety" and "depression," but the words in Urdu had different meanings from Western etic descriptions.

Twenty-five percent of the participants attributed mental disorders to supernatural causes and 35% believed in faith healers.

Most males thought a general practitioner (GP) should be consulted for treatment. Fewer females identified a GP as the first person to consult, but there may be cultural barriers to women getting help from doctors. These difficulties include language barriers, the fact that many doctors are males, and that many Muslim women have difficulty with hospitalization because of the purdah.

One prevalent attitude was that families should cope with mental health problems. Hospitalization was a last resort. Participants were reluctant to discuss intimate family matters with the researchers, even at times saying they did not know someone firsthand with a mental disorder, contradicting previous statements that they did. Pakistanis may fear the **stigma** associated with mental disorder.

Assuming that a researcher of the same ethnic group speaking the same language bridged the barrier between researcher and participant was a mistake. Western research models where individuals respond to interview questions are not always the best way to collect data in collectivist cultures. In addition, the interviewer was known to be a doctor, so social desirability possibly interfered with the responses.

The study successfully identified barriers that women face in getting mental health services. In addition, differences between emic and etic approaches to understanding mental disorder were uncovered.

Implications of the study include physician training and future data collection. Do doctors have enough information about cross-cultural views of abnormality? How can we collect data to accurately identify another culture's views?

## John Berry's comments about using etics and emics properly in research

John Berry (1969) was the first to apply **etics** and **emics** to cultural research in psychology. Berry asked how psychologists could make cross-cultural comparisons without a specifically identified methodology that aided the task.

Etics are pan-cultural groups of continuums and every culture falls onto these continuums in some way (Hank Davis, personal communication, June 2008). Examples of etics are marriage, kinship principles, concepts of intelligence, time orientation and all of the other dimensions of culture, the education of children, and stress.

Examples of emics are specific definitions of marriage and kinship rules, what is valued in educating children, monochronic or polychronic time orientation and how the other dimensions of culture are displayed, and how stress is experienced.

Anthropologists struggled with the dilemma of how to study cultures so they could be understood in their own terms (Berry, 1969). Psychologists shared this dilemma as they became more interested in culture.

Ideally, all cultures should be understood in relation to their own setting.

Berry borrowed the terms emic and etic from anthropologist Kenneth Pike and used them to design a three-step framework for cross-cultural psychology research. Emics and etics were originally used by Pike to distinguish between the sounds particular to a language (emics) and the sounds that could be generalized as universals in language (etics). "By analogy emics apply in only a particular society, while etics are culture-free or universal aspects of our world" (p. 123).

Etics and emics are different ways to gather data about culture. An emic approach studies humans from within their system; the researcher *discovers* cultural practices. On the other hand, an etic approach studies cultures from the outside; researchers collect data that fit into *preexisting categories* assumed to be universal.

Ideally, cultural psychologists should describe both emics specific to a group and etics that make comparisons between cultures possible.

*Historically, psychologists entered cultural systems using emics from their own or some other system or with an imposed etic assumed to be useful. These were not always meaningful to those studied.*

Berry identified three steps to create universal categories that were really useful to make comparisons between cultures.

1. Out of necessity, psychologists may have to start a research study with an *imposed* etic. Psychologists should remain aware that the imposed etic is a poor approximation of what is really needed for the final results, which is to create true emic descriptions of the culture, one that is meaningful to the people in the culture being studied. True emic descriptions of a culture involve continually altering the imposed etic. The researcher moves on to step 2 only if this can be done without completely destroying the original etic categories used for scientific discovery.

2. Researchers create new categories that reflect what is observed in another culture. Berry called these new etics the *derived* etics. The derived etic categories are now useful for making comparisons between two groups.

3. Finally, derived etic categories are applied to new research settings, modified emically again, and then more new etic categories are created. It is only when all groups for comparison have been studied this way that we have real *universals* for comparison.

The goal of this three-step process was to create instruments that were appropriate for measuring behavioral similarities and differences between cultures.

Both Ekman and Cole approached other cultures with one set of imposed etics, realized that they had to modify those etics with emic descriptions, and created new methods that allowed for true comparisons between cultures. Tabassum's research is also valuable for finding future variables that are real comparisons between cultures.

## 5.6 Examine the Role of Two Cultural Dimensions on Behavior: Introduction to the Dimensions of Culture

### Promoting global cooperation with an understanding of others

Did you know that, during experiments, people from the United States trust other people who are identified as belonging to their in-group, even people without obvious connections, more than they trust others from an out-group, even when someone from an out-group is identified as someone with a potential connection? Did you know that in the same experiment, Japanese persons trusted the unconnected in-group member but also trusted an out-group member when the out-group member was identified as having a potential connection? Japanese persons, just like those from the United States, did not trust an unconnected out-group member. (See section 5.13 for definitions of in-group and out-group.)

In experiments, the Japanese conform to the same degree as people from the United States in groups where they have informal ties but conform much more in groups where they have formal ties.

Knowing these things about people's behavior is extremely valuable. *If we want to promote more global cooperation, it is essential that we understand how people are likely to act in the context of different situations.*

By understanding the **dimensions of culture**, we have been able to design studies that show how culture affects individual behavior. *Instead of arming ourselves with guns in the future, might we arm ourselves with good information that helps us understand others?*

The studies introduced above are both detailed in this chapter and are linked to this section, along with any study you ever read about individualism/collectivism or any other dimension of culture. The study about in-group and out-group cooperation is by Masaki Yuki (2005) and is part of section 5.14 about **social identity theory**. The study about conformity is by Yohtaro Takano and Shunya Sogon (2008) and is in section 5.18 about **conformity**.

Many studies in this book examine the dimensions of culture and behavior. You have many behaviors to choose from when answering questions from this heading.

## An introduction to the dimensions of culture

Harry Triandis, Geert Hofstede, and Edward T. Hall are three important contributors to studies of dimensions of culture (Hank Davis, personal communication, June, 2008).

Geert Hofstede and Gert Jan Hofstede (2005) define a dimension of culture as *"an aspect of culture that can be measured relative to other cultures"* (p. 23). The dimensions are research categories that make many psychological concepts applicable cross-culturally. They emerged as psychologists considered how to accurately study behavior cross-culturally, and these applications are always being refined.

The dimensions are **continuums**, such as individualism-collectivism. Cultures fall somewhere on the continuums for each dimension rather than at one extreme or the other. The dimensions categorize behavior on a *social level of analysis* rather than an *individual level of analysis*. They describe the behavior of a *group* and do not always accurately describe individual behavior. Avoid **stereotyping** people by over-identifying them with a dimension of culture. On an individual level, each person has access to both ends of the continuums and displays behavior based on the **situation**.

The dimensions of culture are quite abstract, so *do not oversimplify* them. Here are some basics about the dimensions of cultures:

1. The dimensions of culture are **etics**, or universal behaviors. A dimension of culture must be backed up with research showing that it really is universal.

2. Anything that is an etic can be a dimension of culture. The ones most students recognize were identified in Geert Hofstede's (2001) analysis of a survey conducted at IBM in 1980 (section 5.8). Hofstede originally identified the first four dimensions on this list, *though individualism/collectivism had already been identified and studied.* (Harry Triandis is the expert on individualism/collectivism, see section 5.7).

   a. individualism versus collectivism
   b. masculinity versus femininity
   c. power distance
   d. uncertainty avoidance
   e. long- and short-term orientation—This last dimension was not originally part of Geert Hofstede's IBM survey analysis. It was created after Michael Harris Bond developed the Chinese Value Survey (CVS) to test whether the other four dimensions were valid to the Chinese. He was afraid that questions set by Western researchers would not allow for true responses from non-Western participants. Bond found that, while the first three dimensions were relevant, the fourth was not. Uncertainty avoidance was not correlated to Chinese survey responses. (Keep in mind that we must have research showing that all the identified dimensions apply to everyone for them to be etics. Hofstede did not study everyone. Some of the dimensions are well studied, such as individualism/collectivism, but others still need more research.) Instead, Bond found another dimension that categorized behavior in terms of Confucian dynamism. The positive pole for **Confucian**

**dynamism** reflects an orientation toward the future (with behaviors such as thrift), and the negative pole reflects an orientation toward past and present (with behaviors such as respect for tradition). Hofstede went back and found that other countries also reported values fitting into the Confucian dynamism continuum but that these nations did not recognize Confucian principles. So Hofstede changed the name to long- and short-term orientation, a "label referring to the nature of the values involved, rather than to their origin" (Hofstede & Hofstede, 2005, p. 210). Long- and short-term orientation is addressed in this book under the dimension time orientation.

Descriptions of Hofstede's dimensions are available at www.geerthofstede.com.

3. **Time orientation** (section 5.9) is a dimension of culture that seems to apply to everyone and is related to long and short-term orientation. In *The Silent Language,* Edward T. Hall (1959) coined the terms monochronic (probably correlated with individualism) and polychronic (probably correlated with collectivism) cultures. Time orientation is studied by many others and my example study is from James Jones.

4. It is probable that the **interdependent self/independent self** discussed by Hazel Markus and Shinobu Kitayama is a dimension of culture (Hank Davis, personal communication, June 2008). The concept "self" is an **etic**.

5. A dimension of culture is an *abstraction,* a tendency rather than a real thing. Do not *reify* (make something real that is not) the dimensions, though I know it is tempting.

6. The dimensions of culture are known to exist through correlation studies (statistical relationships between behavior and a dimension). There are no experimental studies verifying their existence. Section 5.8 on Hofstede details the use of **factor analysis**, a method used to identify some dimensions.

7. The dimensions of culture are **ecological level studies**, meaning they are categories used to study populations, such as countries, rather than individuals. Avoid the **ecological fallacy**. We cannot assume that individuals in a population (country in this case) behave the same way as the larger group. While Hofstede's research is *confined* to defining the dimensions of culture in terms of nations, and in addition *only* organizational cultures, other researchers, such as Triandis, show how to use individualism/collectivism to understand an individual's behavior. Triandis makes it clear that *individuals have access to both ends of each continuum* that direct behavior in particular situations and contexts. Albert Bandura agrees with Triandis; it is wrong to categorize people as extremes of individualism and collectivism. However, people in cultural groups have *tendencies* to behave as more one than the other. A behavior should be correlated to both ends of the continuum (Hank Davis, personal communication, June, 2008). For example, a person's score on a locus of control instrument or a self-efficacy scale must first be correlated with individualism and then again with collectivism to see how the individual *uses* the dimension's characteristics. Otherwise, the dimensions are general characteristics of nations.

8. Individualism/collectivism is the most studied dimension of culture. Researchers correlate stereotyping, self-efficacy and depression, aggression, education, and mental disorder with individualism/collectivism. Quasi-experiments compare individualist and collectivist groups on topics such as attributions, compliance, social identity, and conformity. Some lab experiments apply the dimensions to mental processing. This book contains numerous studies about the individualism/collectivism category. The other dimensions are now getting more research attention.

9. Where a nation falls on the dimensions of culture can *change*. Is the world becoming more individualist? There are many implications for behavior if this is true. For example, aggression may increase in traditionally collectivist cultures if people become more individualist. In collectivistic countries, an individual's behavior is constrained by the group far more than it is in individualist cultures.

10. **Cultural neuroscience** is showing neural and genetic differences between persons falling at different ends of the dimension continuums.

## Context for thinking about the dimensions of culture

The dimensions of culture arose out of our attempts to study culture's effects on behavior.

The concept of individualism and collectivism existed for a long time and was discussed in terms of political systems; it was only later that the fields of anthropology and then psychology used them (Triandis, 1995). Margaret Mead was an anthropologist whose gender studies of Tschambuli, Mudugumor, and Arapesh in New Guinea led her to believe that all societies had to manage similar problems (Hofstede and Hofstede, 2005). In 1954, it was formally suggested what these problems actually were. The list included how individuals related to authority, issues with expressing emotions, and how masculinity and femininity were conceptualized. All of these can be viewed as continuums and people within different cultures fall somewhere on these continuums, which we call the "dimensions of culture."

There have been many continuum systems to compare behavior cross-culturally that have been refined over time. The well-known dimensions of Hofstede are refinements of an older continuum.

The dimensions of culture are *assumed* to be correct.

There are four steps (phases) so far in the process of refining the ability to study culture and behavior (Matsumoto & Juang, 2008; Triandis, 2007). The dimensions emerged in phase 2 and have radically changed how we now understand the individual in phase 4.

## Phase 1

Phase 1 researched *individual differences,* such as comparing the scores of individuals from two cultures on an intelligence test (Matsumoto & Juang, 2008). Research questions in these studies simply asked if individuals were different on a variable, such as intelligence scores. Phase 1 research was very limited. Knowing about individual scores in different cultures only shows that there is *a* difference between two subjects in different cultures. We really want to know *why* the differences are there. There is no way to know if a particular aspect of culture explains the differences in phase 1 studies.

## Phase 2

Phase 2 was the initial identification and use of the dimensions of culture. The dimensions came out of trying to answer questions about *why* the differences exist. These studies are *ecological level studies,* meaning that the "country" is what is studied rather than an individual (Matsumoto & Juang, 2008). Individual scores are collected but are averaged into units consisting of one's country. Phase 2 had two advantages over phase 1. First, it gave psychologists a framework for predicting and comparing a wide variety of psychological concepts, leading to knowledge about the general characteristics that were tendencies of one's group. Second, psychologists could correlate how one set of data compared to another, such as Triandis's work on correlating heart disease with individualism/collectivism. Hofstede's 1980 analysis of the IBM survey is another example. The greatest limitation of this group of studies is that they cannot be assumed to explain individual behavior. Hofstede (2001), for example, knew his work was not about individuals and in addition, was confined to explaining the behaviors of organizational cultures.

## Phase 3

Phase 3 studies are **cultural level studies** and build on ecological level studies. Researchers could take the theories identified in ecological level studies and *apply* them. Cultural level studies allow researchers to say that a specific *aspect* of culture explains behavior differences (Matsumoto & Juang, 2008). Triandis was a leader in promoting the use of individualism/collectivism to explain behavior differences. Many of the studies reviewed in this book are cultural level studies, such as the studies about individualism/collectivism and attributions (section 5.12) or compliance (section 5.16).

The greatest limitation of cultural level studies is that they still did not explain individual behavior differences within specific contexts.

## Phase 4

Phase 4 studies bring the dimensions of culture back to *individuals,* but now we can apply the dimensions of culture to the behavior of individuals within specific contexts (Matsumoto & Juang, 2008).

Sometimes, researchers using cultural level studies made mistakes in interpreting the results. For example, if researchers study conformity in a cultural study, they might separate participants into two groups, individualist and collectivist. Perhaps it is found that the collectivist group conforms more than the individualist. However, if the researcher also concludes that participants from the collectivist group conform because of socialization or context without actually gathering data about socialization or context, it is an incorrect interpretation. This is the kind of mistake that led to phase 4 refinements.

Takano's conformity experiment in section 5.18 illustrates phase 4 research. Takano collected data about how conformity works in different contexts, so it is correct to say that context explains the conformity. Yuki's study in section 5.14 on culture, context, and social identity is another example of a phase 4 study. These studies are extremely valuable because now we can predict how an individual might behave in a specific situation. We then avoid **stereotyping** someone as just individualist or collectivist while having knowledge that helps individuals interact in a global community.

Matsumoto and Juang (2008) call phase 4 cross–cultural research *linkage studies.* Cross-cultural linkage studies try to connect culture with a specific concept to be studied, such as individualism/collectivism and the context in which someone identifies with an in-group. The study by Takano on culture and conformity and the study by Yuki on social identity and culture are both linkage studies.

Matsumoto and Juang (2008) further identify two features of linkage studies, unpackaging studies and lab experiments.

In unpackaging studies, the variable for investigation is not an abstract dimension of culture. A **context variable** replaces culture, something that might really explain the differences seen between individuals in the two groups. Takano and Yuki's studies are examples. *The most current kind of context variable used today is an individual level measure of the cultural dimensions.* Michael Harris Bond (2002), who critiques Hofstede, believes we are now ready to really concentrate on individual-level studies. Triandis's work (section 5.7) on horizontal and vertical aspects of individuals in either individualist or collectivist cultures is one example of an unpackaging study where the context of a situation acts as the setting under which a person shows individual aspects of the cultural dimension (Matsumoto & Juang, 2008). Matsumoto also created the IC Interpersonal Assessment Inventory (ICIAI) for use in unpackaging studies where investigators want to see how individuals act on the individualism/collectivism cultural dimension in different situations.

Linkage studies are frequently lab experiments, such as Takano's conformity experiment. In phase 3, the experiments were typically quasi-experiments, where participants were assigned to groups based on culture; there was no random assignment. However, these phase 3 experiments simply confirmed that there were cultural differences in performance. No data were collected showing a clear cause and effect relationship between culture and a specific mental process.

## 5.7 Examine the Contribution of Harry Triandis to Our Understanding of the Individualism/Collectivism Dimension of Culture

Triandis will help you understand why it is incorrect to **stereotype** individuals as strictly individualist or collectivist. While a group has tendencies toward individualism or collectivism, there are many variations of individualism and collectivism that show up if a study is properly designed.

Triandis (1995) discusses applications of individualism and collectivism to abnormal psychology, the expression of emotion, education, social behavior, self-efficacy, communication, prejudice and discrimination, and health behavior, among others.

Individualism and collectivism generally describe everyone, but should we think of individual people as either just individualistic or collectivist? *No one is completely individualist or collectivist*. Rather, think about societies and individual people as combinations of the two poles. In general, people are either **allocentric** or **idiocentric**. Allocentric persons are more likely to emphasize *collectivism* in their behavior and personality, and idiocentric persons are more likely to emphasize *individualism* in their behavior and personality.

Triandis defines the basic characteristics of collectivism.

1. Collectivists are concerned with a group's values and individuals follow group expectations. Correct behavior is determined by group goals.

2. The "self" in collectivist cultures includes the attributes of the larger group. The self is interdependent with others.

3. In-group **norms** establish expected behavior in a collectivist society. Individuals from collectivist societies are socialized to enjoy fulfilling their duty to the group.

Triandis defines the basic characteristics of individualism.

1. Individualists are concerned with one's personal goals, which may be different from the goals of a larger group.

2. The "self" in individualist cultures is based on the independent attributes of a person.

3. Persons living in individualist cultures are not expected to abide by in-group norms. Instead, meeting one's obligations to an in-group is weighed in terms of the rewards or disadvantages it brings to the person.

Many studies validate the concept of individualism/collectivism. Triandis (1995) wrote that Hofstede's individualism/collectivism was similar to what he found when studying traditional Greeks, who were collectivists, and Americans, who were individualists, in 1972.

Triandis believes that there are numerous types of collectivism and individualism. For example, Japanese collectivism is different from other types of collectivism. There is even a **gender** difference in how the Japanese express their collectivism that varies according to rank. It is more acceptable for men to comment to other men than to women on topics such as politics. Another interesting thing is that the Japanese traditionally have a greater difference between their public and private behavior than other groups and individualist societies. For example, private behavior considered immoral by an individualist was not considered immoral in Japan unless knowledge about it became public and tarnished the reputation of the group. Shame is more important to the Japanese and guilt is more important to people in individualist cultures.

Triandis eventually decided that the basic characteristics of both collectivism and individualism could be seen as a mix in everyone. Triandis sums it up well. "*One way of thinking about these constructs is that we are all collectivists but some of us are also individualists*" (p. 37). Children are all very dependent on adults and are essentially collectivists. Some people were encouraged to act more as individuals and even received rewards for individualized behavior. In other places, children were socialized to follow the guidelines of the group more closely, and received rewards for doing their duties. There are a few extreme individualists and collectivists. But most people are some kind of combination, with an emphasis toward one side.

The combination of individualism and collectivism revolves around three main factors.

1. Personal and group goals are closely tied in collectivist groups and are not closely tied in individualist groups.

2. Thinking in collectivist cultures centers on the **norms** and obligations of the group. Thinking in individualist cultures focuses on one's rights and personal needs.

3. Persons living in collectivist societies focus on relationships with each other, even when these relationships are not to the advantage of the individual. Persons living in individualist societies value relationships in terms of their advantages and disadvantages to the individual.

Let's use the factor of "self" as an illustration of how three factors influence behavior. Triandis believes there are really four patterns of self, involving the concepts of similarity/differences and interdependent/dependent.

1. **Horizontal–individualism** (independent/same)
2. **Horizontal–collectivism** (interdependent/same)
3. **Vertical–individualism** (independent/different)
4. **Vertical–collectivism** (interdependent/different)

Horizontal means that people accept the idea that people should behave similarly to some degree. Vertical means that people accept the idea of inequality to some degree.

Here are some examples that Triandis gave about applying the factors of horizontal and vertical.

Sweden has a horizontal–individualist culture. The Swedes are self-reliant and score high on individualism. But at the same time, Swedes want people to be similar and they do not like it when people stand out from the rest.

In another example, Chinese who are vertical–collectivists support reforms and Chinese who are horizontal–collectivists oppose reforms.

The United States is more vertical than the typical individualist society.

Indians are vertical-collectivists. The caste system shows this characteristic.

There could be an unlimited number of specific domains, such as work and school, where people demonstrate their mix of individualism/collectivism. It is hard to study. Perhaps all collectivist cultures are vertical to some extent and individualist cultures are horizontal to some extent. Triandis suggests that the United States might be "horizontal individualist, 40%; vertical individualist, 30%; horizontal collectivist, 20%; and vertical collectivist 10%" (Triandis, 1995, p. 47) and speculates that Germany might have their values at "20, 40, 10, 30 and Japan 20, 5, 25, and 50 respectively" (Triandis, 1995, p. 47).

The concepts individualism and collectivism may be so fundamental that it influences people to prefer particular **political systems** (Triandis, 1995). Surveys asked participants to rank-order 18 values, such as freedom and equality. Participants scoring high on freedom and equality preferred social democratic political systems like Sweden's. Those scoring high on freedom and low on equality preferred the type of free market such as the one seen in the United Stated during the Reagan era.

Triandis examined even more combinations of individualism and collectivism with the concepts **tightness** and **looseness**. The concept of tightness comes from research by Pelto in 1968. Traditional Japanese society is tight and the United States is relatively **loose**. Tightness and looseness refer to the degree to which people agree on which actions to take, the importance of following group **norms**, and who gives or gets criticism.

**Geography** even influences tightness and looseness. Hot climates tend to produce looser cultures and colder climates tend to produce tighter cultures. Both types are probably adaptations to ecological constraints.

Collectivist cultures tend to be tight, but this is not always true. For example, the Thais are considered loose.

**Crime rates** are also affected by tightness and looseness. Crime rates tend to be lower in tight cultures.

## 5.8 Examine the Contribution of Geert Hofstede's Analysis of the IBM Survey to Our Understanding of the Dimensions of Culture

For fun, go to www.geerthofstede.com and compare your country's scores on the dimensions of culture to those from other countries. Keep in mind that these scores represent averages for a country from the individual scores on surveys. See the Web site for definitions of these different types of scores.

The Arab world, using the combined scores of Egypt, Iraq, Kuwait, Lebanon, Libya, Saudi Arabia, and the United Arab Emirates, has a high power distance (PDI) score and uncertainty avoidance (UAI) score.

China also has a high PDI score. In addition, the Chinese have a high long-term orientation (LTO) score and the lowest individualism (IDV) score of all the Asian countries.

The United States and the United Kingdom have somewhat similar profiles. Both have high IDV scores, fairly high masculinity (MAS) scores, and fairly low PDI scores.

Denmark has a high IDV score and a low MAS score. Denmark scores lower than the United States and the United Kingdom on PDI.

Argentina has a middle-range PDI score and a high UAI score.

West Africa, using the combined scores of Ghana, Nigeria, and Sierra Leone, has a high PDI score, a low IDV score, middle range MAS and UAI scores, and is low on LTO.

These scores are a good place to start in understanding others' behavior. If you grow up in one of these countries, you have tendencies to behave according to what you socially learned; it is your norm. You bring your expectations for the norm to your relationships with others. In a global society, it is valuable to know something about others' behavior tendencies.

## How Hofstede identified his dimensions

Hofstede identified his dimensions from analyzing the scores of an existing IBM survey. Since Hofstede is frequently cited in books, it is useful to know something about what he did and how to interpret his findings.

Hofstede's analysis is an example of phase 2 research. It is an ecological-level study that identified some cultural dimensions. In the 1970s, Hofstede had the chance to examine a body of survey data about the values of people in 50 countries. Hofstede says that he gained access to approximately 100,000 questionnaires by accident (Hofstede, no date). All of the survey participants worked for IBM in 50 different countries and were fairly similar except for nationality. Most of the participants were surveyed twice over a four-year period.

**Organizational cultures** were not well studied before Hofstede's IBM survey analysis (Hofstede, no date). The organization is Hofstede's focus. Organizational cultures are a system of values acquired from the job experience and can change easily just by getting a new job. These values are very different from the values we gain from participating in other types of cultures, such as gender or societal cultures, when we internalize these values and they are slow to change, if they ever change.

Hofstede's survey analysis was *really a cross-industry study and not a real cross-cultural study* (Hank Davis, personal communication, June 2008). Hofstede's study *only* applies to behavior of people in organizations that operate in different cultures. In addition, Hofstede warns *that the results of his survey should not be confused with an individual's behavior,* thus avoiding the **ecological fallacy** (Hofstede, no date). Hofstede and colleagues run training programs for international organizations, so their employees can learn to be more successful at relating to people from other organizational cultures.

The IBM surveys were originally analyzed only at the individual level (Hofstede, no date). These results did not make much sense to Hofstede. The correlations started to make sense when Hofstede analyzed them at the *nation* level. Hofstede hypothesized that the data had meaning even outside of the IBM participants. He gave the survey to approximately 400 management-level employees in about 30 countries. As expected, their mean scores correlated with the nation scores from the original IBM survey. "So it seemed that employees of this multinational—a very special kind of people—could serve for identifying differences in national value systems" (Hofstede, no date, p. 4).

Hofstede is well aware of his study's limited applications. However, his study is a famous phase 2 study on culture and behavior that is relevant if properly used.

## The factor analysis method and what it means for identifying dimensions

Hofstede is criticized for how he arrived at his dimensions so it is important to know something about the statistical analysis he used to analyze the IBM surveys.

Hofstede used a statistical technique called **factor analysis** to identify *clusters of values* that distinguished national organizational groups of people. The factor analysis identified four clusters that represented four universal problems that people had to solve. These problems became Hofstede's dimensions of culture.

What is factor analysis? It is a correlation method that identifies a group of factors that answer the question. What do the responses (of the IBM survey in Hofstede's study) have in common? Hugh Coolican (2004) explains that the goal of factor analysis "is to find 'factors' (hidden or 'intervening' variables) that might explain the observed relationships between people's scores on several tests or subtests" (p. 184). Coolican describes the process. After participants fill out a questionnaire, correlations are calculated between all possible pairs of responses in the test and arranged in a matrix. A computer program takes all of the data in the matrix and finds sets of factors that correlate in a meaningful way. *The factors are not real things. They are statistical abstractions.* A refinement process ultimately determines the number of factors that are generated. The researchers may instruct the program to look for a specific number of factors, or the computer may generate what seems appropriate. The researchers continue to look at the data, and in the end, the "most economical or elegant explanation of the data" (p. 185) reveals the right number of factors that explain relationships between items on a questionnaire. In Hofstede's case, this was originally four items. A factor analysis actually takes individual test questions and relates them to a larger concept (in this case, the individual responses of IBM employees were averaged to get a nation's score). For example, a question might be "I consult my family before making decisions." Strongly disagreeing on a Likert scale may be correlated with the factor of individualism. This is how Hofstede got his original four dimensions. Knowing about the method helps you think about the dimensions of culture as statistical in nature rather than real things.

Factor analysis is commonly used. For example, personality and intelligence testing use factor analysis. Coolican says that factor analysis never proves anything for a researcher. The result of factor analysis "provides *supporting evidence* that allows researchers to claim that intelligence or personality *could* be organized in a particular way and that the factor analysis results don't refute this" (p. 187).

Knowing something about the factor analysis method used to come up with the dimensions of culture helps us avoid reifying the categories and thinking that anyone has proven anything in a study. The categories are just useful to researchers.

## See the data for yourself

In addition to reading descriptions of the dimensions, Hofstede provides the correlations for countries in relation to all of his dimensions. It is fascinating to see how countries are different mixes of the dimensions. Never again will the label "Asian" be enough of a distinction. Asian countries vary across the dimensions.

## Hofstede's study has been replicated

The original IBM survey data were replicated in six major studies (Hofstede and Hofstede, 2005). In four of these replications, three of the dimensions were confirmed. The dimension missing in each study is different. Some smaller studies compared two to three countries at a time and confirmed the four dimensions. The strongest correlations were for the individualism dimension.

Next, the original IBM survey findings were correlated with a different variable that was expected to measure something similar. This is called measuring the **validity** of an instrument, or does an instrument measure what the researcher claims it measures? Hofstede and Hofstede report that validity was strong, with examples of correlating power to violence in domestic politics and correlating individualism with national wealth measured as GNP per capita.

Hofstede and Hofstede (2001) write that there are more than 400 correlations of the IBM dimension scores with other measures. They claim that the results obtained in the 1970s were consistent with scores obtained even 30 years later.

However, Brendan McSweeney and Michael Harris Bond criticize Hofstede. I'll address a few of the critiques showing why Hofstede's work should not be blindly accepted and over-generalized.

## Brendan McSweeney attacks Hofstede's research methods and assumptions

McSweeney (2002) believes that the number of questionnaires reported, over 100,000, is misleading. *It just looks like a large sample.* Were there enough participants to draw valid conclusions? The IBM surveys were administered from 1968 to 1969 and 1971 to 1973, and the total number of surveys comes from the combined administrations. In addition, surveys from only 40 countries were used to figure the results rather than those from all the original participating countries. The surveys were given to more than 1000 participants in only six countries, Belgium, France, Great Britain, Germany, Japan, and Sweden. The participant numbers from most of the countries were low. For example, fewer than 200 people were surveyed in 15 of the countries, such as Chile, Iran, Greece, Pakistan, Turkey, and Thailand. Fifty-eight subjects responded to one of the survey administrations in Hong Kong and Singapore. In his defense, Hofstede claimed that that he did not need more than 50 subjects from any country if the participants were all from a homogeneous population. To answer Hofstede, McSweeney asserts that the population was really not homogeneous. Rather, the sample was primarily from marketing and sales employees when Hofstede implied that the results generalized to the entire national culture. McSweeney said that many others, including Triandis, had doubts that the samples were representative of an actual total nation. This is why Hank Davis says that the Hofstede study was really a *cross-industry study* rather than a cross-cultural study.

McSweeney criticizes several of Hofstede's assumptions. As an example, Hofstede assumed that everyone taking the survey shared the same occupational culture, whether they were working in the United States or in Turkey. If the surveys were really comparable, then every laboratory clerk in Germany should share the same "occupational culture" as every laboratory clerk in Chile or Singapore. McSweeney claims that Hofstede's thinking is **reductionist**; it is more likely that the "occupational cultures" in each nation, even with people working for the same company, actually have characteristics reflecting the values of their nations. McSweeney believes that Hofstede could not assume that "national culture" is the same thing as "occupational culture."

Hofstede's answer to McSweeney is available at www.geert-hofstede.com.

## Michael Harris Bond: Reclaim the individual from Hofstede's "national" categories!

Michael Harris Bond (2002) warns that Hofstede's findings should not direct the future of cross-cultural research. Bond believes that cross-cultural psychology must be freed "from the intellectual shackles of Hofstede's achievement" (p. 73).

After reviewing Hofstede's work, it is clear that the IBM survey analysis was never meant to be valid outside of organizational cultures. Hofstede is perhaps the unhappy recipient of the acclaim given to him—that he created a model for studying all cultural variation. It is more likely that psychologists did not look closely at the specifics of Hofstede's research before using his dimensions in research (Bond, 2002).

Bond feels a more productive direction is to identify individual-level concepts that can be correlated with other concepts across cultural groups (phase 4 research). Bond identifies three areas in which these new individual-level concepts should be examined. One example is "extraindividual factors, such as **norms**, roles, and aspects of **language** in generating social cognitions and behavior" (p. 73). This is the kind of thing that Takano did with conformity and Yuki did with social identity. Last, psychologists should come up with new concepts for study that are different from ideas about Western behavior. Recall that Bond refuted Hofstede's idea that the Chinese survey responses were correlated to uncertainty avoidance. Bond does not like that so much of the cross-cultural research from 1980 to 2000 centered on "nation" categories.

## Note to the teacher

I am including this further information so you will know more about the complexities of evaluating Hofstede.

Bond thinks there were some flaws in Hofstede's study. He wonders if Hofstede's results would have been the same if a different decision had been made during the factor analysis. Hofstede had extracted the dimension of individualism/collectivism by subdividing the larger first factor that emerged from his initial "40-nation factor analysis" (p. 74). Originally, there were three factors. The subdivisions of one of the original three gave Hofstede individualism/collectivism and power distance. Bond says that individualism was appropriate, but it is unclear whether some of the nation values making up "collectivism" really were the opposite of individualism. The individualism/collectivism dimension has had a great impact on cross-cultural research since 1980. Perhaps psychologists should have read the report more closely before embracing Hofstede's dimensions. The way that Hofstede defined the dimension placed the U.S. high on individualism and Japan as collectivist. A large amount of research then examined differences on individualism/collectivism comparing subjects from the United States and Japan. In reality, Bond wonders that if the first subdivided factor had been left alone, the United States and Japan would have not been viewed as opposites. Other countries would have been better examples of extremes in individualism/collectivism.

As an example, Takano (2008) argues that the Japanese are not as collectivist as researchers have made it seem. Takano demonstrates that a properly designed study reveals that the Japanese do not strictly conform to certain types of in-groups. Takano's study is reviewed in section 5.18 on factors that affect conformity. Researchers such as Triandis have helped to qualify what is meant by individualism/collectivism *at an individual level*. For example, Bond remarks that instruments to test Markus and Kitayama's independent and interdependent self have shown that at times Japanese individuals are more individualistic than Americans! Bond makes a clear statement that we should never just jump on the bandwagon of something that sounds good.

I conclude by saying that Hofstede's work should be applied as it was originally conceived—a way to describe organizational cultures in a cross-industry study.

## 5.9 Examine the Contribution of Edward T. Hall to Our Understanding of the Time Orientation Dimension of Culture

### Introduction to time orientation, monochronic and polychronic persons

Edward T. Hall's *The Silent Language* (1959) discusses how people's use of time and space convey a large range of social values. **Time orientation** and **proximics**, the social use of space, are etics. My discussion focuses on cultural differences in time use.

Hall is an anthropologist, but his time orientation dimension of culture is relevant to psychology. In fact, much of cultural psychology is borrowed from anthropology; both psychologists and anthropologists are social scientists (Harry Triandis, personal communication with Hank Davis, September 2008).

Hall thought about time orientation as occurring in two opposing categories, **polychronic** and **monochronic** (Hank Davis, personal communication, June 2008). James Jones and William Brown (2005) write that Hall believed time and culture had a reciprocal relationship; time was central to culture but culture also had a great influence on time. Time orientation is important because it "is a cultural value as well as an organizing principle for relationships, **norms**, and expectations" (p. 307).

Monochronic (probably correlated with individualism) includes but is not limited to:

1. People do one thing at a time.

2. People focus on time commitments.

3. The culture is **low-context**. Context refers to the extent to which a culture believes the situation is important in determining behavior. Persons from low-context cultures are more likely to make **dispositional attributions**.

4. People think about deadlines and stick to plans.

5. People follow privacy rules about disturbing others.

6. People "put the job first." Time is a commodity that can be wasted. **Language** reflects time as a commodity, such as "don't waste time."

7. People respect property.

8. People emphasize promptness.

9. People focus on verbal language more than nonverbal language. The literal meaning of words is valued over the context of language use.

Polychronic (probably correlated with collectivism) includes but is not limited to:

1. People do many things at once.

2. People are easily distracted.

3. The culture is **high-context**. Persons in high-context cultures are more likely to make **situational attributions**. The meaning of words is also more dependent on the situation, so nuances such as inflection are more important for understanding than literal meanings.

4. People think in terms of goals and are not as concerned with deadlines. **Language** reflects this, such as "it will get done."

5. People put relationships first.

6. There is more concern toward others who are closely related rather than respecting an individual's privacy.

7. People readily borrow and lend.

8. Promptness is based on relationship factors. For example, polychronic persons may be on time for a respected grandmother but not for someone outside of the family.

9. People pay attention to nonverbal language.

## Time orientation effects on academic achievement, stress management, and mental health

James Jones was leaving Trinidad after a year of researching time orientation. A local journalist threw him a party the night before his morning flight back to the United States. As Jones still had some packing to do, he asked someone at the party for the time (Jones had stopped wearing a watch). It was 1:00. Jones automatically responded that it was time to leave. His announcement was not well received. Why did he want to leave when he was having fun? Jones decided to stay; he knew his host did not value his explanations for packing ahead of time and arriving at the airport on schedule. So Jones stayed at the party and even made the flight on time.

Jones and Brown (2005) used the concepts **temponomic** (similar to monochronic) and **temponostic** (similar to polychronic) to design self-report questionnaires assessing time values and its affects on behavior. They say that one style is not more valuable than the other; a mix is preferable and more adaptable in a global society. Temponomic cultures value time and treat it as an asset. In contrast, temponostic (present oriented) cultures assign no natural value to time. Life in the present is valued and time follows the flow of daily life, a consequence of behavior rather than a determinant.

Jones and Brown theorize that present-oriented cultures evolved out of necessity. Persons coping with oppressive social conditions found it adaptive to value the present over the future. Persons from temponomic cultures are more future oriented because they see that what happens in the present directly determines the future. In contrast, those coping with difficult social conditions cannot reliably count on present behavior to determine the future; the future is unpredictable.

A culture's time orientation affects *individual* behavior, reflecting family relationships and children's socialization as well as strategies for managing health, **stress**, and well-being.

## Note to the teacher

Time orientation might be a good dimension of culture to select if you are also going to teach either the abnormal or health options.

Jones and Brown agree with Hall that persons have access to both ends of the continuum but that one or the other becomes a dominant *pattern* for a culture. One's **language** both reflects and supports a person's time orientation behavior. In many African cultures, the language does not recognize a strict difference between the past (zamani) and the present (sasa). In addition, the "future" is an abstract concept with less importance in an individual's life. The zamani-sasa is a cyclical continuum, where ancestors are an active part of the present. The future depends on one's ancestors and may be part of an individual's awareness for only fleeting moments.

Jones and Brown report the findings of a correlation study by Jones and colleagues from 2004 about past, present, and future time orientation and **academic achievement**. A Temporal Orientation Scale (TOS), a 15-question self-report questionnaire, assessed a person's past, present, and future orientation and its effects on achievement.

A person scoring high on past orientation mulls over the past and wants to relive it. Of interest to students studying abnormal psychology, past orientation is positively correlated with neuroticism, **depression**, and rumination.

A person scoring high on present orientation focuses on the present. Enjoyment is an important behavioral motivation. Present orientation is positively correlated with optimism and impulsiveness and negatively correlated with concern about future consequences.

A person scoring high on future orientation is self-disciplined and plans for the future. Future orientation is positively correlated with concern for future consequences and negatively correlated with impulsiveness.

Earlier research on education and time orientation had established that high academic achievement was correlated with setting academic goals, internalizing the goals, ad having high **self-efficacy** to meet the goals.

In the 2004 study, Jones and colleagues hypothesized that there would be a correlation between future orientation in African American students and academic achievement, but it would be mediated by perceptions about the future value of an education and perceptions about social inequality. The hypothesis was confirmed. African American students scoring high on future orientation had the highest grades and these students also valued the education and had higher personal efficacy to achieve future goals. In contrast, African American students with lower grades also had lower scores on future orientation and perceptions that school systems were unfair.

Jones and Brown (2005) also cite a 2003 correlation study by Jones about time orientation in Trinidad, ATTT, or Any Time is Trinidad Time. Jones says that persons of African origin have a worldview characterized by five interrelating qualities, time, rhythm, improvisation, orality, and spirituality (**TRIOS**). Present-time orientation coordinates these five TRIOS characteristics; "what matters is the life being lived, not the life being planned" (Jones & Brown, 2005, p. 315). *Context* is important to understanding TRIOSity. Present-oriented persons have fewer psychological contextual constraints to manage. Persons high on past or future orientations are very constrained psychologically by past or future events. In contrast, presented-oriented persons attach meaning to present-oriented goals, where the present has everything a person needs.

Cultures high on TRIOSity are high-context language users. The meaning of words depends on knowledge of cultural practices. For example, the Trinidad word "mamaguy" allows words to mean their opposite. If someone says, "Your hair looks great," it means the opposite if the intent is to mamaguy another. Jones says that understanding is not simply a cognitive process in Trinidad; it is also an *emotional* process. The actual semantic context of words is not what gives language meaning. Someone familiar with the cultural meaning behind mamaguying knows to view the context, including inflections and important nonverbal cues. A cultural outsider is stripped of their power to harm others with a little mamaguying. Persons using high-context languages regain personal power through this cultural practice.

Jones developed the TRIOS Scale to show that TRIOSity existed more in African Americans and Africans than in white Americans, Asians, and Latinos. The sample consisted of 1415 participants. Females made up two-thirds of the sample. Approximately 40% were white, 21% were black, 19% were Latino, and 11% were Asian, with an average age of 20 to 21.

As predicted, African Americans scored the highest total and individual component TRIOS scores.

Jones and Brown report other findings that support TRIOS. For example, was TRIOS a factor in the experience of stress and well-being? College students from Ghana attending a largely white U.S. university and a largely black U.S. university filled out the TRIOS Scale, two stress scales, the CES-D Depression Scale, and the Positive and Negative Affect Scale (PANAS).

African American and African students both scored higher on TRIOS than white U.S. students. High TRIOS scores were negatively correlated with stress and a **resilience** factor promoting well-being.

All of the studies in this section are correlation and do not show causes and effects.

## 5.10 Explain and Evaluate Traditional Chinese Medicine (TCM): Its Relevance to Abnormal Psychology and Health Psychology

It is hard to think about what we do each day as culture. But culture is not just what someone else does. The **schemas** learned from culture make it seem that a specific way of doing something is the right way or the only way. It is **ethnocentric** to think of one's culture as the best or only way to do things.

Internationalism is integral to the IB program. But do you really have an international perspective on psychology? Just studying cross-cultural research is not enough. Most students taking the IB psychology exam live in the West, and Western cultural schemas often automatically dictate beliefs about abnormal psychology and health psychology. I challenge you to get outside of your schemas and consider other possibilities.

**Traditional Chinese Medicine** (TCM) is an essential ingredient for an international perspective on abnormal psychology and health psychology.

### What is Traditional Chinese Medicine?

TCM does not make clear distinctions between physical and mental health (Kaptchuk, 1983). Chinese medicine emphasizes aspects of the human body that are unimportant to Western doctors. On the other hand, Western doctors place emphasis on aspects of the human body that are unimportant to Chinese doctors. The logic of Western and Chinese medicine differ fundamentally.

Western medicine focuses on identifying symptoms, finding the specific cause of these symptoms, and then eliminating the cause, if possible, or at least relieving the symptoms. Western medicine is analytical and tends to compartmentalize aspects of a person into narrow areas, such as treating blood pressure separately from depression.

Chinese medicine is different. Chinese doctors consider the entire person, both physically and psychologically. Chinese doctors ask questions about things that seem unrelated to a person's complaint, such as diet and exercise. In addition, a Chinese doctor examines the tongue and takes the pulses (yes, plural). Chinese doctors look for patterns of disharmony in the entire system of a person that show general imbalances (Kaptchuk, 1983). *Finding relationships is far more important than determining cause and effect in TCM.* The pattern of disharmony might even be maintained by one fundamental problem that seems unrelated to the symptom. For example, a food allergy, such as to wheat, might play a fundamental role in maintaining a number of interrelated symptoms, including depressed mood.

The goal of TCM is to treat the whole person, not just the disease (Hammer, 2005). In addition to treating the whole person, TCM's focus is on prevention. Although Western medical doctors talk more now about prevention, Hammer sees clear differences in how TCM and Western medicine view it. Prevention in Western medicine means taking objective tests that show problems only after disease sets in far enough for there to be clear damage. In contrast, TCM views prevention as a lifelong integration of a healthy lifestyle and correct "energy" flows that keep a person in balance. TCM relies on the artistry of a doctor's observation skills to detect small imbalances that occur before a serious problem starts.

Chinese medicine views a person's physiological system as a series of **meridians** (meridians are bioelectrical impulses—an electrical system is the closest thing I can think of in Western terms to describe meridians). "Meridians are the channels or pathways that carry Qi and Blood through the body" (Kaptchuk, 1983, p. 77). **Qi** (chi) means "energy," the life force (Hammer, 2005). It is believed that energy passes through twelve meridians that keep one's physical system in balance (Kaptchuk, 1983). Blood that flows through the meridians is not real blood but "an invisible network that links together all of the fundamental substances and organs" (Kaptchuk, 1983, p. 77). *Meridians connect this interior flow of Qi and Blood with the outer body. This is why acupuncture works.* **Acupuncture, tai chi,** and **herbal medicines** attempt to unblock stagnated Qi and Blood flow and restore balance. Acupuncture points on the exterior body are places along meridians, where needles are inserted to stimulate Qi and Blood flow within the interior system and unblock stagnations. Tai chi practice cultivates Qi within the body. Tai chi practice does this by facilitating a calm strength in the body through the coordination of hands, feet, head, and breathing. Tai chi improves circulation, balance, and flexibility. It relaxes and strengthens the nervous system and relieves many medical problems, such as hypertension, allergies, arthritis, diabetes, **depression, aggressive feelings,** and **anxiety.** An experienced tai chi practitioner can even channel Qi to weak areas of the body to heal the organs that may be contributing to mental or physical distress.

The goal of Chinese medicine is to create harmony and reestablish balance within the meridians. *Western medicine has no concept that is similar to Qi* (Hammer, 2005).

Unblocking stagnated Qi and Blood flow has its roots in the concepts of **yin** and **yang.** Yin and yang represent *balance* (something Westerners often have trouble achieving), and "assumes that a part can be understood only in its relation to the whole" (Kaptchuk, 1983, p. 7).

The Chinese believe that life occurs in circular patterns, such as night and day, good fortune and bad fortune, rain and sunshine. Both occur naturally and in relation to the other in inevitable harmonious patterns. Westerners frequently get upset over setbacks and call them bad luck or blame someone. In contrast, the principles of yin and yang show that both the dark and the light are necessary for a balanced life. The dark turns to light and then goes through the cycle again, but the light always emerges. It is a natural process. The physical world and a person's physiology behave exactly the same way.

Here are two examples in Western terms of how yin and yang work together. Every convenience comes with an inconvenience. The Internet makes some things more convenient, such as comparing airline ticket prices. But the Internet also comes with inconveniences, such as the stress of constant large amounts of information available to a person. The ocean is beautiful; people build waterfront homes to enjoy the view. But the ocean can quickly become deadly during storms.

Chinese doctors do not work in a linear fashion to establish a specific cause to a specific symptom (Kaptchuk, 1983). Though it may be tempting to place a Western notion of cause and effect onto Chinese medical thinking, *TCM really thinks of "causes" as "relationships."* When Chinese doctors are asked why someone is sick, they think of illness as occurring in three domains: environment, such as wind or dampness; emotions; and lifestyle, such as what you eat and how you exercise. The three domains melt together, with each possibly dominant at different times and inseparable. Because of this view, treatments for physical and mental health problems tend to take place in all three domains. TCM doctors in the United States say that many people who come to them want fast cures and have trouble committing to lifestyle changes. However, lifestyle is something we can control.

Many students do not realize that acupuncture is studied experimentally. Modern TCM is evidence based, meaning that TCM has experimental evidence (typically without placebos) to complement case studies and correlation studies. TCM is very *individualized,* which makes it harder to test using Western demands for the "gold standard" of placebo-controlled, randomized experiments (the gold standard is discussed in section 7.13).

Modern TCM doctors use a combination of the best medical practices from a wide variety of sources to treat patients.

TCM fits in well with a level-of-analysis approach. Though the language is a little different from Western medicine, it is a biological theory from a different culture. In addition, the mind-body relationship is central to TCM.

Visit www.bluepoppy.com for research about Chinese medicine and many mental and physical health conditions, including mood disorders, anxiety disorders, eating disorders, obesity, and a variety of diseases.

## Early experimental research on TCM and depression

**Depression** is thought of as **liver Qi stagnation** and is related to the liver organ (Schnyer & Flaws, 1998). The liver regulates emotions, among other things. "If the liver is not able to maintain the free and smooth flow of Qi throughout the body, multiple physical and mental symptoms can develop" (p. 18). Emotional upsets, such as pent-up anger and frustration, easily damage the liver. Liver Qi stagnation contributes to medical conditions such as depression, sleep disturbance, and digestive problems. Sound food choices and exercise habits are important for healthy liver functioning. For example, foods with lots of heat, such as fried or greasy foods, as well as a lack of exercise, can transform into a "depressive heat" and contribute to liver Qi stagnation.

One treatment for depression is **tai chi**. Tai chi is beneficial because it is designed to promote energy flow in the body. Exercise has been found to relieve depressive symptoms by Western scientists. Tai chi is particularly useful because a person cultivates internal energy that circulates in the body with practice. Tai chi is different from running or walking that cultivates external energy.

Another treatment for liver Qi stagnation is **acupuncture**. Experiments validate acupuncture as an effective treatment. Acupuncture stimulates **serotonin**, **endorphins**, and **hormones** (Kemmer, 2007). **Functional MRI** scans show a decreased activity in areas of the hippocampus and hypothalamus related to feeling pain after a needle is inserted. Acupuncture needles are hair thin and patients typically do not feel them. Acupuncture affects many bodily functions, so the concept of **neuroplasticity** is important for understanding its effects.

Rosa Schnyer and Bob Flaws (1998) describe an early experiment on acupuncture and depression that was funded by the U.S. National Institute of Health in 1993. There were two aims of the experiment. One was to see if individualized acupuncture programs could be studied using Western experimental designs. Another was to see if acupuncture was effective in lessening depressive symptoms.

Participants in the study were 38 women between the ages of 18 and 45. The women all met the DSM-IV criteria for major depression. Participants with complicating factors such as suicidal thinking, drug abuse, or hormonal disorders were excluded. Experimental samples must meet a rigid definition of mental disorder, otherwise, the people in the sample are hard to compare and individual differences confound (interfere with) the study. It is hard to generalize the results of experiments using restricted samples to all persons with a disorder; study samples are usually not typical of the cases seen by clinicians. *This same problem with samples occurs in all treatment efficacy studies, not just the studies on acupuncture,* so all of the efficacy studies testing any kind of treatment in section 7.13 are designed with tightly controlled samples. However, experiments are supposed to be artificial so that conditions can be compared. Practitioners know this and read efficacy studies to see how successful treatments are in experimental conditions; this is the only way they know what to offer patients.

Participants were randomly assigned to one of three groups. One group received acupuncture needles at points related to depression symptoms for eight weeks. The second group received acupuncture, but for the first eight weeks, only to points related to their Qi imbalances and not to points specific for treating depression. Group two then received eight weeks of acupuncture for points specific to depression. The third group was put on a waiting list for treatment for eight weeks and then received eight weeks of specific depression-point acupuncture. All women eventually received the acupuncture. Participants were assessed through clinical interviews with the Hamilton Depression Rating Scale, a commonly used instrument to diagnose depression, throughout the experiment. In addition, subjects filled out self-report questionnaires about their symptoms.

Results of this experiment compared well to the results of conventional Western treatments of drugs or talking therapy. Sixty-four percent of the women receiving specific depression acupuncture points achieved full remission and 18% achieved partial remission. The Hamilton Depression Rating Scale showed that 70% of all the women achieved remission. One interesting result is that the drop-out rate for this study was 13%, lower than drop-out rates of many conventional studies where drugs are compared to talking therapy and/or placebos.

This experiment was the first attempt to examine acupuncture in an experiment. The sample was small, and subjects did not all receive the same treatment, something different from the way that Western mental-health treatments are studied (where everyone gets the same treatment, called manualized treatment). Does giving individualized treatment invalidate study results? As you learn more about efficacy testing in section 7.13, you will have to make a decision, but individualized treatments are not viewed as a weakness by TCM practitioners. Some newer research, such as the next study reviewed, used the same acupuncture points for all participants and is more similar to the manualized testing of Western treatments. However, in real practice, while there are some acupuncture points important for treating any specific disorder, the patient may also get other acupuncture needles inserted in points related to their specific needs.

## Newer experimental research comparing acupuncture and Prozac in treating depression

Some newer experimental research compares the effectiveness of acupuncture and Western psychiatric drugs in treating depression.

One example is an experiment by Qi Gui-jun and Sang Peng from 2005 (Wolfe, 2005). The original paper is in Chinese so I am citing a summary of it. The original article is titled "Clinical observations on the acupuncture treatment of 60 cases of depression."

All participants were tested for depression based on the Hamilton Depression Rating Scale and the CCMD-2. The CCMD is the Chinese Classification of Mental Disorders. It is similar to the DSM-IV-R and the ICD-10. While this study used the second edition, the CCMD is now in its third edition, even more similar to the DSM-IV-R and the ICD-10.

None of the participants had previously taken antidepressants. Participants were randomly allocated into two groups of 30 each. Groups received the same acupuncture points or Prozac.

The Hamilton Depression Rating Scale was re-administered after 30 days. Nine of the patients receiving acupuncture and eight taking Prozac were cured, defined as an 80% improvement on the Hamilton scale. Thirteen of the patients receiving acupuncture and 14 of those taking Prozac showed marked improvement, defined as 50%-79% reduction in symptoms. Five of the patients receiving acupuncture and four receiving Prozac showed improvement, defined as 25%-49% reduction of symptoms. Last, three of the patients receiving acupuncture and four taking Prozac showed no improvement.

The results show that both treatments are effective depression treatments. The authors noted that Prozac had to be taken over a period of time, had side effects, and the effects were not always reliable over time. The authors also note that acupuncture can be used in addition to Prozac if medication is desired, and it should reduce the amount of the drug needed and lessen the drug's side effects.

This experiment also did not use a placebo control.

TCM practitioners do not favor placebo controls (Patrick Purdue, Doctor of Oriental Medicine, personal communication, September 2008). A double-blind placebo experiment requires that both the patient and the doctor be blinded. In TCM, the doctor cannot be blinded, only the patient. TCM practitioners do not agree with a "one-size-fits-all" philosophy that is used in Western medicine. Rather, "each patient is viewed as being unique in their symptom presentation." Dr. Purdue uses Lupus as an example. Western medicine experiments investigating Lupus treatments use a single medicine, which is easily tested in double-blind, placebo-controlled experiments. In contrast, a TCM doctor must know each individual's experience with Lupus and their unique symptoms. This way, the doctor can create a customized multiple herb treatment. The TCM doctor may also decide to give the patient acupuncture in addition to the herbal formula, which requires that acupuncture needles be inserted into points specific to an individual's symptoms. Lab blood tests are used to measure the effectiveness of the treatment rather than an experiment. For Lupus, lab blood tests measure markers such as ANA (Anti-nuclear Antibodies, a measurement of autoimmune response). In China, about 80,000 lab blood tests are done each year to test TCM treatment effectiveness. These blood tests are accepted as valid to those practicing TCM.

## Note to the teacher

My classes study tai chi for the health and abnormal psychology options. The health option includes evaluating strategies for coping with stress. Tai chi reduces stress, increases immune responses, and is a treatment for mental and physical illnesses. I recommend the film *Tai Chi 24 Forms* by Dr. Paul Lam, available from *T'ai Chi Magazine*, 800-888-9119.

## 5.11 Describe the Role of Situational and Dispositional Factors in Explaining Behavior

### Definitions and context for situational/ dispositional factors

In 2004, U.S. military personnel committed numerous abuses against prisoners held at the Abu Ghraib prison in Iraq. I highly recommend Philip Zimbardo's *The Lucifer Effect* (2007) for the full story. It was unsettling to see photographs of Americans enjoying the abuse of prisoners. For example, a hooded prisoner with fake electric wires attached to his outstretched arms was led to believe that he would be electrocuted if he fell from a perched position on a box. How long did this man stand in this position fearing for his life? And what was going through the minds of the soldiers as they took trophy pictures to document the abuse? Zimbardo explains how the circumstances at Abu Ghraib remind him of the Stanford Prison Experiment, detailed in this section, and how easy it is for generally decent people to commit atrocities.

Even though people claim that they would never do anything harmful to another person, the research shows that they will in certain situations. In fact, our **belonging** needs, a core principle for the sociocultural level of analysis, explains why. Zimbardo (2007) wrote that the need to belong quickly turned into **conformity** with newly established **norms** defining **in-groups** and **out-groups** in the Stanford Prison Experiment, and it happened far more quickly than expected. The situation at Abu Ghraib is a real-life application of the problem.

Social psychologists study two types of **attributions**, or the way we assign cause to behavior (Fiske, 2004). One type "reflects **dispositional causes**, such as mood, personality traits, values, intentions" (p. 97). All dispositional causes are internal to the person. People automatically try and create stable unchanging explanations about behavior. In contrast, **situational factors** are external causes. Physical, role, rule, **norm**, and law constraints are examples of situational factors. Situational and dispositional causes have application to a wide range of behavior, such as **stereotyping**. When faced with making judgments about others, we use an aspect of social cognition-attributions (Aronson et al., 2007). Stereotyping when making attributions is easy because of the tendency to judge the cause of someone's behavior in terms of dispositions rather than situations.

## Zimbardo's Stanford Prison Experiment

The Stanford Prison Experiment (SPE) illustrates the problem. It is a classic study that is still relevant. I want you to know details of this study and never forget them.

Zimbardo (2007) revisits the Stanford Prison Experiment in *The Lucifer Effect*, a book that examines the power of the situation. Zimbardo believes that most people, even social scientists, underestimate the influence of the situation on behavior. *The tendency in* **individualist** *societies is to attribute behavior to dispositions*, and in everyday life, it appears as if unacceptable behavior must be from something inside a person. We often deny how easily and quickly one's character can be transformed if placed in a particular situation. Zimbardo believes that people have a good-evil dichotomy that they use to view themselves and others that emphasizes dispositional factors. Ultimately, we minimize the role that situations (at least in the West) play in creating and maintaining the conditions under which evil acts are committed. Rather than viewing our personal attributes as fixed, either good or bad, *Zimbardo thinks it is more realistic to think of our attributes in degrees, such as the degree of evil or honesty that we show in different situations.* "People and situations are usually in a state of dynamic tension. Although you probably think of yourself as having a consistent personality across time and space that is likely not to be true" (p. 8). Zimbardo challenges the view that most of us have of ourselves.

The Stanford Prison Experiment took place in 1971 and, in light of atrocities such as Abu Ghraib, is still relevant.

Researchers took 24 healthy male participants, primarily white, middle-class college students, and randomly assigned them to either act as guards or prisoners. The subjects did not know each other prior to the study that took place in the basement of the Stanford University Psychology Department. A mock prison was created with cells, solitary confinement rooms, and an exercise yard. Both guards and prisoners were given clothing that identified the role they were assigned that included khaki pants and mirrored sunglasses (to increase **deindividuation**) for the guards and smocks and ankle locks for the prisoners. Participants were paid $15 for each day of the study. The guards had a brief orientation and were told to maintain order, prevent escapes, that the prisoners should feel helpless, and that there was to be no violence against the prisoners.

The study started with the surprise public arrest (the only deception in the study) of the prisoners by real police. They were processed and placed in the mock prison, remaining there 24 hours a day while the guards worked eight-hour shifts. The researchers were surprised that the assigned roles overtook the participants so quickly. Prisoners experienced a loss of personal identity and arbitrary control from the guards and were deprived of adequate sleep and privacy. They reacted with disbelief, rebellion, and then passiveness. Half of the prisoners were released early because they developed emotional and cognitive disorders. These disorders disappeared after the participants resumed their normal lives. The guards quickly assumed their roles in the mock prison. Some of the guards took the power of establishing and enforcing rules too far and became abusive, especially during the hours when they thought they were not being observed. Though the study was originally designed to last for two weeks, Zimbardo ended it after six days.

The largest lesson of the SPE is that situations are significant. Zimbardo offers many critiques of the study. It was a demonstration rather than an experiment. There was no control group taking the same pre- and post-test assessments but not assigned to be guards or prisoners. Though observations took place 24 hours a day, data used for analysis were selective because of staff and budget limitations. Data consisted of videotapes, audiotapes, questionnaires, personality self-reports, and interviews. Much of the data were analyzed with correlations. Direct cause cannot be established without an experiment using a control group. Another problem about establishing causal directions was that different guard shifts meant that there was inconsistent interaction between guards and prisoners. Zimbardo identified that the only testable variable was guard status versus prisoner status.

Participants took many assessments for the SPE. One self-report inventory used for initial participants was the Comrey Personality Scales. It contains eight personality measurements, such as extroversion, masculinity, empathy, stability, and trustworthiness. The average scores for both prisoners and guards fell into the normal range as defined by Comrey and were identical. This gave support that participants in both groups were normal, healthy, and equivalent to each other. Interesting but nonsignificant differences were found, though, between prisoners who stayed until the end and those released early. Those released scored higher on **conformity**, extroversion, and empathy. As for the guards, the most abusive one scored the lowest on empathy and trustworthiness.

While the Comrey Personality Scale showed that all participants fit the norm before the study, the Mood Adjective Self-Report showed differences between guards and prisoners while playing their assigned roles. Participants filled out this self-report twice during the study and after debriefing. One finding was that prisoners reported three times more negative mood than positive mood during the study. By the debriefing, there were no longer any differences in reported mood between the guards and the prisoners.

## The ethics of the SPE

Be careful about taking an extreme position that the SPE was unethical. There is much to consider. Zimbardo feels that, in some respects, it was unethical. However, he feels that, in some respects, it was ethical.

Here are arguments that it was unethical:

1. The study caused human suffering. Several of the prisoners showed severe stress.
2. The guards suffered because they realized what they did to the prisoners. The abuse to the prisoners put them under greater stress than those participating in Milgram's experiment.
3. The informed-consent form contained nothing about the surprise arrests.
4. The researchers should have ended the study before they did. Zimbardo says he was conflicted over his dual roles of an investigator with research goals and someone who was to uphold ethical principles. Zimbardo said that neither he nor the ethics committee had any idea that the participants would take on their roles so quickly.

Here are some arguments that it was ethical:

1. All participants signed an informed-consent form stating they knew that their privacy would be invaded, that the food would be minimal, that some of their civil rights would be infringed upon, and that they might be harassed.

2. The only deception used in the study was the surprise arrests. All other conditions were disclosed.

3. The mock prison was open for outsiders to inspect. For example, parents could visit and decide that their son was suffering and remove him from the study. However, no parent removed his or her son.

4. There was extensive debriefing.

5. There were some positive outcomes for the participants. Scientific benefit in studies must outweigh the costs to participants. While Zimbardo was not sure that the gains of the study outweighed the immediate suffering of participants, he argued that there were longer-term gains expressed by participants. Many said that it was a valuable learning experience.

## Note to the teacher

Perhaps your class could debate the ethics of the SPE. In addition, situations and dispositions are important components of a full explanation of aggressive behavior, a popular topic with students.

## Staying focused on culture

In keeping with the **culture** theme of the book, the terms *situational* and *dispositional* are relevant for thinking about other social psychology concepts. Culture is the umbrella over how situations and dispositions apply in everyday behavior. For example, individualists are more likely to use dispositions when making attributions and collectivists are more likely to use situations. A study about attributions and culture follows in section 5.12. Another study about culture, situational and dispositional factors, and the self-serving bias is also reviewed in section 5.12.

## 5.12 Discuss Two Errors in Attributions

An important ingredient of human **culture** is the ability to think about others' intentions and process what these intentions mean (Matsumoto & Juang, 2008). **Attributions** help us understand others' intentions. Making attributions is essential to how people explain things that happen; it gives us a sense of order and a feeling of control. Making attributions is universal. Humans are preoccupied with trying to understand the social world, making attributions about every 100 words (Blackwell et al., 2003). Attributions are products of the human mind and research shows they are influenced by culture.

Current research on attributions illustrates viewing humans as **activated actors**. Older attribution research made it seem as if making attributions was a time-consuming cognitive activity (Fiske & Taylor, 2008). Modern research shows that most attributions are made *automatically,* illustrating one end of the **dual-processing model**. We can use more controlled thinking when making attributions, illustrating the other end of the dual-processing model, but this happens primarily when we encounter something unexpected or negative and must take more time making sense of it.

I selected two attribution errors for this section, the **correspondence bias** and the **self-serving attribution**.

Cultural considerations are addressed in both examples. The study on the correspondence bias is about terrorism and aggression. The self-serving bias study illustrates key research decisions that make psychological concepts cross-culturally applicable. In addition to cultural considerations, I give a brief overview of the self-serving bias and the brain to tie the attribution material to the biological level of analysis. Attributions are a product of the human mind, linking the concept to the cognitive level of analysis.

## Definitions and context for the correspondence bias

Elliot Aronson and colleagues (2007) write that the most common **schema** people have to judge anothers' behavior is a **correspondence bias**, that behavior matches a person's **disposition**. In fact, "the correspondence bias is so pervasive that many social psychologists called it the **fundamental attribution error**" (p. 109). At the biological level, it is possible that **mirror neurons**, discussed in section 5.16, are firing when the judgment is made. Even though people do not totally ignore the role of situations, there is far more of a tendency to make attributions according to dispositions, and this is why it is called a fundamental attribution error.

How can we explain the correspondence bias? Janet Riggs and Leah Gumbrecht (2005) think that cognitive factors are at the root. One reason is that we tend to focus on the person rather than a situation, called **perceptual salience**, or "the seeming importance of information that is the focus of people's attention" (Aronson et al., 2007, p. 111). The word salience means the most important or striking feature. Perceptual salience relates to one's visual point of view. It may not be possible to access knowledge about anothers' situation. However, it is possible to see the person and infer from how they look, speak, and behave. It takes more effort to find out important situational factors. Mental shortcuts, such as the **anchoring and adjustment heuristic**, may contribute to what is perceived as most important about someone. Attributions begin with an anchoring position, which is generally the focus of their immediate attention; what is perceptually salient. But as more information becomes available, people should adjust their opinions. Another reason is that expectations can distort perceptions, leading to a correspondence bias (Riggs & Gumbrecht, 2005). Another cause is unrealistic expectations, where comparisons are made between what an individual thinks might happen in a situation with what someone else has done.

Aronson and colleagues (2007) believe that making attributions is a two-step process. First impressions are anchored in dispositions, but then adjustments are made. However, much of the time, these adjustments, which would take into account more of the situational factors contributing to behavior, are not enough to influence the original position.

Making dispositional attributions is *adaptive*. Fiske (2004) uses the concept **spontaneous trait inferences** to suggest that people automatically make inferences about others' behavior. Automatic inference allows people to understand others and have a sense of control, which is one of the core social motives Fiske (2004). The human mind is set up to create categories and abstract images. Social psychologists can provide some perspective on how the correspondence bias happens, but it is unlikely that people can completely avoid making spontaneous inferences.

There are cultural differences that somewhat limit the universality of the correspondence bias (Fiske & Taylor, 2008). It is far stronger in people from **individualist** cultures. People from **collectivist** cultures also use dispositions, but do so to a lesser degree. East Asians tend to use situational factors in judgments. They were socialized by their cultures to have an interdependent self and abide by situational **norms**. In contrast, socialization in individualist cultures produces an independent self, where people feel less compelled to consider the larger group.

## A correspondence bias experiment

The following experiment examines under what conditions Western participants might be persuaded to consider important situational factors. This experiment relates to attitudes about **terrorism**, relating it to our topic of **aggression** and violence, to **situation** and **disposition** factors, and to **stereotyping** and reducing **prejudice**.

Riggs and Gumbrecht (2005) designed an experiment to replicate previous research suggesting that people tended to have a correspondence bias (or dispositions) in an emotionally charged situation during the late fall and early spring after the 9/11 attacks. The authors predicted that, when expectations were violated, use of the correspondence bias would increase or would cause participants to search for situational factors in making a decision.

Ninety-six males and females between the ages of 18 and 21 were recruited from a private college, where most of the students were white and Christian. Participants were told that the experiment was about impression formation, were randomly assigned to eight experimental conditions, and were tested individually or in small groups.

Participants made judgments about a student assigned to write an essay about their reactions to the 9/11 attacks. Assigned groups were given different information about the student essay. Participants read either a pro- or anti-American essay written either by a student named John Miller or one named Mohammed Fatah. In addition, subjects were told that their assigned name either chose the position taken in the essay or that it was assigned. The pro and con essays were similar in length, argument, and writing style.

After reading the essays, participants answered a questionnaire using a Likert scale. The goal of the questionnaire was to assess participants' opinions of the true feelings of the students writing the essays.

The results contradicted researcher predictions. The only variable that seemed important was whether the name of the person writing the essay was John Miller or Mohammed Fatah. Other types of expectations, such as whether the person had a choice whether to write a pro or con essay about the United States was not important, contrary to previous research. Participants reading an essay by John Miller showed an extreme use of the correspondence bias, regardless of whether they were from the group told that John Miller either had a choice in position or did not. The correspondence bias disappeared in participants reading an essay by Mohammed Fatah; situational factors were more important, regardless if participants were told Mohammad Fatah was assigned a pro or con essay.

The authors concluded that participants reading the essay by Mohammed Fatah were concerned about appearing prejudiced. Media campaigns to avoid stereotyped overgeneralizations from the behavior of the terrorists to all Muslims may have been beneficial. Another conclusion was that unrealistic expectations in participants reading the essay by John Miller affected perceptions. It is possible that American participants could not imagine writing an anti-American paper about the 9/11 attacks and therefore ignored the fact that John Miller was assigned to take a con position.

While the correspondence bias is a fundamental human process, there are conditions under which people take situations into account.

The sample in this experiment limits population validity. As typical of much of the social psychology research, it is tested on American college students. Does the study have cross-cultural applications? Since some participants were tested in groups, the influence of others could have introduced social desirability factors into the study. This experiment takes ideas about situations and dispositions in a new direction and needs confirmation in other highly emotional settings and in other sample groups, particularly cross-cultural samples.

## Definition and context for the self-serving bias

The **self-serving bias** means that people are more likely to attribute success to themselves (use dispositional attributes) but place blame for failures on the situation (Aronson et al., 2007). The self-serving bias has been confirmed mainly in Western cultures and is displayed across a wide range of topics, such as education, sport psychology, and mental disorders. People with **depression**, for example, overuse internal attributions when something negative happens (Blackwell et al., 2003).

There are numerous reasons for the self-serving bias. First, we are more likely to use self-serving attributions when our self-worth is threatened. Impression management is a second reason. We want to enhance the self and feel a sense of control; part of the core motives. We behave in order to maximize the chances that we will make good impressions. Third, information might be limited. As in the correspondence bias, without clear information about a situation, it is easier, and probably automatic, to make a dispositional judgment. Last, people will protect themselves when necessary. This is called making **defensive attributions**. Defensive attributions protect us from the idea that the world is uncontrollable and that things can happen by chance. The worse the situation, the more likely we are to blame the individual for what happened (Fiske, 2004). Serious crimes are one example of when people are likely to use defensive attributions. The more serious the crime, the more likely people are to attribute blame on the victim to feel a sense of control; a core motive of the sociocultural level of analysis.

## A cross-cultural correlation study on the self-serving bias

N.C. Higgins and Gira Bhatt (2001) conducted a cross-cultural study on the **self-serving bias**.

Culture is an important factor in how a person views their social world. People from **individualist** societies emphasize the self, and people from **collectivist** societies emphasize the context as explanations for life events. The self in collectivist societies is rarely viewed outside of the group and is influenced by ideology. For example, in Hindu culture, what happens to a person is viewed as often uncontrollable, influenced by past actions in the current or a previous life. People living in individualist cultures are expected to take responsibility for their actions, as there is a distinct separation between individual achievement and relationships with the larger group. Because of these differences, Higgins and Bhatt considered that there would be differences in how people from individualist and collectivist societies made causal attributions.

Higgins and Bhatt explored some methodological issues about studying attributions cross-culturally. Three concepts appeared to be **etics** that allowed for comparison between cultures. These are locus of control (internal or external), controllability (the ability to manage the cause), and stability (if the cause is seen as occurring over time).

Is the self-serving bias universal? The self-serving bias is clearly documented in studies using Western participants. Previous research on culture and the self-serving bias needed clarification because the studies used different measurements to collect data. For example, different variables modify how the self-serving bias is shown, such as whether the study gathers data about achievement or interpersonal relationships.

In addition, Higgins and Bhatt emphasize an important point from Triandis; *any concept in social psychology should have both etic and emic features.* Their questionnaire was specifically designed to show the **emics** of attributions.

With this background information, Higgins and Bhatt designed a study to investigate emics and etics in causal explanations for life events. One prediction was that the self-serving bias would be used by both Canadian and Indian samples, illustrating an etic. Another prediction was that the participants from India would use more contextual causes to explain events than participants from Canada, illustrating emics. Last, it was predicted that the Canadian sample would show more clear distinctions between achievement and interpersonal areas of life, again illustrating emics.

Participants consisted of college students from two universities in India, one an English-speaking university and the other a Gujarati-speaking university (n=195), and one university in Canada (n=162). More females than males participated in both samples.

Data were collected with an open-ended adaptation of the Attributional Style Questionnaire. The researchers were aware that collecting data in a structured format might cause the correspondence bias, where the researchers elicited responses about causes they selected rather than causes that were important to participants. The open-ended questionnaire was an emic approach for the study because it allowed researchers to gather information that was relevant to the person's specific culture. Participants thought about what was important *to them* on topics relating to both interpersonal and achievement domains and rated their responses on a 7-point scale, with 1 meaning "Totally due to others or circumstances," and 7 meaning "Totally due to me." Some of the original questions on the Attributional Scale had to be altered to reflect topics that would have relevance to the specific culture but still be comparable to each other. For example, "You go out on a date and it goes badly" for the Canadian participants was changed to "Your engagement breaks off" for the Indian participants. The questionnaire was written in English and then translated into Gujarati and then **back translated**. The answers to the questionnaires were analyzed with correlations.

Results showed that there were both emic and etic aspects of causal attributions and that *both groups used the self-serving bias* to explain negative events in terms of the situation. Participants from India used the most contextual explanations for both positive and negative events. In addition, participants from both cultures used the self-serving bias for taking credit for positive events, though participants from India used the larger context to take credit for positive events more so than did participants from Canada.

*The authors concluded that the self-serving bias was an etic but also contained emic features,* as participants from Canada and India had culturally relevant ways of using it.

The Higgins and Bhatt study does not show cause and effect as data was analyzed with correlations. The emic approach to gathering data in culturally meaningful ways and back-translating are strengths.

## The brain and the self-serving bias

Nigel Blackwell and colleagues (2003) used **fMRI** in an experiment to investigate the brain and the **self-serving bias**.

The goal of the study was to investigate the neural basis of self-responsibility and of the self-serving bias. Self-responsibility was defined for the study as "a subject's internal attribution of presented positive and negative social events" (p. 1077). The self-serving bias was defined as "the tendency to make internal attributions for positive events and negative attributions for negative events" (p. 1077).

The sample consisted of 12 normal males.

Ten statements from the Internal, Personal, and Situational Attributions Questionnaire were each presented for 30 seconds to participants in an fMRI scanner.

The first statements related to attributions of positive events, such as "A friend brought you a present" and "A friend believes you are honest." Participants read the statements silently and imagined being in the situation described. Next, they decided if the main cause of the situation was internal (if it was something about you), external personal (it was something about the friend), or external situational (it was something about the situation). Participants pressed a button to select one of the three responses.

The second 10 statements related to attributions of negative events, such as "A friend refused to talk to you" and "A friend betrayed the trust you had in her." Once again, participants pushed one of three buttons to indicate their attribution.

The results showed that participants used significantly more external personal attributions than internal or external situational attributions. In addition, participants made more internal attributions for positive events than for negative events.

What was the brain doing?

Self-responsibility activates the bilateral premotor cortex and cerebellum, both related to goal-directed behavior. The premotor cortex is of particular importance because it links attributions to the **theory of mind**. While previous research suggested that the medial premotor cortex was critical to **intersubjective** experiences, the authors report that it was not activated in their study. However, the dorsal premotor cortex was active. This area may be related to understanding others' intentions as well. The authors believe that the medial premotor cortex could be important to making attributions, even if not activated in this study. It was impossible to simulate the complexities of real social interaction in the study. Participants just imagined the situation, possibly preventing important brain activity from surfacing. Blackwell and colleagues realize that real social interactions are not reducible to the study task. The future of fMRI scanning studies should offer chances to see the brain during real social interactions.

In addition, the superior temporal sulcus was active when considering if others were responsible for social interactions. The superior temporal sulcus area is also related to **mirror neurons**, important for understanding others' intentions. Some fundamental concepts related to being human, such as being able to decode others' intentions, keep surfacing as we look deeply into the material.

The self-serving bias is mediated through the dorsal striatum that is related to motivational activity. When someone constructs self-serving biases, they are motivated to come up with explanations that make sense to them, increasing one's sense of control.

Blackwell and colleagues realize that the study sample is small. The study should be replicated using different samples.

## 5.13 Explain the Formation of Stereotypes and Their Effect on Behavior

A common belief is that **stereotyping** is a direct cause of prejudice and discrimination. The belief is incorrect. In this section and the next one about **social identity theory** (SIT), you will learn to distinguish between two types of stereotypes and will learn how both kinds of stereotypes are formed. Stereotypes *can* become activated and turn into prejudice and discrimination (Aronson et al., 2007). However, having a stereotype does not directly lead to prejudice or discrimination. Often, stereotypes are just ways to simplify and organize the world. They can be *adaptive,* as long as they are based on some real experiences and are supported by some truths about others' behaviors.

Stereotyping is universal and there are many similarities in the way that people from different cultures stereotype (Matsumoto & Juang, 2008).

# The activated actor uses two kinds of stereotypes

Stereotypes are *cognitive* inter-group biases and are different from prejudice, *emotional* inter-group biases (Fiske & Taylor, 2008; Aronson et al., 2007). Stereotyping and prejudice are linked through cognition, but the mechanisms explaining each are different (Fiske & Taylor, 2008). Discrimination is the behavior that comes from prejudice (Aronson et al., 2007).

This section in the IB syllabus falls under the category of "sociocultural cognition," so it is important to connect stereotyping to the current focus in social cognitive research on humans as **activated actors**. In addition, while the IB syllabus lists stereotyping and social identity theory as separate, it might be easier to discuss them together under stereotyping, as do Fiske (2004), Fiske and Taylor (2008), Aronson and colleagues (2007), and Matsumoto and Juang (2008). Students must see how everything relates or they tend to get lost in all of the facts.

Fiske and Taylor (2008) divide stereotyping into two types, **blatant stereotyping** and **subtle stereotyping**.

## Note to the teacher

This section focuses on the formation of subtle stereotypes and the effects on gender differences in math performance. If students need a second study about the effects of stereotyping on behavior, use the material from the section 5.14 on social identity theory and blatant stereotyping. Both sections are about stereotyping and I just divided it into two sections to meet the requirements of the syllabus.

The difference between blatant stereotyping and subtle stereotyping relates back to the activated actor and the **dual-processing approach** to social cognition. Blatant stereotyping is primarily controlled and conscious while subtle stereotyping is primarily automatic and unconscious (Fiske & Taylor, 2008).

The formation of blatant stereotypes occurs when people identify with their **in-group** with controlled conscious social thinking. SIT research shows how easily and under what circumstances people express their allegiance to the in-group. We have biases toward an in-group and biases against out-groups (Matsumoto & Juang, 2008). Taken to the extreme, identifying with an in-group can lead to intense competition and **aggression**. Blatant in-group biases take place in response to inter-group threats to one's values and economic resources (Fiske & Taylor, 2008).

In contrast, subtle forms of stereotyping come from interpersonal conflicts. Subtle stereotyping challenges our notions that all stereotypes reflect deliberate prejudice.

The *difference* between automatic and controlled stereotyping matters a great deal when we think about how it *affects behavior*. People are more likely to be held responsible for their actions when they come from controlled, conscious processing than they are if behavior comes from automatic and unintentional processing. For example, the study that will be reviewed in this section under the title "Gender stereotypes in Education," one effect of subtle stereotyping on behavior, is about gender stereotypes and their effects on females' mathematics abilities. Parents and teachers do not intend to negatively affect behavior, even if their stereotyping has great consequence for the girls. In contrast, identifying with an in-group is controlled and conscious stereotyping. The example study on **infrahumanization**, reviewed in the next section, highlights how far consciously identifying with an in-group can go.

## The formation of subtle stereotypes

Here are some factors that contribute to subtle stereotype formation. These factors work together and in reality cannot be separated. *Awareness may prevent the worst effects of subtle stereotyping.*

**1.** Subtle stereotypes form automatically and unintentionally, occur primarily in *ambiguous* and *ambivalent* situations, and stem from inner conflict (Fiske & Taylor, 2008). Advances in research have allowed researchers to show just how subtle stereotyping works. People like to think of themselves as not holding or acting on stereotypes, but research shows that they do both, even if it is accidental and automatic.

**2.** Three of the core principles for the sociocultural level of analysis explain subtle stereotyping, understanding others, belonging to a group, and controlling and predicting situations (Fiske, 2004).

**3.** Everyday cognitive processing, such as selective attention, attributions, concept formation, and memory contribute to the automatic nature of subtle stereotyping (Matsumoto & Juang, 2008). For example, **attributions** contribute to the formation of stereotypes and reinforce them. According to Aronson and colleagues, "Stereotypes are **dispositional attributions**—negative ones" (2007, p. 436). People naturally make dispositional attributions about individuals, and when attributions are placed on an entire group, they may result in the **ultimate attribution error**.

**4.** Our cognitive processes are efficient. **Concept formation** describes how we form categories to organize objects and social relationships (Matsumoto & Juang, 2008). The mind is automatically set up to create **schemas**. Concept formation is part of forming **attributions**. "As a specific type of schema, stereotypes are beliefs about the characteristics of group members and theories about why those attributes go together" (Fiske, 2004, p. 399). Categories are efficient ways of processing large amounts of information (Matsumoto & Juang, 2008). We need schemas. Special schemas help us decode and interact with other people. We create categories about our in-group, called **autostereotypes**, as well as about out-groups, called **heterostereotypes**. Up to a point, both are useful ways of categorizing. However, schematic categories can quickly become destructive and distinctions between in-groups and out-groups can too easily become the blatant stereotypes found in SIT research or even turn into prejudice and discrimination. We grow up viewing the world through **cultural filters** that reflect our **enculturation**. Stereotypes are often based on some truth about a group, which Triandis calls **sociotypes**. But many stereotypes are completely incorrect and come from vicarious learning through others and the media rather than direct experience. We create categories about others *rapidly* to function in human culture. This efficiency can have consequences. One consequence is that categories become too easily accessible and automatic, creating **category confusion** (Fiske & Taylor, 2008). This is when people create general categories, such as gender or race, far faster than they can name individual identities. We get this categorical information primarily from faces. Since categorization happens so rapidly, we tend not to see others as individuals. This is known from studying spontaneous memory. It is easy to confuse one individual with another from the same category. This may be a factor contributing to problems with **eyewitness testimony**.

**5.** The rapidness of automatic categorizing and interpreting **ambiguous situations** cause stereotypes to form (Fiske & Taylor, 2008). Ambiguity is present in most social situations, so we are stuck with making interpretations. The end result of our interpretations can be problematic for others, even if we mean well. For example, priming participants to stereotypes in experiments shows what happens when we must rely on interpretations. In studies on criminal investigations, participants believing in a just world rate women more responsible for an ambiguous aggressive encounter with a man when they are primed with rape-related words. Many **gender stereotypes** come from interpreting ambiguous situations. Facial expressions are interpreted differently depending on whether the person is male or female. In addition, causal attributions are influenced by ambiguous information. Termed the ultimate attribution error, if in-group members do something positive, it is credited to dispositions. However, if an out-group member does something positive, it is credited to the situation. While there can be negative consequences of stereotyping, it creates stability for the in-group.

## Gender stereotypes in education: One effect of subtle stereotyping on behavior

Parents and teachers can unintentionally and automatically teach stereotyped behavior to female children.

Females are still underrepresented in some fields of science and engineering and the underrepresentation is related to mathematics performance. While many parents and teachers try to make females feel that they are as capable at mathematics as males, there is a large body of research suggesting that subtle stereotyping still heavily influences female perceptions of their mathematical capabilities and performance.

These gender stereotypes are not intentional; they come from automatic categorizing and interpreting of ambiguous information. But the consequences are great. Newer research shows how attributions may lead to stereotyping about gender differences in mathematics performance.

Jennifer Herbert and Deborah Stipek (2005) believe that children internalize stereotyped messages from parents about mathematics abilities. The gender gap in mathematics may be smaller now but it is still there. Males outnumber girls in advanced mathematics courses and enter financially profitable careers requiring advanced mathematics skills at a higher rate. Why is there a difference? *Competency beliefs* may be a large factor. Herbert and Stipek examined what these beliefs were, when they emerged, if they were related to actual performance, and how children's beliefs related to parent and teacher ratings of the children's competencies.

The authors conducted a longitudinal study on economically disadvantaged males and females between kindergarten or first grade and the fifth grade. Data were gathered through interviews and achievement test scores. Data were analyzed with correlations.

One prediction was that boys would rate their mathematical abilities higher than girls starting in the first grade but would not actually perform better than the girls on achievement tests. Herbert and Stipek believed that the differences in self-ratings started during elementary school and were visible by the fifth grade.

Previous research on verbal abilities was inconsistent though it generally favored the girls. Herbert and Stipek predicted that girls would rate their performance higher than boys in verbal ability. It was not predicted when the gap appeared.

A third prediction was that parent ratings of verbal abilities would favor the girls and ratings of mathematics abilities would favor the boys.

A fourth prediction was that teacher ratings of verbal abilities would favor the girls and mathematical performance would favor the boys.

A last prediction was that parent and teacher ratings of abilities would predict the children's own ratings. The beliefs of significant adults in a child's life may convey gender stereotypes that the child internalizes.

Participants represented students from 48 school districts in 152 schools and 228 classrooms. Economically disadvantaged girls are not well represented in samples of previous research and the impact of stereotypes may be more harmful to them. Thus, economically disadvantaged students are an important sample for future studies. Parent-education level in the sample was low and 76% had incomes below $15,000. The teachers had an average of 16 years of experience.

Children rated their mathematics and verbal abilities during kindergarten or the 1st grade and then again in the 3rd and 5th grade on the Feelings About School Questionnaire. Trained interviewers administered the questionnaire and children responded on a 1 to 5 scale to questions such as "How good are you at learning new numbers?" and "How good are you at reading compared to all the students in your class?"

Parents were interviewed during a home visit or by telephone and asked to rate their child's mathematical and verbal abilities on a 1 to 5 scale, with 1 meaning "Not as good as the other children" and 5 meaning "Well above children this age."

Teachers filled out questionnaires and returned them to researchers by mail. Teachers rated children using the same 5-point scale as the parents and predicted the children's mathematics and verbal skills for the next school year.

Last, children completed mathematics and verbal achievement tests in kindergarten and again in 3rd and 5th grade.

The results included the following:

1. Boys rated their mathematics abilities higher than the girls starting in the 3rd grade even though performance on achievement tests was similar.

2. Girls performed better than boys on verbal tests but rated their performance lower.

3. Teachers, but not parents, rated girls' verbal skills as higher. Parents, but not teachers, rated boys' mathematics abilities higher than girls'.

4. Parent ratings of mathematics performance by the 5th grade were correlated with their own children's self-ratings. It is interesting that parental lower ratings of math performance emerged during the 3rd grade—*the same time as it emerged in the children.* Teacher ratings overall were more consistent with actual test scores than those of parents.

Herbert and Stipek realize that the results of the study do not show cause and effect. Parent attitudes, as reflected in comments during the interviews, may explain the correlations found in the study. For example, comments included that poor math grades were of little concern and that female parents avoided math-related jobs in the home such as balancing the checkbook.

## 5.14 Evaluate Social Identity Theory (SIT), Making Reference to Relevant Studies

### Some context for SIT: Blatant stereotyping

The **blatant stereotyping** formed from identifying with one's in-group is the topic for this section.

Blatant stereotyping contributes to **aggression**. Blatant stereotyping can even interfere with the trust that is needed for international cooperation.

SIT is one of four psychological theories of group social identity (Fiske & Taylor, 2008). The other three are social categorization theory (SCT), optimal distinctiveness theory (ODT), and subjective reduction theory. I will not review the last two, but you should know they exist.

Favoring one's in-group is something we do on a *controlled, conscious* level as **activated actors**. The tendency to favor one's in-group can even increase under certain circumstances, such as when one's identity is threatened or when a high-status group feels insecure (Fiske & Taylor, 2008).

Social identity with an in-group satisfies some of our **core basic motives**, such as belonging, trusting, and controlling. However, favoring an in-group contributes to the belief that groups are homogeneous. This is a cognitive feature of SIT and it can have a dark side.

SIT is one explanation for the formation of blatant stereotypes and is closely related to the topic of situational and dispositional factors.

SIT is interesting and has many real-life applications. My discussion explains SIT, gives it a **cultural** context, and evaluates some modern research. SIT relates to many other required concepts. The atrocities at Abu Ghraib prison required U.S. military personnel to strongly identify with their in-group. SIT research is also relevant for questions about factors that affect **conformity**.

## An application of SIT: The in-group, the out-group, and justifying violence

It is comforting to categorize others into in-groups and out-groups (Fiske & Taylor, 2008). Categorization relieves ambiguity and ambivalence about others and situations. However, if these categories become *entities,* meaning to take on a reality, strained group relations and even atrocities such as dehumanization and infrahumanization are possible.

You may have studied **dehumanization** and violence. Emanuele Castano and Roger Giner-Sorolla (2006) write that history is full of examples of propaganda that denies an enemy *full human status.* One example concerns Nazi Germany. One survivor of a concentration camp noted that degrading the prisoners was a necessity for the system to work. Someone operating the gas chamber would be severely distressed if they did not rationalize that the people were not really human. Dehumanization is one way that troops get mentally prepared to kill the enemy; most soldiers would never kill anyone in civilian life. Albert Bandura believes that dehumanization increases aggression. Dehumanization requires reduced empathy for the victim, a necessary part of the **moral disengagement**, meaning detaching from the morals that guide your daily life, needed to commit an atrocity. Bandura's thoughts on moral disengagement are reviewed in the next section. What we need to know here is that to commit an act of violence, one must disengage in some way from the victim.

One major consequence of dehumanizing others is that it increases **infrahumanization**, which means that a victim is given a *less than human status* (Fiske & Taylor, 2008). Though most people do not directly participate in killings, research shows that they will participate in infrahumanization. Studies on infrahumanization show that people are likely to justify the atrocities of their in-group members, particularly if the out-group has an emotional meaning for the in-group. Primary emotions, such as anger and happiness, are still attributed to the victims, but the more subtle secondary emotions, such as love, hope, and humiliation are withheld (Castano & Giner-Sorolla, 2006).

Castano and Giner-Sorolla ran three experiments to test the conditions under which infrahumanization occurred. They "hypothesized that when individuals are presented with reminders of violence against the out-group for which their own in-group is held responsible, they infrahumanize the victim more than when such reminders are not included or than when such reminders merely present the fact of large-scale death without in-group responsibility" (p. 806).

Experiment # 1 randomly assigned 68 University of Kent at Canterbury (U.K.) students to two conditions, the accidental killing condition and the in-group responsibility condition.

All participants sat in front of a computer and read a story about humans encountering aliens called the Gs. The story ending depended on the assigned group. One group's story ending was that 10,000 aliens died as a result of an accident. The other group's story was that 10,000 aliens were attacked and killed by soldiers and that few of the military group died. Participants reported their perceptions of how the aliens felt, rating 59 emotions on a Likert scale of 1 (Not at all) to 5 (Very much). As predicted, the in-group responsibility condition had a significantly stronger infrahumanization than the accidental killing group.

Experiment # 2 replicated the original idea but added a real in-group situation for the participants. In addition, the variable of guilt was tested. Fifty-seven University of Kent at Canterbury students were randomly assigned to two conditions. Both groups heard a story about the everyday life of Australian Aborigines before British colonization. The high-impact condition's story ending said that the dramatic decline of Aborigine population happened because of the diseases spread by the colonizers and the wars against them. The low-impact group's story ending said that the decline in the Aborigine population happened shortly after the British arrived but that the Aborigine numbers quickly grew again. Participants rated the emotions felt by the Aborigines as well as the level of guilt they felt toward the Aborigines. The hypothesis was supported. Those in the high-impact condition used a significantly larger amount of infrahumanization than the low-impact group. In addition, the high-impact groups had stronger collective guilt feelings and were more agreeable to giving the Aborigines reparations.

Experiment # 3 replicated the experiments using white Americans of European decent from New York as participants. The stories were about Native Americans. The results supported the research conducted in the United Kingdom.

Castano and Giner-Sorolla suggest that *awareness* of this rather negative human behavior is the start of creating effective public policy. The need to belong to an in-group will probably not go away, so coming up with strategies to defuse violence are not simple.

Future research on infrahumanization should include stories that manipulate different degrees of destruction against an out-group. All three experiments used one-sided stories where the in-group caused all of the destruction. Manipulating the story content will give researchers clues about the extent of in-group infrahumanization to varying situations.

Infrahumanization is an example of the dark side of social identity. We are responsible for learning about it because only then can we use the information to create responsible public policy at an international level.

## The purpose of SIT

We like to think of ourselves as individuals, but groups actually influence us a great deal. The core principles of self-enhancement, belonging, and trusting are highlighted in social identity theory. As all behavior is *adaptive,* an evolutionary advantage for preferring an in-group must exist.

Marilynn Brewer and Masaki Yuki (2007) write that all cultures must meet both individual self-interest needs and social identity group needs as well as provide a way for these needs to coexist. Both **individualist** and **collectivist** cultures meet these needs but differ in *how* they meet them. Remember that *meaning making* is a key component of Matsumoto's definition of culture. Persons from individualist and collectivist cultures have fundamentally different meanings of in-group social identity; *culture shapes and modifies social identity* (Brewer & Yuki, 2007). Working together effectively in a global society rests on understanding the cultural context of social identity and what it means for *trusting* others and for problems of **stereotyping** and discrimination.

Social identity is an **etic**. Individuals need a way to buffer the difficulties of survival; the **evolution** of complex human group living meets this need (Brewer & Yuki, 2007). It makes sense that the most important parts of human biology and cognition were directed at living in social groups. Even though social identity is an etic, "*the locus and content of social identity are clearly culturally defined and regulated*" (p. 307). The categories of individualism and collectivism are the most used way to collect and organize modern data about social identity and culture. The new research provides valuable information about how to interpret another's intragroup (within an in-group) and intergroup (between out-groups) behavior.

SIT and self-categorization theory (SCT), which must be considered together, unite our understanding of group behavior and the cognitive processes that determine a wide range of intragroup and intergroup behavior (Yuki, 2003).

## What is SIT and SCT?

SIT is limited unless it is studied in combination with SCT. In addition, SIT/SCT is limited unless research shows that it applies cross-culturally. Many newer SIT/SCT studies show the cross-cultural applications.

Blatant stereotyping occurs when there is conflict between groups (Fiske & Taylor 2008). One type of conflict is of competing for scarce resources. However, lab and field experiments show that *subjective perceptions* of conflict may be the most important variables. Perceptions of reality are often more important than reality, and these perceptions are what social psychologists study. *Conflict cannot happen unless people perceive themselves as members of distinct groups.* How we behave as members of a distinct group shifts according to the *context* of the situation. Groups compete far more than individuals.

Michael Hogg and colleagues (1995) write that SIT and SCT are social psychology theories that originated in the United Kingdom to explain how an individual's self is intertwined with group behavior and intergroup interaction. Henri Tajfel did the early work on SIT in the 1950s that examined perceptions, cognitions, and belief systems related to discrimination. In the 1980s, John Turner did work on SCT that built on and enhanced SIT. Masaki Yuki (2003) says that the main idea of both SIT and SCT is that "group behaviors derive from cognitive representations of the self in terms of membership in a shared social category, in which, in effect, there is no psychological separation between self and the group as a whole" (166).

SIT claims that people belong to many groups, such as nations, sport teams, and families, and that each group varies in importance to one's *self-concept* (Hogg et al., 1995). Each group is represented in one's mind as a cognitive **schema** that tells us what we should think, feel, and do in particular *contexts*. In specific contexts, a particular social identity with a group becomes the most salient, or noticeable, way of self-regulating behavior in relation to others, fitting in nicely with our definition of human culture. Once the proper social identity for a particular context is identified, those behaviors become **stereotypes** of the in-group and what is considered the **norm**. The behaviors of out-groups are stereotypes of what others are like, and these stereotypes can fuel fierce competition and even discrimination.

Identifying with an in-group is natural but creates cognitive categories, the "us" and "them" categories that **enhance the self** but sharpen the distinctions between in-groups and out-groups (Fiske, 2004). Research shows that people receiving a short-term threat automatically stereotype and stigmatize out-groups. Categorizing and self-enhancement are subjective beliefs that give *meaning* to an in-group (Hogg et al., 1995). These subjective beliefs are not necessarily true; they exist to give behavior meaning. The in-group is always favored. Identification with sport teams is a good example of an in-group that determines behavior in relation to out-groups (other teams). Perhaps the highly competitive nature and aggression in some sports is related to social identity.

SIT emphasized the role of *categorization in maintaining one's self-esteem* (Fiske & Taylor, 2008). As social identity research developed, the emphasis on self-esteem declined in favor of theories emphasizing the cognitive component of categorization.

SCT enhanced SIT. SCT is different from SIT because it changed the focus from self-esteem to how *categories became the cognitions that guided group behavior* (Hogg et al., 1995). People create categories to fulfill **belonging needs**. Categories *magnify* similarities between those of an in-group and those of an out-group (Fiske, 2004). Individuals see their in-group as more varied than they really are and out-groups as more similar to each other than they really are, which promotes belonging but increases out-group stereotyping. Unfortunately, threats to self-enhancement and belonging can lead to stereotypes and discrimination, even by otherwise well-meaning people.

Belonging to an in-group requires group members to share mental representations of the defining features of a group (Hogg et al., 1995). A group's defining features are **prototypes** (norms) for group behavior in a specific context. Creating categories requires **depersonalization**. When depersonalizing, one defines the self in terms of the group category more than the individual self. For example, **aggression** at a sport event is depersonalized as a team behavior; high levels of emotional competition with another team (the out-group) are the norm. Depersonalizing is not the same thing as dehumanizing or deindividuating, it is simply a way to change one's view of the self in a particular context to maintain one's subjective belief of protypical behavior (Hogg et al., 1995). SCT claims that we view groups in terms of prototypes. *Prototypes are cognitive representations,* the characteristics of a group's attitudes, beliefs, and behaviors based on information we have about them. Prototypes are a fuzzy set of context-related expectations of others. Prototypes for out-groups are most influenced by what is salient about a group *in a specific context,* such as a nation or a religion.

Fiske (2004) argues that *stereotyping and discrimination are best framed as in-group preferences rather than out-group disfavor.* People prefer an in-group; they enhance our chances of survival. Any out-group threatening the well being of the in-group is likely to be stigmatized.

## SIT/SCT and culture: Making the theories relevant for everyone

SIT and SCT explain how becoming part of in-groups shapes representations of the individual self. But the self has different meanings in **individualist** and **collectivist** cultures.

Social identity is universal but it has different characteristics in individualist and collectivist cultures (Brewer & Yuki, 2007).

The early research on social identity is from the West. *A cross-cultural view shows that the original SIT/SCT explanations are too simplistic.* The group cognitions that define one's social identity vary and the social self really exists on three levels. One is the *individual level,* where the self is unique. Second is the *relational level,* where the self exists in terms of a harmonious relationship with others. Third is the *collective level,* where the self fits into depersonalized categories of groups that have symbolic value to the person. Obligations to close interpersonal relationships are not required for membership in a collective group. *SIT and SCT explain the social self in the third level, far more appropriate to defining social identity in individualist cultures.*

Social identity in collectivist cultures is **relational**. Harmony and cooperation within collectivist groups are valued. Relational social identities are **personalized** rather than **depersonalized**. Individual self-interest within personalized relational social identities is tied to behaviors that maintain in-group harmony and cooperation. Persons in collectivist cultures have a higher **external locus of control**. The group locus defines the self and behavior. Much of the original data for this cultural view came from studying the Japanese. However, research on the Chinese and West Africans support the view. Each culture has **emic** features of social identity, but in general, collectivistic cultures have social identities that are more relational than categorical.

Why are there differences in social identity between cultures? Identifying with a culture evolved over time to maximize the survival of individuals. The **ecology**, or natural environment we live in, was important to shaping distinct cultural behaviors. One important ecological factor is **mobility**. High mobility is correlated with individualism and low mobility is correlated with collectivism. If you have little chance at mobility, then it is in your interest to behave in ways that promote harmony and cooperation. Groups are still important to people in individualist cultures, but greater mobility allows interests and preferences of each person to define one's relationship and obligations to a group social identity. Thus, *the categorical nature of SIT and SCT is more Western oriented.*

Cross-cultural studies using questionnaires to gather reports about the self find that both individualistic and collectivist participants make reference to their social identity to groups. However, collectivist participants make more references to small group identity and individualist participants make more references to large group identity. We can conclude that social identity is important in all cultures; *the difference is just in emphasis.*

## Social identity has implications for one's sense of self worth and well-being

Masaki Yuki and colleagues (2005) write that relationship-based group orientation is consistent with what we know about the Japanese **interdependent self**. Cognitive representations of the Japanese self are relational. Cognitive representations of the self in the West are far more independent. Western definitions of well-being cannot be applied to all other cultural groups.

Well-being means different things to different groups (Brewer & Yuki, 2007). Identification with the status of an in-group that is compared favorably with those of other in-groups is correlated with well-being and high self-esteem in U.S. samples. The group is a buffer against social isolation. In contrast, East Asian samples show something quite different. Maintaining harmony and cooperation within an in-group is correlated with self-esteem. Collective self-esteem associated with in-group status is not correlated with personal well-being.

At the beginning of this section I raised the issues of discrimination and trust/cooperation. Understanding social identity from a cultural perspective allows us to make some predictions about others' behaviors. *Before we can promote more global cooperation, we must understand how people are likely to act in different situations.*

Are there differences between discriminatory behavior between persons with relational social identity and categorical social identity? The answer is yes. Everyone prefers in-groups to out-groups, but there are cultural differences in how this works. The studies testing these ideas use a **minimal groups format**. Minimal groups have arbitrary categorical distinctions that are depersonalized. It was found that Japanese show in-group favoritism in these experiments *only* when they received cues that everyone in the study was doing the same reward allocation task, making them consider what outsiders were doing. This means that they used relationships to make judgments.

Cultural differences in trusting and cooperating has implications for understanding how social, political, and economic organizations work.

## Two research studies on culture and SIT/SCT

Yuki and colleagues (2005) ran two cross-cultural quasi-experiments testing differences in trusting in-groups and out-groups. The authors believed that all people value in-groups and make distinctions between in-groups and out-groups; they just do it differently.

Both experiments defined trust as "an expectation of beneficent treatment from others in uncertain or risky situations" (p. 50). Both experiments compared U.S. and Japanese university students in three types of depersonalized trust scenarios *before* the participants knew how the other person had acted. One scenario used someone from an in-group. The second used someone defined as part of an out-group, but for which there was a suggestion that there was a potential, though not actual, connection between the out-group member and the participant through an acquaintance. The third was an out-group member with no potential connection to the participant.

It was predicted that both U.S. and Japanese participants would trust the in-group member the most and would trust those in out-groups the least. In addition, differences in why the groups were accepted would relate to culture. U.S. participants were predicted to use categories and Japanese participants were predicted to use relational needs as the primary basis for deciding trust.

Experiment #1 asked 171 male and female Ohio State University students, 171 male and female Hokkaido University students, and 28 male and female Hokkaido Education University students to fill out a questionnaire. Participants had to decide whether to trust an unknown person based on minimal information in different scenarios using the three in-groups and out-groups defined above. The three scenarios were about asking someone to watch luggage in an airport, allowing someone to borrow money at a restaurant, and buying concert tickets online from an individual. The questionnaires were given to participants in their native languages. **Back translation** verified that the Japanese version of the questionnaire had the same meaning as the English original.

Results confirmed the hypothesis that both U.S. and Japanese participants trusted the unknown person from the in-group significantly more than they trusted either out-group person. However, there were differences in trusting the potentially connected and the unconnected out-group member. The Japanese sample was more likely to trust the out-group member if that person had a potential connection to them. In contrast, the U.S. sample did not trust either out-group member, even if the person had a potential connection.

Study #1 had weaknesses that needed clarification. First, the pattern should be replicated in another study. Second, it was not originally predicted that Japanese participants would accept an out-group with a potential link over an unconnected out-group member. Would another study find the same thing? Third, measuring trust outside of a real risky situation might not be meaningful enough for accurate results.

Experiment #2 addressed all three weaknesses. It replicated the first study. In addition, it used a real money allocation game to test trust in an authentic risky situation where participants were told that they would receive money based on their decisions to trust unknown others. The in-group was a person identified as someone attending the same university. The out-group member with a potential connection was identified as someone attending another university where the participant knew someone. The out-group member with no potential connection was identified as someone attending another university where the participant knew no one.

Participants were 146 male and female students from Ohio State University and 122 male and female students from Hokkaido University.

Participants were told that they were part of a real-time online money allocation game. In actuality, the computer never connected them to an online game. It was rigged for the specific conditions of the experiment. Subjects were told that they would be making some decisions with other OSU/Hokkaido University students or with students from other colleges. The decision was how to divide up 11 U.S. dollars, or Yen 1300, between two people. Further, participants were told that the computer would randomly assign one participant the role of deciding who received the money (the allocator) and the other person would be assigned to receive the money (the recipient). The allocator would decide how much money to keep and how much to give to the recipient. There were no rules dictating that any particular amount was to be allocated to any person. In reality, the computer was rigged to always select the other person as the allocator. *The real participant was always assigned the role of recipient and had to decide whether to trust the other unknown person.* Participants were given a choice to either accept a smaller amount of money, 3 U.S. dollars, or Yen 400, a sure thing, or to allow the other person to allocate the larger amount as desired. The dependent variable was either trusting or not trusting the unknown person in each of three conditions. The computer randomly selected either person from the in-group, the potentially connected out-group member, or the unconnected out-group member for the first trial. After the first trial, participants were told that the final amount of money they received was to be determined by a random selection of their decision to trust or not trust from three total trials.

At the end of their participation, subjects filled out a questionnaire that asked about their identification with the in-group. This extra information allowed researchers to correlate trust with being a U.S. participant or a Japanese participant. Subjects were then debriefed about the true nature of the study.

Results showed that the U.S. students trusted the in-group far more than either type of out-group. A significant difference was found between in-group trusting and both out-groups, but no significant difference was found between the trusting of both out-groups. In contrast, Japanese students trusted the in-group and potentially connected out-group far more than the unconnected out-group. No significant difference was found between trusting an in-group and a potentially connected out-group. However, a significant difference was found between trusting the potentially connected and the unconnected out-group.

The results of experiment #2 *replicated* the findings of experiment #1.

In addition to the experimental results, correlations were calculated to see if U.S. and Japanese participants had *different reasons for trusting groups*. U.S. participants had greater identification with an in-group that strongly correlated with their likelihood to trust someone. In contrast, Japanese identification with a group was correlated with the extent to which they felt an indirect connection with a depersonalized group. These correlations are consistent with the theory that East Asians are more likely to make judgments about groups based on relational needs and Americans are more likely to make judgments about depersonalized groups based on categories.

*The authors conclude that cultural differences exist in in-group processing.* Trusting in-groups is the result of different psychological processes, either categorization- or relationship-oriented.

The second experiment has limitations. Watch overgeneralizing the results; university students are not representative of all people. While the research fits into a larger body of research on other Western and eastern countries, future research should measure trust decisions when two people mutually share information about the situation, as opposed to when only one person has information about a situation. Last, the authors wondered why it was more *adaptive* for Americans to perceive in-groups as more trustworthy than a potentially connected out-group member and why it was more adaptive for Japanese persons to find a potential connection with another. *How these differences evolved and how they are advantageous to survival will help us understand why people from different cultures have different points of view.*

## General conclusions about social identity

We can conclude from this entire discussion of social identity theory that the cognitive processing behind group processing is culturally dependent and that social identity must be thought of in a cultural context. The type of social identity one has with in-groups and out-groups is adaptive to the conditions in which people evolved, which ties social identity to the biological level of analysis.

## 5.15 Explain Social Learning Theory, Making Reference to Two Relevant Studies

### Why is social learning theory important?

Social learning theory spans all three levels of analysis and is fundamental to being human. Social learning explains how culture is transmitted to children, explains the cognitive mediation of reinforcement, and is clearly tied to the biological level of analysis through the **cultural acquisition device** (CAD) and **mirror neurons**.

You must understand social learning theory because it is tied to so many other areas of the syllabus.

Albert Bandura is the representative theorist. Social learning theory is a very current explanation of behavior with more strengths than weaknesses.

The Bobo experiments are popular with teachers and students and I review two of them in depth. However, *social learning is not just about Bobo.*

Bandura may be the most cited researcher in the history of psychology. This may be true and I can see why. Social learning theory applies to a wide range of human behaviors. These include mental disorders such as depression, phobias, and eating disorders, education, aggression and delinquency, moral behavior, gender roles and identity, health psychology, sport psychology, careers and organizational psychology, culture and behavior, language, and terrorism. Large amounts of research support social learning theory; it has method, observer, time, space, and combined levels of **triangulation**.

Social learning research about language, depression, and aggression is reviewed in this book.

### Note to the teacher

> You can find a large number of Bandura's original articles at www.des.emory.edu/ mfp/BanduraPubs.html.

### Three key concepts

Three key concepts are important to know. **Modeling** was the focus of Bandura's earliest research. Modeling means to observe the actions of another person, form an idea of how one should behave, and use the ideas as a guide for future behavior (Bandura, 1977). **Self-efficacy**, the belief that one is capable of starting and carrying through a required action, was added a little later. **Moral disengagement**, when someone abandons a moral belief, helps explain terrorism. All three are important in understanding modern uses of social learning theory.

### Social learning theory has a cultural context

Social learning theory is *situated* in a **cultural** context. Modeling and self-efficacy unfold within cultures. Social cognitive theory explains how people grow and change in all cultures (Bandura, 2002). Bandura cautions cross-cultural researchers not to simply view humans as falling into extreme categories such as **individualism** and **collectivism**. Bandura's warning is similar to what Triandis said about the individual and the dimensions of culture; individuals have access to both ends of the continuum. In fact, *self-efficacy is often incorrectly associated just with individualistic cultures* (Bandura, 2002). Successful behavior that adapts to the demands of any culture requires a combination of personal, proxy, and collective **agency**.

Agency means to intentionally influence one's personal and life circumstances. Personal agency is one's own actions. Proxy agency means that one more capable than the individual is selected to guide others' behavior. Collective agency means that people do not behave in a vacuum; they pool together to achieve what they cannot do alone. The *degree* to which these three types of agency exist varies from culture to culture. *Self-efficacy is the key ingredient to agency at all three levels.* "Although efficacy beliefs have generalized functional value, how they are developed and structured, the ways in which they are exercised, and the purposes to which they are put, vary cross-culturally" (p. 273). A large amount of research applies self-efficacy to cultural differences. One example reviewed in this book is about depression and self-efficacy.

## Social learning theory is bidirectional

Bandura frequently uses the term **bidirectional**. Bandura believes in biological predispositions for behavior, such as genes for aggression and an innate capacity for language, but *emphasizes modeling and self-efficacy in a cultural context as the greatest determinants of behavior.* Genes do not directly cause aggression and having innate grammar does not account for how we learn to *use* the grammar. Even in 1977, Bandura wrote that, although extremists existed for both environmental and the biological explanations of behavior, he thought that it was "widely acknowledged that experiential and physiological influences interact in subtle ways to determine behavior and therefore are not easily separable" (p. 16).

## Should we have animal or human research?

Bandura (1973) is critical of using animals in research. Human experiments are necessary because the determinants of behavior are *not the same across species.* In addition, experiments are the only way to see the actual causes of behavior. However, results from controlled experiments should be similar to naturalistic and longitudinal studies before the experiments are accepted.

## Why is social learning theory different from cognitive theory and Skinnerian psychology?

One reason social learning theory is different from cognitive theory is that it focuses on the mental processing of reinforcement. Reinforcement plays a strong role in social learning. *Reinforcement is a generic term.* Social learning reinforcement is not the same as the Skinnerian concepts of positive and negative reinforcement in operant conditioning. Bandura identified numerous types of reinforcement, such as vicarious and self-reinforcement, that relate to symbolic processing. Avoid statements such as "a behavior is due to reinforcement" in essays. Be specific in your word choice. What do you mean by operant conditioning or social learning?

In addition, social learning theorists believe that *self-efficacy is the greatest predictor of behavior, downplaying or even modifying biology.* **Gender** and **culture** affects self-efficacy that in turn affects the **anticipation of reinforcement**. Cognitive psychologists assume that biology is an important determinant of behavior that is closely intertwined with the cognitive processes they study. Cognitive psychologists assume a very important biological basis for the cognitive processes they study, often including biology as too closely intertwined in mental processing the be downplayed.

Bandura's theories on the mental processing of reinforcement are a radical departure from Skinner's operant conditioning. Bandura (1977) says that humans are far too complex to fall under the forces of operant conditioning.

Bandura says that operant conditioning best explains the simple behaviors of animals, which is the kind of evidence that Skinner provided. Humans have a great deal to learn and mistakes can be costly, *so our survival depends on a shorter form of learning.* Humans do not learn about cultural traditions or the dangers of the world through trial and error. "One does not teach children to swim, adolescents to drive, and novice medical students to perform surgery by having them discover the appropriate behavior through the consequences of their successes and failures" (Bandura, 1977, p. 12). The transmission of culture would be hard if members of a cultural group learned about traditions only through trial and error; *models demonstrate appropriate cultural behavior.* A cultural group's language is an example of something so complex that it *cannot* be fully acquired without modeling.

## The basics of social learning: Modeling and self-efficacy

Modeling occurs through four processes, **attention**, **retention**, **reproduction**, and **motivation**.

1. A child pays attention to a model. In Bobo experiment #1, on modeling and aggression, the models were an adult live model, a film of an adult model, or a film of a cartoon character model. The children attended to how the models verbally and physically behaved toward the Bobo doll.

2. Children retain the observations for later use. Retention, or *learning,* was measured by asking the children to repeat the scenes they observed. Both male and female children displayed what they saw.

3. Children's behavior in spontaneous play tested the reproduction of what the children observed. Bandura said that children learn behaviors that are not necessarily reproduced unless the behaviors receive reinforcement. While both male and female children showed that they retained the same behaviors, boys reproduced the aggressive behaviors in spontaneous play far more often than the girls.

4. The motivation is the *anticipated consequences* for reproducing the modeled behaviors. According to social learning theorists, boys receive rewards more often for using aggression than girls. This is the explanation for why boys produce the aggression.

Young children start off **imitating** adult behavior, and their accuracy depends largely on the model's reactions. If young children do not have reinforcement easily available to them, their ability to imitate quickly declines (Bandura, 1977). *Young children without symbolic* **language** *cannot easily store information cognitively for later use and rely on trial and error to learn what to do.*

As children acquire abstract reasoning, they become capable of **delayed imitation** (Bandura, 1977). This is the start of *modeling as the cognitive processing of reinforcement.* Now children use verbal symbols to acquire and retain observed behavior. *Language is the primary way that children model once they have representational thought.* Social learning occurs rapidly once children are able to store and creatively use modeled behavior through verbal symbols.

This is more evidence that language is fundamental to human behavior.

The **anticipation of reinforcement** is a key to explaining which behaviors are actually *performed* in a cultural group. Bandura (1977) discussed two general types of anticipated reinforcement, **extrinsic** and **intrinsic**.

Extrinsic reinforcements are external and arbitrarily associated with a behavior. **External reinforcement** is extrinsic and is socially arranged. Examples of external reinforcement are receiving pay for a job or a car for getting good grades. External reinforcements are successful in reducing many unwanted behaviors, such as **asthma** attacks, **eating disorders**, **aggression**, and **psychosomatic complaints** (Bandura, 1977).

Intrinsic reinforcement is a little harder to understand but applicable to much of the research on social learning. There are many examples of intrinsic reinforcement. If you slip on icy steps, the consequences are external but naturally related (rather than being arbitrarily related) to the behavior and you are more careful in the future. Bandura calls this being regulated by sensory effects. A second type of intrinsic reinforcement is when your sensory effects are internal. During **meditation**, the relaxation you feel is intrinsically motivating and occurs within you. A third kind of intrinsic reinforcement occurs when a person makes a self-judgment about his or her own behavior. You appraise the reinforcement internally, but the motivators for the evaluations are arbitrary. Bandura wrote a lot about **sport psychology** and here is one example where it relates to social learning. A soccer player who spends hours perfecting a skill uses internal self-appraisals but eventually gets the external rewards of an improved performance that helps the team.

Two types of reinforcement are important that regulate behavior extrinsically and intrinsically.

**1. Vicarious reinforcement.** When you see something happen to another person, you process the information and learn from their successes and failures. Vicarious reinforcement is both external and extrinsic. The Bobo experiments demonstrate vicarious reinforcement in the lab. A model rewarded for a behavior is more effective than modeling without a reward. Second, if a model goes unpunished for an undesirable behavior, it increases similar acts in the observer. Third, the vicarious viewing of punished behavior reduces similar acts by the observer. **Symbolic learning**, such as viewing television models, falls under this category. Symbolic learning is one explanation of **phobias**. Monkeys with no prior fear of snakes can develop a fear after viewing a video of monkeys showing fear of snakes (Zinbarg & Mineka, 2000). Girls have been found to model low efficacy of female **math** models (Bandura, 1997). In humans, vicarious reinforcement depends on specific variables, such as the characteristics of the models, the intensity of the consequences, and the ability of the model to justify behavior (Bandura, 1977).

**2. Self-reinforcement**, sometimes called self-generated reinforcement. Much self-reinforcement is intrinsic. The idea behind self-reinforcement is that human behavior is not bound to external reinforcements (Bandura, 1977). People hold firm beliefs that are not easily changed. "Because of their symbolizing and self-reactive capacities, humans are less dependent upon immediate external support for their behavior" (p. 129). Self-regulation is the motivation for much human behavior. Humans have standards of behavior that we model from adults and then we use self-appraisals to judge the quality of our behaviors. Each new behavior is judged against previous behavior. Think of all the behavior we self-regulate, such as school performance, sport performance, gender-role expectations, what is gained in an aggressive or immoral act, or even how terrorists judge the value of a mission.

**Self-efficacy** is important to understanding how humans anticipate reinforcement. Bandura (1997) defines self-efficacy as the "beliefs in one's capabilities to organize and execute the courses of action required to produce given attainments" (p. 3). Highly perceived self-efficacy to follow through on a behavior is related to the performance of both prosocial behaviors and antisocial behaviors. For example, one purpose of schools is to promote high self-efficacy for achievement through teacher models with high self-efficacy for their own understanding of a subject. However, criminals can have high efficacy in their ability to follow through with an antisocial aggressive act.

Gender and culture affect self-efficacy that in turn affects the anticipation of reinforcement. This is a powerful generalization that explains a wide variety of behavior, such as academic abilities, depression, and delinquency.

## Strengths and limitations of social learning theory

### Strengths

1. It has cultural relevance.

2. It has a bidirectional focus.

3. Social learning theory is current; it is even related to biology through the CAD and mirror neurons. Social learning theorists place their emphasis on anticipating reinforcements and self-efficacy as predictors of behavior, factors that modify biology.

4. Bandura used humans in experiments, downplaying animal models as valid for studying humans. This was an advance over theories using animals.

5. Another strong point is the varied research methods and strong triangulation. Social learning theory has method, observer, space, time, and combined levels of triangulation.

6. Social learning research is highly ethical. Even experiments on self-efficacy are ethical, as experiment participants are those with pre-existing low efficacy or efficacy is assessed through in survey studies where there is no manipulation of results. All participants in mental health experiments are worked with until their self-efficacy levels rise. I challenge the criticism that the Bobo studies were unethical. I discuss ethics of the Bobo experiments later in this section. Did participating in the studies really create harm or does it just seem as if it did?

7. Social learning offers explanations of many human behaviors.

### Limitations: They are much harder to find!

1. Social learning theory does not explain certain kinds of behaviors. For example, grammar is something we come biologically equipped with at birth to acquire, though Bandura believes that models help with the learning of grammar. In addition, social learning explanations of mental illness emphasize disorders such as depression, anxiety, and eating disorders. Social learning is not the primary focus of autism and schizophrenia explanations. In these cases, damage to the brain may *affect* social learning, such as recent discoveries about mirror neurons and the inability of autistics to socially learn but are not primary causes.

2. Sometimes students write that the Bobo experiments are artificial and lack population and ecological validity. I put this under limitations only because students often write this on exams, but I challenge the argument that artificiality is a criticism. *Lab experiments are supposed to be artificial.* In addition, modeling research is not method bound; the experiments fit into a wider body of research using other methods. Any *one* experiment lacks ecological validity but Bandura does not make claims based on *one* experiment.

## Mirror neurons: What the brain does during social learning

Mirror neuron research probably applies to all social learning experiences and is likely the biology behind social learning theory. **Mirror neurons** appear to fire automatically during social learning so we should care about the content of television, movies, and video games. Parenting and teaching take on even more importance in light of mirror neuron research.

Mirror neurons keep popping up in studies I read and may be fundamentally important to being human.

Approximately 25% to 30% of juvenile offenders say that they have attempted crimes seen in media (Huesmann & Kirwil, 2007). For example, "A 7-year-old in Texas has been watching wrestling on television when he turns away from the TV and, mimicking a move he has just seen, runs at his 3-year-old brother with his arm extended, hits him in the neck, and kills him" (p. 555).

It is no surprise that **aggression** is popular with students. We are all fascinated and perplexed with why people imitate media. While there are important genetic predispositions to aggression, much of it is socially learned. Violent copycat crimes occur *shortly after witnessing violence* (Huesmann & Kirwil, 2007). Media prime the imitation. But a level of analysis approach tells us that there is more to the story. Something must happen in the brain that affects the mind during social learning. Cultural values mediate the entire process. While the brain is important, the Bobo experiments and related ethnographies show that children do not act aggressively when taught not to do so. The good news is that parents can act as inhibitors to aggression.

Neurons and neural networks are explained in introductory texts. New research adds to our knowledge about neuron systems. The discovery of mirror neurons in the mid 1990s may be the biological basis of social learning. The first experiments showed that mirror neurons fire in the premotor cortex of monkeys when they performed hand actions, when they saw another perform hand actions, and when they heard the sound of a task they had experienced, such as the sound of paper tearing (Dobbs, 2006). We now know that human mirror neurons are more numerous and complicated than those in monkeys. In addition to firing in the premotor cortex, human mirror neurons fire in brain areas related to language, such as **Broca's area**.

Primates and humans imitate hand movements from early life. The hitting and grabbing that children observe from media sources are similar to all of the other motor functions imitated in mirror neuron experiments (Huesmann & Kirwil, 2007). In addition, research shows that babies imitate facial expressions. Facial expressions appear linked to one's emotions. Psychologists think that imitating another's facial expression automatically activates emotions that then activate **schemas** and **scripts** about how to behave.

Mirror neurons are part of our theme about humans living together in cultures. Social learning is one category of the cultural acquisition device (CAD), so mirror neurons help explain how humans develop cultures. As social learning is an **etic**, it is likely an evolutionary adaptation. V.S. Ramachandran (no date) believes that human cultural inheritance "characterizes our species and liberates us from the constraints of a purely gene based evolution" (p. 5).

Marco Iacoboni and colleagues (2005) write that scientists are learning more all the time about the functions of mirror neurons. Early monkey experiments show that mirror neurons are active in recognizing others' actions, showing *what* mirror neurons do. For example, "John sees Mary grasp an apple" (p. 1). Studies now show that mirror neurons help humans understand others' **intentions**, *why* another is doing an action. For example, why is Mary grasping the apple? Perhaps she will eat it or throw it. *Context* is necessary for understanding others' intentions. If Mary has a scowl on her face, she may throw the apple.

Iacoboni and colleagues designed a correlation study to see how mirror neurons networks helped in decoding another's intentions.

Participants were 23 right-handed males and females with an average age of 26.3. They were recruited from newspaper ads.

This study used repeated measures. Participants watched three movie clips showing context alone, action alone, and then context with actions (the intentions clips). A blank resting screen appeared between each clip. The context movie showed two pictures of a tea service, one before tea and the other after tea. The action movie featured a coffee mug on a blank background and a person either grasping it with the entire hand or just on the handle. The intention movie showed both types of grasping interspersed in the before and after tea clips.

The action- and context-only movies did not contain information that allowed participants to infer intention. Some participants were told to just watch the clips and others were told to pay attention to the grasping and try and decide what the intention was.

**Functional MRI** scans recorded brain activity in all conditions, including the resting time. Brain areas were correlated with watching the different clips and with the instructions given to only watch the movies or to pay attention to the intentions.

More neural activity was recorded when participants watched all three movie clips over the resting time. The most important scans examined differences between the intention condition and the action/context conditions. There was no difference between the scans of those told to just watch the clips and those told to pay attention to the intentions. Both groups showed an understanding of the intentions when debriefed. Understanding another's intentions is automatic, activating the left frontal lobes of everyone. The differences occurred between the intention clip and the other two. Reading another's intentions activates neurons in the interior frontal cortex, an area known to have mirror neurons.

The authors concluded that mirror neurons are active when decoding another's intentions. This is not a cause-and-effect experiment; it just shows that certain brain parts are active at the same time a person is doing a different task. The study is important because it is the first evidence that specific neurons fire when someone tries to figure out what another is doing, a process called "logically related neurons" (Iacobani et al., 2005, p.5). Motor neurons fire in chains that are logically related to each other.

V. S. Ramachandran (no date) believes "that mirror neurons will do for psychology what DNA did for biology; they will provide a unifying framework and help explain a host of mental abilities that have hitherto remained mysterious and inaccessible to experiments" (p. 1). Ramachandran thinks that mirror neurons are a key ingredient for explaining language evolution. Mirror neurons might be responsible for humans being able to understand the gestures of others that then provided the chance for language to evolve. One case of an autistic child shows that his mirror neurons do not fire properly. Ramachandran expects that mirror neuron theory will help explain and possibly treat the problems that people with **autism** have understanding and empathizing with others.

## Aggression and social learning explanations: An introduction

Albert Bandura makes many contributions to explanations of **aggression**. I review modeling, self-efficacy, and moral disengagement in each of the next three sections.

Bandura emphasizes the social determinants of behavior over biological predispositions. Bandura believes there is too much emphasis on the biology of aggression (Bandura, 2001). "People possess the biological potential for aggression, but the answer to the cultural variation in aggressiveness lies more in ideology than in biology" (p. 20).

## Bobo study #1: Aggression—learning versus performance

The Bobo studies are popular; they are experiments from the 1960s showing how normal children model aggression. Each Bobo experiment has a specific purpose. In addition, criticisms about the ethics and the artificial nature of the Bobo studies require some investigation.

One purpose of modeling research is to show *the difference between learning aggression and actually performing it* (Bandura, 1973). One of the Bobo experiments examined "the hypothesis that reinforcements administered to a model influence the performance but not the acquisition" of behavior (Bandura, 1965, p. 589). Even today, the implications of these findings are great. It is important to Bandura that the theory be tested in tightly controlled experiments *before* it is applied. This particular Bobo experiment confirms that children only perform what they learn in the presence of reinforcement. The experiment fits into a larger body of research that includes observations from cultural psychologists and anthropologists.

Experiment participants were 33 boys and 33 girls from the Stanford Nursery School between the ages of 42 and 71 months. Participants were randomly assigned to one of three groups and each group contained males and females. A female administered the study and the models were males.

Children were tested individually. The female experimenter told the children she had some work to do before going to the "surprise playroom," but that the child could watch a television show while waiting. The film showed a man ordering the Bobo doll to move. When the Bobo doll did not move, the model used four *novel* physical and verbal types of aggression against it. One example was that the model "pummeled it on the head with a mallet. Each response was accompanied by the verbalization, "Sockeroo... stay down" (p. 590–591). In the first condition, the model was rewarded with verbal praise and food treats for showing aggression to the Bobo doll. In the second condition, the model was punished with a scolding for showing aggression to the Bobo doll. In the third condition, a model received no consequences.

Two people collected data for the experiment using observation. It is a mistake to think of the Bobo experiments as observation studies. Observation was a technique used to gather the experimental data.

To test for *performance,* observers watched as the children were brought into the "surprise playroom" right after they saw the model. The room contained a variety of toys, including anything used by the model against the Bobo doll. Each child spent 10 minutes in the playroom with the Bobo doll and toys and did whatever they wished during the time. Observers recorded behavior every 5 seconds. Rater reliability between the observers was 99% correct.

To test for *learning,* the experimenter next entered the room with juice and booklets of stickers. The children were instructed that for each modeled verbal and physical behavior they demonstrated, they would receive a sticker and juice.

Results showed that the performance of modeled aggression was different than demonstrations of what was learned. Children seeing a model rewarded or receiving no consequences modeled more aggression than those seeing the model punished. A **gender difference** was found. Boys modeled aggression more than girls in all three conditions. There was especially a difference when the model was punished. Interestingly, boys performed a large amount of aggression even when the model was punished. However, gender differences disappeared when the children were asked to show what they learned. When given a positive incentive to show aggression, both males and females demonstrated what they learned.

Two important conclusions come from these results. First, learned behaviors are modeled only when they receive reinforcement. Second, the models acted as *disinhibitors* for the boys far more than the girls, reflecting the differences in reinforcement that males and females receive for aggression throughout their lives from models.

## Why was it important to study aggression in a lab experiment?

The Bobo experiments are tightly controlled lab experiments where the researchers have full control over the independent variable. Students frequently have two criticisms about the experiments. One is that the experiments are too artificial. The second is that the experiments lack ecological validity. Ecological validity is the extent to which the conditions of the investigation can be generalized outside of the study. But are these valid criticisms?

Experiments are too often criticized for investigating exactly what people wish to know—the cause of behavior (Bandura, 1973). Experiments pinpoint specific causes. Cause cannot be known from naturalistic observations or from correlations. Lab conditions hold one variable constant while others are manipulated. Criticisms that experiments are artificial reflect a misunderstanding of how knowledge advances. "Experiments are not intended to duplicate events as they occur in real life, and they would lose their value if they did" (p. 63). Theories are tested in the lab, not real life. As a funny example, Bandura points out that airline travelers do not rely on actual flights to determine the safety of new airplane designs. New airplanes are first tested in labs. Once a cause is established in a lab, it can be tested in the field. Results of lab experiments should be consistent with other types of research. This same idea applies to interpreting all tightly controlled experiments. Look to see if the experiment has **method triangulation**. If so, then its lack of ecological validity is diluted.

In addition to these two criticisms, many are concerned about the novel behaviors used by the models, saying that the novel behaviors are different from what the children know. However, the experimental design *deliberately* used novel behaviors. Novel behaviors act as controls for previous learning. Prior aggressive behavior *confounds* the experiment. Criticisms that the novel behaviors taught to children do not reflect their real-life aggression are superficial. The intent was to see if the child modeled the model's behaviors. The novel behaviors may not reflect what the children do in real life but testing real life was not the purpose of the experiment. The experiment meant to predict the conditions under which someone would perform aggression. Again, experiments must be artificial in order to test a theory. No one should make a claim based on the results of one experiment. Alone, an experiment lacks ecological validity. Poor ecological validity is not as much of a problem the study is placed within a larger body of research.

## Are the Bobo experiments unethical?

Two ethical issues to consider are *potential harm* and *removing adverse effects*. Critics claim that the children were harmed because they were exposed to novel forms of aggression that they did not already know. In addition, the children might continue to perform the aggression. Here are some things to consider. The sample used normal children, not delinquents or those at risk for delinquency. The parents were likely to act as inhibitors of aggression. Even if they learned it, did they perform it? There is no evidence that the children continued to use the aggressive behaviors modeled in the experiments. Watch having an automatic response that the Bobo studies were unethical.

With this said about artificiality and ethics, here is another Bobo experiment.

## Bobo study #2: Aggression—the effect of symbolic modeling on behavior

The experiment investigated the effect of symbolic models on behavior. Bandura (1973) writes that humans do not learn simply through direct experiences in daily life. Instead, much of our modeling is vicarious, or through symbols given symbolic value. Symbolic modeling has the potential to account for large amounts of social learning.

Forty-eight boys and 48 girls from the Stanford Nursery School were randomly assigned to one of three conditions experimental conditions, a live model, a film model of a real person, and a cartoon model. The live model condition and the film model condition used both a male and female. Each model showed physical and verbal aggression to a Bobo doll. Control subjects observed either a nonaggressive model or no model. Each participant group contained half males and half females. Participants were equally allocated to the conditions based on ratings of their baseline aggressive interactions at the school to ensure that participant variables did not affect the results. A female conducted the experiment.

Each participant was tested individually in a playroom. The children sat a table containing many toys. The live model was escorted into the room after the child and given a separate play table. After a minute, the live model turned to the Bobo doll and spent the rest of the 10-minute time period behaving aggressively toward the doll. The film of the live model and the cartoon model performed the same aggressive acts as the live model, such as kicking it around the room and tossing it in the air, saying, "Sock him in the nose" or "Kick him." The cartoon model was a female dressed as a black cat similar to popular cartoon figures. The space was made to look like a cartoon with artificial grass and a backdrop of trees and birds.

Next, the participants were tested for modeled aggression in a different room. The goal of the experiment required that the children display *delayed* modeling, as it was thought that a model's greatest influence on aggression occurred in later situations, when the use of the behavior was beneficial. To achieve this effect, participants were taken to a room that contained toys and told they could play. Quickly though, the experimenter interrupted the play, saying that those toys were really reserved for other children but another set of toys could be played with in another room. Each child was then escorted to another playroom and they could play with a variety of toys, including both nonaggressive toys and those used in the model's behavior toward the Bobo doll. Observations of 20 minutes of play were gathered by independent raters, coded as imitative (including strikes with the mallet), partially imitative, mallet aggression (actually aggression with objects other than the mallet), nonimitative aggression, and aggressive gun play.

As predicted, seeing aggressive models increased a child's aggression. Mildly frustrating the children by interrupting their play ensured that researchers were testing delayed aggression. Children seeing a nonaggressive model showed the least amount of aggression toward the Bobo doll. Females showed less overall aggression than males. Children in all three experimental conditions modeled aggression significantly more than both control groups. Of the three experimental conditions, the children modeled the most aggression from the films of the human model, including more gun and mallet aggression, suggesting that film models are important teachers of aggression.

## Ethnographies support Bandura's Bobo experiments

The differences between learning and performance and the importance of symbolic modeling are applicable to considering **cultural** differences in aggression. Experimental results about the social modeling of aggression are confirmed with ethnographies. *Societies that value and reinforce aggression display more aggression.*

Bandura (1973) writes that the Dugum Dani of New Guinea is an aggressive society. Many of their social and religious practices surround warfare. Children are carefully prepared to take part in planned aggressive displays on specially prepared battlefields. The Dani believe that spirits have the ability to cause damage and sickness in a family unless the family takes the life of an enemy. So warfare is started and maintained by a fear that one has not avenged the spirits. Families are known to even amputate the fingers of female children in order to further console the spirits. Male children go through elaborate war game training. For example, boys fight with grass blades that are not sharp enough to cause injury but mimic the skills needed for battle.

In contrast, the Polynesians of the Society Islands do not value aggression and actively discourage its use. Tahitians are slow to become angry and get over it quickly. They use verbal aggression more than physical aggression. Parents discourage aggression. Verbal aggression typically receives no consequences so that it does not continue. The strongest deterrent for aggression probably comes from the Polynesian belief that sickness and accidents are punishment from spirits for past actions.

The Bobo experiments and the cross-cultural ethnographies show that modeling is important in aggression. But modeling is just one several factor explaining aggressive behavior.

## Aggression: The role of self-efficacy

**Peer groups** are important places for children to "broaden and validate self-efficacy" (Bandura, 1997, p. 173). Children have a greater risk for using aggression in peer groups when they have high self-efficacy beliefs to use and carry out aggressive acts. In addition, children are at greater risk for delinquency when they generalize aggressive behavior learned from parent models to peer groups and other relationships.

Children have different beliefs about their ability to carry out either prosocial or antisocial acts. *Self-efficacy is a mediator of self-attributions to carry our prosocial or antisocial behaviors.* High self-efficacy beliefs for prosocial behavior result in the use of peaceful means to achieve goals. In contrast, some children have high self-efficacy to use aggression to get what they want and believe they can successfully carry out these acts. These children are more likely to use aggression with peers. Children with low beliefs about their ability to carry out an aggressive act are unlikely to use aggression, even when faced with the hostile intentions.

Peer groups form around similar beliefs and interests. It is likely that children with high self-efficacy beliefs in their ability to use aggression to get what they want attract others with similar beliefs. The peer group then reinforces each other's behavior. Where does the aggression start? Children model much of their self-efficacy beliefs to start and carry out aggressive acts from parents. Parent models are more likely to use punishment and coercion to control children's behavior and are less likely to have positive interactions with their children. Power struggles result where the parents either give in or continue with the punishment until the child gives up. Children generalize their way of handling relationships to relationships outside of the family, including peers.

## Aggression: Terrorism and social learning

### Note to the teacher

> It is well worth the time to consider some causes of terrorism and the challenges of a solution. It takes several days to complete this activity. First, each student finds something that interests them about terrorism in the media and brings it to class. We then share the information. Next, the class brainstorms questions about terrorism that a psychologist might be able to answer. Now we turn to Bandura's explanation. Students print out a copy of Bandura's 2004 writing "The Role of Selective Moral Disengagement in Terrorism and Counterterrorism" from www.des.emory.edu/mfp/BanduraPubs.html. Small groups find Bandura's answers to their questions. It is a humbling activity. Some students start out thinking that there are easy solutions to terrorism but quickly learn about its real complexities.

Bandura writes that one must **morally disengage** to commit a terrorist act.

We are agents of our own behavior, meaning that we judge our actions as right or wrong against certain standards and self-regulate behavior accordingly (Bandura, 2001). These standards come from a variety of sources.

1. Personal ideals

2. Situational circumstances

3. The anticipation of reinforcement from others viewed as more capable. Sometimes we give **proxy control** for our behavior standards to another. Leaders determine accepted behavior in terrorist groups.

4. The anticipation of reinforcement from the larger cultural group. Bandura believes that a group's ideology maintains behavior far more than biology. Adults teach accepted standards to children early.

Humans are self-directed; we make choices to meet goals. Persons in both **individualist** and **collectivist** cultures are self directed, though the standards for choices vary. Moral standards primarily come from childhood teachings.

Morals are fairly stable over time. Core moral values that guide behavior do not change on a regular basis. This is why there must be moral disengagement for someone to commit a terrorist act.

Most of the research on moral disengagement examines military and political aggression (Bandura, 2004). Because of this limited focus, it may appear that moral disengagement happens only in extreme circumstances. In reality, moral disengagement is part of everyday life. Think of moral disengagement in terms of *degrees*. Terrorism is extreme disengagement, but moral disengagement also takes place in corporate misbehavior, politics, and personal relationships. There are plenty of examples where typically honest people further their own interests at the expense of others. Telling a lie to a friend, cheating on one's income taxes, or giving and accepting insider information about a company stock all require disengagement from moral beliefs against lying and cheating. Disengaging requires justifying the behavior, which Bandura calls **self-exonerations**.

People have the ability to choose humane behavior or inhumane behavior, even in the face of extreme circumstances (Bandura, 2001). There are many examples where even under severe pressure, many choose strongly held moral convictions to behave humanely, even receiving punishment for these actions. Deviating from core moral standards requires mental disengagement.

Committing terrorist acts that kill many people by blowing up buses or flying planes into buildings need *special training* that builds on childhood learning. Terrorist training includes morally justifying these actions (Bandura, 2004). For example, Bin Laden portrayed the attacks on the United States as a religious duty, a defensive jihad.

There are many ways to psychologically disengage (Bandura, 2001). They are part of everyday life as well as terrorist training. Again, these take place in *degrees*.

1. The behavior is cognitively restructured. Here are three examples of the process.
   a. The behavior is framed as socially or morally worthy.
   b. Euphemistic language makes the behavior seem appropriate. This means that words making an action seem inoffensive are substituted for distasteful words. Bandura (2004) uses the example of bombs being called "vertically deployed anti-personal devices." People are more likely to commit aggressive acts if the acts are called something else.
   c. **Advantageous comparisons** justify behavior by making a comparison with worse behavior. Here is an everyday example. My husband has justified watching television when I want it turned off by saying "I watch very little television compared to other husbands." At an extreme level, some terrorist groups feel they are less of a problem than other groups because they attack only military targets.

Bandura (2004) uses the example that terrorists sometimes minimize their cruelty by saying it is a way to end the worse cruelty of the existing government. Counterterrorist activities are often justified by claims that they must use violence to end the attacks of terrorists. Each side minimizes their cruelty and condemns the other side, citing their "just causes." It is a real dilemma for groups wanting to use military retaliation against a terrorist act. Moral disengagement must be high for citizens to support the policies.

2. A person lessens their personal responsibility for an action by displacing the responsibility.

3. A person minimizes or challenges the effects of their behavior on others.

4. The victim is dehumanized. Dehumanizing another involves giving them animal qualities or blaming them for bringing on their own suffering.

5. Terrorist activities sometimes have the support from legitimate organizations that may provide indirect support for the violence, such as providing financial assistance.

Bandura (2004) sees no quick fixes for terrorism. Solutions include addressing social situations that drive people to commit terrorist acts. For example, "Islamic terrorists come mainly from populations living in an environment of poverty, political oppression, gross inequities, illiteracy, and a paucity of (means a lack of) opportunities to improve their lives" (p. 150). Bandura writes that Islamic terrorists learned to value suicide bombing from early childhood. It is not easy to reverse values instilled in childhood.

## Modeling and language

**Language** is important to social learning in two ways. First, language is necessary for modeling; it is the primary mode of modeling retention in children with symbolic thinking. By age 3 or 4, children have progressed from using simple imitations to storing information for later creative use. Second, children may benefit from modeling the language use of more capable adults.

The acquisition of normal language is biologically based; social learning does not account for the evolved capacity that children have to acquire language. Dan Slobin (1968) wanted to know if the social learning process was helpful in some way to learning to use our biologically based language.

Slobin believes that the natural environment is the best place to study a child's spontaneous language after an exchange with an adult. Slobin used transcripts from a naturalistic study by Roger Brown and Ursula Bellugi in 1964 to test his ideas. The transcripts were from two children called Adam and Eve for the study. Exchanges between Adam and Eve and their parents were recorded between the ages of 18 months and 3 years in the home setting. Slobin studied the exchanges where a parent first expanded upon what the child said and then the child modeled these expansions in their own speech. Would the modeling of parental expansions benefit the child in some way? Adam and Eve had three possible ways of responding after the parent expanded on their speech. First, they could simply imitate. Second, they could reduce, or even shorten what was said. Third, they could add necessary words to the adult's sentence, such as an article or a pronoun. Here is an example from Slobin's research illustrating the third option. Adam and Eve used the third option more than the other two.

Child: "Pick 'mato."
Adult: "Picking tomatoes up?"
Child: "Pick 'mato up." (p. 171)

The modeling of parental expansions may be helpful to a child in learning to use language.

Slobin thinks that there is a *critical period* for the modeling of expansions. Modeling of expansions may be most beneficial when a child is in the *telegraphic phase,* when children use two-word phrases such as "cookie get." The benefits of modeling parental expansions taper off at 3, when children start constructing full sentence.

Do children learn to construct grammatical sentences without modeling? It is impossible to know because children are not raised without hearing adults use language. Cases of feral children who did not hear human language suggest that we do need to hear language from other humans. Perhaps there is an important role for modeling in activating evolved language capacities.

## Depression and social learning theory

This material is also relevant for section 7.9 on the etiologies of depression.

Everyone faces obstacles and experiences failures (Bandura, 1997). Why can some people manage obstacles and failures while others become depressed? Perceived self-efficacy is the key. *Self-efficacy is the mental mediator that pulls together all other cognitive and behavioral theories of depression.* Self-efficacy is the greatest determinant of how one manages cognitions and analyzes behavior.

Self-efficacy contributes to depression in four ways. First, social support is a big factor in stress **resilience**. To what extent does a person have the self-efficacy to build and maintain social support systems? Second, to what extent is a person able to turn off negative thoughts? Third, how does a person set and evaluate goals? Fourth, to what extent does a person judge their personal experiences in relation to the experiences of others?

Good social support is critical for coping effectively with stressors. "A sense of personal efficacy not only mediates the impact of social support on depression but also functions as a determinant of social support" (p. 158). People with high self-efficacy beliefs for creating and maintaining social support systems have a lower risk of depression. Social networks in turn enhance a person's self-efficacy. Others in a social network act as models for effective problem solving. Social networks are created; those with low self-efficacy are more isolated and at greater risk for depression. While most of the self-efficacy and depression research uses adults as subjects, some research on teenagers reveals why **gender differences** in coping with stressors become evident at puberty. Both male and female adolescents with depression report low self-efficacy to manage academic demands. However, females also report low efficacy to manage social relationships and in managing the self.

Depressed persons have lower self-efficacy to turn off negative thoughts than nondepressed persons. They realize that distractions from negative thoughts are beneficial but tend to use other negative thoughts as distractions. Depressed persons get into a cycle where one negative thought leads to another. Unfortunately, they are good at turning off positive thoughts. In addition, depressed persons tend to ruminate over setbacks. The time spent ruminating over failures is a predictor of both the severity and length of depression.

Depressed persons have trouble setting realistic goals. They are more likely to set vague, idealistic, and unattainable goals. When depressed persons fail to achieve goals, their motivation falls and their sad mood rises. Nondepressed persons set attainable specific goals, and when they fail, they have greater motivation to move forward more quickly.

Depressed persons frequently judge their performance against that of others and use the conclusions as evidence that they are worthless. Depressed persons are more likely to judge themselves against the successes of others without a realistic picture of how much effort another expended. Females are more likely than males to devalue themselves in relation to others.

Many studies on the etiology (contributing factors) of depression have found correlations between self-efficacy and depression. But some questions remain. Next, we will review a study clarifying the relationships between gender, culture, self-efficacy, relationship harmony, and depressed symptoms in adolescents.

Sylvia Chen and colleagues (2006) compared the etiology of depression in adolescents from the United States and Hong Kong. Data were gathered with questionnaires and analyzed with means, standard deviations, and correlations.

The authors write that both self-efficacy and good relationships are important to adolescent development. However, individualist cultures valuing an independent self emphasize one's personal self-efficacy and collectivist cultures valuing an interdependent self emphasize relationship harmony. The authors believed that different cultural values related to **individualism** or **collectivism** might make adolescents more sensitive to either self-efficacy or relationship harmony as an etiology for depression.

The authors predicted "that both self-efficacy and relationship harmony will significantly predict depressed symptoms in each of these two cultural groups, and that the pathway of self-efficacy to depression will be stronger among American adolescents, whereas that of relationship harmony will be stronger among Hong Kong adolescents" (p. 646).

The sample included 1171 Hong Kong (873 males, 898 females) and 501 U.S. (198 males, 303 females) participants from secondary school volunteers with an average age of 15. Questionnaires were completed during class time.

Three separate questionnaires measured the degree of self-efficacy, the degree of relationship harmony, and depressed symptoms.

The 10-item General Self-Efficacy Scale (GSE) measured perceived self-efficacy. "I can solve most problems if I invest the necessary effort" is one example of a question.

The scale used a 4-point Likert scale of "not at all true" to "exactly true."

The 5-item Interrelationship Harmony Inventory (IH) measured relationship harmony. "My parents and I have a harmonious relationship" is one example of a question. Students rated their responses on a scale of 1, very low, to 7, very high.

Self-reports about depression symptoms were obtained with an adapted Beck Depression Inventory (BDI) and its Chinese version. The BDI has tested well for cross-cultural **validity**, so it is a good choice to measure depressive symptoms. The BDI contains questions about how someone is feeling and participants rate themselves on a Likert scale from 0, "I do not feel sad," to 3, "I am so sad or unhappy that I can't stand it."

The results include the following:

1. The means showed that self-efficacy differed between males and females. Males had higher mean self-efficacy scores in both cultures.

2. Differences in mean scores were found between the two cultures in both self-efficacy and in family harmony, with the U.S. sample higher on both.

3. Culture was correlated to how participants became depressed (the two pathways). While self-efficacy was correlated with depression in both cultures, it was a stronger pathway for depression in the U.S. adolescents than it was for Hong Kong adolescents. However, both pathways supplemented the other in both samples, so future research should investigate the role of self-efficacy and relationship harmony in adolescent depression.

4. The authors believe that individualism and collectivism contributed to the differences found in self-efficacy and depressed mood. While no data were directly collected on individualism and collectivism, the results from Chen and colleagues are consistent with other research suggesting that personal capabilities and autonomy are more related to mood in individualistic cultures. Chen and colleagues speculate that other di-

mensions of culture could help explain the differences in pathways, such as **tightness**, **looseness**, the **independent self**, and the **interdependent self**.

It is typical that etiologies of mental illness in humans use correlations to analyze data. It would be unethical to create conditions that cause mental illness. This means that the variables are related and that no variable is known as a cause of depression.

## 5.16 Discuss the Use of Compliance Techniques

### Social influence is adaptive behavior

This section and the next two are unified under the study of **social influence**, or how interpersonal interactions shape the expected behaviors of a group (Fiske, 2004).

**Compliance**, **conformity**, and **obedience** are three general types of social influence and the five **core social motives** explain why people respond to them. For example, belonging needs make sure that we respond to others' requests. All three forms of social influence fit under the general theme of this book; humans evolved a **social intelligence** (section 3.5) that allowed us to live together in **cultures**. Without the ability to socially influence each other, we would not function well in groups. It is *adaptive* to belong to a group.

Cross-cultural research is one focus of new research investigating how social influence theories apply to everyone.

### What is compliance and what are some common techniques?

Compliance is "yielding to social pressure in one's public behavior, even though one's private beliefs may not have changed" (Matsumoto, 2008, p. 369).

Robert Cialdini and Brad Sagarin (2005) write that compliance techniques are used both professionally, in sales and fundraising, and in everyday life. *It is easiest to study compliance techniques through the behavior of compliance professionals and then generalize the knowledge to understanding how humans exert social influence over each other in everyday life.*

Compliance techniques socially evolved. The **evolution** of social influences ties social psychology to the biological level of analysis. Compliance professionals who use the techniques successfully prosper and survive, passing their success to the next generation.

Cialdini and Sagarin (2005) identify and analyze six psychological principles that organize compliance techniques.

1. **Reciprocity.** People are more likely to comply with requests from someone who has already done them a favor. Reciprocity served an evolutionary purpose. People could give away things without really giving them away because another person is likely to return the favor. The **door-in-the-face** concession is one variation where an extreme request is made, refused, and then the person makes a less demanding request, actually the real request.

2. **Social validation.** People are more likely to comply with persons who think and do things in a similar way. Looking for social validation frequently works, as we are correct much of the time when we look to others for guidance. In addition, it may be easier to get someone from a collectivist culture to comply.

3. **Commitment/consistency.** Humans want consistency and are more likely to comply with a request if they have already committed to a similar request. Leon Festinger studied how people struggle to keep consistency. Professionals use a variety of strategies

that capitalize on getting a person to comply to a request that is consistent with a previous commitment.

    a. **Foot-in-the-door** techniques involve a person making a small request that will surely be granted. The initial request is followed by a greater request. To remain consistent, the second request will likely be granted.

    b. **Bait-and-switch procedures** are sales strategies where one item is advertised but when a person arrives at the store, the item is no longer available. However, other items are available, often at a greater price.

    c. **Low-ball techniques** are part of sales pitches where an item is offered at a low amount, but when the customer agrees to purchase the item, suddenly there is some reason, perhaps a calculation error, that interferes with the initial low price. The person is likely to agree to purchase the item because of the initial commitment.

4. **Friendship/liking.** People are more likely to comply with requests from those who are liked. The point of this strategy is to get others to like you first. Tupperware is a company with success at using the friendship/liking strategy. Attractiveness, similarity, such as wearing the same types of clothing, giving compliments, having a previous relationship with a person, and using a similar type of communication are factors that increase the intensity of the friendship/liking strategy. **Gender differences** exist in the friendship/liking principle. Females are more likely to comply with a face-to-face request than an e-mail request. Males comply equally to either personal or e-mail requests.

5. **Scarcity.** If an item is perceived as scarce, people are more likely to try and get it. Scarce items are more attractive. We lose a sense of freedom if an item is unavailable so it is best to get it when obtainable. The **psychological reactance theory** explains that, when people perceive a freedom as limited, such as the ability to acquire a good, it becomes more desirable. The **limited number** and **deadline technique** are two sales strategies that use the scarcity principle.

6. **Authority.** Requests from legitimate authority figures are more likely to be followed. Sales professionals benefit from describing themselves as experts in a field. Stanley Milgram was successful in getting people to comply to obedience demands because he appeared an authority; the man in the white coat.

At what point is the use of compliance techniques unethical? *Most uses of the strategies are probably ethical, as they are an adaptive part of living in groups.* However, falsifying information to gain compliance is unethical. Education may prevent people's naive obedience with compliance techniques.

## A correlation study on culture and compliance

This study tests the social validation and commitment/consistency compliance techniques as well as the individualism/collectivism dimension of **culture**.

    Petia Petrova and colleagues (2007) write that most of the research on social influence uses North American samples. The authors aimed to strengthen the research on the **foot-in-the-door** technique with research in the natural setting.

    There is little direct research on culture and compliance but related research suggests that **individualism** and **collectivism** are important variables. Existing research shows that individualists use **dispositions** more frequently and collectivists use **situations** more frequently in self-descriptions. Therefore, individualists are more likely to have consistent views of the self and thus behave more consistently in their choices. Previous research suggests that freely making a personal choice has a strong impact on the later behavior of individualist persons. Petrova and colleagues reason that persons from individualist cultures are more likely to be consistent with previous choices than those from collectivist choices, but research needs to test the idea.

The authors cite one previous quasi-experiment on compliance and consistency as support for their idea that previous commitments have strong effects on future commitments in people from individualist cultures. Students from the United States and Poland read a hypothetical situation where they judged their likelihood to respond to a request by a Coca-Cola staff member based on their previous actual compliance to similar requests. U.S. students were more likely to take into account their previous behavior. The level of individualism accounted for the difference between the two groups.

Petrova and colleagues *wanted more evidence that the differences in compliance were actually related to personal levels of individualism and collectivism.* Field research in a natural setting would increase the **method triangulation** of the earlier experiment. The authors thought that **social desirability** might explain why some participants altered their real responses in the experimental setting.

There were three hypotheses. First, participants who agreed to the first request would comply more frequently to the second request. Second, compliance would be greater in the U.S. students than the Asian students. Third, personal orientations of individualism and collectivism would account for the compliance differences.

Both the U.S. and Asian participants attended Arizona State University. All surveys were in English. The authors thought that translation problems often interfered with research goals. The sample consisted of 1287 Asian international students and 2253 U.S. students. The researchers got student e-mail addresses from the university database. The sample contained students from all majors in all departments, though as it turned out, major and department had no effect on the results.

E-mails requested that students take an online survey containing questions on numerous topics, such as education and career goals. The researchers included questions about individualism and collectivism from the Cultural Orientation Scale (COS) throughout the survey. The COS contains 13 pairs of items. One pair measured the frequency of behaviors in the student's native culture, such as the frequency of consulting family members in decision-making, with 0 meaning not at all and 6 meaning always. Another pair measured student perceptions of these behaviors, with 0 meaning very bad and 6 meaning very good.

One month after the first request, participants received a second e-mail asking them to fill out another online survey related to the first one.

Results showed that 10.2% of the Asian sample and 8% of the U.S. sample complied with the first request. Interestingly, more males complied than the females in both groups. Even though a smaller percentage of the U.S. students complied with the first request, 21.6% responded to the second request. In contrast, only 9.9% of the Asian students complied with the second request. In addition, 69% of the U.S students who complied with the first request also complied with the second request. Only 44.8% of the Asian students who complied with the first request complied with the second request.

The authors conclude that "Although both cultures' participants were more likely to comply with a request if they had chosen to comply with a similar request one month earlier, this tendency was more pronounced among the U.S. participants than among Asian participants" (p. 15). In addition, an individualist personal orientation is correlated with compliance to a second request after a first request.

The researchers believe strengths of this study include its measurement of behavior in a natural setting and the ability to use surveys for both groups in English.

However, one limitation was that the differences between the samples were not large. It is possible that Asian students attending U.S. universities have more characteristics of individualist cultures than Asian students living in Asia. Another limitation is that the study uses correlation and cannot provide cause and effect explanations for the results.

Using e-mail as a way to collect data has strengths and limitations. It is easy to distribute e-mail surveys and participants remain anonymous. However, it is impossible to verify who fills out the surveys. Last, participants cannot ask immediate questions about the informed consent forms unless they are present with researchers. This could be an ethical concern for the study.

Petrova and colleagues see many implications of their findings. More evidence is now available about compliance and culture and data actually reflects individualism and collectivism. In addition, marketing campaigns aimed at Asian might be more effective if requests are framed in terms of expected **in-group** behavior.

## 5.17 Evaluate Research on Conformity to Group Norms

### Our tendency to conform

Although you may deny that you conform, the research shows otherwise. Humans are social creatures and **belonging needs** are strong. Philip Zimbardo (2007) warns that the worst abuses that humans commit against other humans "are not the consequences of exotic forms of influence, such as hypnosis, psychotropic drugs, or "brainwashing," but rather the systematic manipulation of the most mundane aspects of human nature over time in confining settings" (p. 259). **Self-serving biases** make us believe we are not vulnerable to social influence. Zimbardo warns that simply because we hold self-serving biases, we tend to underestimate **situational** influences on behavior. The five **core motives** are biases toward social influences, and the same characteristics that help us live with others in cultural groups can make us vulnerable.

### Conformity, social influence, and social norms

I am not surprised at the great interest in studying **conformity** to social **norms** since Muzafer Sherif and Solomon Asch's early research. It is interesting and relevant. Some conformity is natural and adaptive but too much conformity can have dire consequences.

Learn about the original Asch experiment in your introductory text before reading the rest of this section.

Conformity research investigates a particular kind of social influence, how a majority influences individual behavior. Conformity serves two general purposes (Aronson et al., 2007). It is a way to get information from others to interpret ambiguous situations. We conform in simple ways after getting information from others, such as how to address a professor; what is everyone else doing? In addition, it serves a normative purpose, satisfying the need to belong to a group. These two purposes fit in with the idea that humans evolved to interact with others in cultural groups.

### Research directions: The brain, culture, and conformity

Between Asch's experiment in 1955 and 1994, there were 94 experiments using Asch's original model and 39 modifications of the original model, with 17 of these testing conformity cross-culturally (Fiske, 2004).

The study of conformity did not end in 1994. More recent studies asked two questions. First, what is the brain doing when someone conforms? Second, are there really cross-cultural differences in conformity?

Besides knowing the Asch study, I recommend that you know the one reviewed in section 3.11 using fMRI to examine the brain during conformity and something about culture and conformity. This way, evaluations reflect more recent knowledge. *Conclusions about conformity based only on the original Asch experiment are limited.*

## The relationship between conformity, cultural evolution, and genetics

Some context about conformity as part of **cultural evolution** is needed, defined as the way that cultures change and show diversity over time (Newsone et al., 2007). *This discussion will help you understand why conformity must be viewed from a cultural perspective.*

Lesley Newsone and colleagues (2007) suggest that conformity is an important feature of cultural evolution; humans are socially oriented and so much of our behavior is socially learned. It is *adaptive* to conform. It increases one's chances of survival.

The mass media have made most people generally aware that DNA carries information about inheritance. But do people know much about cultural evolution?

Genetic evolution and cultural evolution are intertwined in humans. *Any genetic limit on cultural evolution must also be seen in light of how culture affects genetics.* For example, cultural preferences for attractiveness define who is selected for mating. The genes of these people are then more likely to survive. In addition, cultural practices can even shield people from natural selection. For example, even though people with round, high surface-to-volume body types can survive in colder climates more easily, cultural inventions of warm clothing allowed a greater variation of body types to develop in cold regions.

Culture and genes evolving together allowed for practices that might not have evolved simply through natural selection or genes. Human culture is the result of thousands of years of interplay between biological and cultural factors. When humans acquired **language**, cultural evolution got a large boost. Now adults could symbolically transmit the culture to children. Think of language as one of the human **cultural tools**, which also includes the ability to create categorize human groups and a set of built-in biases that help people quickly decide which cultural variations to acquire. Biases help us make decisions quickly, and those people making good decisions quickly have a greater chance for survival.

This brings me to conformity. When we see others doing something, we have to decide whether or not to do the same thing. Which behaviors are the best to adopt? "A good rule of thumb to follow when contemplating what cultural variants to adopt is to imitate behaviors that are popular with people similar to oneself, who seem confident in what they are doing or are considered worthy of admiration" (p. 463). Asch's experiment supports the idea that people have these preferences and use them to decide to conform to norms.

Cultural evolution is different from genetic evolution in that cultural evolution depends on decision-making forces in people. Psychologists have studied the decision-making forces that give us social norms. Asch's experiment is one example. An evolutionary framework fits in with our study of levels of analysis. We must take every opportunity to draw relationships between ideas; we need a larger frame of reference. Findings from social psychology research fit into the larger framework.

Benefits of conforming include expanding one's knowledge through social networking and preventing individuals from breaking rules and suffering punishment (Newsone et al., 2007). It is hard to be part of human culture without *some* conforming.

## A meta-analysis about culture and conformity

Ron Bond and Peter Smith (1996) conducted a meta-analysis using 133 studies from 17 countries. They asked two questions. First, has the tendency to conform changed over time? Second, is conformity modified by culture?

There are many variations of the Asch study and the results are sometimes contradictory. Few of the studies collected data cross-culturally. Some reviews of the studies following Asch concluded that to some extent his work was a "child of its time," meaning time bound. In contrast, other studies found results similar to Asch's original experiment. At least one study found higher levels of conformity than what Asch reported.

Bond and Smith selected studies that met the following criteria. The studies used the Asch format, used Asch's line test, and were designed so that participants responded to group members (typically three, as this was the number that caused conformity) who were all present during the study. In addition, the meta-analysis included samples with female participants.

Bond and Smith made three main conclusions.

1. Conformity was higher in study participants when the size of the majority was large, when it included a larger proportion of females, when ambiguity was high, and when the majority consisted of **in-group** members. These factors determined conformity only in the studies that used the Asch line stimulus. This conclusion was based on studies run in the United States.

2. Levels of conformity steadily declined since the 1950s. This conclusion was based on the studies run in the United States.

3. Conformity was higher in cultures with a tendency toward **collectivism**.

Bond and Smith identified several limitations of their meta-analysis. First, meta-analyses are correlation studies. The interpretation is limited to relationships rather than cause and effect. Second, the sampled studies did not allow the authors to draw conclusions about gender and the topic of culture and conformity. It was *assumed* that since gender has an effect on conformity, it would also affect conformity in collectivist cultures. However, the studies in the meta-analysis did not include gender and culture. Strengths of the study included using strict criteria for selecting studies to appear in the meta-analysis so that they were really comparable.

## Other research results on culture and conformity

Michael Harris Bond and Peter Smith (1996) reported that conformity may work very differently in some cultures. For example, they reported that Dols found "perverse norms" in Spanish culture that did not exist in Anglo culture. Perverse norms are norms that are agreed to exist but are not frequently enforced. The Asch experiments found that people conformed to a *majority*. In a perverse norm system, people can conform to an individual authority figure. This authority has control over behavior because he or she has the ability to decide when a norm is enforced.

 This information on perverse norms adds to the body of research suggesting that specific aspects of cultures affect conformity.

### Note to the teacher

In the next section, I review two experiments about how culture affects conformity, one by Matsuda (1985) and one by Takano and Sogon (2008). Students may use both studies for exam questions coming from this learning outcome or the next. It is a good chance for students to the same studies for two learning outcomes.

## Conformity: A summary of strengths and limitations

Conformity research has strengths.

1. Conformity research has time, observer, and space triangulation. These replications generally had results that were similar to Asch's original findings when the studies used the Asch model, ambiguous information, and in-group members as social influence.

2. Bond and Smith's meta-analysis was well designed and allowed the authors to make some clear generalizations about conformity.

Though many studies investigate conformity, there are still limitations (Fiske, 2004).

1. The impact of gender in conformity research is inconsistent. Some studies show that women conform more than men. Other experiments found that apparent gender differences were really attributable to lack of expertise on the tasks.

2. Asch's conformity studies did not examine group processes; they looked at how an individual reacts to a group.

3. Ethical considerations are another limitation. Participants are deceived in conformity studies. Does the scientific benefit of the study outweigh the rights of participants? Under what circumstance can the researcher dispense with informed consent? Can the researchers keep participant performance confidential? The ethics of conformity studies remain controversial.

# 5.18 Discuss Factors Influencing Conformity

Numerous factors affect one's **conformity** to social **norms** (Aronson et al., 2007; Fiske, 2004).

1. One is **culture**.

2. Another is the **minority opinion**, an automatic response to **in-groups** and **out-groups**.

3. A factor related to minority opinion is when one consciously decides to conform because of **in-group social identity (SIT)/social categorization (SCT)**.

4. The **false consensus effect** affects conformity when one automatically thinks that the thoughts and behavior of others are the same as theirs.

5. Another factor comes from **social impact theory**. This means that the importance of the group (if you have friendships or other close relationships with group members), the number of people in the group (3 or more), the physical closeness of group members (for example, living in a sorority house), and whether or not you have allies in the group have a large impact on the likelihood that you will conform.

6. **Gender** affects conformity, but only in some instances, such as when an audience is present. Gender differences are not seen in all situations when someone might conform.

7. **Memes** (reviewed in section 3.12) probably affect conformity. Current research is limited but this may change in the future.

Two of the factors are selected for this section, social identity theory/social categorization theory and culture.

## How to reuse some previous research on SIT/SCT for "factors influencing conformity"

Investigations into **SIT/SCT** showed the large effect that in-groups have on conformity. *Conformity may be at its greatest in SCT* (Fiske, 2004). Much of the traditional literature views conforming as an automatic process. However, identifying with one's in-group is powerful. It is an example of controlled conscious (the opposite side of the **dual-processing model** for **activated actors** from automatic processing) behavior, where people conform to the point of view of their in-group because it seems most appropriate. People have less uncertainty about what to do by conforming to an in-group. The in-group defines social norms. Errors are not as important as similarity in creating a socially shared understanding. Experiments using the Asch format that manipulate in-group identity find that conformity is greatest to an in-group. Experiments also show that in-group members punish those who go against the in-group.

The experiments from section 5.14 on **infrahumanization** and SIT/SCT and culture are also studies about factors that affect conformity.

## Cultural factors that affect conformity

I introduced the concepts **tightness** and **looseness** in section 5.7 on Harry Triandis. Tightness and looseness affect conformity. "The degree of **individualism** and **collectivism** in any given culture is influenced by certain factors, including two specific cultural syndromes: cultural tightness versus looseness and cultural complexity versus simplicity (Triandis, 1995, p. 52).

According to Triandis, people from collectivist cultures conform more strongly than people from individualist cultures. People from tight cultures conform more than people form loose cultures. Japan is an example of a tight culture, though modern Japan is not as tight as it was historically. The United States is an example of a loose culture.

Triandis (1994) tells a story about something that happened when he was in Japan in 1990. "I read an account in the English language *Japan Times* about a startling event. A teacher slammed a heavy door on the head of a student who was two minutes late for class, killing her" (p. 159). Triandis was intrigued that there were varied opinions in public discussions about the killing. Some of the opinions showed an understanding of the teacher's attempts to train students to be on time.

Another story from Triandis (1995) told about a 13-year-old Japanese student, Yuhei Komada, who was **bullied** by classmates. Yuhei endured jeers and shoves from the group and was later found suffocated in a closet. Triandis was not sure if Yuhei did anything to start the bullying but remarked that the bullying, called *ijime,* happened when someone did not fit into the **in-group**. How was Yuhei different? He did not use the Japanese dialect of the community, his father was educated in Tokyo, and his family had only lived in the community for 17 years.

Both stories are about people conforming to social norms. Historically, when the Japanese were a very tight culture, Japanese samurai were even allowed to kill anyone of a lesser rank if they thought their behavior deviated from expected norms.

Japanese children conform to age-appropriate norms to a great extent. However, the Japanese are more likely to conform to an in-group's norm expectations than they are to outgroups (Aronson et al., 2007). Some of the Asch study replications found that Japanese participants would not conform to the opinions of strangers. This finding is clarified in the Matsuda experiment reviewed below. Japanese children are protected when they identify with an in-group. In tight cultures, people are expected behave as others behave. Conforming shields people from making social judgments that bring criticism and have unfortunate effects on one's social position (Triandis, 1994).

Tightness requires homogeneous groups where the rules are clear. In contrast, in less homogeneous cultures, the norms are not always so clear or enforced.

Triandis (1994) points out that the strict rules of a tight culture have benefits. For example, crime is lower in cities such as Tokyo. Crime is high in U.S. cities.

## A study showing that culture affects conformity

This study is one of the cross-cultural replications of the Asch experiment, though it included modifications of the original task.

Noriyuki Matsuda (1985) conducted an experiment that clarified some of the inconsistencies in experiments that found less conformity in Japanese samples than Asch found in the American samples.

Matsuda thought that studies showing less conformity in Japanese samples were misinterpreted. He designed an experiment using the kinds of in-groups specific to Japanese culture and how participants conformed to each. Matsuda believed a properly designed study would show that Japanese persons *do* conform.

Matsuda thought that previous researchers failed to control for the *readiness* of participants to interact with three specific types of groups. Matsuda's experiment distinguished between three types of Japanese relationships, *uchi, seken,* and *soto.* The Japanese select appropriate behavior based on the kind of relationship they have with a group and these relationships impact the level of conformity in an experiment. Uchi relationships are the most intimate of the three. Seken is an intermediate level of intimacy. Soto relationships are when there are few ties between people. Matsuda says that the concept *amae* confounds studying Japanese relationships. Amae applies mainly to uchi relationships. Amae is a "mutual understanding among members that allows moderate deviation" (p. 86). Amae permits a Japanese person to feel less pressure to conform to another. Amae does not allow the person to fully deviate. However, a person can carefully compare their view to that of others and decide on an appropriate range of deviation. Amae does not exist in seken relationships so there is little room for deviation to those groups. As Soto relationships are not important, people are generally indifferent to the other's opinions.

Matsuda hypothesized that the most conformity took place in seken relationships. Conformity to uchi relationships would come next. He expected the least conformity from soto relationships.

In addition to clearly defining the *kinds* of relationships the Japanese participants experienced, Matsuda operationalized the definition of conformity for his study as a change in judgment to the group view. However, the change must occur from an initial correct choice. This is a modification of the Asch study.

Matsuda's experiment differed in one other way from previous experiments. Rather than just see if participants changed their view to the majority view, Matsuda wanted to see the *degree* to which participants perceived the similarity of each figure with the standard one.

The sample was 84 females from the University of Tsukuba. Seven total groups were formed based on the 3 intimacy levels of uchi, seken, and soto. The uchi groups were made up of girls that selected each other as important in-group members. Having a group of girls give self-presentations to the others created the moderate intimacy seken groups. The soto groups were not given any instructions to get to know each other.

Each participant sat in front of a computer and could not see each other's answers. Participants saw a figure on the screen and compared it to three other figures. Participants rated how close the figure was to the other three, with answers ranging from 0 to 5. After all four team members completed the task, each were told the mean response of the group. Seventeen trials were conducted, and for all but 3, the girls were given the correct mean of the group. The three trials used for the experiment gave an incorrect mean. Participants were then asked to confirm their answers. They could change their answer or keep their original answer. Responses were anonymous.

Matsuda made two general conclusions.

First, conformity was high. Matsuda felt the degree of conformity was great, especially since the conditions of the experiment made it easy to avoid conforming. The girl's responses were anonymous and there was no face-to-face interaction. In fact, the degree of conformity exceeded Matsuda's expectations.

Second, there was some inconsistency among the degree of conformity among the three types of relationship groups. However, Matsuda concluded that most of the changes in judgment occurred because of **normative** comparisons, meaning that the girls were more likely to change their judgments based on the behavior expectations from the other group members. Normative comparisons occurred more in the seken group as expected. Amae made it easier to disagree in the uchi group and the relationships in the soto group were not judged as important.

This is an important study. It showed that the Japanese do conform but *only in specific contexts*. Matsuda's conclusions fit in with a larger body of evidence showing that context is an important determinant of behavior.

The study has limitations. First, the sample used all females. Females may conform more than males. This study investigates conformity only in Japanese samples and does not compare the Japanese to other kinds of samples. However, it was Matsuda's goal to clarify research on the Japanese in particular. Second, Matsuda's experiment is a modification of Asch's original study so it is not completely comparable to it.

The next study brings research on conformity and culture up to the present.

## A study challenging the idea that the Japanese conform more than others

Although important cross-cultural researchers believe that the Japanese conform more as a collectivist culture, Yohtaro Takano and Shunya Sogon (2008) suggest that this generalization is not entirely true. I want you to be *aware of a current controversy in studying conformity cross-culturally*. Takano attacks the designs of studies claiming that the Japanese conform more than Americans and refines the study of conformity and culture by investigating conformity in specific contexts (a phase 4 study about the dimensions of culture, section 5.6).

Concluding that the Japanese are more collectivist because of conformity research is misleading. For example, research by Williams and Sogon from 1984 showing that the Japanese conform really confounds, meaning it confuses, conformity with the kind of discipline used in different sport club groups (Takano & Sogon, 2008). Williams created groups for the study based on association with a sport club. There are two kinds of sport clubs in Japan, informal clubs (doukoukai) and formal sport clubs (taikukai). The discipline in formal clubs is strict and vertical. The discipline in informal clubs is looser.

To control for discipline, Takano and Sogon created groups from only informal *non-sport* clubs. The study was a *strict replication of Asch's experiment* so that the results could be weighed against the original findings. Remember that Matsuda used a modification of the Asch study.

Results showed less conformity in non-sport clubs than previous reports from studies creating groups using sport clubs. The percentage of conformity reported in Takano's findings were similar to those found in American samples.

What does this mean? A lot of time has passed since Asch's original study. Both Takano and Matsuda found that conformity occurred more frequently in specific *contexts*. So context is a key variable. One lesson from Matsuda and Takano's work is that we should *never make sweeping generalizations about one's individualism or collectivism*. Broad generalizations too easily turn into **stereotypes**. As Triandis said, everyone has access to both individualistic and collectivistic behaviors. These behaviors are demonstrated in specific contexts.

# 6 What Should We Do with Behaviorism?

## 6.1 Evaluate Behaviorism: Some Context

Traditional behaviorism includes **classical conditioning** (CC) and **operant conditioning** (OC). CC means to condition biologically based reflexes. OC means that an organism operates, or behaves, in an environment and receives either reinforcement or punishment. Reinforcement increases the chances that an organism is likely to behave in the same way in the future. B. F. Skinner identified two kinds of reinforcement, positive and negative. Reinforcement is distinguished from punishment. Both positive and negative reinforcement strengthen behavior while punishment decreases behavior. Introductory textbooks describe the basics of CC and OC.

It is important to understand CC and OC, as both are forms of learning. But it is important to also understand how CC and OC apply to a level of analysis approach.

### Note to the teacher

> I recommend that you teach CC in depth, particularly if you select the health psychology option. CC has narrow applications but is an important type of human learning. CC is part of the biological level of analysis and is a component of the Cultural Acquisition Device (CAD) (reviewed in section 3.5), which organizes CC under culture.
>
> In contrast, I recommend that you teach OC mainly as part of psychology's history. OC is limited as a *thread* through a level of analysis approach. The IB syllabus guide warns students to avoid oversimplification and recognize reductionism. The whole idea of a level of analysis approach calls into question the oversimplified and reductionist nature of Skinnerian behaviorism.
>
> The IB syllabus guide is designed so that teachers can bring in any material that they find relevant to their courses. But because of the large scope of the syllabus, I recommend topics that easily thread through the learning outcomes.

## 6.2 Examine Classical Conditioning: Two Applications to Studying Health Psychology

Ivan Pavlov's dog experiment is usually the introduction to classical conditioning. Pavlov's experiment is the easiest way to learn how CC works but we need to go beyond Pavlov to study CC's relevance to modern psychology.

The **cultural acquisition device** (CAD) includes the innate reactive process of CC (Konner, 2007). CC primes infants to sift through a flood of unconditioned stimuli from a culture. Unconditioned stimuli are connected to the neural circuits for reflexes. For example, "If being in church calms the mother, then this setting will gain the power to calm the

**183**

child, because the unconditioned stimulus (calm mother) becomes associated with conditioned stimuli such as liturgical music" (p. 95).

Innate CC behaviors increase an infant's chance of survival. As the child develops, many innate reflexes are replaced with cognitions that mediate culture. For example, a child will start to understand what music represents in their culture. However, CC primes the child to live in culture.

Two modern examples of classical conditioning are **addiction relapse** research and **immune system** research. Both are part of the biological level of analysis for the health psychology option. There are plenty of other modern examples, such as the classical conditioning of implicit memories about fear, but space limits the number I review.

## CC and addictions

Why do alcoholics and drug addicts relapse? These people can have terrible cravings for their drug of choice and frequently go back to using it. Addicts can relapse as soon as they get out of rehabilitation programs or years later, risking the loss of family and careers.

### Note to the teacher

> Anna Rose Childress is an important addiction relapse researcher. She is featured in the films "The Hijacked Brain," available from Films for the Humanities and Sciences, and "The Secret Life of the Brain," available from www.pbs.org.
> Addiction is a required topic for the health psychology option.

A series of experiments researching cue reactivity in the brains of cocaine addicts tests the hypothesis that "the powerful craving and arousal responses to drug-related cues are based on simple classical conditioning" (Childress et al., 2002, p. 1).

Classical conditioning theory predicts that cocaine cues trigger emotional biological responses because the cues are *reliable predictors of real drug experiences.* Cocaine cues provide two kinds of conditioned responses. One is that addicts experience feelings similar to being on the drug. Addicts express that they feel as though they can actually feel the drug, even though they have not yet had it. The other is a drug-opposite effect, where addicts respond to cocaine cues with withdrawal feelings of nausea or sweating. Both types of conditioned responses can trigger relapse.

Conditioned stimuli come from both external sources and internal sources. External sources include seeing other users or drug paraphernalia. Internal sources are dreams or memories about the drug. Both sources can lead to relapse.

Video-induced cravings have been studied in many experiments using a variety of brain imaging techniques, such as **SPECT**, **PET**, and **fMRI**. Childress remarks that using a variety of imaging techniques in different labs ensures that study results are not simply the effect of a particular lab on participant behavior.

One experiment by Childress randomly allocated addicts (who were free of drugs for at least two weeks) to either watch a narrative nondrug video or watch a video of other addicts using and talking about cocaine. PET scans showed that the **amygdala** and the **anterior cingulate**, among other brain parts, were active in the group watching the videos of addicts using and talking about cocaine. One important job of the amygdala is to signal the learning of important biological incidents. The anterior cingulate is active in selective attention and emotional reactions to important events. Both brain parts are located in the **limbic system**. The limbic system is partially responsible for motivation and emotion.

Six independent experiments followed Childress' study on similar or related topics. Childress hopes to discover a clear pattern of brain reactivity related to relapse. Future medical treatments might moderate cravings.

As you can guess, CC's role in relapse is far more complicated than the original study suggests. There was no clear pattern of brain activity in follow-up studies. While the amygdala and the anterior cingulate were found active in all of the relapse studies, other brain parts were active in some of the experiments but not in others. The most effective medical interventions target specific brain areas, so relapse treatments are in the beginning stages of refinement.

The **ethics** of conducting drug craving experiments are complicated. There are several key points to consider. The informed consent form must state the nature of the study and inform participants of all potential risks. Childress must show that the study is of great scientific benefit in order to place participants at risk for relapse. Can Childress remove the adverse effects of study participation? Some participants experienced intense drug cravings. Childress says that she works with participants to make sure all induced cravings are eliminated. Weigh the evidence and make your own decision.

## CC and the immune system

We are learning a lot about CC and the immune system that might have future applications for healthcare.

Robert Ader (2005) was the first to identify the **bidirectional** connection between the brain and the immune system. In 1975, he published a CC experiment that demonstrated the process and concluded that it was possible to condition the immune system.

Three groups of mice were part of Ader's taste-aversion experiment, which was one way to study CC and immune suppression.

Group #1: The mice received a saccharin drink (conditioned stimulus CS) that they liked before it was paired with an immunosuppressive drug (unconditioned stimulus UCS). From studying Pavlov's experiment, students will guess that the UCS would produce an unconditioned response (UCR) of a lowered immune system. Next, the mice were injected with an antigen, a substance that stimulates the antibody production meant to fight off foreign substances. Then, they were reexposed to the CS, the saccharin drink.

Group #2: These mice also received the saccharin drink (CS) that they liked before it was paired with an immunosuppressive drug. Next, the mice were injected with an antigen, a substance that stimulates the antibody production meant to fight off foreign substances. They were not reexposed to the CS, the saccharin drink.

Group#3: The control mice that were not given the saccharin drink with the drug (CS). They next were injected with an antigen, a substance that stimulates the antibody production meant to fight off foreign substances. They were not exposed to the CS following the injection.

Results showed that the mice from group #1 showed a lowered immune response in relation to the mice in groups #2 and #3.

Ader's experiment was successfully replicated numerous times, opening the door for a new field of study about the immune system.

Animal and some human experiments as well as correlation and case studies on humans are investigating the mechanisms of CC on immunity. We now have some good **method triangulation** on CC and immune suppression.

In one experiment, mice received a flu virus and then were exposed to stress. These mice had suppressed NK cell activity and delayed production of virus killing antibodies (Ader, 2005). Other experiments designed to see the effect of disruption of social structures on mice find that, among other things, the HPA axis is activated and the cells needed to suppress the spread of lung tumors decrease in numbers.

Human studies on conditioning and health are often nonexperimental for ethical reasons. Anticipating **chemotherapy** appears to condition the immune functioning. There is a correlation between humans anticipating nausea from cancer chemotherapy and lowered ability of lymphocytes to respond to foreign stimuli. In addition, depression is correlated with declines in several aspects of immune functioning. Just remember that human cognitions are complicated to study and are unaccounted for in animal experiments. However, animal models are a basis for thinking about the human immune system.

One application of animal experiments was documented in a case study about a child with **lupus** who was successfully treated with conditioning to reduce the amount of immunosuppressor drug needed (Ader, 2005). This child's treatment was based on the findings of mice experiments. In this case, mice had overactive immune systems that contributed to spontaneous cases of lupus. It is valuable to lupus patients to be able to suppress immune responses. The mice were conditioned to suppress their immune systems with a CS, which consisted of receiving injections without the active drug. There was a delay in the onset of lupus using an amount of the drug that would not have been enough to actually impact the course of lupus. It is possible that even small changes in the immune system have large effects on the development and course of illness.

Maj-Britt Niemi (2009) describes one human CC experiment by Marion Goebel suggesting that **placebos** (discussed in detail in section 7.13) can suppress overactive immune responses and lessen allergies. Thirty people with an allergy to dust mites were given a novel tasting drink paired with the allergy drug desloratadine every day for five days. Then, 11 of the original sample received the same drink paired with a placebo pill. The rest of the sample received either just a placebo, water, or the allergy medication. Participants who received the novel drink and the placebo showed reduced allergic symptoms and lower immune reactivity similar to the level of people taking the drug.

We have even identified the brain area important for conditioning, the **insular cortex**, which modulates sensory experiences as well as emotions and the physiological state of the body (Niemi, 2009). Animals with damage to the insular cortex show no conditioning responses, regardless of where lesions are placed.

Niemi writes that some physicians are considering the benefits of using placebos to enhance drug treatments and surgeries and are thinking through the ethics of their use.

## 6.3 Examine Operant Conditioning

Radical behaviorism lost its most passionate defender when B. F. Skinner died in 1990. By this time, most behaviorists had already changed their ideas because of evidence provided by cognitive psychologists. Skinner argued until the end of his life that even if cognitive psychologists figured out what was in the "black box" of the mind, understanding human behavior still rested on studying the contingencies that shaped behavior.

### Note to the teacher

Skinner can be difficult for students. He sounds good at first but further investigation reveals flawed assumptions, unsound explanations of complex human behavior, and destructive reductionism contrary to a level of analysis approach.

Keep in mind as you read about Skinner that he meant to universally apply his animal studies to explain all complex human behavior. This is why students must take operant conditioning past the animal studies. Skinner controlled for culture and language in his animal studies, precisely what modern psychologists want to investigate. The result is that OC does not explain the complex mental life of humans that is imbedded in a culture and requires symbolic thought and language.

While mental health treatments such as biofeedback and systematic desensitization stem from Skinnerian concepts and are still used, many behavioral treatments are now used as supplements to other primary treatments.

## Skinner's assumptions and research methods

Skinner agreed with John Watson that only observable behavior was worthy of science. In addition, Skinner believed in the **continuity of species**, an assumption that behavior was fairly similar across species. Skinner thought that human behavior was similar to that of animals, just more complex, with the largest difference in **verbal behavior**. Skinner used the continuity of species to defend animal experimentation as a basis for explaining human behavior; *a science of human behavior supported by the science of animal behavior.* Skinner taught pigeons and rats to do amazing things, such as pressing levers, twirling in circles, and pecking pianos. Animal research showed the mechanisms of operant conditioning in experiments that *controlled for human culture and language but were meant to apply to all complex human behavior.*

As it turned out, Skinner controlled for exactly what modern psychologists want to know about humans! We should study humans within the sociocultural context. Thus, Skinner's research format is flawed. Skinner envisioned a future scientific study of psychology that used behavioral principles to identify the **successive approximations**, or steps that needed reinforcement, to create and maintain human complex behavior. However, no research successfully shows these steps for complex human behaviors and modern researchers show that learning relies on efficient cognitive systems.

## Skinner's beliefs about reinforcement in humans

Skinner thought that the most important reinforcer for humans was *success.* Think about it; success is different for everyone. Consider how hard it would be to operationally define success for each individual and then maintain the contingencies for each individual in experiments! Skinner said this task was a project for future psychology.

Three topics—verbal behavior, culture and genes, and education—will help you see how Skinner meant to apply the principles obtained from animal studies.

## Skinner's views on verbal behavior (language)

Skinner thought verbal behavior was the main difference between animals and humans. *Verbal behavior is the part of Skinnerian principles that generated the most criticism.* Skinner thought language was a behavior like any other behavior and was under the forces of operant conditioning. We just do not speak in behaviorism. For example, hunger in behavioral terms is "I have been deprived of food for six hours." Love in behavioral terms is really "Honey, you reinforce my behavior." Skinner wrote that humans just say hunger and love because we have internal state languages.

Skinner said there were six verbal operants that maintained chains of human verbal behavior. These verbal behaviors took place in cultural environments. One verbal operant is *mands,* or commands. If a person mands "give me water," it sets the occasion on which another behaves. Another is *echoic,* where the sound of someone's voice sets the occasion on which you respond. Verbal operants set up *chains* of accepted cultural verbal exchanges. For example, in the United States, "How are you?" prompts the conditioned response "I am fine."

Skinner (1985) demonstrated verbal operants on pigeons Jack and Jill. Jack and Jill were operantly conditioned to use symbolic communication, the verbal equivalent in animals lacking the physical structures to produce speech. Jack was separated from Jill by a curtain and signaled Jill to press correct levers. Jack gave Jill reinforcement and then was reinforced for his part. This was an elaborate training program and these pigeons performed more than you might expect a pigeon to do; but it is not how humans use language.

No one has produced research breaking down the steps needed to reinforce language. There could be thousands. Biological and cognitive explanations are more elegant.

## Skinner's views on culture

Skinner said that **culture** was the primary reinforcement for human behavior, including verbal behavior. Skinner (1989) defined culture "as the contingencies of reinforcement maintained by a group" (p. 52). Contingencies shaped members of a group and these practices were passed down to new members. As an example, Skinner said that if a monkey accidentally dipped a sweet potato into the ocean to wash it off and the clean and salty flavor left on the potatoes was reinforcing, then the others would also pick up the behavior. The practice had to promote the survival of the group in some way for it to be reinforcing. If the monkeys got sick from eating the potato after it was washed in the ocean, this would not be reinforcing and the practice would stop. Skinner said psychologists sometimes called these new behaviors cultural practices; however, culture was just a series of reinforced behaviors.

Skinner said that **genes** were important to behavior only so far as they were shaped by the contingencies of reinforcement, primarily through sociocultural practices. Skinner wrote that even the behavior of lower animals was not completely determined by genes. The environment acted on the genes to shape behaviors. He used the example of a wasp gathering food (Skinner, 1989). "Some features of the wasp's behavior must have been affected by incidental features of the setting" (p. 49). Skinner said that the wasp's setting had varied features such as the types of soil and available food sources. It was unlikely that the wasp had a large bank of evolved behaviors to prepare it for varying circumstances. It was more likely that the specific actions of the wasp were selected by specific consequences following each step of gathering food such as a grasshopper struggling to get away after the wasp stung it.

Does research show that operant conditioning explains gene expression? Research now correlates the interaction between genes and stressful events in increasing the risk for **depression** (see section 3.4), but Caspi's study is completely different from operant conditioning explanations. Caspi showed that people with two short alleles of the serotonin transporter gene were more reactive to stressful events; that the gene is important. The effect of the gene was not fully noticed before gene-environment correlation studies.

## Skinner's views on education

Skinner argued that schools did things haphazardly; they were too large and inefficient (Skinner, 1989). It might be better if they used operant reinforcements.

Before language, all species had an actual acquaintance with what they learned via contingencies of reinforcement. Developing a physical system that allowed humans to acquire verbal behavior created a situation where people could learn through *descriptions of contingencies*. The distinction between learning by acquaintance and learning by description was important to Skinner because it explained what was wrong with education. Skinner used the example of opening a door. You watch a friend trying to open a door without success and say, "Open it by sliding it to the right," because this is how it works for you. Skinner says that the friend just has knowledge by description until he or she actually opens the door.

The person giving the direction has knowledge by acquaintance, or knowledge based on the contingencies encountered when opening the door. When the friend tries the door, then he or she also has knowledge by acquaintance.

Skinner thought that learning was efficient only when students had knowledge by acquaintance, or behaved and were reinforced. Skinner said that most of what happened in schools was descriptive knowledge that was not directly related to any behavior a student actually did. Students went to school and "paid attention" because they were punished if they did not. "The fact is that neither rewards nor punishments have anything to do with teaching if they merely keep students in contact with teachers and books. Teachers and books cannot teach because they are not properly contingent on the behavior we take to show the possession of knowledge" (p. 89).

Skinner proposed a more efficient educational system based on *priming* and *prompting*. Priming is getting a behavior to occur for the first time. Prompting means to give the student cues to maintain the behavior after it is primed. Skinner used origami, Japanese paper folding, as an example. The origami master primes the student by demonstrating the first fold on the paper. The student copies it. The process continues until complete. Now the prompting begins. The student tries to fold the shape on his or her own, with cues from the teacher. Eventually, the teacher removes all prompting as the student folds the paper alone. The task is mastered and the student has the knowledge by acquaintance.

Skinner also promoted **teaching machines**. "Teaching machines were designed to take advantage of the reinforcing power of immediate consequences" (p. 92). These machines were efficient and made sure that students progressed at their own rate while having direct experience, or acquaintance, with the material. The process worked on the concept of *shaping*. Small steps toward the desired end, or successive approximations, were broken down and presented to students on a screen. Students immediately saw if they were correct, and could move on or go back and study the material. Skinner says one U.S. teacher in Roanoke, Virginia, taught eighth graders the ninth-grade math material in half a school year with the machines.

There are numerous problems with Skinner's ideas about education. One is a lack of empirical research. Skinner's own demonstrations were with animals. The examples of closing doors and origami are anecdotes and do no resemble the kind of higher level thinking human students are expected to master. It is one thing to clearly break down the steps to origami, but how many steps are needed to master chemistry or psychology? Skinner said this was the task of future research. The issue with teaching machines is similar. How many steps must be reinforced to get to the final product for high level material? Skinner said that it took 600 steps to teach the numbers 1 through 5. How many steps does it take to learn calculus? Operant conditioning in education seems overly cumbersome when we consider putting it in practice. Social learning theory and cognitive theory have more elegant theories and research to back up their claims.

## Modern applications of Skinner

Current applications of operant conditioning include animal training and some mental health therapies. Anyone training animals uses operant conditioning. It is very effective. I trained a cat to walk on a leash and use a toilet with operant conditioning.

**Biofeedback** has been used, for example, to train children diagnosed with ADHD to better attend to their behavior.

Be aware that **behavior modification's** effectiveness is not always easy to measure because it is frequently used along with other treatments. Section 7.13 contains a case study showing how behavior modification is part of an **eclectic**, or combination, treatment plan for **depression**. However, the behavior modification supplements the primary treatments.

Many students study **systematic desensitization** as a phobia treatment. Jeffrey Hecker and Geoffrey Thorpe (2005) write that although systematic desensitization is still used, most behavioral treatments have been modified to include cognitive factors or they support other treatments. "Today systematic desensitization has been supplemented by such methods as graduated practice in real-life situations" (p. 99). This sounds similar to Bandura's **guided mastery** treatment, where models demonstrate, for example, the handling of feared animals. Bandura has experimental research showing that snake phobics improve through guided mastery, and that the improvements in **self-efficacy** modify biological systems by affecting **neurotransmitters** (a level of analysis approach). Systematic desensitization appears most effective for phobias acquired through direct experience. Social learning researchers claim that most phobias are not acquired through direct experience.

Animal research is a limited way to study human cultures where complex cognitive abilities embedded in language are required. Skinner does not have adequate explanations of humans living together in cultures.

# 7 Abnormal Psychology

## 7.1 Introduction

### The future of global mental health

We have the power to significantly reduce mental illness. While there are no simple answers to why people get mental disorders and how best to treat them, I want you to come away from my discussions with a sense of empowerment. I firmly believe that **stress** is a concept that unifies the study of mental disorders. We have the power to do something about stress but must understand its sources in order to tackle it, both personally and as a global community.

The World Health Report (World Health Organization, 2001) contains a warning that "one person in four will be affected by a mental disorder at some stage of life" (p.1). The World Health Organization (WHO) Director-General writes that major depression is the leading cause of disability globally and has the potential to become a major cause of disease. The WHO reports that along with the escalation of depression, 70 million people have alcoholism, 24 million have schizophrenia, and 1 million people commit suicide each year.

With all that modern medicine offers to combat mental illness, why is the problem growing? Could the benefits of modernization and globalization also increase our stress?

I originally trained as a family therapist but decided I could make a greater impact as a teacher. I highlight three themes in this chapter that have emerged in the field of abnormal psychology over the course of my career.

**1.** We must reduce stress to reduce mental illness. I agree with Robert Sapolsky; stress is a good organizing concept. Sapolsky's ideas on stress, depression, and genes were reviewed in section 3.4. But stress contributes to all mental illness, even the disorders that students most associate with genetics, such as schizophrenia and autism. The genetic contribution to schizophrenia is about 50%, leaving room for many other factors. Stress is one of those. Twins are not 100% concordant for autism, so sociocultural factors must place stress on the developing brain.

**2. Bad reductionism** has no place in thinking about mental disorders. The Walker-Tessner model (section 3.4) for psychiatric outcome will help us avoid bad reductionism. This model is a modern view of **diathesis–stress**. Historical views of diathesis, meaning a predisposition for disorder, were reductionist. Older theories saw diathesis as biological, such as genes, and stress as something in the environment that triggered the genes. *We know now that diathesis is* **bidirectional** *and interactive.* A diathesis is a mixture of inherited and acquired factors. Stress comes from many sources and interacts with genes.

The Walker-Tessner model shows all of the factors *contributing* to mental illness. It is not helpful to use the term "causes." It is more helpful to look at the factors that contribute to an increased risk of disorder. Modern psychologists view causation as bidirectional, where no single factor "causes" a mental disorder. In fact, many of the single factors cannot affect behavior unless they interact with other factors, as gene-environment correlation studies show. *So no one level of analysis fully explains mental disorder.* **Neuroplasticity** allows the levels of analysis to work together to modify the brain over the lifespan, creating a richer but more complex view of mental illness. *Tolerate uncertainty;* a more complicated view is the reality of mental disorder. This more complicated view has its benefits; it is becoming clearer that we can control many factors that must be present for mental illness to surface, in particular, stress.

While the levels of analysis work together to produce mental illness, different aspects of the Walker-Tessner model are *emphasized* in different disorders and by different researchers. In the end, many contributing factors fit together in ways we are just beginning to understand to create mental disorder. Much is to be learned about **resilience** as we think through modern research.

A *risk model* is an elegant way to view vulnerability to mental disorder. If a person has no contributing factors, then the risk for the disorder is low. Add one factor and the risk increases. Two contributing factors increase the risk, and so on.

**3.** An international perspective on mental illness is necessary to understand the required concepts.

## A cultural approach to abnormal psychology

While the IB syllabus has two specific headings for "culture and diagnosis" and "culture and prevalence," the entire option is organized under culture. *Otherwise, I am afraid that students will approach mental illness with the frame of reference of their own cultures, looking at cultural differences as variations of the "real" way to view mental disorder.* A more realistic approach is to recognize that beliefs about mental illness come from **cultural schemas**, reviewed in section 4.4. Taking a broader perspective helps us avoid the urge to **reify** mental disorders as specific things.

The classifications in the **DSM-IV** and the **ICD-10** (see section 7.5, a brief history of the DSM and the ICD) are *evolving*. While some other cultures have created categorical systems that are similar to these Western systems, such as the Chinese Classification of Mental Disorder (**CCMD-3**), these systems retain culture-specific features useful for their populations. The fourth edition of the DSM contained the first acknowledgment that culture was important for thinking about mental illness, but culture is still not essential to diagnosis. The DSM-V is expected in 2012. The agenda for the fifth edition, published by the American Psychiatric Association, contains ideas for expanding cultural considerations.

It is not easy to come up with one clear definition of any mental disorder (Castillo, 1997). Definitions change over time and continually evolve. Psychologists now understand that mental disorder results from the complex interplay between biology, cognitions, and the sociocultural experience. In addition, there is no definite and clear distinction between mental health and mental disorder. The DSM-IV-TR (2000) includes this statement: "There is no assumption that each category of mental disorder is a complete discrete entity with absolute boundaries dividing it from other mental disorders or from no mental disorder" (p. xxxi). While the DSM-IV organizes mental illness into categories, it is done this way for a reason— to increase **reliability** and to stimulate research. Increasing reliability does not ensure that **validity** increases, referring to the extent to which a disorder really exists in clinical practice (Castillo, 1997). In fact, the choice to use categories as a way to organize mental disorder is simply *one* way to organize the disorders, not the *only* way. See section 7.5 for more on classification and diagnosis.

Castillo stresses that it is dehumanizing when clinicians fail to treat the whole person. A large amount of new research has pushed Western psychiatry to take a cultural approach. One example concerns schizophrenia. It is now known that the course of schizophrenia is less chronic in non-Western countries, where the family is expected to support individuals. If a doctor approaches people with the attitude that schizophrenia is chronic, it may affect the prognosis of the patient.

In addition, Castillo writes that research on the "neuroplasticity of adaptation and learning" (p. 4) challenges strict disease-centered views of mental illness and promotes more holistic views. Any brain changes noted by a physician could be the result of experience but could also be *the result of the disorder rather than the cause.*

And last, the IB is an *international* program, so students preparing for its exams should have a balanced, cross-cultural perspective on human behavior.

Depression and eating disorders (particularly anorexia nervosa) are my main examples.

## 7.2 To What Extent Do Biological, Cognitive, and Sociocultural Factors Influence Abnormal Behavior?

Biological, cognitive, and sociocultural factors influence abnormal behavior to different *degrees* depending on the disorder.

The three levels of analysis all influence mental illnesses in a bidirectional way. Many students come into the class with the idea that genes cause mental illness. The discussion in Chapter 3 on gene expression should straighten out this belief.

### Note to the teacher

> Draw the Walker-Tessner model for each disorder to see the contributions of each level of analysis. I have students draw a new model for each disorder studied.

Theorists representing each level of analysis have opinions about the strength of different contributing factors. For example, Caspi claims that persons with two short risk alleles of the 5-HTT gene are more reactive to stressful life situations and have a greater risk of depression. In contrast, Bandura says that genes may predispose someone to depression, but one's self-efficacy is the greatest determinant of vulnerability. Bandura acknowledges the genetic contribution but downplays it. You must decide which theories have the most defensible research. Just remember that all modern theories are bidirectional.

Some information needed to respond to an IB exam question from this learning outcome is included in other sections. Section 3.4 contains Caspi's study on genes and depression. Section 7.13 contains information on the cognitive theory of depression. Section 3.8 covers diet and depression. Section 5.10 discusses Traditional Chinese Medicine (TCM) and depression. Section 5.15 contains the social learning theory point of view on depression. Section 7.10 contains a discussion of genes and eating disorders and a study on eating disorders and information-processing biases. Sections 7.6 and 7.8 cover culture and eating disorders.

## 7.3 Evaluate Psychological Research Relevant to the Study of Abnormal Behavior

Evaluations are included within my discussions of research. Consider the following when evaluating research:

1. Many of the researchers recommend replication or additional research testing different variables or using different samples.

2. Pay attention to *who is included in the sample.* Many studies exclude those not meeting strict criteria and use opportunity samples (nonrepresentative sampling).

3. Human studies about "causation" (contributing risk factors) are primarily correlation studies.

4. To what extent do concepts created and studied in the West apply cross-culturally? Look for cross-cultural verification of Western theories and findings.

5. It is hard to know if a therapy works. It might depend on how one defines "work." Also, it is hard to know which therapies are better than others because no study compares all available treatments.

6. Many of the theories about the "causes" and treatments of mental illness have different assumptions. For example, TCM, Western medicine, cognitive theory, and social learning theory all have different assumptions about the causes and proper treatment of mental illness.

## 7.4 Examine the Concepts of Normality and Abnormality

### Defining normality and abnormality: The elements of abnormality

There is no definition of **normality** and **abnormality** that is agreed on by all; cultural context is critical. While some behaviors are considered abnormal in most cultures, such as schizophrenia and autism, others are more debatable, such as the group of symptoms called depression in Western societies. This is because schizophrenic and autistic behavior is more clearly outside of normal behavior for any culture.

Many, such as Allan Horwitz, think that mental illness exists but believe that some groups of symptoms have been **over-pathologized**, such as "depressive" symptoms (except when someone has depression that includes suicidal thoughts and/or psychotic symptoms). He raises questions about the **validity** of the DSM-IV diagnosis for major depression and wonders if changing assumptions about normality and abnormality have turned everyday unhappiness into a disorder. Horwitz's (2005) article "The Age of Depression" is a clear account of his views. It is free at http://findarticles.com. Google the title and click on the "find articles" Web site pathway.

James Butcher, Susan Mineka, and Jill Hooley (2007) created a list of concepts called **elements of abnormality**. Each element alone may not make someone abnormal. The risk of abnormality increases with each addition of an element.

1. Suffering
2. Maladaptiveness
3. Deviancy
4. Violation of the standards of society
5. Social discomfort
6. Irrationality and unpredictability

### Note to the teacher

I ask students to consider the meaning of each item and rank them in order of importance, noting that one is not necessarily enough to call someone mentally ill. We have a discussion where students defend their responses and challenge each other, citing examples of disorders.

## Culture, normality, and abnormality

Anthony Marsella and Ann Marie Yamada (2007) think a person's cultural context is critical to considering the concepts of normality and abnormality. Their views are closely tied to cultural considerations in **diagnosis**. *Culture complicates thinking about normality and abnormality, but a diagnosis without it is incomplete.*

We must understand a person's cultural construction of reality to avoid calling them abnormal when they are not. Otherwise, we run the chance of over or under-diagnosing people and giving destructive treatments.

Almost every culture has its own system of diagnosis (Marsella & Yamada, 2007). While I highlight the **CCMD-3** (Chinese Classification of Mental Disorders) as an example of a non-Western classification system, I do not suggest that it is the only alternative to the **DSM-IV** and the **ICD-10**. While other diagnostic systems appear similar to Western classification systems to some degree, it cannot be assumed that they really are the same (Marsella & Yamada, 2007). For example, section 5.5 contains a study about how the meaning of the word depression is different for ethnic Pakistani living in the United Kingdom than it is for Western psychiatrists. *Marsella and Yamada say that we must avoid* **decontextualizing** *disorders.* A disorder is not automatically similar for another culture. For example, **susto** is a folk "fright illness" for Hispanics (http://altmed.creighton.edu/MexicanFolk/Susto.htm, 2008). The cause of susto is the soul leaving the body during a stressful event. Symptoms include sleep difficulties, withdrawal, loss of appetite, and listlessness. Treatment for susto in some Hispanic cultures involves "passing a chicken egg and herbs over a person's body" (p. 1). The symptoms of susto are similar to Western depression. But should we consider susto a kind of depressive disorder? *Do any similarities mean that the disorder shares the same causes, expression and course as those in the West?* Marsella and Yamada say absolutely not! "How can we separate a disorder from the very psyche in which it is construed and the very social context in which people respond to it?" (pp. 807–808).

## 7.5 Discuss Validity and Reliability of Diagnosis

### Can we end automatic reifying?

The biggest hurdle I face in teaching abnormal psychology is that students think of disorders as real things. *Reifying is automatic unless I make a big deal about it.* Even the DSM-IV-TR warns, "A common misconception is that a classification system of mental disorders classifies people, when really what are being classified are disorders that people have" (p. xxxi). It is much better to think about someone as "meeting the criteria for major depression" than to say "the depressed person." In addition, **cultural schemas** must never be far from your thoughts since culture affects the expression and course of mental illnesses.

The following situations might help reduce reifying. If a person reports symptoms such as blurry vision, itchy skin, cuts and sores healing slowly, increased thirst, frequent urination, and leg pain, a doctor thinks, "This person may have diabetes." The doctor then sends the person for a blood test to verify if diabetes is the correct diagnosis. Physical disorders are far more concrete than mental illnesses, plus there are lab tests to verify a diagnosis. But if a person reports symptoms such as sadness, difficulty sleeping, feelings of worthlessness, decreased appetite, and thoughts of suicide, a doctor thinks, "This person may have major depression." But the doctor cannot order a blood test to confirm the suspicion. In fact, it is possible that if a male and a female approach the same doctor with symptoms of depression, females may get the depression diagnosis more often than the male! To complicate matters even more, some people may seem "crazy" but are really just expressing behavior that is part of their culture. We have mental illness diagnostic systems, but that doesn't mean that a particular classification system is "right" (they change over time so ideas of mental illness are not static) or that there is only one way to look at a person's symptoms. As we studied before, TCM doesn't even distinguish between mental and physical health.

## Setting the stage for discussing reliability and validity

Are diagnostic manuals reliable and valid? The dominant manuals, the DSM-IV and the ICD-10, have evolved over time and as a result have become more reliable. But to what degree are the manuals valid? *That depends on whom you ask.* Validity is more controversial. Right now my answer is that diagnostic manuals are valid to *some* extent. Here is another place where Allan Horwitz's article, "The Age of Depression," is useful. Horwitz believes that validity should be valued over reliability. DSM-I and DSM-II situated a diagnosis within one's life context. The move to symptom-based diagnosis in the DSM-III improved reliability but compromised validity.

Increasing reliability decreases validity and vice versa. No one agrees on which is more valuable.

While there are many aspects to the validity debate, I ask the question "Do the manuals have cross-cultural validity?"

## A brief history of the DSM and ICD

A brief history of three diagnostic systems, the DSM-IV-TR, published in 2000 as a revision of the 1994 **DSM-IV**, the **ICD-10**, published in 1992, and the **CCMD-3**, published in 2001, will help clarify that mental disorders are abstractions and should not be reified. The DSM and the ICD are the most dominant of the diagnostic systems. The CCMD is a national classification system (Parker et al., 2001). It is a post–Mao science product. The first CCMD was published in 1979 and gave respectability to Chinese psychiatry. The CCMD has been revised several times, with the CCMD-1 appearing in 1981, CCMD-2 in 1984, and CCMD-3 in 2001. The CCMD-2 was revised primarily to be consistent (reliable) with the DSM and the ICD manuals. The CCMD is similar to the DSM and the ICD but retains numerous culture-bound disorders such as neurasthenia, Qi Kung disorder, and disorders due to witchcraft.

Let it be known that most cultures have a way of classifying mental disorder. Sometimes a cultural group does not even believe that sets of symptoms similar to Western "mental illnesses" are real mental disorders. So while I discuss the DSM, the ICD, and the CCMD as examples of classification, I refer now and again to disorders as they are thought of in other cultures.

Understanding the *assumptions* of diagnostic manuals helps in evaluating their reliability and validity.

The authors of the DSM-IV-TR (2000) include a section outlining its history and that of the ICD, suggesting that physicians have always needed to classify mental illnesses. The authors include a blunt statement that "there has been little agreement on which disorders should be included and the optimal method for their organization" (p. xxiv). The problem continues. The development of the DSM-V, expected in 2012, is laced with some contentious disagreements about what should be included.

Before I do anything else, you should know the definition of **nosology**. It is a branch of medicine that describes and classifies physical and mental diseases. A nosological system is just a classification system, such as Chinese nosology or the nosological system of the DSM. The term nosology pops up frequently in articles about classification.

The classification of mental disorders has varied in purpose and organization over the past two centuries (DSM-IV-TR, 2000). The number of disorders included in each system varied and sometimes the purpose was to collect statistical data while other times the purpose was to assist clinicians in getting the right help for patients.

Collecting statistical data was the objective of the first U.S. classification systems, starting with the 1840 census report that had just one classification, idiocy/insanity. Seven categories were used in the 1880 census, including mania and melancholia. Even in 1917, data on mental health, though evolving, were still used primarily for statistical purposes. After 1917, the American Medical Association included psychiatric disorder in its Standard Classified Nomenclature of disease.

Responding to the needs of World War II Veterans, the U.S. Army and the Veterans Administration developed a broader classification system for mental disorders. At the same time, the World Health Organization (WHO), heavily influenced by the U.S. Veterans Administration's efforts, included mental disorders into the sixth edition of the ICD for the first time. The ICD-6 had 10 psychotic disorders, nine neurotic disorders, and seven disorders of character, behavior, and intelligence. Each new edition of the DSM and the ICD were now made in collaboration with each other.

The first official DSM appeared in 1952, a modification of the ICD-6. The American Psychiatric Association conceived DSM-I as an official way to help practitioners get the right treatment for patients. The DSM-I used the term *reaction* throughout the manual to mean that mental disorder was a reaction to biological, social, and psychological factors. *This makes* **etiology**, *or causes, a primary assumption of DSM-I; diagnosis identified causation.*

The next important step for classification was the WHO's attempt to improve the sixth and seventh editions of the ICD, which were not popular. British psychiatrist Stengel headed the task force. Stengel suggested that each disorder needed a specific definition. The goal was to make diagnosis more *reliable*. While the DSM-II and ICD-8 did not follow Stengel's suggestions, *the present emphasis of the DSM-IV and the ICD-10 is on definitions that promote reliability.*

DSM-II was pretty much the same as DSM-I except that the term *reaction* was removed. *This was a move away from diagnosing mental illness in terms of causation.*

The DSM-III, which appeared in 1980, was developed in coordination with the ICD-9, which appeared in 1978. The DSM-III was very different from the previous manuals. The DSM-III was a *symptom-based* manual where the *context* of the illness was eliminated (Horwitz, 2005). The move to a symptom-based system increased reliability. Horwitz writes that it was easier for clinicians with different theoretical orientations to agree on lists of symptoms. But did the move away from context increase reliability at the expense of validity? The DSM-III was *neutral to causation,* contained specific *descriptions* of disorders, and included a multiaxial system (DSM-IV-TR, 2000). As the psychiatric manuals evolved, more and more research facilitated the changes. This research included the development of valid diagnostic assessments, such as semi-structured diagnostic interviews. The ICD-9 did not include two of the big changes in DSM-III, the diagnostic definitions and multiaxial system because its purpose was to gather statistics on mental disorder worldwide. The 1987 DSM-III-R's purpose was to clarify problems with the DSM-III.

The increasing research base about mental illness aided DSM-IV development. Committees reviewed the literature on each disorder in the DSM-III-R. Any time a disorder was backed up with only a small amount of research, a decision was made to keep or eliminate it based on field trials; did the disorder really exist in clinical practice? The field trials tested diagnostic criteria from the DSM-III, the DSM-III-R, the ICD-10 (published in 1992), and new proposals at 70 cites on over 6000 participants from many sociocultural groups. Field tests made sure that any difficult diagnostic category could be *reliably applied across many samples.*

The American Psychiatric Association task force for DSM-IV admitted that coming up with "absolute and infallible criteria" (DSM-IV-TR, 2000, p. xxviii) was impossible, though some organizing principles guided decisions. First, anything that appeared in the DSM-IV must be backed up with research. Second, the diagnostic criteria were simplified whenever possible. Third, the task force made the DSM-IV compatible with all of the following: the ICD-10, current research, opinions from unpublished research, field testing results, and "consensus of the field" (p. xxvii). The phrase "consensus of the field" was not defined.

Many proposals for new diagnoses were considered. These proposals were made based on patients seen in real clinical practice who did not fit an existing diagnosis. The only ones added to DSM-IV were those based on research. The writers of DSM-IV admitted that there was no way to include everything seen in clinics into the manual. Therefore, *the authors of DSM-IV know that there are limits to its categories.* There is no assumption that categories are discrete. In addition, a category system works best if everyone is homogeneous and there are "clear boundaries between cases" (p. xxxi). The obvious problem in applying a category system is that the problems of real clients seen in clinical practice do not fit neatly into a discrete category.

**Cultural** considerations were new to the DSM-IV, though *culture is not essential to DSM-IV diagnosis and thus limits its validity.* Validity concerns are intertwined with discussions about prevalence, cultural considerations in diagnosis, and gender and culture variations in prevalence. The discussion continues in section 7.6 and section 7.11.

Section 7.7 contains a history of the CCMD.

## What might we expect to see in the DSM-V?

Google "DSM-V" to see a wide range of proposals and some very heated debates. In addition, the entire book titled *A Research Agenda for DSM-V* is free at the American Psychiatric Association's Web site. Access it by Googling the title or go to www.appi.org/pdf/kuper_2292.pdf.

Several proposals interest me because they would add new disorders, improve classification, and increase cultural validity in diagnosis.

The proposals for new mental disorders are interesting, such as Internet addiction.

Another is the idea to simplify the way mood disorders are diagnosed. Daniel Klein (2008) suggests changing the symptom-based system for diagnosing depression to a two-dimensional system of severity and chronicity. The book *A Research Agenda for DSM-V* has a chapter devoted to the possibility of using continuums for all diagnostic categories in the chapter about validity.

Renato Alarcon and colleagues (2002) want culture to be more central to diagnosis. Their arguments appear in one chapter of the book *A Research Agenda for DSM-V.*

The ICD is also under revision. The ICD-11 is expected after the publication of the DSM-V. The document about the ICD revision process is available free at www.who.int/classifications/icd/ICDRevision.pdf.

## 7.6 Discuss Cultural and Ethical Considerations in Diagnosis

Prevalence rates are incorrect unless psychologists diagnose persons from all cultures accurately. Both over- and under-diagnosis are the potentially dangerous and *unethical* results of applying Western diagnostic criteria cross-culturally. If culture affects diagnosis significantly and these concerns are left unaddressed, then the **validity** of diagnostic systems is compromised.

Be careful with the phrase "cultural variation." The term "variation" is appropriate only as long as it is not interpreted as deviating from a "real" standard that is set out in a Western diagnostic manual. Otherwise, you run the risk of **ethnocentrism**.

# General concerns about culture and the validity of diagnosis

Marsella and Yamada (2007) highlight a statement by Lawrence Kirmayer that appeared in *Transcultural Psychiatry*. Kirmayer stressed that the aim of cultural psychiatry was to consider behavior within someone's cultural context but that diagnostic manuals did just the opposite—they **decontextualized** mental illness. Western diagnostic manuals situate the problem within the brain or as a psychological state rather than looking at **situational** factors affecting the person. Many mental illnesses stem from family and community problems.

In addition, Marsella and Yamada draw attention to a statement from Asian Indian psychiatrist Chalraborty. He claims that studies investigating culture and mental illness originate from Western thinking, even if they are meant to be cross-cultural. These studies take the point of view that mental illness in another culture is a variation of a "real" mental disorder seen in the West. Psychiatrists practicing in non-Western countries use the Western standards but find that they are not really useful for behaviors in other cultural contexts. Marsella and Yamada therefore view Western diagnostic systems as *dominant* rather than *accurate*.

Marsella and Yamada (2007) list seven factors that contribute to mental illness across culture, particularly depression.

1. Social conditions such as "war, natural disasters, racism, poverty, cultural collapse, aging populations, urbanization, and rapid social and technological changes" (p. 811) are important.

2. Western experiences with depression may be linked to an abstract language that separates the person from their experiences, emphasizes guilt, and emphasizes the characteristics associated with **individualism**. In contrast, people in non-Western cultures experience depression primarily through somatic symptoms that show a unity of mind and body.

3. Messages from the media contribute to the experience of depression.

4. The way that people know their world is through the "self." How the self is represented in each culture affects the interpretation of everything from emotions to relationships with others.

5. Social class is a factor. There is an inverse correlation between depression and social class. This means that, as depression rates rise, social class lowers.

6. Powerlessness, inequality, racism, and cultural disintegration contribute to poor mental health.

7. The **stigma** of mental illness prevents some people from getting help. My discussion on the symptoms and prevalence of depression in China highlights the concern. If Western definitions are used to categorize someone as depressed, might practitioners be creating stigmas? Parker and colleagues (2001) make it clear that supporters of Chinese categorization systems think that many cases of depression can be re-diagnosed as neurasthenia. Creating stigmas is particularly a problem with ethnic minorities within a larger group, especially if the diagnosis contributes to cultural breakdown for the person. Stigmatization and cultural disintegration are potential *ethical* problems.

## Classification and **eating disorders**: A specific example of the concern

Anne Becker (2007) writes that using Western classifications to diagnose eating disorders cross-culturally prevents psychologists from getting accurate **prevalence** rates. In addition, many persons may be either under- or over-diagnosed.

**Norms** about food consumption and accepted body shape differ across cultures. It then follows that symptoms of body shape distortions and disordered eating differ across culture. In addition, the way that **stress** is experienced and expressed varies across culture. The challenge is to come up with a way to collect *comparable* data about the prevalence of eating disorders cross-culturally while respecting cultural variations. This is a huge challenge.

The challenge involves the proper use of **etics** and **emics**. Etic approaches apply universal diagnostic systems, usually based on Western classifications. Assessment tests that are translated and **back translated**, such as the Eating Disorders Attitude Scale (EAT-26), are *intended* to have cross-cultural **reliability** and **validity**.

The etic approach is inadequate, though it is designed to make cross-cultural data comparable.

The other way to collect data is through an emic approach that starts with locally meaningful contexts for eating disordered symptoms. Becker writes that "To the extent that core cultural values are represented in body shape ideals and dietary norms, rationale for food refusal, concern for body shape, and distress associated with overeating will be culturally particular" (p. S112).

An emic approach may be the best way to collect data, though it compromises comparability.

Here are some problems that come up when researchers fail to take emics into account. A fat phobia is important to Western diagnoses of anorexia nervosa (AN). But persons from Hong Kong, Japan, Singapore, Malaysia, South Africa, and India can have all the other symptoms of AN except the fat phobia. Becker says that persons from Hong Kong have been misclassified as non-cases of eating disorders based on the EAT-26 simply because they lacked a fat phobia. Black adolescents from South Africa who tested positively for eating disorders by the EAT-26 later clarified in follow-up interviews that they were preoccupied with food because of poverty, hunger, and food shortages, not because they had an eating disorder. Too many mistakes happen without knowledge of a person's social context.

Attitudes about food consumption also complicate the etic approach. During Fijian feasting, local herbal tonics are used for purging after culturally sanctioned overeating. This behavior may look like bingeing and purging, but traditional Fijian culture does not consider it disordered. Traditional Fijian culture lacks eating disorder classifications that are similar to Western ones. A local Fijian diagnosis exists for **macake**, an appetite disorder that is not similar to anything in the West. Persons with macake refuse food and have poor appetites, behaviors that arouse great social concern. Macake is usually brief since persons are willing to take herbal supplements to restore their appetite. The behaviors lack meaning unless we are aware of the social context.

Becker adds that persons *within* Western populations are frequently misdiagnosed because classifications are too limited. For example, the most frequent eating disorder in the West is actually "eating disorder not otherwise specified" (EDNOS), those with atypical symptoms. Some recurring purging without bingeing goes undiagnosed because it does not fit into existing classifications. Perhaps the DSM-IV is not currently designed to pick up the wide range of disordered eating even within Western persons.

Part of the problem lies with professional journals. Only about 6% of the articles that appear in the major psychiatric journals report research on persons representing 90% of the world's population. These journals give off the impression that Western classification is the norm and are guilty of *reifying* these "norms" as universals. The potential to **stigmatize** and **stereotype** is great from these Western points of view.

The question remains, to what extent is it possible to have both an etic approach for cross-cultural comparison while using emic features that are meaningful in specific social contexts?

## Culture-bound disorders

**Culture-bound disorders** deserve a separate subheading.

The DSM-IV was the first edition to contain a section on culture-bound disorders, but they are listed *as an appendix at the end of the manual.* Appendix I in the DSM-IV-TR is titled "Outline for Cultural Formulation and Glossary of Culture-Bound Syndromes." Cultural information *supplements* the diagnostic categories and helps practitioners apply DSM-IV classifications to someone from another culture. Clinicians are directed to take a person's cultural background into account each time they apply a DSM-IV diagnosis. Culture-bound disorders are defined as "recurrent, locality-specific patterns of aberrant behavior and troubling experience that may or may not be linked to a particular DSM-IV diagnostic category" (p. 898). The manual explains that culture-bound disorders are typically limited to one culture and are considered localized folk "illnesses" (the DSM-IV-TR uses quotes here) with local names. No DSM diagnoses are equivalent to culture-bound disorders.

Examples of culture-bound disorders listed in the DSM-IV-TR are **susto**, **shenjing shuairuo** (**neurasthenia** in China that involves many somatic, or bodily, symptoms), **Shin-byung** (a Korean disorder where the person has anxiety, somatic complaints, dissociation, and spirit possession), **zar** (spirit possession in some North African and Middle Eastern societies), and **brain fag** (a West African disorder that students get as the result of school demands).

Considering culture-bound disorders raises some larger questions for mental health clinicians (Marsella & Yamada, 2007). How should we think about any mental disorder? *Are disorders **etics** or responses to one's cultural context?* Perhaps they are both. At least we should consider the implications of the view we take. Can any disorder really be interpreted outside of its cultural context? If the DSM-IV-TR lists groups of mental disorders and then includes a list of non-Western disorders in the Appendix that are viewed as "exotic," can we make a case that the categories are really a product of Western **cultural schema**? Are all disorders culture bound? Are culture-bound disorders variations of Western anxiety or depression? Should culture-bound disorders be classified as personality, neurotic, or psychotic disorders?

## Note to the teacher

These questions should create some good class debate. Several studies in this book will help the class think about culture and ethics in diagnosis. A study about diagnosing depression in Uganda is in this section. A discussion of culture, diagnosis, and depression in China is in the next section. Traditional Chinese culture **stigmatizes** persons with a mental health problem. The family and extended family "loses face" (Parker et al., 2001). The study about the Pakistani in section 5.5 shows how the word depression can mean different things to different ethnic groups living in the West.

## Diagnosis and prevalence of depression in Uganda's Baganda

Try and answer this question. Should the Ugandan people described below be diagnosed with major depression as defined in Western psychiatric manuals? There is not one right answer, but it makes for good class discussion about cultural and ethical concerns in diagnosis, prevalence rates, causes, and treatments of depression. In addition, knowledge of **individual interviews** and **focus group interviews** is required for HL Paper 3.

Elialilia Okello and Solvig Ekblad (2006) used individual interviews and focus group interviews in the form of case vignettes to explore lay perceptions of "depression" in the

Baganda of Uganda. Vignettes are short stories. The goal of this pilot study was to see if case vignettes were a feasible method for gathering data on lay views on the causes, behavioral effects, and treatments of depression.

Okello and Ekblad write that "depression" in Uganda is often expressed and referred to as an "**illness of thoughts**" rather than an emotional illness. Illnesses of thoughts do not require medicine, as there is no medicine for thinking. Medical help is required only in cases of chronic or recurring illness.

The Bagandan view shows the complexities of diagnosis. If the lay population does not recognize the symptoms as depression, it is unlikely to be received as a diagnosis. This is not to suggest that the Baganda change. They have their own history of thinking about mental illness that fits with their cultural expectations.

Okello and Ekblad claim that the prevalence of depressive symptoms in Uganda is high, between 10% and 25%, largely because of its violent history and the large number of HIV/AIDS cases in the population. While observations made in psychiatric clinics in Uganda suggest that depression is one of the most common disorders, the people of Uganda rarely recognize it as such, and about 70%–90% of mental health problems in Uganda never reach mental health services.

## Note to the teacher

Your class must decide if the Bagandan symptoms should be considered "depression" and treated as such or if the symptoms should be handled locally with accordance with local custom.

The interviews took place in Bajjo, a small district close to the capital. Bajjo is semirural and a good place to test the methods that were to be used in a larger study with both rural and urban participants.

Here is some background on the Baganda that is needed to interpret the case vignettes.

The clan system dominates how Bagandans think about others. No one is thought about without reference to patrilineal descent. Clan members are extended family members where people are thought of as family even if blood ties are distant. The clan is a hierarchy, with the clan leader at the top. All clans have a primary and secondary totem, a symbol for the clan that often takes the form of an animal or plant. Everyone introduces themselves to others in the context of the clan.

The Baganda believe in superhuman spirits and that a person's spirit remains after death. Many other African cultures share this belief. Several types of spirits are recognized. One is *mizimu,* ghosts of the dead. These spirits seek out those that the dead person holds a grudge against. *Misambwa* are objects that the mizimu has entered. *Balubaale* are spirits that have the talents of outstanding men. All three spirits are called *byekika,* or "the clan things." Spirits are believed to influence health and are divided into two general groups, the family/community spirits that aid in health unless they are upset and alien/evil ones that cause most of the trouble.

The Baganda connect illnesses with body parts. For example, a cough is labeled "chest." "Depressive symptoms" stem from thoughts and from the heart, so depression is connected to either, such as "illness of thoughts." Illnesses are further broken down into those that are treated by traditional healers or folk remedies and those that are treated by Western doctors. The way the Baganda think about illness and treatment affect **help–seeking behavior**.

Five individual participants responded to the vignettes, including three traditional healers and one faith healer. Other participants took part in four different focus groups of six each representing different layers of society. The focus groups were secondary school girls, village women, village men, and primary level teachers (the only mixed gender group). The researchers made sure that variables that might influence the perception of individuals in each focus group, such as age and educational level, were controlled.

The DSM-IV was used to create the vignettes. The authors created a series of stories illustrating different experiences with depression so that participants could consider if anyone they knew fit the descriptions. The vignettes and interview questions about the vignettes were translated into Luganda, the local language and then **back translated** into English.

The researchers used five vignettes for the study. I will describe two.

One case was a 28-year-old person with major depression symptoms without psychotic features. The symptoms included unhappiness, a lack of enjoyment of usual activities, a closed mind, feelings of emptiness, sleeping difficulties, a change in eating habits, no energy, thoughts that life was no longer worth living, wandering thoughts, and thoughts of death and suicide.

All 30 participants were able to connect the vignette with their own experience or someone they knew. Most everyone described the symptoms as "too many worrisome thoughts." The thoughts were judged to be under a person's control and the person should avoid the thoughts. While most of the participants thought that the vignette described mental illness or a sickness of one's soul, they did not consider the person to be "mad." While these "illnesses of thought" were considered a mental illness, most of the participants thought that it was the kind of illness that should be treated by traditional healers rather than Western medicine. Traditional healers in the individual interviews characterized the symptoms as "mild madness" that were the result of witchcraft. The view of the traditional healers was a little different from that of the lay community members. But both the lay participants and traditional healers supported local interpretations; traditional healers should treat all illnesses that are the result of community or cultural causes.

Another case was a 38-year-old person with recurring dysthymia over four years. This person felt uncomfortable, complained of bodily aches and pains, and thought a neighbor was bewitching him/her. This person had received treatment from both a local mental health clinic, without success, and a local healer. The focus group members thought that these symptoms were the result of a family disease (genetic), HIV, and/or witchcraft. The explanations for the symptoms are a combination of biomedical and local beliefs. The men's focus group added that these symptoms were a recent problem and had no formal name in their language, though they believed it to be the result of everyday life conditions, such as lacking money.

The results from all the vignettes showed that the Baganda categorized the causes of mental disorder into four groups. One cause is psychological factors that come from thinking too much about things such as relationship problems. A second cause is socioeconomic factors such as job loss. A third cause is spiritual factors such as witchcraft and angry ancestral gods. The last cause is biological/physical factors such as genes or chronic physical illness, which is reserved for cases with recurrent symptoms. Eighty percent of the participants perceived depression to be primarily the result of social stress. Most cases of "depression" are viewed as an "illness of thoughts" that were not chronic and best treated by spiritual healers. Only symptoms that are recurring are considered linked to genetics or chronic illness requiring Western medical care, and even if the person might benefit from Western medicine, local healers still consulted with the cases.

All participants stressed the importance of getting help from family, friends, clan elders, and religious leaders as well as traditional healers. Traditional healers were recommended when the illness was caused by witchcraft, angry ancestral gods, or if the illness had an unknown cause. One focus group member said that the lack of Western mental health services available was a reason that Western medicine was not used.

The authors write that the findings of this pilot study should be viewed as tentative. There are some limitations of the use of focus groups in this study. The authors relied heavily on **informants** for assistance. These informants were local authorities and could have biased the study by recommending that certain persons become participants. The use of specifically designed vignettes in the individual interviews may have limited the discussion to just those situations. Future research will either confirm the findings from the present study or take the research into new directions.

## 7.7 Describe Symptoms and Prevalence of Major Depression: Affective (Mood) Disorders

The WHO (2001) reports on the **prevalence** of **depression** vary substantially across cultures. For example, point prevalence for depression in a 1995 report shows 6.3% in Seattle, Washington, 4% in China, 4.7% in Verona, Italy, 15.9% in Groningen, Germany, 16.9% in Manchester, United Kingdom, 11.6% in Ankara, Turkey, and 2.6% in Nagasaki, Japan.

So even though the examples of symptoms and prevalence that follow come from the DSM-IV-TR and the CCMD-3, keep in mind that these two classification systems do not necessarily represent the symptoms and prevalence rates from other cultures.

You need to know what **point prevalence** and **lifetime prevalence** mean. Point prevalence is the percentage of people with a disorder at one time. Lifetime prevalence refers to the risk over one's life of having a disorder.

"Major depressive disorder, also called major depression, is characterized by a combination of symptoms that interfere with a person's ability to work, sleep, study, eat, and enjoy once-pleasurable activities. Major depression is disabling and prevents a person from functioning normally. An episode of major depression may occur only once in a person's lifetime, but more often, it recurs throughout a person's life" (NIMH, 2008).

Let's compare how the **DSM-IV** and the **CCMD-3** define the symptoms and report prevalence rates for major depression.

### DSM-IV-TR diagnosis for major depression and prevalence reports

To receive a diagnosis of major depressive disorder, single episode, five symptoms from the list must occur during a two week period (DSM-IV-TR, 2000). These symptoms must be very different from the regular behavior of a person.

1. Self-reports or information from others show that the person has depressed mood most of the day each day.

2. Self-reports or information from others show that the person has a significantly lowered interest and pleasure in activities all day almost every day.

3. The person experiences changes in appetite and/or weight. This means that a 5% weight gain or loss occurs, or one's appetite increases or decreases most every day.

4. Almost every day, the person suffers from insomnia or hypersomnia (extreme sleepiness).

5. Reports from others show that the person is physically too active or not active enough.

6. The person is tired or has low energy almost every day.

7. The person feels worthless or shows too much or inappropriate guilt almost every day.

8. The person cannot concentrate or is indecisive almost every day.

9. The person has frequent thoughts of dying that are not just fears of dying. The person may have thoughts of suicide without a plan, has plans for suicide, or has attempted suicide.

The prevalence rate varies among U.S. samples. According to the DSM-IV-TR, the lifetime prevalence for major depressive disorder is from 10%–25% for females and from 5%–12% for males. The chance of having major depressive disorder at one point in time is from 5%–9% in females and from 2%–3% in males. The average age to have the first episode of major depression is the mid-20s. Studies show that the age when someone first experiences major depression is *decreasing*. Some people have one episode of major depression and others have recurring problems. Those with one episode have a 60% chance of having a second episode. Those with two episodes have a 70% chance of a third one. Those with three episodes have a 90% chance of a fourth. Studies show that one year after diagnosis, 40% are free of symptoms, 20% have some symptoms, and 40% still meet the criteria for the disorder.

## CCMD-3 diagnosis for depressive episode

The CCMD-3 contains a disorder called "depressive episode" that is similar to the DSM-IV major depressive disorder but with some differences that reflect its use in Chinese culture. To receive this diagnosis, a person must have a depressed mood that does not fit with the person's situation. The depressed mood must also include four of the following symptoms. These symptoms refer to a single episode of depression. There are separate diagnoses for recurrent depression and mild depression. A diagnosis of recurrent depression requires that any type of depression must occur within the past two months. Mild depression is the same as depressive episode but the impairment in social behavior is mild. The DSM-IV-TR does not contain a diagnosis of mild depression.

1. The person has a loss of interest in or loss of enjoyment.

2. The person has low energy or fatigue.

3. The person is either physically agitated or shows little motor activity.

4. The person has low self-esteem, feels worthless, is self-blaming, or is preoccupied with guilt.

5. The person is unable to focus his or her thinking.

6. The person has attempted some kind of self-harm or suicide or has thoughts of doing either.

7. The person has insomnia, wakes to early in the morning, or has hypersomnia.

8. The person has little appetite or obvious weight loss (no percentage of weight loss is given).

9. The person has a decreased libido.

The CCMD-3 also contains a diagnosis of **neurasthenia**. Chinese persons often express depressive symptoms as somatic complaints. Neurasthenia is then a more appropriate diagnosis, though it is not used as widely as it once was (Chinese Society of Psychiatry, 2003). Neurasthenia is classified in the group of disorders called "Hysteria, Stress-related disorders, Neurosis." Neurasthenia is not a DSM-IV-TR diagnosis.

Neurasthenia is listed as a *neurosis*. The main symptoms are mental and physical weaknesses. The person is easily excited and fatigued and is tense, annoyed, or irritated. The person has sleep problems and muscle tension or pain. These symptoms are not part of another disorder and usually persist over several months. The person may be experiencing great stress and may suddenly start to have headaches and difficulty sleeping.

Neurasthenia includes the following symptoms:

1. The person meets the criteria for neurosis. Neurosis is classified as a stress-related disorder in the CCMD-3, which also includes phobias, panic attacks, and obsessive behavior. For those students studying **anxiety disorders**, it is interesting that the CCMD-3 classifies them under stress-related disorders. For a person to have any of the neurotic disorders, they must have some insight about the problems but the symptoms must be out of proportion to the person's actual circumstances.

2. The person has mental and physical weakness, such as a lack of vigor, problems with concentration and memory, and physical fatigue that are recovered by rest, along with two of the following:

   a. The person has emotional difficulties, such as tenseness, anxiety and depression that are not the prominent symptoms, irritability and difficulty in coping with daily life.
   b. The person is easily excited (meaning agitated), such as difficulty concentrating on one thing at a time.
   c. The person has muscle aches and pains or dizziness.
   d. The person has problems sleeping, such as insomnia.
   e. The person has other psychological or physical problems, such as rapid heartbeat or tinnitus (ringing or roaring noises in the ears).

## Prevalence of depression in China

The CCMD-3 does not contain prevalence rates. It is hard to pinpoint exact prevalence rates in China, which probably vary a great deal by region.

Cultural values affect the expression and diagnosis of mental illness. Understanding symptoms and prevalence rates of depression in China requires a history lesson about mental health in China.

The Chinese are the world's largest ethnic group, representing approximately 22% of the world's population (Parker et al., 2001). But do not assume that everyone in China thinks about mental health the same way. *Many factors make understanding the symptoms and prevalence rates complex.* For example, there are 55 official and numerous unofficial ethnic groups within China and the rapid changes occurring since the end of Mao's regime have affected the *layers* of society differently. Some parts of China have adopted Western psychiatric views, some combine Western and traditional Chinese views, and others have kept their beliefs exclusive to Traditional Chinese Medicine.

Depression was rarely diagnosed in China in the 1980s. A psychiatric study was conducted in 1982 and again in 1993 using a combination of the ICD and Chinese classification. In 1993, only 16 of 19,223 persons met the criteria for an affective disorder, and this was higher than the rate found in 1982. The study showed that the lifetime prevalence rate for affective disorder was 0.08%; several hundred times lower than the rate of affective disorder in the United States.

Even studies on the prevalence from Taiwan between 1982 and 1986, a more industrialized nation, show that the prevalence of depression is low.

Why is the rate so low in comparison with U.S. rates? There are many possibilities, including an actual low rate, low reporting because of social **stigma**, sampling problems, the presence of other disorders that are similar to depression and more culturally valid for the Chinese, and cultural differences in **help-seeking behavior**.

Chinese psychiatrists have not historically diagnosed depression as often as they have other equivalent disorders. For example, during a one-week period in Hunan province, only 1%

of the patients were diagnosed with depression while 30% received the diagnosis for neurasthenia. Adding to the complexities is the attitude of the typical person toward doctors. For example, people are more likely to consult a TCM practitioner for problems they consider "illnesses" and a Western-type doctor for problems they categorize as "diseases." *Chinese persons do not generally consider emotional upset a disease.*

So does a true Western depression exist in China? Yes, but depression is embedded in the history of how the Chinese think about mental illness. *The Chinese may de-emphasize depressive symptoms as defined by Western standards, but in turn, depression may be overemphasized and pathologized in the West.* You need to understand neurasthenia and **Traditional Chinese Medicine** to understand why the Chinese think about depression the way they do.

TCM was the primary care for mental health problems in China until the beginning of the 1900s (Chinese Society of Psychiatry, 2005). Remember from section 5.10 that TCM makes no distinction between mental and physical health. All mental and physical health problems are Qi imbalances that are treated with acupuncture, herbs, and lifestyle changes.

In the early 1900s, new ideas came to China and neurasthenia was one of those new ideas (Parker et al., 2001). Neurasthenia was a neurological concept, a condition where a person experiences primarily somatic symptoms. In China, neurasthenia was called **shenjing shuairuo**, meaning neurological weakness. Shenjing shuairuo was a common Chinese illness. Approximately 80% of psychiatric patients in China received the diagnosis of neurasthenia by the 1980s. People without much experience and knowledge of Western mental disorders experience distress physically and report these symptoms to doctors. In addition, the experience of mental health as a physical problem is less **stigmatizing**, something that is still a concern for Chinese persons. Chinese psychiatrists also prefer not to call someone depressed because of the social stigma for people.

Another concern is the various translations of the word depression, which can mean "repress," "gloomy," or "disorder," all of which are unpopular with the Chinese.

Last, political history influences attitudes toward depression. Mao thought that psychology was "90 percent useless" and mental illnesses were incorrect political thinking. Political policy amplified the social stigma of mental illness, *making neurasthenia a socially acceptable diagnosis.* There are plenty of words in the Chinese language for emotions, so it is not a language problem that makes the Chinese prefer to report somatic symptoms. Rather, *it is a cultural preference, a "display rule," that dictates what the Chinese report to doctors.* Chinese persons find it more acceptable to seek medical help for physical problems rather than emotional problems. Perhaps the way that the Chinese express their emotions helps to define the somatic symptoms. The Chinese do not always directly use specific emotion words but rather speak in metaphors that relate to their emotions. These metaphors tend to be physical in nature and may define the symptoms that are reported.

In the 1980s, China opened to Western influence, which included Western psychiatric practice. By the time that the DSM-III was published in 1983, Western-influenced psychiatrists in China thought that most neurasthenia cases could be re-diagnosed as depression. Chinese doctors realized that the diagnosis of depression gave them a new treatment option—antidepressant drugs. There were no anti-neurasthenia drugs.

But while neurasthenia became less popular with modern Chinese psychiatrists, it was still preferred by the typical person as a diagnosis throughout the 1990s. So even today, neurasthenia is used, though not as much as before. *However, those supporting the Chinese classification system argue that cases of depression can be re-diagnosed a neurasthenia!*

Diagnostic systems continue to evolve, so the Chinese interpretation of "depressive symptoms" will continue to evolve. Just understand that the use of TCM in China is still widespread and is embedded in Chinese culture. Currently, less than 10% of people suffering from depression get Western psychiatric treatment (Chinese Society of Psychiatry, 2005). Both Western psychiatrists and TCM practitioners work at Chinese hospitals and it is common for persons getting Western psychiatric help to also get TCM treatments. It is accepted that the two forms of medicine are complementary. Please refer to the studies on acupuncture and depression in section 5.10 and section 7.13 on eclectic treatments for example studies.

To further complicate matters, TCM is gaining in popularity in the West, as a supplement or replacement for Western medicine.

*Prevalence rates may be affected by the style of diagnosis used by Chinese psychiatrists* (Parker et al., 2001). For example, Chinese psychiatrists take a broader perspective of schizophrenia, and some cases of depression may be diagnosed as schizophrenia. Parker and colleagues report the results of a 1988 study comparing diagnoses of 116 patients in Shanghai made by Western psychiatrists and Chinese psychiatrists. Half of these patients who were diagnosed by Western psychiatrists as depressed using the DSM-III were given a different diagnosis by Chinese psychiatrists. Patients reporting anxiety and depression along with somatic complaints were given something other than depression, showing that Chinese psychiatrists placed emphasis on somatic complaints.

A shortage of Chinese psychiatrists may be another reason that patients are not classified as depressed. Because of budget limitations, a small number of Chinese psychiatrists sometimes have only a short time to diagnosis patients. Parker and colleagues wonder if Chinese psychiatrists would select depression as a diagnosis more frequently if they had more time to evaluate a patient.

But even if a Chinese person is diagnosed with depression, it does not mean that they use Western treatments. Even today, shortages in budgets and personnel as well as attitudes against depression as stigmatizing affect the use of Western psychiatric treatments (Chinese Society of Psychiatry, 2005). In addition, doctors practicing TCM have efficacy studies showing that their treatments can be just as effective and have fewer side effects, cost less, and do not stigmatize.

Does a low rate of depression also occur in Chinese populations outside of China? Studies show that the rates are still lower in Westernized Chinese populations (Parker et al., 2001). Parker and colleagues report a 1998 study conducted in Los Angeles on 1,747 Chinese Americans. Their lifetime prevalence rate for major depression is 6.9%, much less than the 17.1% rate of the general U.S. population rate. Watch jumping to conclusions about the reason for these low rates. Perhaps health-seeking behavior differences in the Chinese account for these results.

Are the Chinese just more **resilient** to depression? Parker and colleagues list several sociocultural factors that promote resilience in the Chinese. There is a long tradition in Chinese culture of accepting hardship, interdependence with family members who provide social support, and an attitude that the family is responsible for taking care of individual family members.

Assessments used to diagnose mental disorder need cross-cultural relevance. Is part of the problem the assessment instruments? For example, Parker and colleagues report that the Zung Self-Rating Depression Scale identifies different ways that people express depressive symptoms. A study comparing white, black, and Chinese students from China using the Zung scale shows that white students report cognitive symptoms, black students report a mix of somatic and emotional symptoms, and Chinese students report mainly somatic symptoms. The Chinese also have a Chinese Depressive Symptom Scale (CDSS), which is designed to give Chinese patients the chance to report a wider variety of symptoms. But even the CDSS collected more somatic symptoms. *Perhaps we should think of the emphasis of somatic complaints as a culturally accepted cognitive style.*

## 7.8 Describe Symptoms and Prevalence of Anorexia Nervosa: Eating Disorders

Most of the symptoms for **anorexia nervosa** (AN) are similar in the DSM-IV-TR and the CCMD-3. One difference that stands out relates to the *fear of getting fat*. A fat phobia is part of the DSM-IV diagnosis. The ICD-10 also contains a requirement for an intense fear of getting fat. In contrast, fear of getting fat is *possible but not required* for a CCMD-3 diagnosis. This difference is most likely because of cultural differences in attitudes about weight.

Pamela Keel (2005) writes that "anorexia nervosa" as a medical term first appeared in 1874 as the way William Gull described the symptoms of four girls who deliberately lost weight. So eating disorders existed before modern times. Historically, AN was not linked to a fear of fat. Instead, it was self-starvation related to moral beliefs and attention seeking. The diagnosis for AN has *changed over time* to include modern, perhaps Western, cultural influences concerning weight and body shape. Since the fear of being fat and concerns about body shape are relatively new to AN diagnoses, there are arguments about whether either should be required to diagnose AN.

In any case, while AN exists historically, there has been a modest increase in its diagnosis over time.

### DSM-IV-TR diagnosis for anorexia nervosa

The DSM-IV-TR (2000) categorizes anorexia nervosa (AN) under the heading "Eating Disorders." Eating disorders are severe disturbances in eating behavior and includes AN and bulimia nervosa (BN). A person diagnosed with AN is "characterized by a refusal to maintain a minimally normal body weight, is intensely afraid of gaining weight, and exhibits a significant disturbance in the perception of the shape or size of his or her body" (p. 583).

### Note to the teacher

The health psychology option includes the study of **obesity**. Note that obesity is not included as an eating disorder in the DSM-IV because psychological factors are not linked consistently to obesity. If it is determined that psychological factors are important to obesity in a person, the DSM allows it to be diagnosed under the category "Psychological Conditions Affecting Medical Condition." The ICD also does not include obesity as a mental disorder, and instead lists it as a general medical condition.

The DSM-IV-TR lists the symptoms of AN as follows:

1. The person will not maintain normal weight for their age and height. The person is 85% of an appropriate weight because of weight loss or failing to gain the appropriate weight during a developmental period.
2. The person is extremely fearful of gaining weight or being fat, even though he/she is already underweight.
3. The person denies that his/her weight loss or lack of weight gain is a serious problem, has a distorted view of body shape and weight, or places too great an emphasis on weight or body shape in self-reports.
4. Amenorrhea, meaning that a female misses three menstrual cycles in a row.

The DSM-IV-TR lists two types of AN, Restricting and Binge-Eating/Purging Type. Restricting types engage in extreme fasting, dieting, or exercising. Restricting types do not binge/purge, where large amounts of food are consumed and are followed by self-induced vomiting or the use of laxatives, diuretics, or enemas.

The lifetime prevalence rate of AN in females is 0.5%. Males are one-tenth as likely to get AN as females. Rates of AN have increased significantly but modestly during the 20th century (Keel, 2005).

AN typically starts between the ages of 14 and 18 (DSM-IV-TR). Stressful events often proceed AN. The length of time someone has AN and the level of recovery varies. Some fully recover after one episode of AN, some have problems with fluctuating weight and then relapse, and some people have chronic problems and even die from AN. Sometimes persons with AN are hospitalized in an attempt to stabilize weight. Of those admitted to hospitals, about 10% eventually die of AN.

## CCMD-3 diagnosis for anorexia nervosa

Eating disorders are classified as part of a group of disorders called "Physiological disorders related to psychological disorders" (Chinese Society of Psychiatry, 2003) in the CCMD-3. Eating disorders include AN, BN, and disordered vomiting. AN is described as primarily a disorder of adolescent females where they deliberately eat less and weigh less than is considered normal. Patients often worry about being fat even when they are already underweight and if a doctor tells them they are not fat. AN patients usually suffer from the consequences of poor nutrition as well as metabolism and hormone imbalances.

The symptoms include the following:

1. A person shows a large amount of weight loss of at least 15% below the expected weight.

2. A person deliberately loses weight and has at least one of the following:
   a. The person avoids fatty foods.
   b. The person uses self-induced vomiting to purge food.
   c. The person exercises in the extreme.
   d. The person uses drugs to lessen appetite and/or diuretics.

3. The person typically has a fear of getting fat, *but is not required to have this fear to get a diagnosis of AN.*

4. The person's endocrine system is out of balance. The imbalance can take numerous forms, such as amenorrhea, heightened levels of growth hormone, high cortisol levels, and insulin abnormalities.

5. The person has had the symptoms for at least three months.

6. The person may also show signs of depression or obsessive behavior. In these cases, the person should receive a second diagnosis.

Prevalence rates of AN are not in the CCMD-3. Prevalence rates of AN in China are included in a study reviewed in the next section comparing the prevalence of eating disorders and differences in attitudes toward eating in Western and non-Western countries (Makino, Tsuboi, & Dennerstein, 2004). Generally, AN is more prevalent in Western countries but is *increasing* in non-Western countries. While rates are increasing in non-Western countries, remember that people in non-Western cultures may have different experiences with eating disorders than the experiences categorized in diagnostic systems using Western **norms**.

Makino and colleagues conducted a search of MEDLINE and Medscape between 1982 and 2003 for English-language articles about prevalence rates. In addition, any survey using the Eating Disorders Attitudes Test-26 (EAT-26) was included to compare Western and non-Western attitudes toward eating. The EAT-26 is thought to predict the development of an eating disorder.

The authors realize that there are methodological limitations to their study. First, diagnoses of AN were made with either the DSM-IV or the ICD-10. Second, the EAT-26 was created in the West but was translated and used to gather data in non-Western countries. Third, because eating disorder rates are lower in non-Western countries, larger samples are necessary to see prevalence rates. Last, most of the participants are from convenience samples from schools or medical facilities.

Results on prevalence rates of AN in non-Western countries, including China, showed:

1. In 1989, there were few cases of AN recorded in Hong Kong.
2. By 1991, there was a small rise of reported AN cases in Hong Kong to 0.46%
3. In 1996, 6.5% of females in Hong Kong showed disordered eating attitudes on the EAT-26.
4. In 1998, 8.5% of both male and female adults in Korea showed disordered eating attitudes on the EAT-26.
5. In 1999, 5.4% of both male and female Japanese high school students showed disordered eating attitudes on the EAT-26. Another survey in 2000 showed that 4.1% of both Japanese males and females showed disordered eating attitudes on the EAT-26.
6. By 2003, the percentage increased to 11.2% in Japanese female high school samples for disordered eating attitudes on the EAT-26.
7. In 1982, seven cases of AN were reported in Chinese females living in Singapore.
8. By 1997, 50 cases of AN were reported in Chinese females living in Singapore.
9. Survey studies using the EAT-26 show an equal amount of disordered eating attitudes between male and female college students in China.

The prevalence of AN in China may be correlated with Westernization. Sing Lee (2000) said that in the previous decade, AN became more prominent in many Asian countries, such as Japan, Hong Kong, Taiwan, and the Republic of Korea. Lee noticed that when restrictions on advertising were loosened, rates of AN rose in lower income Asian countries such as China, India, and the Philippines. However, cases of self-starvation existed in China before Westernization, so AN was never exclusive to the West. Would cases of AN in the East start showing more of the fat phobia symptom? In addition, Sing Lee and colleagues (1993) wrote that of 70 cases examined, only 41 showed a fear of getting fat. These persons had other reasons for refusing to eat, such as having no appetite or bloating. However, it was predicted that more cases would show a fear of fat as time progressed.

*AN is not culture bound.* There is evidence for self-starvation cases all over the world (Keel, 2005). *The fat phobia is not universal.* "When the fear of fat criteria is removed, AN is seen with equal frequency in Western and non-Western cultures" (p. 23). AN is reported in Africa, Middle Eastern cultures, East Asia, India, and Southeast Asia, as well as in Western countries. However, it does seem that many cases of AN in non-Western cultures involve females who have been exposed to Western culture.

For example, Keel reports the lifetime prevalence rate for AN as 0.9% for Iranian schoolgirls. Somewhere between 0.05% and 0.16% of mental health cases in Malaysia were related to AN, and Egyptian mental health cases were related to AN 0.19% of the time according to a 1977 report.

## 7.9 Analyze Etiologies of Major Depression

I start with a statement from the *New England Journal of Medicine:* "**Depression** is a heterogeneous disorder with a highly variable course, an inconsistent response to treatment, and no established mechanism" (Belmaker & Agam, 2008, p. 55). This means that persons have an assortment of symptoms, have different experiences with depression, respond differently to treatments, and there is no agreement about cause.

This is the reality; there are no simple answers. Discard any preexisting ideas that depression is a specific thing. Any text that identifies "causes" in such a way as to make them appear distinct and easy to verify is oversimplified and misleading. This is another time when students must *tolerate uncertainty.*

So then how should we think about depression? Keep the concepts **stress** and **cultural schema** in mind at all times.

First, stress unifies all of the factors *contributing* to depression. "Contributing" factors is a more realistic framework than "causes." Our *risk model* is the best way to study factors contributing to depression and is essential to thinking through the Walker-Tessner model. The risk of depression increases with the addition of each risk factor.

Second, the concept of cultural schema is important. Depressive-type symptoms are universal and rates are increasing. But at the same time there are many ways to experience and treat depression. "The way in which depression is confronted, discussed, and managed varies among social worlds, and cultural meanings and practices shape its course" (Kleinman, 2004, p. 1).

My list of factors that contribute to depression is long. You might be able to add some things.

### An international list of factors that increases one's risk of depression

**Biological level of analysis:**

genes

sleep patterns—For example, EEGs show that some depressed persons go into REM sleep rapidly, just after 60 minutes, about 20 minutes earlier than nondepressed persons (Butcher et al., 2007).

hormone imbalances

neurotransmitter imbalances

asymmetry of brain hemispheres—EEGs show that some depressed persons have lower activity in the left prefrontal region (Butcher et al., 2007).

Qi liver imbalance

poor diet

lack of proper exercise

chronic illness or the presence of another mental disorder—For example, AN is associated with depression, heart disease is associated with depression.

techno-brain burnout (Small & Vorgan, 2008)

One's effort-driven rewards system is under-stimulated (Lambert, 2008).

**Cognitive level of analysis:**

cognitive style

reformulated helplessness theory (Butcher et al., 2007)—negative attribution style

**Sociocultural level of analysis:**

low self-efficacy

marital problems

being a female

the view of the self, which relates to cultural factors

parental maltreatment

neighborhood factors

poverty

discrimination and prejudice

war

social class

grieving a loss

aging populations

natural disasters

increased urbanization

media messages

lack of social support

witchcraft

spirits and other culturally based community causes

If a person has none of these factors, then the risk of getting depression is low. If a person has the two short alleles of the 5-HTT gene, the risk increases. If the person also has stressful life events, such as parent maltreatment, the risk increases a little more. If the person also lives in poverty, the risk further increases. Add low self-efficacy or a negative cognitive style and the risk increases even more. We can put together many combinations of risk factors.

No one has all of these risk factors. But you see how it works. The reason thinking about the etiologies of depression is complex is because there are so many factors that contribute to it; one factor is unlikely to be enough for someone to actually get depressed and culture mediates all of the factors. *Any answer to exam questions asking for one etiology of mental disorder should include a discussion of how the selected factor interacts with other factors as shown on the Walker-Tessner model.* Any mental disorder studied has the same general framework.

It might be hard to ever know the *exact* cause of someone's depression. Two more concerns come to mind when I think about the causes of depression.

First, the "causation" pattern is **bidirectional**. Sometimes students incorrectly say that "neurotransmitter imbalances cause depression." Scientists are not even sure that serotonin is the main neurotransmitter responsible for depression (Lambert, 2008; Sapolsky, 2004). Be aware that many things contribute to neurotransmitter imbalance, such as genes, low self-efficacy, poor diet, or even being depressed. The argument is circular. Factors such as hormone imbalance and sleep disturbance work the same way. *This is why treatments are not always linked to cause.*

Second, "causation" for humans is primarily known through *correlation* studies. Strict "causation" cannot be inferred from correlation studies. While animal experiments add to our understanding of causation, animal lives are not exactly the same as human lives.

## Where to find all the studies in this book on the etiologies of depression

I include many studies about depression throughout this book. While I cannot review studies on every contributing factor, I try to cover a variety of factors that are not typically reviewed in introductory texts.

A **gene-environment correlation** study is reviewed in section 3.4. Information on **diet** and depression is reviewed in section 3.8. A cross-cultural correlation study on **self-efficacy** is reviewed in section 5.15. A discussion on **Qi liver imbalance** is located in section 5.10. **Spirits/community factors** are addressed in section 7.6.

## Note to the teacher

I start the depression unit with the film *Deeply Depressed* (2006) available from the Films for the Humanities and Sciences. The film distinguishes between ordinary sadness and clinical depression and discusses the serotonin transporter gene. While the film has a Western perspective, it is a good place to start.

Next, I present research on how neighborhoods and technology may increase one's risk for depression.

## Neighborhood effects: A sociocultural risk factor

A growing body of research shows that neighborhoods contribute to depression. Neighborhood factors contribute in a number of places on the Walker-Tessner model. For example, neighborhoods are part of one's life stressors. However, they also contribute to pre- and postnatal stress for the developing brain. Unfortunately, stress hormones can pass through the placenta and interfere with the development and functioning of neurotransmitters and activate the HPA axis, possibly damaging the hippocampus.

Cutrona, Wallace, and Wesner (2006) summarize a range of findings on how neighborhoods contribute to the risk model. **Stress** *is the variable that links neighborhood traits and depression.* Specific kinds of living conditions increase stress. One is physical characteristics such as poor-quality housing and high traffic zones. Second are high levels of social disorder that increase fears of victimization. Third, experiencing life stressors leads to depression more frequently if someone also lives in an unfavorable neighborhood. Fourth, people in adverse neighborhoods are less likely to know their neighbors so there is less social control and support. Fifth, married couples in adverse neighborhoods respond to each other with less warmth than couples in better neighborhoods. Marital stress is correlated with depression.

**Resilience** to the stress of living in a neighborhood rated high in social disorder is correlated with women's ratings of themselves as high on perceived **self-efficacy** and hope for the future. Experiencing life stressors did not predict depression in women with these coping skills.

Studies on neighborhood effects are collected through interviews, self-report questionnaires, and naturalistic observation. Data is analyzed using descriptive statistics such as mean, standard deviation, and correlation. Cause and effect cannot be determined with this information. Definitions of neighborhoods come from census studies, but it is likely that neighborhood characteristics change more quickly than census data indicates. The accuracy of census data may be a weakness of the study. Researchers try their best to make sure they are really measuring neighborhood effects and not individual and family characteristics that might confound, or interfere, with study results.

One example of a neighborhood study from 2005 by Cutrona, Russell, and Brown tested whether or not neighborhood settings, life stressors, and personality traits predicted the start of major depression (Cutrona, Wallace, & Wesner, 2006).

The key research question asked in this study was whether living under adverse neighborhood conditions was correlated with two factors, negative life stressors and the personality type of negative emotionality. The authors believed that poor neighborhood conditions would amplify these two depression predictors.

Study participants were 720 African American women between the ages of 24 and 80 from a large range of neighborhoods and income levels. All participants were primary caregivers for children 10 to 12 years old. Neighborhoods were operationally defined as block group areas (BGA), a group of blocks within a census tract. Census data from 1990 was used to define these clusters of neighborhood blocks. The sample is not a random sample. It was more important to select participants from every type of neighborhood, something random sampling would not achieve.

Participants were interviewed twice, in 1997 and 1999, labeled wave 1 and wave 2. Wave 1 data are cross-sectional; they are collected at that one time. Wave 2 data are longitudinal; they are data collected over a span of two years and are independent of the data from wave 1. The authors took numerous steps to ensure as much rigor as possible in data collection. All interviewers were African American. Interviewers received a one-week training program to make sure that question asking, probing, and clarifying were consistent. Administration of interview questions was further controlled because all questions were preprogrammed into a computer.

Many demographic characteristics of subjects were gathered such as age, marital status, and education.

A structured psychiatric diagnostic scale using DSM-IV guidelines for major depression designed for lay interviewers was administered to each participant. It was critical to the study that the women were not depressed before moving to the neighborhood.

A 29-item checklist that included experiences such as being a crime victim assessed severe life stressors during the 12-month period prior to the start of the study. It is known that being depressed increases the likelihood that a person experiences negative events. Researchers ensured that the items from the checklist were independent of any stressors associated with already being depressed. Interviews at wave 1 were conducted only with women diagnosed with depression within the previous six-month period and who also lived in the neighborhood six months before becoming depressed. Wave 2 interviews included only those women who were not depressed at wave 1 and had not moved in two years. This ensured that wave two participants were not simply showing the same depression symptoms from wave 1.

Personality traits were investigated using the Clark and Watson Brief Temperament Survey. The questionnaire measures three general subscales of personality: negative temperament, positive temperament, and disinhibition. Negative emotion was operationalized as the results of the negative temperament scale.

Results showed the following:

*The most important neighborhood variables found in the study were economic disadvantage and social disorder.* As these two variables correlated with each other, they were used as the definition of important neighborhood characteristics. Economic disadvantage/social disorder was then tested for its interaction with the number of life events and negative emotionality as a personality trait.

Data for both wave 1 and wave 2 participants showed that women reporting greater numbers of negative life stressors who lived in neighborhoods high on economic disadvantage/social disorder also had a disproportionately high rate of depression.

Negative emotionality as a personality trait did not correlate with high economic disadvantage/social disorder for either group as an important factor in showing depressed symptoms. This is the opposite of the predictions of the authors. It appears that negative personality traits are not an important risk factor on their own.

What do the study results mean? *Women from neighborhoods scoring low on disadvantage/disorder had lower rates of depression associated with the neighborhood context.* One advantage of this study is its use of multiple types of neighborhoods and socioeconomic levels. This way, the researchers could determine which types of clusters of neighborhoods might correlate with the onset of depression.

The other finding of interest is that *personality was not a predictor of depression in relation to neighborhood context.* Having a positive outlook and productive coping skills may be a **resilience** factor against depression. Community-based mental health services should offer programs to increase coping skills.

Moving away from low income neighborhoods is beneficial for both cognitive development and mental health (Cutrona et al., 2006; Leventhal & Brooks-Gunn, 2004). Programs supporting these moves are Habitat for Humanity and government-sponsored voucher programs. These findings are a challenge for future public policy.

## Depression and the under-stimulation of the brain's effort-driven reward system

Kelly Lambert is a neuroscientist with an idea that may help us to have a sense of control over our future. Perhaps something as simple as adding a hands-on creative activity to our day can decrease stress and our risk of depression.

Lambert's Web site, www.kellylambert.com, summarizes the concerns that led her to study depression's relationship to the brain's reward circuits.

Lambert cites startling statistics. Besides what I already covered from the WHO statistics, Lambert writes that:

1. About 25% of all visits to health care practitioners involve depressed or anxious symptoms.

2. In 2005 alone, about 189 million prescriptions written in the United States were for depression.

3. Between 1994 and 2002, antidepressant use tripled in adults. In addition, one of three women visiting a doctor in 2002 received an antidepressant.

4. Antidepressants work about 60% of the time and placebos work about 47% of the time. Cognitive-behavioral and interpersonal therapy have about the same effectiveness rate as drug therapy without the side effects.

5. No one is in agreement that serotonin is the main neurotransmitter involved in depression.

As of the writing of this book in 2008, no one is totally sure what causes depression. Lambert is concerned that because of drug company's marketing, people think they know what causes depression and how to treat it.

*Lambert wants to know why depression rates are soaring if serotonin is the actual cause of depression and antidepressant drugs the best treatment.*

Lambert (2008) wonders if easy, technological lifestyles raise stress that then contributes to depression. Lambert's premise is similar to my book's theme: can we gain a sense of control over our lives and become more resilient to stress?

Think about your daily life. You get information from the Internet instead of going to a library and searching reference books. You talk and text with others on cell phones instead of mailing letters or traveling long distances to see others. You microwave food from grocery stores instead of growing and cooking it from scratch. You drive to school and work instead of walking or riding a horse. Vacuum cleaners and washing machines make household chores easier. Perhaps you have a lot to do, but modern life is very different from the lives of those in the not-so-distant past. Even refrigeration is a fairly new invention. It is a recent phenomenon that people can buy food in bulk and keep it in a freezer. Is it possible that a lack of effort in daily activities is part of the problem? New research says yes.

Lambert's theories unite **evolution**, the brain, and lifestyle to create a theory of depression **resilience**.

When Lambert attended a lecture by Martin Seligman, she was surprised to learn that younger people are more likely to have depression than older people over their lifetime. People born in the early third of the 20th century have lower rates of depression than those born in the middle third. One difference between the two groups is the amount of physical exercise.

Lambert is not suggesting that we get rid of modern technology. But neuroscience evidence shows that "pushing buttons instead of plowing fields" (p. 33) has removed something important to our resilience to depression. *Can living more balanced lives reduce depression rates?*

Lambert says the human brain is hardwired for satisfaction from meaningful physical work. She refers to this hardwiring as an "effort-driven rewards system."

Having a brain-based reward system for meaningful physical labor was *adaptive*. The reward system is activated when complex movements, particularly hand movements, are combined with complex thinking. In addition, anticipating the pleasure of a reward motivated task completion.

Here is an example of something very simple that stimulates the brain's reward centers. I recall when my mother taught me how to bake chocolate chip cookies from scratch. It took some time, but I anticipated the reward the entire time. Making the cookies required coordinated hand movements as I measured the right amount of ingredients and cracked eggs without getting the shell in the batter. I still bake cookies from scratch and feel the same anticipation of a reward each time and the cookies are better than anything purchased ready-made.

Lambert wondered if depressive symptoms were related to a *specific brain circuit*. She started with the **nucleus accumbens**, the reward center of the brain, and its connections with other brain parts. These other parts are the **striatum**, which controls movement, the **limbic system** (which includes the **hippocampus**), brain parts associated with learning and emotion, and the **prefrontal cortex**, the part of the brain associated with thinking. Lambert was interested in the connections between them and realized that she could "correlate every symptom of depression with a part on this circuit" (p. 35). Lambert believed that the more this rewards circuit was stimulated, the more **neurogenesis** occurred. Neurogenesis is important for recovering from depression.

An experiment on rats tested Lambert's hypothesis. Rats were divided into two groups, the worker rats and the "trust fund rats." The effort group rats were trained every day for five weeks to find fruit loop cereal (a treat they loved) that was hidden in different mounds of cage bedding every day. These rats had to work for their reward. The trust fund rats also were given the mounds of cage bedding, but no matter what level of effort they showed to try and find the buried fruit loops in the bedding mounds, they were given a fruit loop treat in the corner of the cage.

After five weeks of training, all of the rats had to solve a novel problem. A fruit loop was placed inside a plastic toy. The rats could see and smell the food inside the toy but the fruit loop was too large to push through holes in the plastic. In actuality, there was no way to open the toy. Which group persevered more? The worker rats worked on opening the toy 60% longer and attempted the task 30% more often than the trust fund rats. Both groups of rats were similarly motivated to get the food as they were on restricted diets. Were the worker rats telling Lambert that their training made them more persistent problem solvers?

Lambert thinks that her findings give new insight to the problem of **learned helplessness**. Perhaps we know more things, do more things, and do things more rapidly than earlier generations, but are we increasing stress in the process? Possibly even small hobbies and regular exercise that stimulate the effort-driven rewards brain circuits are important in managing stress should be part of our daily lives.

Lambert's theory is new so the research needs replication as well as **method triangulation** with human studies.

## Note to the teacher

Here is a project idea. Assign students to do something that stimulates their effort-driven rewards system. The activity must be something that is regularly integrated into student lives and must be a hands-on activity not related to technology. For example, students could plant and tend a vegetable garden, learn to cook from scratch, take up knitting or scrapbooking, build furniture, or build homes with Habitat for Humanity. Have students keep a log containing the date and time of the activity as well as their reactions. I recommend that the project last at least a month so that students can see the benefits of a lifestyle change. This activity might even qualify for **CAS** if it goes beyond the class assignment.

## Techno-brain burnout

This study on how technology alters the brain can also be used to answer questions about the effects of the environment on physiological processes in section 3.7.

*Technology has the power to reshape neural networks.* Using technology has positive and negative affects on human behavior. While technology use has increased some skills and even improved IQ scores, it comes with a price—increased **stress**. Chronic stress causes changes in adrenal functioning that affects the brain and in turn increases one's risk for depression.

By no means am I suggesting that we get rid of technology. I love my computer, particularly the convenience of shopping on Amazon, buying airline tickets, and finding psychology studies. But my theme of gaining control over our lives challenges students to consider the effects of technology on their lives. *Has it affected the way they learn in school? Is it contributing to stress and higher rates of depression?* What are the implications of these changes?

It is hard to think about how technology affects learning and mental health because we are living in the midst of it. Imagine what the human mind was like before the written word. Everything had to be remembered. I bet that the first printing press had critics claiming that the written word would mean an end to people having excellent memories!

The concept of **neuroplasticity** reminds us that the brain changes in response to the environment. Each era of information probably ushered in different underlying brain processing. Human information started with storytelling and then changed to the written word, to television, and then to the computer. I think it is safe to say that the brain in the computer era is different from the brains of the past. The students I now teach grew up with computers and cell phones and do not know a world without them.

Gary Small and Gigi Vorgan (2008) conducted a quasi-experiment using **fMRI** to compare the brains of people who had never used a computer with the brains of people using computers regularly.

Both groups first participated in a control condition that involved reading simulated book text. Small and Vorgan wanted to make sure they were just measuring brain changes from computer use. The brain activity specific to text reading could be subtracted from the scans collected during computer use. The brain activity for both groups while reading text was similar.

Next, both groups started an Internet search task. The scans showed different brain activity. A specific neural network in the dorsolateral prefrontal cortex was recruited in the computer savvy group. This brain area is associated with decision making, integrating complex information, thoughts, and sensations, as well as working memory. Scans from computer-naive participants did not show the same brain activation.

In order to train the brain, all participants were asked to conduct an Internet search each day for five days. After five days, the groups without computer experience showed the exact same brain activity as those with previous computer experience.

Small and Vorgan write that we expose our brains to technology for long periods of time each day, citing research that people from ages 8 to 18 get an average of 8.5 hours of technology stimulation every day. This includes television, video and DVD movies, computer games, and computer use.

Are there some potential consequences of all this technology stimulation? The authors write that constant computer exposure has trained our brains to be in a state of "**continuous partial attention**," where we are always busy, monitoring the Internet and the phone for bits of information but never actually focusing on one task at a time. This is different from multitasking. Multitasking is when we have a purpose for our activities and try and improve efficiency. Continuous partial attention keeps us alert for *any* contact, such as news alerts, an e-mail, or text message. Everything is in our peripheral attention.

Stress increases when we are in a state of continuous partial attention. People "no longer have time to reflect, contemplate or make thoughtful decisions. Instead they exist in a sense of constant crisis-on alert for a new contact or bit of exciting news or information at any moment" (Small & Vorgan, 2008, p. 47).

A person's sense of control is correlated with the size of the hippocampus. Losing a sense of control may be a consequence of long-term continuous partial attention. Persons using computers for long periods of time report fatigue, irritability, and distractedness. Small and Vorgan suggest that techno-brain burnout is becoming epidemic. The stress of constantly being alert signals the fight-or-flight system, and the adrenal glands continually produce the stress hormone cortisol.

Unfortunately, cortisol can damage the brain, particularly the developing brain. High cortisol levels *can contribute to depression* and change the neural circuits in brain areas such as the hippocampus, needed for memory and emotional stability.

## 7.10 Analyze Etiologies of Anorexia Nervosa

Use the same risk-model approach to consider the etiology of **anorexia nervosa** (AN). It is unlikely that one factor is enough to explain AN. The etiologies of AN and BN are different, so my list is only for AN.

## A list of factors that increase one's risk of AN

**Biological level of analysis:**

genes

appetite and weight regulation imbalance—the hypothalamus

neurotransmitters—Those studied are serotonin, norepinephrine, and dopamine.

neuropeptides—Neuropeptides are similar to neurotransmitters; they work to increase (neuropeptide Y) or decrease (cholecystokinin and leptin) appetite. Decreased leptin is the neuropeptide most associated with AN.

**Cognitive level of analysis:**

cognitive factors, such as attentional biases toward food and body-related cues; cognitive distortions, such as dichotomous thinking

perfectionism

reward sensitivity—Those with AN report higher reward dependence, meaning that they have a higher need for reward (more sensitive to rewards and praise) than those without AN, and continue a rewarded behavior, even if they are exhausted.

**Sociocultural level of analysis:**

media portrayals of cultural attitudes toward thinness

family interaction

social learning, including modeling from parents and low self-efficacy

## Note to the teacher

I start this unit with the *NOVA* film "Dying to be Thin," available from www.pbs.org. The film is a good overview of anorexia and bulimia. Teachers selecting the sport psychology option can make a good link between sport psychology and mental health.

I have three research examples of etiology spanning the three levels of analysis—genes, cognitive style, and the role of the media. Remember that all three levels of analysis work together, so for example, genes or the media alone are not enough for someone to develop AN. Use the Walker-Tessner model to show how the factors work together.

## Genetic risk factors: The biological level of analysis

Suzanne Mazzeo and Cynthia Bulik (2009) write that, while family-based association studies and twin studies suggest an important genetic contribution to eating disorders, molecular genetic studies are still inconsistent in identifying specific risk alleles (gene variations). This means that we still are not sure which genes are the problems. Pamela Keel (2005) said the same thing and reported that several genes were identified in molecular genetic studies. These include the 5-HTT (serotonin transporter gene) and several 5HTT receptor genes, estrogen receptor genes, and two dopamine receptor genes. However, none have emerged in enough of a pattern to be clear candidates.

Please do not get the idea that one gene will be discovered to explain eating disorders. We are not moving toward more reductionist thinking with molecular genetic research. Quite the contrary. We are moving to complex models where identified risk alleles interact with other genes and environmental factors in a complex way.

Mazzeo and Bulik focus their article on helping people understand how gene-environment (GXE) correlations *probably* work for eating disorders, discussing passive, evocative, and active GXE correlations. Recall that I discussed how gene-environment correlations were the focus of newer genetic research and defined passive, evocative, and active GXE correlations in section 3.4.

Mazzeo and Bulik clarify which environmental risk factors are most likely to interact with genetic vulnerabilities. This is the most current thinking on gene-environment correlations and eating disorders as of the publication of this book. Mazzeo and Bulik write that advances in genetic research methodology will aid future researchers in identifying the specific alleles that make certain people more reactive to environmental risk factors.

First let's talk about **parenting**. It is unfair and out of date to simply say that parents are a direct cause of a child's eating disorders. A **passive GXE correlation** probably exists between parental models and child disordered eating behavior. For example, studies show that mothers' *comments and complaints about their own weight* are correlated with the esteem of their fourth- and fifth-grade children as well as the concern level that their daughters have about their own weight. It is a passive GXE correlation because these parents pass on genes to their children *and* provide an environment for their children. The children get what Mazzeo and Bulik call a "double dose" of risk factors for eating disorders without doing anything.

There are many other passive GXE interactions that increase a child's risk of eating disorders. Here are two more examples. One factor is a *mother's own problematic feeding behavior.* There is a correlation between a mother's restrictive eating behavior and the degree to which 5-year-old female children restrict their own eating. A second factor is *parental overemphasis on weight.* Women with eating disorders may become overly focused on the weight of their children. One study found that a mother's satisfaction level with their child's body size was negatively correlated with the severity level of her own eating disorder.

**Evocative GXE correlations** also contribute to AN. In this type of GXE interaction, a person with a specific genetic makeup evokes, or brings about, specific types of responses from the environment. **Perfectionism** is one example. While temperament is influenced by genetic factors, a person's temperament also influences how a person interacts with the environment. Research shows that persons with perfectionist temperaments *seek out demanding environments and hold themselves to very high standards.* These persons seek evaluations from others about their performance. Perfectionist persons evoke comments from others, and even positive feedback reinforces a perfectionist personality. In addition, MZ (monozygotic, or identical) twin research on AN and BN shows that sometimes one twin receives more critical evaluation from parents. While both twins may carry a genetic predisposition for eating disorders, only the one twin expresses it, possibly the one with a temperament that evokes more criticism from the parent.

Mazzeo and Bulik think the *media* is part of an **active GXE correlation** contributing to eating disorders. All girls do not develop eating disorders even though most are exposed to Western media that idolizes thinness. Girls with a genetic vulnerability for eating disorders might actively seek out media highlighting thinness that then reinforces negative views of their own body shape. Longitudinal research analyzing data with correlations supports this hypothesis. One study found that girls whose eating disorder symptoms increased over a 16-month time period also reported reading more fashion magazines during that time. In addition, research suggests that girls with genetic vulnerabilities to eating disorders actively select peer groups with the same ideals. European-American girls in sororities have high rates of eating disorder symptoms. Longitudinal research shows that girls in sororities have significantly greater eating disorder symptoms than girls not in sororities after a three-year period.

We cannot currently change our genes. But we can create **resilience** programs based on knowledge about the environmental factors that interact with genes. For example, two resilience factors, eating regular breakfasts with the family and training aimed at emotional regulation are attracting attention.

## Information processing biases: The cognitive level of analysis

Keel (2005) identifies two types of cognitive factors that increase the risk for eating disorders. These are **attentional biases** toward food and body and **cognitive styles** that distort reality. Research about cognition is valuable for understanding the symptoms and personality traits of persons with eating disorders, making predictions about the severity of an individual's disorder, and designing treatment plans.

Laura Southgate and colleagues (2008) ran a quasi-experiment comparing the information processing biases of girls with AN and BN with normal controls.

Previous research suggests that cognitive styles of persons with AN predict having eating disorder symptoms. For example, persons with AN have obsessive-compulsive personalities, meaning they are perfectionists, preoccupied with details, lists, order, and have rigid thinking. These personality traits are correlated with inflexibility on cognitive tests. In addition, persons with AN perform better on cognitive tasks requiring local cognitive processing as opposed to global cognitive processing. This means that they pay more attention to detail than to the larger picture, a cognitive style that reflects enduring personalities of persons with eating disorders. In addition, self-reports show that persons with BN are impulsive, a trait that is correlated with binging and purging.

Southgate and colleagues aimed to expand on previous studies and hypothesized that participants with eating disorders would show information processing biases toward *impulsivity* or *efficiency* as compared to normal controls. Persons with AN would show the greatest efficiency and persons with BN would show the greatest impulsivity.

The researchers collected data a little differently from the way it was collected in the past. This is the first study to collect data by dimensions (continuums), where *accuracy* (efficiency, or perfectionistic, local processing) at a cognitive task was at one extreme and *speed* (impulsivity) was at the other extreme. Data were gathered through the Matching Familiar Figures Test (MFFT), a demanding task where persons are shown a target picture, a single picture of a familiar object. Then one at a time, eight other similar pictures are shown. Only one is identical to the target picture. Persons must identify the correct match. When the first target picture is correctly matched, the person moves on to the next target picture until all are correctly identified. If an incorrect response is given, the person is asked to try again. Participants in this study were told that both speed and accuracy were measured but that neither was valued over the other.

The sample included 60 females from the United Kingdom, 20 with AN, 14 with BN, and 26 normal controls. All participants were females aged 16 to 57. Participants with substance-abuse problems, a history of psychiatric illness, head injury, or those taking psychiatric drugs were excluded from the study. All AN and BN participants met the DSM-IV criteria for an eating disorder.

Experimental results showed that persons with AN were significantly more efficient than controls. This finding supports the hypothesis predicting that persons with AN pay more attention to detail. Southgate and colleagues conclude that their findings support what is known about the clinical symptoms of AN. Self-starvation is correlated with cognitive deficits. Persons with AN suffer from "hyperarousal," where "individuals are often so focused on maintaining their maladaptive behaviors they are unable to see the 'bigger picture' and the severe consequences these behaviors have on their life" (p. 225).

The hypothesis that persons with BN would show more impulsivity, meaning to have a faster time but less accuracy, was insignificant. While this finding contrasts previous research, the authors wonder if the sample or study procedures account for the differences. The definition of impulsivity for this study, a trade-off between accuracy and speed, may not pick up impulsivity in persons with BN. Impulsiveness can refer to a wide range of behaviors.

Southgate and colleagues acknowledge some limitations of the study. This is the first study to use a continuum to gather data, so it needs replication. In addition, it was impossible to make the researcher administering the MFFT blind to each participant group. It was obvious who made up the AN group. Standardized instructions helped minimize experimenter bias.

## Television exposure: The sociocultural level of analysis

Anyone thinking that the media are not a risk factor for developing disordered eating habits should read Anne Becker's research. While clinical diagnoses of eating disorders were not part of this study, Becker and colleagues (2002) documented large changes in attitudes toward body image and risky eating disordered behavior after the introduction of television to Fiji in the 1990s. Becker's findings fit in well with other research showing that the risk of eating disorders increases after exposure to Western culture.

Becker and colleagues write that existing studies on the role that television plays on disordered eating are limited because no control condition compares participants without access to television with those with access. Fijian adolescent girls were the perfect solution. Prior to 1995, television access was limited in Fiji. In addition, traditional Fijian culture valued hearty eating habits and robust figures.

Was exposure to Western television a risk factor for developing disordered eating behavior despite traditional cultural values?

Quantitative and qualitative data were collected. HL students will find this study beneficial for understanding some of the concepts required for Paper 3.

First, data for a field experiment tested the existence of disordered eating in 1995 before exposure to television and again in 1998 after three years of Western television. Data for the field experiment were collected through a self-report questionnaire, a modification of the EAT-26, about attitudes toward eating. Extra questions were added for the 1998 sample asking about intergenerational differences between participants and their parents with respect to dieting and eating values. Most of these data were analyzed with correlations. Second, qualitative data were gathered through a **semi-structured interview**. The interviews collected **narratives** from a **purposive sample** covering a range of disordered eating from the 1998 sample. The narratives reflected opinions about diet and weight control in relation to traditional Fijian values. The narratives were analyzed with **content analysis** methodology aimed at identifying important themes.

The sample consisted of all ethnic Fijian adolescent girls from two schools in Nadroga, Fiji. The 1995 sample included 63 girls, with a mean age of 17.3. The 1998 sample included 65 girls with a mean age of 16.9.

The results include the following:

**1.** Field experiment data showed numerous significant findings. First, there was a significant difference between disordered eating scores on the EAT-26 between the 1995 and 1998 samples. Second, within the 1998 sample, high EAT-26 scores were significantly correlated with dieting and self-induced vomiting. Third, a significant difference was found between the 1995 and 1998 samples about using self-induced vomiting to diet. No one in 1995 sample used self-induced vomiting to diet, but by 1998, 11.3% of the girls did. Fourth, 74% of the 1998 sample said they sometimes felt "too fat." There was a significant correlation between feeling "too fat" and dieting. Fifth, a significant correlation was found between girls in the 1998 sample who perceived large differences in intergenerational values and also used self-induced vomiting to control weight.

2. Several themes emerged from the qualitative data. First, the girls admired the television characters and wanted to be like them by changing their hairstyle and body shape. Second, 83% of the purposive sample said that television changed the way they and their friends felt about their body type. Third, 40% of the purposive sample felt they had a better chance at advancing in a career if they were slimmer. Last, everyone was aware that the younger generation's values about desired body shape were very different from those of traditional Fijian culture.

Becker and colleagues realize that television is not a direct cause of disordered eating, it is just one *risk factor*. In addition, television is just one of many effects of increased participation in a global society. The Fiji economy had shifted away from subsistence agriculture to one producing the necessary cash to meet consumerist demands.

The authors do feel that the data, particularly the narrative data, suggest that television has played a significant role in changing values toward body shape and eating behaviors. The following excerpt from the narratives is a theme found in the reports from the entire group: "When I look at the characters on TV, the way they act on TV and I just look at the body, the figure of that body, so I say 'look at them, they are thin and they all have this figure' so I myself want to become like that, to become thin" (p. 513).

Limitations of the study include the following:

1. Official diagnoses of eating disorders were not part of the study. While it is not known if these girls had an official eating disorder, the EAT-26 scores worry the authors.

2. Some of the measures between the 1995 and 1998 samples were not significant. For example, there was no significant change in the use of laxatives to control weight and in binge eating behavior between the samples.

3. Were the samples really comparable? The same girls were not in both samples so it is unknown if the 1998 sample had disordered eating before the arrival of television. However, the authors feel it is unlikely that these girls had disordered eating before 1995. There was only one report of AN in Fiji before 1995.

## 7.11 Discuss Cultural and Gender Variations in Prevalence of Mental Disorders

Be careful with the phrase "variation." The term "variation" is fine as long as it is not interpreted to mean a variation of the "real" Western disorder or a disorder that is studied primarily on just males or females. Prevalence rates that do not take culture and gender variations into account run the risk of *over- or underrepresenting* the actual occurrence of a disorder. So this material is also relevant for sections 7.7 and 7.8. For example, **stereotypes** about female gender roles may cause them to be overrepresented in depression prevalence rates. In addition, males may be underrepresented in eating disorder prevalence rates because they are rarely included in research samples.

## Why it is hard to know about culture and prevalence

It is hard to know about cultural variations in the prevalence of mental illness. It is a complicated topic that is related to **emics** and **etics** as well as strengths and limitations of ethnographies and surveys. I identify and explain some of the challenges researchers face when trying to research cultural variations in the prevalence of mental illness.

Think about how hard it is to design a study to get accurate percentages for both lifetime and point prevalence of mental illnesses across numerous cultures. *In order to compare prevalence rates, the data must be comparable.* Credible data is hard to gather so all current estimates are tentative and possibly inaccurate (Marsella & Yamada, 2007). Much of the prevalence data comes from surveys. Data interpretation is affected by the biases of those collecting the data, the source of the data, and the **reliability** and **validity** of the assessment tools (such as the WHO CIDI, a structured survey that is used in the study reviewed later in this section). Given differences in the expression and course of mental illnesses across cultures, to what extent can we compare data from different cultures?

*Researchers can look at prevalence in individual countries, but we cannot study variations or say that one group has more mental illness than another without running a cross-cultural study where numerous cultures are surveyed and compared.*

Think of all the things needing standardization before accurate cross-cultural comparisons are possible. Marsella and Yamada list five things that must be done to plan and run a comparable survey. While this list calls attention to the complexity of knowing about the prevalence of mental illness across cultures, following the guidelines does not guarantee that any set of data is accurate.

1.  Ethnographies must be used to define the symptoms that are used to create research categories that are appropriate for all cultures. The WHO survey reviewed below primarily used the DSM-IV categories but made some adjustments for cultural differences. Refer back to section 5.5; John Berry identified the challenges of collecting etic and emic data for useful cross-cultural studies. The point is that researchers must create etics for the mental disorders but should use the ethnographies to make sure that emic data is also included. This is hard enough to do for one culture, and so it is a real challenge for a study comparing mental illness rates across numerous cultures.

2.  All words and concepts for the comparisons must be clearly defined. The translation process should include **back translation**.

3.  Categories for the comparison study should come from the results of ethnographies. While multivariate statistical methods can create appropriate categories, these categories cannot just come from those already established in Western research.

4.  Case examples must be equivalent across cultures. For example, if people from different cultures report sleep difficulties, low energy, and sadness, do they all have depression?

5.  All assessments must measure symptoms that are appropriate for each culture.

6.  A clearly defined baseline must be established for **normality** and **abnormality**.

## A World Health Organization study on culture and prevalence

One study of cross-cultural prevalence rates for mental illness is the World Health Organization (WHO) (2004) survey of the prevalence, severity, and unmet needs of people with mental disorders across 14 countries. Many of the things on Marsella's and Yamada's list were challenges for the creation, administration, and analysis of these data.

Surveys were administered to 60,463 participants from 14 countries. The countries were Belgium, Colombia, France, Germany, Italy, Japan, Lebanon, Mexico, Netherlands, Nigeria, People's Republic of China (in Beijing and Shanghai), Spain, Ukraine, and the United States. Efforts were made to recruit other countries, but only those countries with funding for the study participated.

Data was gathered through face-to-face household surveys. The survey was a structured interview using the WHO Composite International Diagnostic Interview (CIDI). It was administered by trained lay persons. The sample was obtained from a variety of databases within each country, such as national registers and telephone directories. The CIDI assessed the amount of many disorders, including depression, phobias, PTSD, ADHD, and eating disorders. The survey excluded severe disorders such as schizophrenia. The disorders were assessed using the definitions in the DSM-IV. The definitions were determined to be both reliable and valid. The article does not say how reliability and validity are established.

Results showed that prevalence over a 12-month period varied a great deal, from 4.3% in Shanghai to 26.4% in the United States. The incidence for having all of the disorders was:

Colombia—17.8%

Mexico—12.2 %

United States—16.3

Belgium—12%

France—18.4

Germany—9.1%

Italy—8.2%

Netherlands—14.8%

Spain—9.2%

Ukraine—20.4%

Lebanon—16.9%

Nigeria—4.7%

Japan—8.8%

People's Republic of China, Shanghai—4.3% and Beijing—9.1%

The prevalence of mild disorders varied from 1.8% in Shanghai to 9.2% in the United States. The prevalence of moderate disorders ranged from a low of 1.4% in Shanghai to 9.4% in the United States. The prevalence of severe disorders ranged from 0.4% in Nigeria to 7.7% in the United States.

Anxiety disorders were the most prevalent of the disorders in all but the Ukraine, where mood disorders were most prevalent. Mood disorders were the second most prevalent disorder except in Nigeria and Beijing, where substance abuse disorders ranked second.

The amount of persons with disorders receiving treatment in the 12 months prior to the interview varied a great deal. Nigeria reported the lowest amount of treatment, 0.8% and the United States reported the highest level, 15.3%. There are many people not receiving treatment. Up to 50.3% of the severe cases in less developed countries and up to 85.4% of severe cases in developed countries received no treatment. It appears that some of the treatment resources are going to less severe cases. The WHO recommends that treatment resources be allocated so that more serious mental health cases get treatment. The WHO realizes that it is easy to suggest reallocation and hard to do so effectively. For example, it makes little sense to leave mild cases untreated, as many with mild cases go on to develop more serious cases if left untreated. In addition, there is no model of optimal allocation of treatment resources.

The WHO report contained a list of survey limitations. One limitation is wide variation in survey response, with some of the response rate even too low for an accepted standard. This means that cross-national comparisons may be distorted. Another limitation was that the surveys deleted some disorders that were not considered relevant for a particular country, making comparisons difficult in some cases. I wonder how much this problem limits the **validity** of the CIDI. Each disorder measured must have "clinical reality," meaning that it is seen in clinics, to be a valid disorder. Did the DSM-IV criteria account for any culture-bound symptoms? The earliest versions of the CIDI were standardized in the West, so "performance . . . could be worse in other parts of the world either because the concepts or phrases used to describe mental syndromes are less consonant (in agreement) with cultural concepts than in developed Western countries or because absence of a tradition of free speech and anonymous public opinion surveying causes greater reluctance to admit emotional or substance-abuse problems than in developed West countries" (WHO, 2004, p. 2587). A third limitation is that schizophrenia and some other severe disorders were not included in the survey. The WHO decided that persons with schizophrenia typically met the criteria for other disorders on the survey, such as mood or anxiety disorders, and were captured in these statistics. Still, the results for specific disorders may not be completely accurate.

Strengths of the WHO survey include that it is consistent (has high **reliability**) with other surveys showing that mental disorders are very prevalent around the world and often are not treated. However, one thing to keep in mind when interpreting this study is that the most severely disordered persons are unlikely to respond to a survey, so it is possible that the results are lower than they are in reality.

Marsella and Yamada (2007) criticize the WHO survey. While it is possible that these variations reflect real rates, the validity of the interviews cannot go unchallenged. Using the DSM-IV categories does not include culture-bound disorders relevant to each individual culture. *Prevalence rates are distorted if interview respondents are not all talking about the same thing.* Should we conclude that Chinese persons experience little stress? In addition, any study is designed in accordance with the *values* of the researchers. Researcher *values* should never be assumed to represent the "authority."

What conclusions can we draw about prevalence of mental illness across culture? First, it is hard to design a credible survey that has relevance for all cultures studied. Even the results of the WHO study must be taken as tentative. Second, it does appear that persons in all cultures experience mental illness. Third, mental health services are not reaching everyone who needs help.

## Generalizations about gender and prevalence of mental illness

Hilary Lips (2005) makes some useful generalizations about **gender** variations in the prevalence of mental illness.

**1.** Generally, males and females have similar overall rates of mental illness but vary according to specific disorders. Women have higher prevalence rates of depression, eating disorders, and specific phobias such as agoraphobia. Males have higher rates of antisocial behavior, substance abuse, and childhood disorders such as autism. But watch making claims that females are not substance abusers or that males do not have eating disorders or depression. Perhaps male and female expressions of these disorders are different and classification systems are inadequate to show us the reality of male depression and female alcoholism. For example, Pamela Keel (2005) writes that men are typically excluded from samples in eating disorders studies, even though they make up about 40% of people with binge eating disorders. Future research must examine how both males and females express each disorder.

**2. Gender stereotypes** may affect expectations of how someone should cope with distress.

**3.** Male and female **gender role** expectations may affect how others respond to mental illness symptoms. Diagnosis may be made according to expectations about one's gender role.

**4.** A "politics of diagnosis" reflects gender stereotypes and role expectations. Lips writes that "sex-biases built into diagnostic categories may well influence perceptions of whether women and men are psychologically healthy" (p. 373). The field of psychiatry is dominated by males and biases may surround diagnostic categories that use male behavior as the "**norm**." Females who behave along the lines of their socialization may be diagnosed as abnormal. The danger is that diagnostic categories are assigned according to gender stereotypes. Would males and females reporting similar symptoms to a doctor get the same diagnosis and treatment?

**5. Stress** is a factor. Males and females both experience stressful events (such accidents or divorce), but there are *good reasons to believe that women experience stress differently than men and have more life-long stressors* (chronic conditions, such as poverty). Susan Nolan-Hoeksema (2004) identifies the stressors specific to females *that have research support* in section 3.4. Stress affects gene expression, so it is important to identify and address stressful events and life-long stressors. Lips raises three questions regarding research on stress and gender. Question-naires are a popular research tool where participants select all of the stressful events that apply to them. First, could these lists be biased toward male experiences? Second, could the life-changing events experienced by men be more positive than those experienced by women? Third, could women respond more strongly to stressful events? All three questions have been studied. Lips says that sometimes lists of stressful life events fail to include stressful events of great significance to women, such as rape and difficulties managing child care. If males and females are to be compared, then assessment instruments must include comparable items. In addition, women tend to rate experiencing stressors at greater intensities than men. Lips reports a study by Klonoff and Landrine in 1995 that investigated gender differences in experiences with stress. Klonoff and Landrine created the Schedule of Sexist Events (SSE) to measure a stressor that females endure more frequently than males: sexist behavior. The SSE included events such as degrading jokes and sexual harassment at work. Half of the participants reported being picked on, threatened, and even hit because they were female. Forty percent said they were denied a raise or promotion because they were a woman. In terms of life-long stressors, women are more likely to be living in poverty, endure life-long and unpredictable family violence, and are more likely than men to work outside the home and do most of the housework and child care.

## Gender and depression

Prevalence rates for major depression are reported in section 7.7.

Section 3.4 contains a review of Susan Nolan-Hoeksema's research about females and depression. Nolan-Hoeksema highlights the theories about the female experience of stressful events and the life-long stressors that have research support.

Males may be underrepresented in depression statistics. Females meet diagnostic criteria for major depression more often than males but *males may just experience depression differently.* Six million men in the United States experience depression each year (NIMH, 2008). While both men and women can show the standard symptoms, research suggests that there are gender differences in experiencing and coping with depression. Females are more open to talking about emotions and seek health care more often than men. Men are more willing to report physical symptoms, such as sleep difficulties and irritability. Some researchers even believe that the DSM-IV diagnostic criteria are inadequate to describe male depression. For example, men are more likely to be diagnosed with substance abuse and dependence. Is substance use really a symptom of depression? In addition, men are more likely to throw themselves into their jobs or engage in reckless behavior than females, perhaps other signs of depression in men. Many psychologists worry that the higher rates of suicide for men reflect the tendency of males to avoid seeking help for depression.

## A study on gender and culture differences in the prevalence of eating disorders

Prevalence rates for anorexia nervosa (AN) are reported in section 7.8. Lifetime rates for bulimia nervosa (BN) in U.S. samples are 1%–3% in females, with the rate for males 1/10 that of females (APA, 2001). Pamela Keel (2005) writes that the most common of the eating disorders not otherwise specified (EDNOS) is binge eating disorder (BED). BED occurs more frequently in women. Samples from weight-loss centers show that women are 1.5 times more likely to have BED than men. In community samples, the ratio of BED in females and males is a little different, 60:40. This means that men account for 40% of BED cases.

The following study is terrific because it examines *both gender and cultural variations* in the prevalence of eating disorders.

Recent research challenges the widely held notion that only white Western women suffer from eating disorders. Eating disorders occur in other cultures and in males.

Margarita Alegria and colleagues (2007) conducted *the first study about 12-month and lifetime prevalence rates of eating disorders in Latino ethnic groups living in the United States*. While some studies report that Latino females have higher rates of eating disorders than other ethnic minorities, including Asian Americans and African Americans, no systematic study exists about specific prevalence rates. In addition, clarification was needed about the extent to which **acculturation**, meaning to adopt behaviors that represent the **norms** and values of the dominant culture, was the reason for the eating disorders.

Survey data were collected from a sample of 2554 English- and Spanish-speaking Latinos living in the United States. Four Latino subgroups were identified: 868 Mexicans, 495 Puerto Ricans, 577 Cubans, and 614 other Latinos.

The survey was conducted in English or Spanish as needed and all materials were translated and **back translated**. Researchers gathered three categories of data for the survey: prevalence rate of eating disorder, acculturation, and body mass index (BMI).

Lay persons collected the survey data through structured interviews.

Presence of an eating disorder was determined by DSM-IV criteria. Four eating disorder categories were created: AN, BN, BED, and Any Binge Eating.

Acculturation was measured as being native or foreign born, if one or both parents were born in the United States, and percentage of one's life spent in the United States.

Participants were organized into four weight categories based on BMI: underweight, normal weight, overweight, and severely obese.

The results showed the following:

1. No one, male or female, met the criteria for AN.

2. Females had a higher lifetime and 12-month prevalence rate for BN, BED, and Any Binge Disorder than males, but the differences were not significant.

3. There was no significant difference in prevalence for BN, BED, and Any Binge Disorder across ethnic subgroup.

4. Participants under 30 years of age had a significantly higher rate of BN than those over 30. The incidence of BED did not vary by age.

5. Participants living in the United States the longest had significantly higher lifetime prevalence rates for eating disorders than those new to the United States.

6. Controlling for age and gender, persons with a BMI over 40 had significantly higher rates of lifetime BN.

Alegria and colleagues made numerous conclusions.

1. The findings support the idea that binge eating disorders are a serious health problem for ethnic Latinos living in the United States.

2. AN is not common in ethnic Latinos living in the United States. The authors note that their results may not be accurate; the way ethnic Latinos express AN just may be different. A *fear of getting fat,* part of the DSM-IV diagnosis, may not be relevant for Latinos. While 102 persons were underweight according to BMI, only 6 participants reported a fear of getting fat. Future research should include culturally relevant assessments (must collect data about **emics**) for ethnic groups living in the United States.

3. The gender differences found in the Latino sample greatly contrasts with gender differences found in white U.S. samples. The lack of a significant difference in male and female ethnic Latinos may be real or the result of a fairly small sample.

4. Rates of eating disorders may be increasing in ethnic Latinos. Persons living in the United States for more than 70% of their lifetime had the highest lifetime prevalence rates of BN.

5. Persons with the most education had greater rates of BED.

Alegria and colleagues acknowledge several weaknesses that limit the interpretation of their data. First, the survey was conducted on a small sample. Second, self-reports could have been contaminated by recall biases. Third, the structured interviews were conducted by lay persons. The authors suggest that longitudinal studies follow up on their results.

## Risk factors for male eating disorders

Males account for 10% of eating disorders, though they are most likely to have BED when they have an eating disorder (Keel, 2005). Most of the research on eating disorders is on females, so psychologists do not know as much about the male experience with them. Men account for 40% of BED but are generally excluded from samples studying it.

Keel raises some good questions about males and eating disorders. First, do the findings from studies using female participants apply to males? Second, are there risk factors for eating disorders specific to males that are unknown from studying females? Third, do males show symptoms of eating disorders that differ from those women display? If so, then perhaps males are underrepresented in eating disorder statistics.

Keel thinks that there are some *risk factors* specific to men that need more research. Could there be correlations between each risk factor and having an eating disorder? One risk factor is that males are more likely to be overweight or obese before the onset of their eating disorder. A second risk factor is participating in **sports** that require low body weight (wrestling weight classes) or a low percentage of body fat (body building). A third risk factor is homosexuality. Last, pursuing an extreme masculine role may be a risk factor, called **reverse anorexia**. Reverse anorexia is when males perceive their bodies as too small, even when bodybuilding has greatly increased overall body mass.

## 7.12 Examine Biomedical, Individual, and Group Approaches to Treatment

Answers to questions about this heading are primarily addressed in other sections. I will provide a summary of the assumptions for each approach and direct you to appropriate studies. *All treatments probably affect neurotransmission and neural circuitry.* So it is up to the clinician and patient to decide which approach is the "best fit."

It is important that you understand that all treatments probably do the same thing to the brain. The Goldapple study reviewed in section 7.13 documents that the prefrontal cortex-limbic system pathway is altered with both antidepressants and cognitive therapy. However, the way that the pathway is altered differs. The end result is the same though. Other treatment studies should document brain changes in patients as therapy progresses. Bandura writes that raising self-efficacy alters neurotransmitters. Acupuncture, exercise, and diet also alter neurotransmitters. But different treatments alter neurotransmitters at different rates. Drug therapies probably work the fastest, for example. Decisions about which treatment to use depend on the situation of the patient as well as the preference of the practitioner, which tend to relate to their training.

1. **Biomedical treatments.**

   a. Western psychiatric biomedical treatments. Clinicians taking this approach view mental illnesses as diseases that are treated with drugs and/or, for example, electro-convulsive therapy. The treatments "work" if symptoms are reduced. Hecker and Thorpe (2005) warn that common errors in thinking about Western psychiatric treatments lie in several areas. First, it is wrong to assume that biomedical treatments are the only logical treatments for disorders with strong biological abnormalities. Second, it is wrong to assume that, if a biomedical treatment reduces symptoms, then psychological factors are not important. The opposite claim is also problematic, that psychological treatments reducing symptoms rule out the importance of biological factors. Taking a bidirectional approach should reduce making these thinking mistakes. Section 7.13 includes a discussion of drug treatments, including two experiments.

   b. TCM. Refer to section 5.10 for the assumptions and philosophy of TCM along with experiments on acupuncture and depression. Section 7.15 includes an eclectic approach that involves Chinese herbal medicines.

   c. Dietary treatments. Refer to section 3.8 for the assumptions and goals of dietary treatments for depression and an experiment.

2. **Individual treatments.** There are many types of individual treatment. I highlight cognitive therapy. Section 7.13 includes assumptions and goals of cognitive therapy and representative studies.

3. **Group treatments.** The IB syllabus lists therapies that are delivered to more than one person at a time as "group therapy." Most therapies can be administered to more than one person at a time. This is how I define group therapy as separate from family therapy, where the group is the family. Even though I trained as a family therapist and recognize its effectiveness for treating many disorders, such as schizophrenia, bipolar disorder, and AN, I selected **mindfulness-based cognitive therapy** (MBCT) and **group interpersonal therapy** (IPT) as my examples for depression treatment. Section 7.13 includes a group MBCT and an IPT efficacy study for treating depression. **Family therapy** is not as effective in treating depression as other therapies, though research suggests that marital therapy is beneficial. In addition, there are *so many types of family therapy* that efficacy studies are very challenging to design.

Avoid making a sweeping claim that "family therapy" works. Identify which type is used, learn its assumptions and techniques, and evaluate relevant efficacy studies.

Paula Truax (2001) writes that group therapy is effective for treating depression *as long as the client is enthusiastic about getting therapy in a group setting and has mild to moderate symptoms.* Persons with severe depression, suicidal tendencies, or with other mental illness in addition to depression are usually excluded from samples so it is not known if group therapy is effective for them.

Truax's opinions are based on McDermott's 2001 meta-analysis on group depression treatment. The general results of the meta-analysis are as follows: 48 studies conducted between 1970 and 1998 were included in the study; the average age of study participants was 44; and 70% were women. All but one study used CT and/or behavioral therapy. Several findings are important. First, depressed persons receiving group psychotherapy improved significantly more than those getting no treatment. Second, there was no significant difference between the progress of depressed persons getting group psychotherapy and those getting individual treatment. Last, CT and psychodynamic therapy was compared in eight of the studies, and in all eight, depressed persons receiving group CT improved significantly over those getting psychodynamic group therapy.

It is no surprise to me that the therapies with good **outcome research**—meaning studied in experiments—results for individual therapy also have good outcome results when used in groups. The client's preference is probably the key to selecting the right treatment setting. Is the person enthusiastic about group therapy? If not, individual therapy is just as effective.

The group therapies supported with outcome research, such as CT and interpersonal therapy (IPT), appear more effective than group therapies supported with **process research**, meaning it relies on nonexperimental evidence, such as psychodynamic. Truax thinks that counselors should use therapies supported with outcome research, where it is easier to show that the therapy reduces depressive symptoms. Truax's opinion does not mean that process-oriented therapies are useless. However, the short-term nature of most outcome research is not appropriate for process-oriented therapies. Many therapies using outcome research seek to reduce symptoms, while the therapies using process research seek to restructure the personality.

## Note to the teacher

If your students study treatments for AN, Google the free publication, *The Maudsley family-based treatment for adolescent anorexia nervosa,* by Daniel LeGrange. Pamela Keel (2005) writes that family-based treatments are probably the most effective ones for AN and the Maudsley program has some good results.

Hecker and Thorpe (2005) write that most all psychotherapies originated from psychoanalysis. As Freudian assumptions about the therapy process were challenged, one of the questions asked was, why not have others present during therapy? In addition, offering therapies in groups addresses a logistical concern for therapists. How can hardworking therapists deliver counseling to everyone needing it? At best, it is only possible to deliver individual therapy to a small number of persons at a time.

I expect to see more therapies conducted in groups in the future, as health-care dollars are limited.

Hecker and Thorpe claim that group counseling is beneficial for many reasons. These include acceptance by peers and belonging to a group, particularly for lonely persons living in a depersonalized world. Any individual therapy can be administered in a group settings, but make sure that efficacy studies support the therapies both individually and in groups. Hecker and Thorpe identified 10 therapeutic factors that are common to all therapies offered in a group setting. These are "instilling hope, universality (the person is not the only one with the problem), imparting information, altruism (group members helping each other), corrective recapitulation of problems from a person's original family, developing social skills, imitating others, emotional processing and cognitive reflection, interpersonal learning, and group cohesiveness" (p. 376).

## 7.13 Examine Biomedical, Individual, and Group Approaches to the Treatment of One Disorder

### Taking a level of analysis point of view

A wide variety of treatments are available for depression. While I use the categories listed in the IB syllabus, treatments affect people at all three levels of analysis. First, treatments affect the brain. Second, treatments affect a person's thinking. Last, Arthur Kleinman (2004) says that culture affects the perception and acceptance of treatments, even affecting how drugs alter the brain.

Any source claiming that a particular treatment is best for everyone with a set of symptoms is guilty of *oversimplification*. Treatment choice really depends on many factors, such as the severity of the symptoms, the cause of the problem if one can be identified, cultural beliefs, and the presence of other mental and/or physical health problems. No one treatment works for everyone. Some people do not respond to any treatment. Some people get better without any formal treatment. Helping professionals often use more than one treatment at the same time, called an **eclectic**, or combination, approach.

### Note to the teacher

> I included a lot of information in this section. The purpose of all this information is to show why evaluating treatments cannot be oversimplified and why students must tolerate uncertainty.
>
> I suggest that students read the material and then practice summing up the main points. This way they can make useful generalizations about the material on the IB exam.

### A cross-cultural list of depression treatments

Depression treatments include but are not limited to the following:

**Biomedical treatments**

drug therapy

ECT

acupuncture

herbal medicine, such as St. John's Wort

dietary change

exercise

vagus nerve stimulation

transcranial magnetic stimulation

### Individual treatments

Biomedical treatments are given individually, but the IB syllabus uses the term "individual" to refer to treatments that attend to the specific needs of a person and involve one-on-one therapy sessions or community-based cultural treatment.

cognitive therapy (CT)

mindfulness-based cognitive therapy (MBCT)—a combination of meditation and CT

interpersonal therapy (IPT)

well-being therapy

psychodynamic therapy

humanistic therapy

behavior therapy

guided mastery therapy to raise self-efficacy

faith healers, shaman, or other culture-based community treatments

### Group treatments

family therapy

marital therapy

group psychotherapy

Some treatments are more effective than others. The IB syllabus suggests that therapies should have a high degree of **efficacy**. The studies reviewed in this book meet this standard. After the next section that outlines some key questions we need to ask to determine whether or not treatments are successful, I discuss some treatments that represent a variety of opinions and highlight some newer research. I cannot review all available treatments, but *my goal is to provide a more balanced, cross-cultural view of treatment than is found in most introductory texts.*

The hardest thing about evaluating treatment is that *no efficacy study compares all available treatments.* So we cannot rank them in order of effectiveness. In fact, all the treatments reviewed in this book have evidence showing that they are effective. Researchers typically test a treatment against one or two others. Sometimes, drug studies only compare antidepressants to other antidepressants and maybe placebos and leave out talking therapies. Sometimes, study results conflict. Ask the question, to what extent are the samples and study conditions comparable? Always remain aware of which treatments are used for comparisons.

## Some things to think about when evaluating treatments

The direction that treatments should have high efficacy requires that we tackle the question, what counts as evidence?

Each treatment has strengths and limitations. How do clinicians know if a treatment "works"? Is one better than another? *It might depend on whom you ask.*

Consider the following:

1. Treatment selection should reflect the *potential benefits versus potential risks* of the treatment.

2. Modern-day clinicians want **evidence-based treatments** from efficacy experiments. *But clinicians do not all value the same kind of evidence.* What does it mean for a treatment to "work"? Does it mean to reduce the symptoms? Does it mean to restructure the personality? Does it mean to change an underlying pattern of thinking? Does it mean to change an underlying physical problem that contributes to the symptoms? Does it

mean to do something to increase one's resilience to the symptoms in the future? Does it mean that clients say they feel better?

3. *The questions in #2 are controversial.* Jeffrey Hecker and Geoffrey Thorpe (2005) divide research into two categories, **outcome research** and **process research**. Both categories reflect different research values and goals.

4. Outcome researchers seek evidence-based treatments with efficacy, meaning that an experiment shows that a treatment causes a change. Efficacy studies use **randomized clinical trials** (RCTs). There is currently a debate about the extent to which these RCTs must use experiments that are double-blind and placebo controlled, referred to as the gold standard in Western psychiatric treatments (and physical health treatments). Should all treatments have to meet this gold standard? Many drug efficacy studies adhere to this gold standard. Some talking therapies, such as cognitive therapy, can be tested in RCTs meeting the "gold standard," sometimes testing cognitive therapy against drugs and placebo controls. But many drug or talking therapy efficacy studies use the RCT format without a placebo control. Clinicians using other types of talking therapies often view RCTs as restrictive. In addition, modern TCM practitioners use evidence-based medicine but do not favor placebo controls. The standard for outcome research is debated.

5. What place should **process research** have in modern evidence-based psychology? Any therapy that takes a long time to "work," such as psychodynamic therapy, is best suited to process research. The goal of psychodynamic therapies is to restructure the personality and this takes a long time, perhaps two years. While some brief psychodynamic therapy is experimental in an attempt to work within the demands of the accepted gold standard, the brief duration violates its main goal. Process research is also best for humanistic therapy. Carl Rogers (1961) produced a large amount of process research showing that a person's ideal self and actual self became more strongly correlated during therapy and after a follow-up period. Process research relies on correlation studies or case studies.

6. Sometimes clinicians do not follow the research and have an allegiance to the theories they studied in college. Should any treatment ever be used when there is no evidence (either outcome or process evidence) for its effectiveness?

7. Placebos are problematic for all depression treatments. However, new research may reduce the impact of placebos. This research is reviewed later in this section.

8. How do we know that any treatment works in the long run?

9. Why do some people get better without any formal treatment?

10. How does culture affect treatment?

11. To complicate the study of treatments, *there are no studies that compare all available treatments.* A study comparing all available treatments is not really practical.

12. *The fact is that depression is increasing.* Why are rates increasing when so many treatments are available?

There is no *one* answer to which kind of evidence is best. There are just opinions, each with advantages and disadvantages. The debate is important because *what is accepted as evidence determines which treatments those who control health care monies offer.*

No one in a modern society is against evidence-based practices. "What is seldom appreciated, however, is that evidence-based practice is a *construct* (i.e., an idea, abstraction, or theoretical entity) and thus must be *operationalized* (turned into something concrete)" (Weston

& Bradley, 2005, p. 266). There are many ways to operationalize the concept "evidence" and debates focus on the extent to which all evidence should meet the **gold standard**.

A gold standard of mental health treatment evidence was established in the mid 1990s that gave RCTs using placebo controls top status (Weston & Bradley, 2005). An APA task force and other research that followed it distinguished empirically supported outcome-based treatments from less structured longer-term process-based treatments process that many practicing psychotherapists used (Weston et al., 2004).

Long-term therapies do not fit neatly into this gold standard, which uses the U.S. Food and Drug Administration (FDA) model of RCTs. In addition, TCM treatments are evidence-based, but do not typically use a placebo control.

The gold standard reflects very specific *values*. A list is then generated of either "supported" and approved treatments, or "unsupported" or unapproved treatments (Weston & Bradley, 2005). The argument is that any other type of study contains too many confounding variables to be credible. Included in the argument is that clinicians need standardized diagnoses and manualized treatment plans where every clinician administers the therapy the same way (Weston et al., 2004).

Weston & Bradley believe that RCTs have their place, but are they the best way to test treatments for *all* disorders?

Strengths of RCTs include the following:

1. They establish clear cause and effect.
2. They use tightly defined samples to control for confounding variables.
3. They seek to keep harmful therapies from being used.
4. Mental health care is expensive. Is it harmful to society to spend money on treatments that are not supported by RCTs?

Disadvantages of using RCTs include the following:

1. Many therapy applications emerge from practice and are applied individually in accordance with an individual's personality. Weston and Bradley believe the best results from the most experienced therapists should be compared to other treatments in RCTs, but only after best practices are established in the field.
2. The samples used in RCTs are limited to patients with clearly defined single diagnoses. For example, in an RCT on depression, participants cannot be too severely depressed, cannot be suicidal, or have a second mental health problem, such as substance abuse. These homogeneous participants are rarely what clinicians encounter in practice.
3. Using a manualized approach to treatment does not guarantee that a clinician applies the treatment correctly and effectively.
4. How is improvement defined? A treatment can appear supported using one way of examining outcome and unsuccessful using other criteria. Symptoms reduced over the course of a brief trial are not the same thing as recovery over a longer time frame. Sometimes patients test as improved in brief RCTs but are not followed over the long term. When followed, there are mixed results. For example, depressed patients tend to show poorer progress over time than patients with panic disorder.

Do the advantages of using RCTs outweigh their limitations? Should long-term therapies and TCM not be used because they do not fit a particular research model?

There are outcome experiments investigating *brief* psychodynamic therapies. In addition, there are studies, though not all controlled, investigating the outcome of humanistic therapies and longer-term psychodynamic therapies. For students studying psychodynamic and humanistic therapies, here is an overview of the research.

Short-term **psychodynamic therapy** (STPP) is studied in experiments but with no placebo control. Moran (2005) reviewed a meta-analysis of the effectiveness of 17 STPP experiments. These experiments randomly assigned participants to get STPP, another treatment, or a waiting list. In addition, all the therapists were trained to use a manualized approach, and data were collected so that a comparison could be made on client progress. The disorders treated were depression PTSD, AN, social phobia, and cocaine dependence. Results showed that those getting STPP were better off than those receiving other treatments or on the waiting list. In addition, 95% of the STPP group was still better than those in the other two conditions after a 13-month follow-up period.

Short-term psychodynamic therapy was designed to fit into RCTs lasting from eight to about 16 weeks.

Hecker and Thorpe (2005) reviewed a meta-analysis from Elliott in 2002 about the effectiveness of **humanistic therapy**. Elliot concluded that persons getting humanistic therapies made large gains. These gains were stable even after a follow-up time of a year or more. The gains made during humanistic therapy were similar to the gains made in other types of therapy. However, any time that humanistic therapy was compared to cognitive therapy (CT), those getting CT made changes more rapidly. Elliott points out many criticisms of humanistic studies. Many of the studies were uncontrolled, the therapists did not use manuals, and many of the participants in the studies did not have a formal diagnose. Elliott admitted that scientific minded persons examining his meta-analysis would not be happy.

Let's examine some treatments and see what must be considered.

**Acupuncture**, a biomedical treatment, is reviewed in section 5.10. The authors wrote that acupuncture could be used alone or in combination with drug therapy. **Dietary change**, a biomedical treatment, is included in section 3.8. Christensen (1990) wrote that persons using dietary treatments should be screened to make sure that diet is a factor in the depression.

This chapter includes discussions on drug therapy, exercise, cognitive therapy, group mindfulness-based cognitive therapy, and group interpersonal therapy. Section 7.14 examines eclectic treatments for depression.

## Treatment #1: Biomedical treatment— antidepressant drugs

Western psychiatrists often prescribe **antidepressants** as the "first line of defense" against depression, though drugs are sometimes combined with psychotherapy. There is a long list of antidepressant medications. One group is the SSRIs, the selective serotonin reuptake inhibitors, such as Prozac. Other drugs affect more than one neurotransmitter. For example, the SNRIs, such as Cymbalta, affect serotonin and norepinephrine reuptake inhibitors. New drugs are undergoing efficacy testing all of the time.

### A few words about the future of antidepressants

Leonard Rappa and colleagues (2001) write that future antidepressants may be very different from today's antidepressants. The first antidepressants became available about 50 years ago. *The trend over time is to find drugs with fewer side effects that help persons with depression fully recover.*

Rappa and colleagues, as well as Sapolsky (2004) and Lambert (2008), say that many questions remain about what causes depression and what helps people get better. While many of the existing antidepressants target **serotonin** and/or **norepinephrine**, it is not really clear that these neurotransmitters explain depression. The fact that current antidepressant drugs are effective for only 56%–60% of the patients using them is evidence that currently available antidepressants have not ended depression (Lambert, 2008). Please refer back to section 3.4 for Sapolsky's discussion of depression and section 7.9 for Lambert's views.

New drugs are being studied to treat depression all the time. Researchers were already investigating about 26 new substances in 2001 (Rappa et al., 2001). Two promising candidates are **substance P** and drugs targeting **stress** hormones.

Substance P is a neuropeptide, which acts like a neurotransmitter. Substance P is found in the brain, spinal cord tissue, and in other parts of the body. Substance P has a receptor in the brain called NK, is known to interact with serotonin, and coexists with norepinephrine. The theory is that blocking substance P receptors reduces depression. While initial tests were encouraging, a second round of tests was inconsistent. Substance P is used now to treat pain and the side effects of chemotherapy.

Another promising research area targets stress hormones. Depressed persons over-produce stress hormones. Samuel Barondes (2003) describes the potential benefit of a drug that targets overactive stress systems. Pharmaceutical companies are trying to develop a drug that binds to corticotrophin releasing hormone (CRH) receptors. CRH is a hormone that stops the secretion of cortisol in normal persons. Depressed persons may have an abnormally functioning hypothalamus, which means that cortisol production continues when it should stop. Theoretically, a drug blocking CRH stimulation in the pituitary gland would lower cortisol levels in depressed persons. This idea is still under investigation.

Many other substances are being studied to treat depression (Rappa et al., 2001). One example is **nitric oxide** (NO). Recall that one study from section 3.4 about genetics and aggression investigated NO. Higher levels of NO are associated with lower aggression. This is particularly interesting because studies on meditation show that NO increases during the relaxation response in meditators (Dusek et al., 2006). However, NO only increases after extensive meditation training and practice. Just understand that any drug developed in the future to increase NO levels will give the brain a greater "punch" of NO than meditation, just as SSRIs gives the brain far more serotonin than a turkey sandwich (which contains tryptophan that the body converts into serotonin). We'll see what happens with NO research.

Rappa and colleagues warn that theories about these new substances are still in their conceptual stages. Most of the efficacy trials on new drugs, which can take years to complete, drugs are variations of those already in use. The most promising of the new drugs is substance P.

## Antidepressants: The case of Lauren Slater

*Clearly, there are people who need drug therapy and benefit from it.*

Take Lauren Slater's case from the impressive PBS series called *The Secret Life of the Brain*. Lauren Slater is featured in the depression segment. Lauren, author of the book *The Prozac Diary*, talks candidly about managing severe depression and taking Prozac over the 10-year period the film covers. Her experiences might surprise you and elicit your empathy. There is generally a humble silence in my classroom after the film has been shown. Those students who believed that drugs are a simple solution now understand differently, and those who spoke out against prescription drugs see that drugs can be helpful. Prozac clearly helped Lauren, but as the drugs reduced one set of problems, another set emerged.

After five hospitalizations, Lauren started taking Prozac in 1988, the year Eli Lilly and Company released it (Slater, 1999). Lauren had an immediate positive benefit. Her symptoms melted away after just five days on the drug; the world was a new and wonderful place. Within a year, Lauren was accepted into Harvard and she earned a doctorate in psychology. Lauren married, had a child, and became a therapist. Lauren was one of the first people to take Prozac for a decade.

But life is never so simple. Lauren experienced what patients call "**Prozac Poop-Out**," even though "poop-outs" can happen with many drugs. Prozac Poop-Out means that the brain develops a *tolerance* to the drug and its effectiveness diminishes. This is one of the limitations of antidepressant drugs, and as reported in a study by Maurizio Fava in 1995, Fava found that about one third of people taking Prozac experience tolerance problems after one year of taking the drug (Lambert, 2000).

Along with tolerance problems, Lauren experienced other side effects of taking Prozac, such as a loss of creativity (Slater, 1999). Over the first 12 years of taking Prozac, Lauren's doctor raised her dosage from 10 milligrams each day to 80, the top limit approved by the U.S. Food and Drug Administration (FDA). Sometimes, Lauren's doctor switched her to other types of antidepressant drugs when Prozac was not working at all and her symptoms returned.

*The Prozac Diary* is meant to describe both the benefits and the risks of taking an antidepressant drug. Lauren raises many ethical questions about her use of Prozac, such as "Am I really myself on the drug?" and "Is taking the drug robbing me of important experiences?"

Lauren continued to take the drug because her symptoms were so bad. After the film, Lauren's doctor increased her dosage to levels higher than recommended by the FDA. Lauren's plan was to wait and see what happened. She embraced the reduction of depressive symptoms yet was fearful of the potential increases in side effects, cognitive damage, toxicity, or a time when Prozac does not work at all for her. Why did Lauren continue to take Prozac? *Because the benefits still outweighed the risks.*

I recommend that you watch the film and hear Lauren in her own words.

When faced with long-term severe depressive symptoms, might the benefits of taking the drugs outweigh its risks? There is much to consider before someone takes an antidepressant. Some people respond to one drug and not another. Some people have side effects from drugs, though the SSRIs and SNRIs are generally well tolerated. Some people cannot take drugs at all. Anyone taking a drug must have symptoms regularly monitored. The brain sometimes begins resisting the drug, and patients must switch drugs for periods of time or increase the dosage.

## Drug efficacy testing: The FDA approval process

Drug companies must provide randomized double-blind placebo controlled experiments (the gold standard for RCTs) showing that the drug performs better than a **placebo** in reducing symptoms before the FDA approves it for use. Make sure you understand that FDA approval does not mean that the drug is 100% safe.

For example, Cymbalta was shown to be more effective than a placebo in four different trials on people ranging in age from 18 to 83 (FDA Web site). These experiments are **efficacy trials**, meaning that the drug must do what the drug claims it does. In two of the trials, participants were randomly assigned to receive either Cymbalta (N=122 and N=128) or a placebo (N=122 and N=139) for nine weeks. How did researchers know that the drug worked? "Working" is defined as symptom reduction and measured by the **Hamilton Rating Scale for Depression**. The Hamilton Rating Scale is a multiple-choice questionnaire administered by a health-care professional during an interview with a patient. The results of all four of Cymbalta efficacy trials showed that race, gender, and age did not affect the results.

Here are some things to consider when evaluating drug efficacy trials. Besides the FDA efficacy studies, there are plenty of other RCTs showing that drugs are effective when compared either to a placebo and/or another drug, and against psychotherapy.

1. FDA experiments compare drugs to placebos. The purpose of FDA studies is to show that the drug has effectiveness over a placebo and does not pose obvious dangers to people.

2. Drug companies typically sponsor the efficacy trials. To what extent do the researchers conducting the trials, who are also associated with drug companies, have a conflict of interest?

3. Doctors prescribing drug therapies say that a drug is "working" if symptoms are reduced. The Hamilton Rating Scale for Depression is a common assessment instrument to identify baseline symptoms and progress. But the Hamilton Rating Scale has some critics. For example, Bagby and colleagues (2004) claim that, while the Hamilton Rating Scale has high internal reliability, its test-retest, interrater reliability, and content and discriminant validity are poor.

5. Is the data from *all* efficacy trials available to physicians and the public? Erick Turner and colleagues (2008) wrote in the *New England Journal of Medicine* that health-care professionals did not get to see all of the research on antidepressants. Turner claims that drug companies and sponsors may have been selective about which studies to submit, that journal editors did not publish all of them, or both. Turner examined experiment results for 74 registered FDA studies of 12 antidepressants tested on 12,564 patients. Twenty-three studies representing 31% of the total number using 3449 subjects were not published. Whether the 74 studies were published or not seemed related to whether positive or negative outcomes were obtained. Paxil and Zoloft have some of the worst ratings. For example, seven Paxil trials with positive outcomes were published. Only two Paxil trials with negative results were published. Five Paxil trials with negative outcomes were not published. Prozac and Cymbalta have better profiles. Turner found no negative trials for Cymbalta. Both Prozac and Cymbalta had four positive outcomes published. Turner says that his team found two questionable Cymbalta trials that were not published. This is just some of the data that Turner reports. *Watch out for popular news stories making sweeping claims that antidepressants do not work.* Examine the real data; the results for some antidepressants are better than others. Doctors just want the facts so they can prescribe the best medicine.

## A short introduction to drug efficacy studies

In *The Prozac Diary,* Lauren tried everything she could think of to get better before Prozac went on the market. But Prozac was the first treatment that helped.

Lauren's case shows that it is not always helpful to tell someone to go to a therapist, meditate, or make dietary changes. While other treatments also alter neurotransmitters, they do so with less of a "punch." Drugs give the brain a big boost of neurotransmitters.

Just remember that, like any treatment, drugs have strengths and limitations. Lauren's case is a good example of the strengths and limitations.

There is more than one way that Western scientists study the efficacy of antidepressants. One way is to compare one antidepressant to a different antidepressant. Another way is to compare an antidepressant to a placebo. The best placebo controlled experiments have a no-treatment group. Sometimes this group is made up of people on a waiting list for treatment, in order to answer the question, did the placebo group do better than the group who got nothing? However, some consider no-treatment groups to be unethical. Other efficacy studies compare antidepressant drugs to CT and sometimes include a comparison group getting a combination of drugs/psychotherapy. Drug studies are generally RCTs. But in fact, some of the RCTs do not use a placebo control, and when they do use one, they often lack a no-treatment group.

Even outside of Western medicine, antidepressant drugs are still part of efficacy studies. For example, drugs are compared to acupuncture or Chinese herbal medicines.

## An efficacy study comparing antidepressants, cognitive therapy, and their combination

Martin Keller and colleagues (2008) designed an experiment to compare the effectiveness of the antidepressant nefazodone with CT or with a combination of the drug and CT. This experiment is also useful for section 7.14 about eclectic treatment approaches.

The aim of the study was to clarify some of the existing research inconsistencies. Published studies show that antidepressants have efficacy for treating depression in both the initial stage of treatment and the maintenance phase of treatment (after the symptoms go into remission). But it is less clear if combination treatments are really better than either a drug or CT alone.

Participants were 681 persons with depression from 12 different outpatient clinics as measured by the Hamilton Rating Scale for Depression. Participants were between the ages of 18 and 75. As typical of most efficacy studies, participants must be homogeneous for comparison purposes. This means that persons with certain characteristics are excluded. Some of the exclusion characteristics were high risk for suicide, the presence of a second mental health problem such as OCD, substance abuse, or schizophrenia, and previous failure to respond to nefazodone.

Participants were randomly assigned to receive nefazodone, CT, or a combination for 12 weeks. Progress was measured with the Hamilton Rating Scale. Twenty-four percent of all participants did not complete the full 12 weeks, with 14% of the drug group, 7% of the combination group, and 1% of the CT group withdrawing.

Results showed several things. First, participants in all three groups showed significant improvement. Second, persons in the drug alone group improved more rapidly than persons in the CT group during weeks 1 through 4. Third, by week 12, the efficacy for the drug alone (55% improvement) and for CT (52% improvement) was the same; it just took longer for the CT to have an impact. Last, the combination group showed the greatest change, an 85% improvement.

Keller and colleagues noted some limitations to their study. One, there was no **placebo** group. However, previous research showed that the drug was more effective than a placebo. Another limitation is the exclusion guidelines for the sample that restrict the study's generaliziability. Last, while drug companies typically provide financial support for any drug efficacy study, you should know that Bristol-Myers Squibb, the makers of nefazodone, financially supported the experiment.

## A meta-analysis on the efficacy of SSRIs and TCAs against placebo controls

Here is a second experiment about the efficacy of **antidepressants** in a particular kind of setting—treatment by a primary care physician.

This meta-analysis is important because primary care physicians are often the first to see mental health complaints. Bruce Arroll and colleagues (2005) asked if antidepressants were effective treatments when prescribed by primary care physicians in a primary care setting.

The authors believe that this is the first comprehensive review of primary care physicians and depression treatments. The study is necessary. *While most persons with depression are first seen and treated by primary care physicians, most of the research targets secondary care provided by psychiatrists.* Arroll and colleagues write that care for depressed persons by primary care physicians varies a great deal, probably because of doubts about the effectiveness of different drugs and psychotherapies. Arroll and colleagues state that up to 40% of depressed persons fail to respond to an antidepressant. Of those patients who do respond, few are considered cured. This meta-analysis sought to clarify the role of antidepressants in primary care practices.

The meta-analysis included all efficacy studies from numerous databases, such as MEDLINE, that met certain requirements. All of the studies selected for the meta-analysis were required to be RCTs that compared either a tricyclic antidepressant (TCA), an SSRI, or both with a placebo. The meta-analysis targeted adults with depression and left out studies on adolescents and the elderly.

Arroll and colleagues located 12 studies that met the meta-analysis requirements. Some tested SSRIs against a placebo, some tested TCAs against a placebo, and some tested both SSRIs and TCAs against a placebo. The sample size of participants taking SSRIs (sertaline, escitalopram, or citalopram) was 890. The sample size of participants taking a TCA (dothiepin, amitriptyline, mianserin, or imipramine) was 596. The sample size of persons taking placebos was 1267. The participants included both mild cases and persons with major depression.

Results of the meta-analysis showed that both SSRIs and TCAs were significantly more effective than taking a placebo when prescribed by a primary care physician. The results suggest that antidepressants are effective for reducing a range of depressive symptoms.

These conclusions come with a warning that many of the studies available for the meta-analysis contain design flaws. The concerns include the following:

1. There were few available experiments on primary care treatment and most of those were small-scale studies. If primary care physicians treat most depression, why do most efficacy studies target persons treated in other settings? More research should be conducted about primary care treatment of depression.

2. All of the SSRI versus placebo experiments had commercial ties.

3. Arroll noted that many of the reviewed studies contained selection biases and handled the withdrawal of participants (such as after experiencing side effects) incorrectly. When poor-quality studies are pooled with all the others, the positive treatments are exaggerated as much as 30%–50%.

4. The meta-analysis findings agreed with research suggesting that TCAs may take as long as two weeks to become effective and those patients might be able to take lower doses.

5. Depressed persons do not necessarily need to see a psychiatrist. However, more research should be conducted on the primary care doctor and depression treatment.

## Culture and antidepressants: The example of Japan

What happens when **antidepressants** become popular in non-Western cultures? Thinking about the increasing use of antidepressants in Japan gives us a chance to consider both the positive and the negative consequences of exporting Western biomedical treatments to non-Western cultures.

Laurence Kirmayer (2002) wrote that 2001 marked a turning point in Japanese psychiatry. Before 2001, antidepressants were rarely used. After 2001, antidepressant use dramatically increased. Its popularity may continue to grow in a globalizing world.

How can we explain the surge of interest in antidepressants? Might the use of antidepressants help more people get the treatment they need? Or might taking antidepressant drugs conflict with the values of traditional Japanese culture? What are the implications of answers to these questions?

Kirmayer writes that Japan's case gives us a chance to really think through some "cultural assumptions about the nature of depression, emotion, personality, and the good life" (p. 296).

Antidepressant medications, particularly the SSRIs, are popular Western biomedical treatments. Japan has a tradition of using drug treatments for physical and mental health other than antidepressants. In addition, Japan offers more mental health services than most Asian countries. So the problem is not a reluctance to use biomedical treatments. *The reluctance is specific to antidepressants.*

Antidepressants had a small market in Japan up until 2001. After 2001, SSRI use increased to the equivalent of 25 million U.S. dollars every month.

Depression symptoms are a problem in Japan. So why did it take so long for antidepressant drugs to become popular? Kirmayer identifies many factors.

1. The history of Japanese psychiatry

2. Japanese persons tend to view distress in terms of psychosomatic symptoms.

3. The Japanese government requires new efficacy trials using Japanese samples before any drug is adopted for use.

4. Cultural variations in the social meaningfulness of a group of symptoms

5. The Japanese view of the self

Let's talk a little about each.

Historically, severe psychotic disorders were the focus of Japanese psychiatry and treatment took place in hospital settings. This emphasis probably contributed to the **stigma** of mental illness throughout Japan.

Perhaps to reduce stigmatization and also to conform to socially defined perceptions of distress in Japan (these perceptions are socially meaningful and reified by the group), Japanese persons with "depressive" symptoms preferred to see internal medicine doctors for psychosomatic complaints. Although it is estimated that about 20% of patients seen by clinicians are "depressed," Japanese doctors have traditionally prescribed antianxiety drugs or just told patients to "relax."

Regulatory bodies in Japan are another limiting factor. Government policy requires new efficacy trials on Japanese samples showing that the drug is effective for use with Japanese patients. Remember that culture affects responses to drug treatments, so it makes sense to require new efficacy testing. These efficacy trials are in addition to those already conducted in the West. RCTs are hard to conduct in Japan for many reasons, such as the stigma of participation. In addition, it is costly to run efficacy trials, so those running them must perceive an economic benefit from marketing the drug in Japan. Both Zoloft and Buspar were not accepted for use in Japan because efficacy trials were unsuccessful. The negative results could have been a real failure of the drug to work in Japanese persons or problems with the samples. But since efficacy trials in Japan involve the use of many clinics and include both mild and severe cases, positive effects of the drugs might not be detected. The result is that the drugs are not as widely available as they are in the West.

Between traditions of doctoring in Japan, the problem of stigma, the use of psychosomatic medicine, and the difficulty of running efficacy trials, it is not surprising that antidepressant use in Japan got off to a slow start.

But despite these factors, Kirmayer thinks that *cultural variation is the key to understanding the reluctance of the Japanese to use antidepressants.* Each culture has a set of socially meaningful values that defines groups of symptoms. The historical practice of treating "depression" as anxiety reflects values of traditional Japanese culture and influences how a set of symptoms are classified by physicians.

The DSM-IV and the ICD-10 reflect socially meaningful ways of classifying a set of symptoms in the West. But is the category "major depression" meaningful to the Japanese? While new and younger Japanese psychiatrists are now promoting antidepressants, cultural values still keep them from widespread use in psychosomatic medicine. Kirmayer quoted Kobayakama Toshi-Hiro, an important psychopharmacologist. Toshi-Hiro made several important points. First, mental disease is less prevalent in the Japanese than in Westerners, perhaps because Westerners are more preoccupied with themselves. This is in contrast with the Japanese, who focus on interrelatedness. Since Western behavior is already exaggerated, the use of a drug that heightens a person's individual performance is accepted. The Japanese do not want their behavior exaggerated, so sedative drugs are more popular.

Perhaps these comments from a Japanese psychopharmacologist help situate what is socially meaningful for Japanese persons. *It challenges the notion that diagnosing and treating depression can be universal.*

Is the reluctance to use antidepressants in Japan simply their failure to adapt to modern times? Or is the reluctance an expression of traditional culture?

Personality differs according to culture and SSRIs modify a person's personality.

Do the Japanese think it is acceptable to enhance one's individual personality? The desired effects of taking an antidepressant are not the same in Japan as they are in the West. Before taking an SSRI, a person in the West may be sad and say, "I am depressed," meaning the individual is generally unhappy. Antidepressants make a person more outgoing and extroverted, an **individualist** view of the self. But in Japan, a **collectivist** culture, calmness, containment, and focusing on the larger social group are valued. Taking an SSRI might make the individual stand out, something not valued in Japan. In addition, the Japanese tend to view mood disturbance as social or moral problems. There is not even a word in Japanese that is the exact equivalent of depression. There are related Japanese expressions, such as *yuutsu,* meaning grief, but it also refers to gloominess of spirits and weather.

Kirmayer gives a second example from Sri Lanka. Many persons in Sri Lanka meet the Western diagnostic category of depression. But their Buddhist point of view keeps them from being disabled. To a Buddhist, "depressive symptoms" show one's wisdom. Antidepressants interfere with the meditations that transform the self to the ultimate goal of enlightenment.

Kirmayer writes that antidepressants alter one's **narrative** construction of the self, the self-talk that makes meaning of human lives, in three ways. First, taking a drug often energizes an individual, and narratives reflect this enhancement. Second, one's **attributions** have a new target after taking antidepressants; the drug is responsible for behavior. Third, taking a drug may make a person less empathetic to others, changing the very nature of social relationships.

Kirmayer concludes that the consequences are great for a culture when individuals take antidepressants. As Western psychiatry influences non–Western cultures more and more, perhaps we should take some time and think about the consequences. For example, the WHO Nations for Mental Health Program promotes biomedical treatments throughout the world. This program is supported by Eli Lilly and other drug companies. To what extent is the promotion of biomedicine beneficial?

Arthur Kleinman (2004) also asks questions about exporting Western biomedical treatments and writes, "The professional culture, driven by the political economy of the pharmaceutical industry, may represent the leading edge of a worldwide shift in norms" (p. 2). The shift in **norms** comes with both benefits and consequences.

We don't want to keep people from getting help when needed, but do cultural considerations make taking antidepressants less of a clear solution?

## The problem of placebos

**Placebos** complicate depression research. Participants in antidepressant efficacy trials respond positively to placebos almost as often as they respond positively to antidepressants.

While high placebo responses to depression treatments currently complicate treatment outcome research evaluation, new research may reduce those concerns.

Two themes emerge from new research on placebos.

1. Placebos are assumed by many, but not all, Western physicians to be useful in RCTs of mental health treatments. A placebo is defined in RCTs as an inactive substance, something that has no effect on the patient. Placebos keep the experiments double-blind. *But recent research suggests that placebos are not inert substances.* What does this mean for the interpretation of research using placebo controls?

2. If placebos are not inert substances, is there a way to control for placebo effects so they do not confound RCTs? At the same time, might controlling for placebo effects enhance the **ethics** of including placebo controls in RCTs?

Let's explore the first problem.

Donald Price and colleagues (2008) write that a shift has occurred in our understanding of placebos. *The older view that placebos are inert substances comes with a paradox; how can an inert substance have an effect?*

Scientists now think that the placebo effect is a real effect resulting from the "stimulation of an active therapy within a psychosocial context" (Price et al., 2008, p. 2.3). Many environmental, psychosocial, cognitive, and emotional factors, as well as the perception of somatic sensations, affect the expectations that may lead to a placebo effect.

Environmental and psychosocial factors include classical conditioning as well as the verbal and nonverbal behaviors of the person running the study. For example, research investigating placebos and pain medications use an *open-hidden method* to study researcher verbal and nonverbal behaviors. In these studies, participants either receive a drug openly from a person or in the hidden condition from a computerized dispenser. Those in the open condition respond better to the pain medication than those receiving it from the machine. This is one way to see the placebo effect in pain medications. In other research, those told that the drug was a potent painkiller responded more positively to the drug than those told either nothing or that it might or might not be effective.

Cognitive and emotional factors influencing the placebo effect include expectancy combined with emotions related to the desire to change or a combination of expectancy and memories of the effectiveness of past treatments.

Somatic perceptions also play a role. Some studies ask participants if they think they are getting the real treatment or a placebo. Participants who think they are getting the real drug report more positive physical changes.

Positive responses experienced by study participants are not just figments of the mind. Actual brain changes accompany the reported positive changes. Here is **neuroplasticity** at work again.

To sum up, real biological and cognitive changes occur during a placebo response.

*If placebo control groups are such a problem, why not just stop using them?* There are even professionals who argue that placebo groups are unethical. But Price and colleagues feel it is essential to drug efficacy trials that changes in the drug condition be significantly different from changes in placebo controls *and* a no-treatment group (which many have argued is also unethical). Without a no-treatment group, it is impossible to see a true placebo effect.

How do new findings about placebos affect the questions raised in problem #2?

Advances in neuroimaging now allow scientists to see the brain at work when responding to a placebo. *It may be possible to screen study participants for the likelihood that they are placebo responders.* Being a placebo responder might become a subject variable that is controlled in future research. This is potentially advantageous for future antidepressant efficacy studies because, right now, the evidence is not clearly in the favor of antidepressants.

Michael Craig Miller (2003) reviewed and commented on placebos in the *Harvard Mental Health Letter.* Studies over time report better results for placebo groups than for groups taking the drugs, but perhaps this is because of sampling limitations. Early antidepressant research primarily used participants with severe symptoms; those more likely to respond to the real drug. But now persons with severe symptoms are diagnosed earlier and are less likely to be referred to efficacy studies. *More recent studies use patients with milder symptoms, those more likely to respond to influences, such as hope.* Miller warns not to overvalue currently available antidepressants, but they are probably very effective for at least a minority of patients.

Is it possible to create profiles of **placebo responders**, non-placebo responders, medication responders, and medication nonresponders? And if so, might this help identify the real effects of a drug in clinical efficacy studies? Andrew Leuchter (2002, 2004) says yes to both questions.

In a neuroimaging study about the brain and placebos, 51 participants were randomly assigned to one of two placebo controlled RCTs testing the effectiveness of flouxetine (the SSRI Prozac) or venlafaxine (the SNRI Effexor) for nine weeks (Leuchter et al., 2002). **Cordance**, or data about regional brain activity, was collected by qualitative electroencephalography (**QEEG**) before the start of the study and at the end of one-, two-, four-, and eight-week periods. At the end of the study, 51% of persons getting the antidepressants and 38% getting the placebos responded positively. It is interesting that the drug and placebo responders could not be distinguished by the results of the Hamilton Rating Scale for Depression. But QEEG results showed great differences in the prefrontal cordance between the groups. The placebo responders showed *an increase* in prefrontal cordance, very different from even their baseline brain activity, and the medication responders showed *a decrease* in prefrontal cordance.

Leuchter and colleagues believed the results showed two things. First, the placebo response is really an active treatment rather than an inactive treatment. Second, the placebo response is really very different from the drug response. This is of particular interest to researchers because it is reported that 50%–75% of the positive response in antidepressant efficacy studies is because of the placebo effect. Leuchter's results suggest that placebo responders are entirely different from drug responders. Replication was suggested using different samples.

In an attempt to further identify distinguishing characteristics between placebo responders and drug responders, Leuchter and colleagues (2004) analyzed data on the same participants. Placebo responders can possibly be identified before the start of an efficacy study. Placebo responders start off with lower cordance in the frontocentral brain region and have somewhat faster cognitive processing than placebo nonresponders, meaning that the depressive symptoms affected their cognitive processing less than placebo nonresponders. Again, the authors suggest replication. Since the medication responders in the study may have responded positively because of things other than the medication, including a placebo response not measured, the study results are tentative.

Perhaps in the near future scientists will use this information to know more about the mechanisms by which drugs and placebos work, something Lambert, Sapolsky, and others say need clarification. In addition, for those who consider placebo controls to be unethical, perhaps future drug trials will help screen participants for studies and also help to understand what is happening to those patients responding to placebos.

## Treatment #2: Biomedical treatment—exercise

**Exercise** may be a good choice for certain types of patients. Exercise probably affects the brain by releasing **serotonin** and endorphins, though more research needs to confirm the exact effects.

Michael Babyak and colleagues (2000) conducted an experiment and found that exercise was as effective as drug treatments and combination treatments of drugs and exercise in patients with major depression. A 10-month follow-up found that those continuing to exercise had fewer depression relapses than those taking medication.

Through advertisements, researchers recruited 156 experiment participants interested in exercise. Subjects were aged 50 and older and met specific guidelines. For example, they were not taking medication at the time of the study, were not substance abusers, were not suicidal, and were not in psychotherapy that started in the year prior to the study.

All met the DSM-IV requirements for major depression as determined by the Hamilton Rating Scale for Depression and the Beck Depression Inventory.

Participants were randomly assigned to one of three groups. The first group received three aerobic exercise sessions each week for 16 weeks. The second group took Zoloft, an SSRI. The third group took both the exercise program and Zoloft.

Patient depression symptoms were measured at the start of treatment, at the end of the 16-week period, and six months after the end of the experiment, for a total of 10 months.

All three groups showed similar remission rates at the end of the 16-week period, 60.4% for the exercise group, 65.5% for the medication group, and 68.8% for the combined group. But the most interesting results were those after six months. Follow-up was possible with 133 of the original 156 participants. The Beck Depression Inventory (self-report) was used to measure follow-up success. After the full 10-month period, those who exercised reported lower depression rates than those taking medication, even those taking medication along with an aerobic program.

The authors conclude that exercise is a valuable depression treatment. The finding that those exercising had fewer relapses than those in the combination group was unexpected. The researchers considered several reasons for the success of the exercise group. These reasons are related to the sample. In initial interviews, people who responded to study advertisements were more likely to show negative attitudes toward drug treatments. Some of the participants in the combined group reported that they thought the drug interfered with the exercise. It is possible that exercise increases one's sense of high personal **self-efficacy** for mastering a task, and taking a drug at the same time as exercising interferes with setting priorities. Expectations for improvement were also likely from the beginning of the study, as participants were motivated enough to respond to an advertisement for an exercise experiment.

Setting manageable priorities is an essential feature of high self-efficacy. The exercise study may be related to social learning factors of depression and the role that increased self-efficacy plays in treatment.

Babyak and colleagues write that it is impossible to infer that continued exercise between the end of the original 16 weeks and the end of the six-month follow-up period was the *cause* of continued depression relief. Participants may have continued to exercise because they were less depressed. The authors speculate that "these results suggest a potential reciprocal relationship between exercise and depression: feeling less depressed may make it more likely that patients will continue to exercise, and continuing to exercise make it less likely that the patient will suffer a return of depression symptoms" (p. 637).

## Treatment #3: Individual treatment—cognitive therapy

### Assumptions and goals of cognitive therapy

Aaron Beck, the founder of cognitive theory (CT), writes that our thoughts are primarily responsible for how we feel and behave (Engler, 2007). Negative cognitive style is a *risk factor* for developing depressive symptoms. The following explanation is from Barbara Engler's text.

The **cognitive triad**—thoughts about the self, the world, and the future—are the result of cognitive **schemas**. Schemas develop in the context of our experiences and often mirror the schemas of significant others, particularly parents. These schemas become the individual rules and beliefs that guide behavior.

Schemas of depressed persons are negative and pessimistic. Beck divides thoughts into *automatic* or *controlled*. Automatic beliefs occur just below one's surface awareness and are more difficult to change than conscious controlled thoughts. Destructive self-monologues are examples of automatic thoughts in depressed persons, such as "Things are never going to work out because it has always been this way in the past."

The automatic thoughts of depressed people are full of **cognitive distortions**. One kind of distortion magnifies problems, making things worse than they are in reality. An example of magnification is "anything less than an A on a test is a failure; I will never go to college and have a good future." Another cognitive distortion is **dichotomous thinking**, or thinking in extremes. An example of dichotomous thinking is "I am either a total failure or a complete success."

Negative and pessimistic cognitive distortions become part of a depressed person's cognitive triads. A depressed person believes that he/she is incapable of managing life, that the world is difficult and harsh, and views the future with pessimism.

*Cognitive therapy attempts to bring negative automatic thoughts to conscious awareness.* The therapy focuses on present perceptions of events and the automatic distortions that are applied to the events. The therapist challenges the client to examine the validity of automatic thoughts.

### Is CT effective?

A large body of research shows that CT is beneficial for persons with depression and is cross-culturally applicable. CT is the most studied psychotherapy and is frequently compared to drug treatments.

Specific themes emerge from studying CT. First, CT appears to make important changes in the brain. Second, CT is often as effective as or better than drug treatments and placebos. Third, CT works well with mild to moderate cases of depression. Fourth, some believe that CT is also effective with severe cases, though this finding is more controversial. Fifth, CT is frequently used in combination with drug therapy. Last, CT is relevant cross-culturally. Surveys and case studies investigate CT cross-culturally, sometimes as part of **eclectic** treatments.

Examine research with a critical eye. Here are some things to consider. Subject characteristics vary by study and population validity is limited. Individual study designs also limit ecological validity. Do the researchers represent particular biases? For example, do researchers have ties to drug companies, or are they associated with the creation of a particular therapy?

The following are two different kinds of studies on the efficacy of CT. The first examines important brain changes after getting CT. The second examines the effectiveness of CT for severe depression that also illustrates how to use a placebo control ethically. However, the study does not have a no-treatment group, probably for ethical reasons.

I conclude with a brief discussion about cross-cultural applications of CT, citing a survey on Thai individuals receiving CT and a case study about a Native American Indian.

## Study #1: A PET scan study about brain changes during CT

Kimberly Goldapple and colleagues (2004) used **PET scans** to document brain activity before and after 15 to 20 sessions of CT therapy over seven weeks in 14 patients. This is a small sample and there is no control group. PET scans from a previous study of patients taking Paxil were used for comparison. This study is also useful for section 3.7 on how the environment affects physiology.

Patients were measured as responders or nonresponders to therapy by the Beck Depression Inventory and the Hamilton Rating Scale for Depression. There were significant brain changes from baseline data of participants after therapy. The authors *assumed* that getting CT caused the brain changes. The authors recognized that future research needed experiments where patients were randomly assigned to CT, drugs, placebos, and no treatment to confirm the results.

Participants were recruited through newspaper advertisements in Toronto, Canada. Participants met the DSM-IV criteria for major depression. Patients were screened to ensure that they had, for example, no substance abuse problems or antidepressant treatment within the month prior to the study.

PET scans measured changes in glucose metabolism in specific brain regions. The authors concluded that "each treatment targets different primary sites with differential top-down and bottom-up effects—medial frontal and cingulate cortices with cognitive therapy and limbic and subcortical regions with pharmacology, both resulting in a net change in critical prefrontal-hippocampal pathways" (p. 39). Both CT and drugs affect a complex system of brain parts rather than one specific brain area, and the changes are the same after treatment. If you receive CT, the brain changes start in the cortex and work their way down to the limbic system (top-down). If you take antidepressants, the brain changes start at the subcortical level and work their way up to the cortex (bottom-up).

This is valuable evidence; CT has the same net effect on the brain as drug therapies.

The authors found no significant difference between the pattern of brain changes in milder and in severe cases. As the sample is small, this finding needs replication.

It is important to note that the brain changes made during CT are different from the brain changes made in previous studies investigating placebo controls in drug efficacy studies. Research shows that Prozac placebos mimic brain changes made with the real drug. The authors predict that placebos will mimic the effects in the brain of any treatment with which they are compared. Studies should investigate this prediction and include a no-treatment group for comparison, though using a no-treatment group raises some ethical concerns.

The authors believe there could be a selection bias in their study. Some of the participants reported previous negative experiences with drug therapy. Might these people be more motivated to be part of a CT study, and might their motivation affect the brain changes?

It makes sense that all therapies affect the brain and the evidence is growing. This is why Goldapple's research is so important; it is one of the first to document the process.

## Study #2: Is CT effective for severely depressed persons?

Robert DeRubeis and colleagues (2005) compared CT to antidepressant drugs in a randomized placebo controlled experiment. The sample included both moderately and severely depressed patients.

Previous literature suggests that drug therapy is the most used therapy in the United States to treat *severe* depression. But is this the best practice? Outcome research shows that CT is effective with mild and moderate cases. Is it also effective for severe cases?

An early experiment showed that CT was more effective than drug treatments, even in severe cases. But several criticisms limit the interpretation of that study. First, Aaron Beck was one of the researchers and his interests may have biased the study. Second, patients received low doses of the drugs, which were tapered off before the final results were tallied. Third, a study funded by the National Institute of Mental Health (NIMH) found, among other things, that the skill of cognitive therapists was not equal at all of the research sites, perhaps influencing patient progress. The NIMH position is that drugs are the most effective treatment for severe depression. The NIMH position is very influential in practice.

The varied findings about treating severe depression needed clarification.

The aim of the DeRubeis experiment was to see how to best treat severe depression in a randomized placebo controlled experiment. DeRubeis said that many other researchers supported Beck's findings, contrary to the NIMH position.

The 240 participants recruited from media advertisements who met DSM-IV diagnoses for depression by clinical interviews and the Hamilton Rating Scale were randomly assigned to one of three groups. One group received Paxil (n=120), one group was assigned a drug placebo (n=60), and one group was assigned CT (n=60). Treatment was given for 16 weeks for the Paxil and CT groups, but for ethical reasons, placebo treatment ended after eight weeks, long enough to see differences between it and Paxil. For the first eight weeks, double-blind procedures were used with the Paxil and drug placebo groups. At the end of eight weeks, placebo patients were offered other treatment at no cost, and those taking but not responding to Paxil had their treatment supplemented with other medications.

The experiment was administered at two sites, Vanderbilt University and the University of Pennsylvania. Participants were primarily middle-aged, white, and had some college education. Males dominated the Pennsylvania sample. "Overall, but especially at Vanderbilt, the sample was highly chronic or recurrent, with early onsets and a substantial rate of hospitalization" (p. 412). This means that most of the participants had severe symptoms. Many of the patients also had other mental disorders, something that usually excludes participants from efficacy studies. The authors believed that having another disorder would not affect treatment response.

Data on symptom reduction were gathered through the Hamilton Rating Scale at the end of eight weeks for all three treatments and then 16 weeks for CT and Paxil. At the end of eight weeks, 50% of the Paxil group, 43% of the CT group, and 25% of the placebo group showed positive symptom reduction. At the end of 16 weeks, there was no overall significant difference between the responses of those receiving Paxil and those receiving CT when data from both sites were combined. However, the results differed between the sites. There was no significant difference at the Pennsylvania site and a significant difference at the Vanderbilt site.

The authors concluded that both moderate and severe cases responded better to both drugs and CT than a placebo. The different findings from the Vanderbilt and Pennsylvania sites were probably related to therapist skill rather than characteristics of the sample. The results of this experiment do not support American Psychological Association and NIMH recommendations that severely depressed patients need drug treatments. The authors conclude that when administered by a qualified therapist, CT is just as effective as drugs for severely depressed patients.

## Culture and CT for depression

James Scorzelli (2001) suggests that CT is applicable cross-culturally as long as therapists take both the **etics** of counseling theory and **emic** features of a person's cultural context into account. Etics refer to aspects of a therapy that are universally beneficial, such as the way that a therapist establishes a relationship with a client. Emic approaches apply the therapy in culturally meaningful ways, such as using a culture's specific way of problem solving in counseling sessions.

An opportunity sample of 58 school and rehabilitation counselors in Thailand responded to survey questions about perceptions of using cognitive therapy in Thailand. Participants also wrote down the reasons for their responses. Results showed that 93.1% of the sample said that cognitive approaches to counseling did not conflict with their beliefs. Buddhist beliefs that the mind is the creator of problems were a theme that emerged in a content analysis of participant reasoning. Religion was not the primary reason given in the 6.9% who said that cognitive therapy conflicted with cultural beliefs. Instead, they said things such as "Thai families decide for the person."

Scorzelli writes that perceptions about the cross-cultural applicability of CT *may vary considerably*. The results of Scorzelli's 1994 survey of psychology and special education graduate students from India shows some variations. The students said that CT conflicted with cultural values; however, there were no consistent themes to their reasons.

Scorzelli believes that the backgrounds of the two research groups probably account for the different opinions. The Thai participants were all professional counselors and the Indian participants were students. Religion also varied. The Thai participants were primarily Buddhists and the Indian participants were primarily Hindu.

The results are not generalizable to all Thai therapists or Indian students because the samples are nonrepresentative.

Scorzelli warns therapists to consider cultural values of clients but to avoid applying presumed group norms to individuals.

Case studies also support cross-cultural applications of CT. Maureen Kenny (2006) documented the case of Andrea, a 37-year-old Native American (Seminole) Indian. Andrea's treatment was **eclectic**, involving CT, antidepressants, Alcoholics Anonymous (AA), client-centered therapy, and behavioral therapy. Andrea's case is also useful for section 7.14 on eclectic treatments. While Andrea's combination treatment included client-centered and behavioral therapies, they *supplemented* CT, antidepressants, and AA (Andrea also had substance-abuse problems). Sensitivity to Andrea's cultural background was essential throughout the therapy.

Andrea's case adds something valuable to the scant research available on treating depressive symptoms in Native American Indians.

Andrea had many stressors, such as her grandmother and brother's death, her adolescent daughter's pregnancy, a difficult divorce, a new relationship, and struggles to maintain an eight-year sobriety. Andrea reported many symptoms, such as headaches, excessive worrying, inferiority, anxiety (though not enough to receive a diagnosis for an anxiety disorder), hypersomnia, fatigue, low energy, irritability, and fear of losing control. Andrea met the DSM-IV requirements for major depression.

Kenny treated Andrea in 49 sessions over 22 months. Please note that Andrea's insurance plan did not limit the number of counseling sessions.

Andrea's primary treatment consisted of CT, antidepressants, which were reduced by a consulting psychiatrist after eight months of treatment, and AA. Client-centered therapy techniques, such as active listening and reflection of feeling, were used throughout the 49 sessions as "supportive therapy." Behavioral therapy consisted of assertiveness training (role-playing rehearsal) and was added three months into the treatment to help Andrea set limits on taking responsibility for others, especially her daughter, and attend to her own needs. The behavioral therapy helped Andrea develop "cognitive rehearsal strategies" to cope with everyday life demands.

Andrea made numerous changes after 22 months of treatment. She started and maintained a new relationship, coped better with her daughter, and reported improved mood and higher energy levels. In addition, Andrea stopped taking antidepressants. Kenny reports that it took a long time for Andrea to share her cultural values. For example, it took several months for Andrea to discuss a cultural event, a corn dance. It may take a long time to develop a productive client-counselor relationship with persons outside of Western culture. In particular, Native American Indians are unlikely to share sacred practices with a therapist early in treatment. This report raises concerns about using brief therapies with persons outside of Western cultures; will the therapy last long enough for the client-therapist relationship to develop?

Kenny warns that case studies are unique to an individual, so Andrea's treatment plan cannot be generalized to all Native American Indians with depressive symptoms. The case does provide insights into an approach that may help others.

I end the discussion of culture and CT with two observations. First, surveys and case studies are **process research**. It is unknown if Andrea's eclectic treatments "caused" her changes. In addition, Scorzelli's survey study was meant to show if CT was compatible to non-Western cultures. Second, future research about cross-cultural applications of CT must take into account the different ways that persons display cognitive distortions. I expect this to vary considerable depending on one's culture.

## Treatment #4: Group treatment—mindfulness-based cognitive therapy

John Teasdale and colleagues (2000) ran an experiment investigating the idea that **mindfulness-based cognitive therapy** (MBCT) reduced the risk of relapse after depressive symptoms were in remission. MBCT is *not* recommended as a primary treatment for depression.

### Note to the teacher

I highly recommend the film *Alternative Therapies: A Scientific Exploration: Meditation* (2008), available from the Films for the Humanities and Sciences. It reviews MBCT and other scientific research, such as Sarah Lazar's brain imaging studies about how meditation changes the brain. Lazar's research is also relevant for section 3.7 on the effects of the environment on physiology.

The purpose of the film is to see how science is quantifying meditation. Meditation research is new and we are directed to take a tentative view pending more investigation.

Students studying the health option are required to "evaluate strategies for coping with stress," so the material has another use.

The Web site www.mbct.com is a resource for this therapy. According to the Web site, MBCT "combines ideas of CT with meditative practices and attitudes based on the cultivation of mindfulness."

Relapse or recurrent depression is a common and costly problem. Teasdale and colleagues write that antidepressants are an effective and cost-efficient way to stabilize depression but that patients do not need to continue taking the drugs for a lengthy time period. Could MBCT as a follow-up therapy keep patients stable after the symptoms are in remission?

MBCT can easily be delivered as a *group skills training program* rather than individual therapy in order to further promote cost effectiveness.

MBCT practitioners believe that "when a negative mood happens again, a relatively small amount of such mood can trigger or reactivate the old thinking pattern" (www.mbct.com) in persons who have successfully completed their primary treatment. Learning to be mindful of such triggers, which means to be aware of negative thoughts and feelings and then disengage from them, can help limit relapse.

MBCT is different from CT. CT aims to change the content or meanings of thoughts. MBCT involves learning to *disengage* from thinking, where thoughts are reframed as "mental events" (Teasedale et al., 2000, p. 616). Thoughts are just thoughts, and they do not always represent reality. This way, a person can acknowledge the existence of the thoughts or emotions without having them trigger the negative associations that start a relapse. MBCT gives people a different way to relate to their thoughts and emotions.

The sample consisted of 145 depressed patients in remission or recovery from major depression. Participants were randomly assigned to receive treatment as usual (TAU) or to attend MBCT training. The researchers followed the progress of participants for one year. Those assigned to the TAU condition were told to consult their family doctor or get any other help they would normally choose if their symptoms returned. The MBCT program was delivered in eight weekly sessions, each lasting two hours. Between sessions, participants completed homework, which consisted of listening to both guided (through tapes) and unguided imagery exercises as well as exercises to apply their skills to everyday life situations.

Key components of MBCT training were *empowerment* and having *an open and accepting response* to all thoughts and emotions. Participants learned that they had a choice; they no longer had to automatically accept and react to negative thoughts and emotions as they did in the past. Teasdale and colleagues used the analogy of driving on a familiar road, "of suddenly realizing that one has been driving for miles 'on automatic pilot' unaware of the road or other vehicles, preoccupied with planning future activities or ruminating on a current concern" (p. 618) to describe automatic responses to thoughts and emotions. MBCT teaches "mindful driving," where one is fully conscious of each moment and responds without the shackles of old habits.

Results showed that relapse rates of participants in MBCT were approximately 50% less than the relapse rates of participants in the TAU condition. The effectiveness was strongest for participants with three or more episodes of depression. Why does MBCT appear more suitable for persons with three or more episodes of depression? The authors speculate that persons with three or more episodes were most likely to have had their relapses triggered by negative thoughts.

These findings were replicated by S. Helen Ma and John Teasdale (2004). It appears that MBCT is an effective and cost efficient way to prevent relapse in persons with three or more depressive episodes.

## Treatment #5: Group treatment—interpersonal therapy

### A cross-cultural experiment on group interpersonal therapy with adolescent war survivors

Paul Bolton's experiment on group interpersonal therapy (IPT) for depression relates to the IB course in four ways. First, it is an outcome study about group therapy for this option. Second, this experiment is an example of how a therapy developed in the West, IPT, is also useful cross-culturally. Third, this study relates to a topic in the human relations option titled "Discuss the effects of short-term and long-term exposure to violence." One effect of long-term exposure to violence *is an increased risk of mental illness,* including depression and anxiety. Fourth, this study is also useful for evaluating treatments for anxiety disorders.

Paul Bolton and colleagues (2007) write that the war in Uganda is extremely violent and persistent, with about 1.8 million people, particularly ethnic Acholi, displaced over 20 years of fighting. Although existing qualitative research shows that children exposed to war have an increased risk of mental illness, few studies evaluate intervention strategies with RCTs. The existing research needed **method triangulation**.

Participants were 14- to 17-year-old Acholi adolescents who were internally displaced because of war and currently living in one of two camps in Northern Uganda.

Adolescents were selected for the study based on the results of the Acholi Psychosocial Assessment Instrument (APAI). The APAI was developed to study locally defined depression-like and anxiety-like disorders that are similar in many, but not all, respects to the DSM-IV categories. Depression-like symptoms were created by combining the definitions of three categories of locally defined behaviors. One category is *Par,* which includes "Has lots of thoughts, wants to be alone, is easily annoyed, holds head, drinks alcohol, and has lots of worries" (p. 520). Another category is *Two Tam,* which includes "Experiences body pain, feels that brain isn't functioning, and thinks of self as being of no use" (p. 520). The last category is *Kumu,* which includes "Has loss of appetite, feels pain in the heart, does not sleep at night, and feels cold" (p. 520). The APAI also assessed anxiety-like symptoms. The local population used the term *Ma Lwor,* which includes "Clings to elders, constantly runs, dislikes noise, has fast heart rate, and thinks people are chasing him/her" (p. 520). The APAI was tested for reliability and validity on a similar sample before use in this RCT.

IPT was selected because of the strong outcome research supporting its effectiveness as an individual depression treatment. IPT was designed in the 1970s to treat depression (Hecker & Thorpe, 2005). IPT examines the person's past and current social roles and assumes that mental illness occurs within a social system and that one's social (interpersonal) roles are keys for recovery.

In addition to IPT, Bolton and colleagues thought that creative play (CP) was also beneficial. CP was thought to strengthen **resilience** through creative verbal and nonverbal activities.

Participants were randomly assigned to receive group IPT, CP, or to a waiting list (the no-treatment control). The treatment consisted of 16 weekly sessions.

Results showed that participants in the IPT group had a significant reduction of depression-like symptoms (the definition for a cure was a 50% reduction in symptoms) over the waiting list controls. When the data were analyzed by **gender**, the significance differences were just for girls. Those in the CP group showed no significant depression-like symptom reduction over the waiting list controls. Further, anxiety-like symptoms failed to improve in either IPT or CP.

Bolton and colleagues conclude that group IPT effectively treats depression symptoms in girls displaced by war. Why did the boys fail to improve? Perhaps boys are less willing to share emotions in group settings. Even though the depression symptoms of girls were significantly reduced, neither girls nor boys tested as improving in day-to-day functioning right after the study. It may be that improved functioning may follow improvement in symptoms after more time passes. Remember, this study defined the treatment as "working" if there was a reduction of symptoms.

## 7.14 Discuss the Use of Eclectic Approaches to Treatment

**Eclectic** approaches to treatment, sometimes called combination or integrative approaches, means to combine two or more therapies to maximize a person's progress.

Sometimes helping professionals have a primary orientation, such as cognitive, but supplement it with techniques from family therapy. Other combinations are drug therapies and CT, drug therapies and acupuncture, and CT and meditation therapy (meditation helps to maintain change after symptoms are in remission). Many other combination treatments are possible.

I discuss two studies about the efficacy of eclectic approaches for treating depression. The first examines the combination of antidepressant drugs and psychotherapy. The second is the combination of antidepressants and Traditional Chinese Medicine (TCM).

### Advantages of using an eclectic approach

This list of advantages comes from a discussion of integrative approaches for family therapists (Lebow, 2003), but I find these ideas useful for evaluating any eclectic approach.

1. Eclectic approaches have a broader theoretical base and may be more sophisticated than approaches using a single theory.
2. Eclectic approaches offer the clinician greater flexibility in treatment. Individual needs are better matched to treatments when more options are available.
3. There are more chances for finding efficacious treatments if two or more treatments are studied in combination.
4. Eclectic treatments apply to a broader range of clients. Failure to offer eclectic approaches may limit clinicians to helping only clients suitable for a single approach.
5. The clinician using eclectic approaches is not biased toward one treatment and may have greater objectivity about selecting different treatments.
6. Clinicians using an eclectic approach adapt their primary treatment with the benefits of other treatments that have evidence of effectiveness.

### Limitations of using an eclectic approach

Lebow lists some disadvantages of eclectic approaches.

1. Sometimes clinicians use eclectic approaches in place of a clear theory. Eclectic approaches are not substitutes for having a clear orientation that is supplemented with other tested treatments.
2. Sometimes eclectic approaches are applied inconsistently. It takes knowledge and skill to deliver eclectic approaches effectively.
3. At what point does using an eclectic approach turn into setting grandiose goals for the client?
4. Sometimes eclectic approaches are too complex for one clinician to manage.
5. There is always a danger that clinicians might call themselves "eclectic" when they really have no clear direction for treatment.
6. I added this last one to Lebow's list: Eclectic approaches should be backed up by efficacy studies that examine if specific combinations of treatment "work." Sometimes,

clinicians use eclectic approaches without examining the evidence. I know that eclectic approaches are sometimes hard to study. *But treatments that lack evidence are potentially dangerous.*

## Eclectic approach #1: Antidepressants and cognitive therapy

Timothy Peterson (2006) writes that drug/psychotherapy combinations are valuable *as long as the two are combined in specific ways.*

Peterson cites both the Goldapple and DeRubeis studies reviewed in section 7.13 and challenges some of their interpretations. *Tolerate uncertainty.* There is disagreement about which treatments work. No one can "prove" their argument anyway. Weigh the strengths and limitations of all of the viewpoints before coming to a conclusion.

Peterson says that there are many good reasons for using drug/psychotherapy combination treatments. For example, studies by Hollan as well as those sponsored by the American Psychiatric Association show that when a patient has, for example, social problems, psychotherapy ensures that the problems do not undermine the benefits of the drug therapy. In addition, Hollan found that even when combined, both psychotherapy and drugs maintain their individual benefits, giving the patient a more complete treatment. These complementary benefits reduce relapse. Last, a study by Segal noted that about 40% of patients do not take antidepressants as directed. Compliance with doctor's instructions increases after psychotherapy.

Peterson examined research on drug and psychotherapy combination treatments when they were used in three different ways. The first combination is the *simultaneous* use of drugs and psychotherapy. The second is when drugs and psychotherapy are combined *sequentially,* meaning that one or the other is used in addition to the first as needed to control symptoms. The third is *stage-oriented* use of antidepressants and psychotherapy, meaning that drugs are used in the acute phase and psychotherapy is used alone or in addition to continued drug therapy during the maintenance phase.

Peterson makes these claims about the effectiveness of drug/psychotherapy combinations:

**1.** The *strongest evidence* is for the *stage-oriented* combination treatment. Antidepressants are the most beneficial treatment during the acute phase. After a patient's symptoms go away, psychotherapy either alone or combined with continued antidepressants is the most effective way to prevent relapse. Patients first responding to drug therapy during the maintenance phase maintained their remission best if the psychotherapy was CT.

**2.** Research on the *simultaneous* use of drugs and psychotherapy during the acute phase of depression shows only a *moderate* increase in the reduction of symptoms. Peterson does say that combining antidepressants and psychotherapy in the acute phase *may* prevent or delay relapse, but the evidence is inconsistent. There is contrasting evidence about the simultaneous use of drugs and psychotherapy either in the acute or maintenance treatment phases. One study reviewed was the DeRubeis experiment. DeRubeis found that CT alone was just as effective for treating severely depressed patients, contrary to the claim that drugs were the best acute phase treatment. But there is more to the DeRubeis study than the results reported in section 7.13. Participants who responded to CT in the first eight weeks were removed from the study and compared to those who responded to antidepressants. Now, these participants were assigned to either continue antidepressants or a placebo in a 12-month maintenance-phase period. DeRubeis found that those receiving three more CT therapy sessions in this 12-month maintenance phase had fewer relapses (37%) than those who continued on the drug (27%) or a placebo (16%). However, CT was only significant *statistically* over the placebo group and not the group taking the drug. To complicate the argument, contrasting research to the DeRubeis experiment found something different. A larger study with chronically depressed outpatients showed that patients getting combined nefazodone/CT had the lowest relapse rates during the maintenance phase. *It is the reality of treatment outcome research; different studies have different findings and are sometimes hard to compare.*

**3.** There is some evidence that the *sequential* use of drugs and psychotherapy is beneficial. For example, an experiment by Frank in 2000 found that women with chronic depression were best treated first with IPT. Those who still needed help to reduce symptoms were given SSRIs to supplement the IPT.

**4.** Peterson agrees that Goodapple's neuroimaging study shows that both drug therapy and CT cause changes in the brain. Peterson believes that many questions still remain about the brain changes. Do the different pathways to brain changes have the same end effect? Are the effects complementary in some way?

## Eclectic approach #2: Antidepressants and Chinese herbal medicine combinations

Antidepressants are one strategy Chinese psychiatrists use to treat depression. However, they seek ways to minimize the amount of the drug needed to reduce symptoms. Bob Flaws (2003) translated an article from Chinese to English written by Liu Jing-feng and Zhang Hong-xue in 2002. The study tested the effectiveness of combing antidepressants and Chinese herbal medicine to treat depression.

One hundred twenty participants were assigned to receive either a Chinese herbal formula/antidepressant combination treatment or antidepressants alone.

The combination treatment used 11 Chinese medicinal herbs thought to "calm the spirit" plus others if the participant also had other symptoms. In addition, this group took both chlorpromazine and amitriptyline.

The comparison group took a larger dose of both chlorpromazine and amitriptyline.

Results showed that 41 participants in the combination treatment groups were pronounced cured, meaning that all symptoms disappeared and they returned to their normal work and personal lives. Twelve participants had a marked improvement, meaning most of their symptoms disappeared and they regained part of their work and personal life routine. Seven improved somewhat, meaning some of their symptoms ended though they did not return to their normal work and personal lives. All of the participants in this condition experienced some improvement.

A total of 36 participants in the drug only comparison group were cured, eight achieved marked improvement, 14 improved, and two showed no change.

The Chinese researchers wrote that "all depression damages the spirit; [therefore,] to treat depression [one] must calm the spirit" (p. 2). The Chinese herbal formula used in the experiment was designed more than 40 years ago.

Flaws noticed that, when Chinese medicinal herbs were combined with smaller doses of antidepressants, "the treatment effect is better, the course of treatment is shorter, and side effects are less" (p. 2). Western doctors know that the greater the dose and the longer patients stay on drug therapy, the greater the risk of side effects. The participants in the combination treatment had better results with one-third less of the antidepressant drugs than the comparison group.

# 7.15 Discuss the Relationship between Etiology and Therapeutic Approach in Relation to One Disorder

Modern models of "causation" are more complex than older models. The older models suggesting one "cause" are **reductionist**. Here are nine points to consider about the relationship between etiology and therapeutic approach. Depression is my primary example, but the same reasoning applies to any mental illness.

**1.** No one treatment works for everyone. Even if "causation" is established, the selected therapeutic approach should take into account a client's **cultural** values, a client's ability to tolerate drug treatments, a client's enthusiasm for group therapy, a client's willingness to address negative cognitive style, or a client's ability to start and follow through (self-efficacy) with the lifestyle changes necessary for dietary or exercise treatments.

**2.** It is often difficult or impossible to identify a specific "cause" of any mental disorder. Walker-Tesser model shows that causation is really an interrelated group of contributing factors. *One risk factor is not enough to cause any disorder.* The more risk factors, the greater the risk of mental illness. Besides, correlation studies are the main research method used to investigate "cause."

**3.** It is still possible to treat "symptoms," even when causes are unknown. For example, antidepressants or cognitive therapy treat depressive symptoms. Many clinicians measure symptoms before and after treatment with assessment instruments such as the Hamilton Rating Scale for Depression and the Beck Depression Inventory. Many consider a treatment to "work" if the symptoms are reduced. Just keep in mind that not everyone agrees with this definition of "work." For example, TCM practitioners do not think that treating "symptoms" is enough.

**4.** A primary therapeutic approach is frequently aimed at reducing the greatest risk factor. *Genetics is not the greatest risk factor.* Genetics are predispositions that increase one's risk of developing a disorder. We presently cannot change genes. Those thinking that advances in genetic engineering will end mental illness need to think through all of the biological and ethical implications of genetic engineering. Genetics do not determine behavior anyway. Gene expression depends on many factors. For example, the Caspi study (2003) about depression in section 3.4 shows that genes predispose someone for greater reactivity toward stress. The best therapeutic approaches for someone with two short risk alleles might be those reducing stress. While drug therapies reduce symptoms for many persons, the drugs do not improve one's stress management. Cognitive therapy or treatment involving lifestyle changes may help someone reactive to stress acquire greater coping skills.

**5. Culture** affects beliefs about "causes" and treatments. First, *cultural differences in gene expression complicate how we think about selecting a therapeutic approach.* Japanese samples carry 70%–80% of the two short risk alleles for 5-HTT and Caucasian samples carry 40%–45%. However, depression rates in the West are greater than they are in non-Western countries. Are there culturally based protective factors against mental illness in Japan that say something about the cause of mental illness? Refer to section 7.13 for the discussion about Japanese attitudes toward using antidepressants. Perhaps the Japanese will use more antidepressants in the future, but at least now, they are in a transition period where traditional Japanese culture still determines a lot of what is valued. How does traditional Japanese culture manage "depressive" symptoms? Does the answer to this question change your view of how to treat depression in non-Western countries? Second, *cultural values affect what is viewed as disordered.* For example, the Bagandan people in Uganda do not even think that many of the "symptoms" labeled mental illness in the West are actually illnesses requiring medical treatment. Their view affects what is considered a "cause."

**6. Gender** considerations affect knowledge about causation. Depression or eating disorder diagnoses may not take into account the way that both males and females express the disorders. Beliefs about "causes" and treatments then run the risk of reinforcing **stereotypes**.

**7.** If a "cause" *is* known, then treat it. For example, Larry Christensen developed a questionnaire to assess the extent to which diet was a primary contributing factor to depression (section 3.8). Participants in his studies were only persons whose diet was a factor.

**8.** The desire to locate specific "causes" is part of Western medical thinking. TCM practitioners do not look for a cause. Instead, physical and mental illnesses are considered interrelated. TCM practitioners claim that, if a person suffers from liver Qi imbalance, then acupuncture to rebalance liver Qi is necessary. But diet and other lifestyle habits also play a role and must change as well for a person to regain balance. Section 5.10 reviews TCM assumptions and acupuncture research.

**9. Eclectic** treatments may be the best approach when more than one "cause" of a disorder is known.

I advise taking a tentative approach to answering IB questions from this heading. Use the existing studies in this book for support.

# Appendix

# The Food and Sleep Challenge

The purpose of this assignment is to experience the benefits that lifestyle changes have on physiology. Choose either the **sleep challenge** or the **food challenge**—or both if you like. People frequently say they will *try* to get more sleep and eat properly but end up doing so irregularly that there is never any real benefit. This project runs for four weeks. No cheating allowed! It is worth a test grade, but it is only possible to earn either an A or an F; it is either completed or not completed. We will all make a commitment and stick with it.

This project is a chance for you to get some control over your life so that the day-to-day demands of an increasingly technological world do not increase your risk of poor health. After the project is over, you can decide if you want to control day-to-day demands or if you are going to let day-to-day demands control you.

I randomly contact parents to see how things are going. Parents must be fully aware of what you are doing and how you are progressing.

## The Sleep Challenge

It is clearly documented that adolescents need eight or more hours of sleep each night, with nine and one quarter hours as the ideal amount. Sleep deprivation effects include lowered immunity, irritability, decreased attention, and decreased memory consolidation. People often say that sleep deprivation does not affect them but the research shows otherwise.

Students selecting the sleep challenge must document at least eight hours of sleep each night, including weekends. Depending on your current level of sleep deprivation, you may feel drowsy until you pay back your **sleep debt**, a term used by William Dement (1999). Dement writes that "We discovered that the effect of each successive night of partial sleep carried over, and the effect appeared to accumulate in a precisely additive fashion" (p. 60). This means that, if you sleep six hours each night, you will get progressively more tired each day, even with the same six hours of sleep. To feel normal again, you must make up the lost sleep. While you might feel a little better after catching up on a little sleep, the rest of the debt is still there. Dement recommends keeping a sleep diary. Document your sleep and wake times for a week before the project starts and how you feel throughout the next day to get a baseline standard for which to gage your improvement. After paying back the sleep debt, you should feel more alert in the morning (no more sleepiness during first period), more relaxed, and better able to manage everyday stressors.

You may have to reorganize your life to get enough sleep but it is worth it. Good time management is practice for a future balanced life.

Keep a log and record your sleep and wake times as well as how you feel throughout the day. Both the student and parent must sign the log each day. Naps do not count toward the eight hours—if you have a sleep debt, it must added to the eight hours you sleep at night.

There are cases where entire families took the sleep challenge and later reported that they got along much better!

# The Food Challenge

I have three goals for the food challenge. One is adding good (meaning real) foods to your diet. A second goal is for you to eat regular meals. Third is to have you balance proteins, carbohydrates, and fats in order to stay healthy and maintain an ideal weight. Every meal must be balanced. As the food challenge progresses, you should feel more energetic, with fewer energy dips throughout the day. In addition, a proper diet decreases stress.

Be clear on this direction: *There are no food restrictions for this project.* You may eat anything you or your parents wish as long as you also follow the guidelines.

Keep a food log of everything you eat for a week before the challenge starts as a baseline measurement. Include how you feel throughout the day. During the challenge, log all meals and snacks and come up with a highlighting system to designate carbs, proteins, and fats, which must be present in all meals and snacks. Include how you feel throughout the day. Students and parents must sign the logs each day.

## Goal #1: Adding good (real) foods to your diet

I wonder if you have considered the role that sugar, processed foods, nonorganic foods, and caffeine have on your health. Many regard food as the best medicine. Hippocrates (460–377 B.C.) said, "Let food be your medicine and medicine be your food."

Let me say this again, *there are no food restrictions during this project,* though you only get points for eating *real foods.*

Any foods selected for the balanced meals must be unprocessed and free of refined sugars. You are not required to buy organic foods but I want you to learn about them. I notice that prices have come down as the public demands more organic products.

You must become educated about the food you eat. Only then can you make good choices. Get used to reading food labels! For example, the supermarkets are full of food labels that promise a product is "low in carbs." But all carbs are not created equal. Fruit is a common carb; it contains sugar, but it is a naturally occurring sugar that is better for you than refined sugars. However, you might find that eating fruit alone is not enough for you. It can give you a quick boost of energy but also cause a rapid energy plunge after the boost. A balanced snack might include an apple with peanut butter on it for proteins and fats that provide balance. See section 3.8 for a discussion on sugar's effect on mood. Another example is chicken. It is a good protein, but if you eat it from a frozen, prepackaged meal, it is probably processed with unhealthy additives. As with carbs, all fats are not bad for you. Good fats include olive oil and nuts. You have to eat some good fats in order to maintain an ideal weight. Processed foods tend to contain unhealthy fats, such as hydrogenated oils, many types of sugar, grains stripped of their nutrients, and chemicals.

All enriched grain products, such as white enriched bread and white pasta and rice (not basmati rice, which is whole grain), do not count toward a balanced meal. Instead, try whole-grain breads, pastas, and rice. You might even try grains other than wheat, which is a common allergen, such as spelt and quinoa.

White potatoes do not count toward anything in the food challenge. No fast foods count as real foods, unless restaurants such as EVOS or Chipotle, which are natural fast food chains, are in your area.

Here is a list of processed foods that do not count for the food challenge:

1. All products containing enriched grains
2. Most meal-replacement bars

3. Most lunch meats

4. All frozen meals

5. Soft drinks

6. Most bread

7. Chips and other bagged, bottled, or canned snacks

8. Many salad dressings, mayonnaises, pasta sauces, breakfast cereals, some nut butters

9. Sugar goes by many names, so read labels carefully. Labels including sugar, corn syrup, high fructose corn syrup, and anything else ending in "ose" are sugars. None of these are organic or unrefined sugars. I allow only foods with organic or unrefined sugars.

Please learn about the **glycemic index** for foods. You might want to eat high-glycemic foods only occasionally.

If you are addicted to sugar and caffeine, it is not the goal of this project for you to suffer withdrawal, unless your parents want you off of the products. Although sugar and caffeine do not count toward anything for the food challenge, you may consume them anytime you wish.

I highly recommend learning to bake. Try baking your own bread. If you like chocolate chip cookies, follow any recipe but use unrefined or organic sugar. This includes choosing chocolate chips that are without refined sugars. As Kelly Lambert believes, baking may stimulate your brain's reward system in the process!

Sometimes parents add their own restrictions. Sometimes the entire family takes the food challenge. I encourage parents to get involved. One family even planted an organic vegetable garden.

## Goal #2: Number of meals

NO SKIPPING MEALS ALLOWED!

It is up to individuals to choose three meals a day or four or five smaller meals. If you have lots of energy dips, try more frequent, smaller meals. Energy dips can be related to skipping meals or eating too many carbs at one time. A snack of a soda and chips is all carb!

The minimum requirement is three meals a day: breakfast, lunch, dinner, and one healthy snack. Log how the meals and snacks are balanced. For example, put peanut butter or almond butter on celery for a balanced snack. Meal-replacement bars are acceptable for snacks only if they do not contain added sugars, processed foods, and chemicals. Unfortunately, most of the meal bars my students have do not qualify.

## Goal #3: Balancing meals

You are required to show how each meal and snack is balanced for carbs, proteins, and fats. There are many philosophies on how to balance meals. Here are three examples:

1. One philosophy, adopted by the Zone Diet and many training programs, is to have 40% proteins, 30% carbs, and 30% fats at each meal. This is known as the 40/30/30 diet.

2. Some organizations, such as the American Heart Association (AHA), believe the 40/30/30 diet contains too much fat. Follow the AHA guidelines if you wish. Their Web site lists their guidelines and has a cookbook with great meal ideas.

3. Another perspective is the metabolic typing diet. It is based on the idea that everyone needs a balance of proteins, carbs, and fats, but that individuals fall into one of three

categories. These are the protein type, the mixed type, and the carb type. The balance requirement for each type differs. If you select this method, then you must know your metabolic type. One source for the test is *The Metabolic Typing Diet* by William Wolcott and Trish Fahey. Another source is Dr. Mercola's Web site, www.mercola.com.

Please note!!! Your parents' wishes are the bottom line on how you decide to balance meals.

I recommend Elizabeth Somer's book *Food and Mood*. Somer has good ideas about healthy balanced meals.

You will have to spend more time preparing food during the food challenge. But consider this—why do so many people view taking responsibility for their health a chore? Anything that reduces stress is valuable and is something you can control.

# References

Ader, R. (2005). Psychoneuroimmunology. In G. Miller, & E. Chen (Eds.), *Current directions in health psychology.* Upper Saddle River, NJ: Pearson Prentice Hall.

Alarcon, R. D., Alegria, M., Bell. C. C., Boyce, C., Kirmayer, L. J., Lin, K., Lopez, S., Ustun, B., & Wisner, K. L. (2002). Beyond the funhouse mirrors: Research agenda on culture and psychiatric disorders. In D. J. Kupfer, M. B. First, & D. A. Regier, (Eds.), *A research agenda for DSM-V.* Washington, DC: American Psychiatric Association.

Alegria, M., Woo, M., Cao, Z., Torres, M., Meng, X., & Striegel-Moore, R. (2007). Prevalence and correlates of eating disorders in Latinos in the United States. *International Journal of Eating Disorders, 40,* S15–S21.

American Psychiatric Association. (2000). Autistic disorder. *The diagnostic and statistical manual of mental disorders (DSM-IV-TR)* (4th ed.). Washington, DC: American Psychiatric Association.

American Psychological Association. (2000). Behavioral genetics. In A. E. Kazdin (Ed.), *Encyclopedia of psychology* (pp. 379–384). Oxford: Oxford University Press.

American Psychological Association. (2002). *Ethical principles of psychologists and code of conduct.* Available from http://www.apa.org/ethics/code2002.html

Aronson, E., Wilson, T. D., & Akert, R. M. (2007). *Social psychology* (6th ed.). Upper Saddle River, NJ: Pearson Prentice Hall.

Arroll, B., Macgillivray, S., Ogston, S., Reid, I., Sullivan, F., Williams, B., & Crombie, I. (2005). Efficacy and tolerability of Tricyclic antidepressants and SSRIs compared with placebo for treatment of depression in primary care: A meta-analysis. *Annals of Family Medicine, 3,* 449–456. Retrieved October 28, 2008, from http://www.annfammed.org

Babyak, M., Blumenthal, J. A., Herman, S., Khatri, P., Doraiswamy, M., Moore, K., Craighead, E., Baldewicz, T. T., & Krishnam, K. R. (2000). Exercise treatment for major depression: Maintenance of therapeutic benefit at 10 months. *Psychosomatic Medicine, 62,* 633–638. Retrieved March 11, 2008, from http://www.psychosomaticmedicine.org/cgi/reprint/62/5/633

Bagby, R. M., Ryder, A. G., Schuller, M. D., & Marshall, M. B. (2004). The Hamilton Depression Rating Scale: Has the gold standard become a lead weight? *American Journal of Psychiatry, 161,* 2163–2177.

Bandura, A. (1965). Influence of model's reinforcement contingencies on the acquisition of imitative responses. *Journal of Personality and Social Psychology, 1*(6).

Bandura, A. (1973). *Aggression: A social learning analysis.* Englewood Cliffs, NJ: Prentice Hall.

Bandura, A. (1977). *Social learning theory.* Englewood Cliffs, NJ: Prentice Hall.

Bandura, A. (1997). *Self-efficacy: The exercise of control.* New York: W. H. Freeman.

Bandura, A. (2001). Social cognitive theory: An agentic perspective. *Annual Review of Psychology, 52,* 1–26.

Bandura, A. (2002). Social cognitive theory in cultural context. *Applied Psychology: An International Review, 51*(2), 269–290.

Bandura, A. (2004). The role of selective moral disengagement in terrorism and counterterrorism. In F. M. Mogahaddam, & A. J. Marsella (Eds.), *Understanding terrorism: Psychological roots, consequences and interventions* (pp. 121–150). Washington, DC: American Psychological Association Press.

Bandura, A., Ross, D., & Ross, S. (1963). Imitation of film-mediated aggressive models. *Journal of Abnormal and Social Psychology, 66*(1), 3–11.

Baron-Cohen, S. (1995). *Mindblindness: An essay on autism and theory of mind.* Cambridge, MA: MIT Press.

Barondes, S. (2003). *Better than Prozac.* Oxford: Oxford University Press.

Becker, A. E. (2007). Culture and eating disorders classification. *International Journal of Eating Disorders, 40,* S111–S116.

Becker, A. E., Burwell, R. A., Gilman, S. E., Herzog, D. B., & Hamburg, P. (2002). Eating behaviors and attitudes following prolonged exposure to television among ethnic Fijian adolescent girls. *British Journal of Psychiatry, 180,* 509–514.

Belmaker. R. H., & Agam, G. (2008, January 3). Mechanisms of disease: Major depressive disorder. *The New England Journal of Medicine, 358,* 55–68.

Bem, S. (1998). Gender schema theory and its implications for child development: Raising gender-aschematic children in a gender-schematic society. In D. Anselmi, & A. Law (Eds.), *Questions of gender: Perspectives and paradoxes.* New York: McGraw-Hill.

Berns, G. S., Chappelow, J., Zink, C. F., Pagoni, G., Martin-Skurski, M. E., & Richards, J. (2005). Neurobiological correlates of social conformity and independence during mental rotation. *Biological Psychiatry, 58,* 245–253. Retrieved April 6, 2008, from http://www.ccnl.emory.edu/greg/Berns%20Conformity%20final%20printed.pdf

Berry, J. (1969). On cross-cultural comparability. *International Journal of Psychology, 4*(2), 119–128.

Blackwell, N. J., Bentall, R. P., ffytche, D. H., Simmons, A., Murray, R. M., & Howard, R. J. (2003). Self-responsibility and the self-serving bias: An fMRI investigation of causal attributions. *NeuroImage, 20,* 1076–1085.

Blakemore, S. (2000). The power of memes. *Scientific American, 283*(4), 64–6.

Bolton, P., Bass, J., Betancourt, T., Speelman, L., Onyango, G., Clougherty, K. F., Neugebauer, R., Murray, L., & Verdeli, H. (2007). Interventions for depression symptoms among adolescent survivors of war and displacement in northern Uganda: A randomized controlled trial. *Journal of the American Medical Association, 298*(5). Retrieved March 2, 2008, from http://www.jama.com

Bond, M. H. (1991). *Beyond the Chinese face: Insights from psychology.* Oxford: Oxford University Press.

Bond, M. H. (2002). Reclaiming the individual from Hofstede's ecological analysis—a 20-year odyssey: Comment on Oyserman et al. (2002). *Psychological Bulletin, 128*(1), 73–77.

Bond, M. H., & Smith, P. B. (1996). Cross-cultural social and organizational psychology. *Annual Review of Psychology, 47,* 205–35.

Bond, R., & Smith, P. H. (1996). Culture and conformity: A meta-analysis of studies using Asch's (1952b, 1956) line judgment task. *Psychological Bulletin, 119*(1), 111–137. Retrieved July 12, 2008, from http://www.runet.edu/~jaspeine/_private/gradsoc_articles/individualism_collectivism/conformity%20and%20culture.pdf

Bookheimer, S. (2002). Functional MRI of language: New approaches to understanding the cortical organization of semantic processing. *Annual Review of Neuroscience, 25,* 151–188.

Brewer, M. B., & Yuki, M. (2007). Culture and social identity. In S. Kitayama, & D. Cohen (Eds.), *Handbook of cultural psychology.* New York: The Guilford Press.

Brown, R., & Kulik, J. (1977) Flashbulb memories. In U. Neisser, & I. E. Hyman (Eds.), *Memory observed: Remembering in natural contexts* (2nd ed.). New York: Worth Publishers. (Reprinted from *Cognition, 5,* 73–99).

Bruner, J. (1977). *The process of education.* Cambridge, MA: Harvard University Press.

Bruner, J. (1978). Learning to do things with words. In J. Bruner, & A. Garton (Eds.), *Human growth and development.* Oxford: Clarendon Press.

Bruner, J. (1983). *Child's talk: Learning to use language.* New York: W. W. Norton.

Bruner, J. (1990). *Acts of meaning.* Cambridge, MA: Harvard University Press.

Bruner, J. (1996). *The culture of education.* Cambridge, MA: Harvard University Press.

Buller, D. J. (2009). Four fallacies of pop evolutionary psychology. *Scientific American, 300*(1). Retrieved February 9, 2009, from http://www.sciam.com

Butcher, J. N., Mineka, S., I Hooley, J. M. (2007). *Abnormal psychology and modern life* (13th ed.). Boston: Pearson Education, Inc.

Call, J., & Tomasello, M. (2008). Does the chimpanzee have a theory of mind? 30 years later. *Trends in Cognitive Science, 12*(5), 187–192.

Cantlon, J. F., & Brannon, E. M. (2006). Adding up the effects of cultural experience on the brain. *Trends in Cognitive Sciences, 11*(1). Retrieved May 5, 2008, from http://www.sciencedirect.com

Carey, G. (2003). *Human genetics for the social sciences.* Thousand Oaks, CA: Sage Publications.

Carreiras, M., Lopez, J., Rivero, F., & Corina, D. (2005, January 6). Neural processing of a whistled language. *Nature, 433,* 31–32.

Caspi, A., McClay, J., Moffitt, T. E., Mill, J., Martin, J., Craig, I. W., Taylor, A., & Poulton, R. (2002, August). Role of genotype in the cycle of violence in maltreated children. *Science, 297,* 851–854. Retrieved March 18, 2008, from http://www.sciencemag.org

Caspi. A., & Moffitt, T. E. (2006, July). Gene-environment interactions in psychiatry: Joining forces with neuro-science. *Neuroscience, 7.*

Caspi, A., Sugden, K., Moffitt, T. E., Taylor, A., Craig, I. W., Harrington, H., McClay, J., Mill, J., Martin, J., Braith-waite, A., & Poulton, R. (2003, July 18). Influence of life stress on depression: Moderation by a polymorphism in the 5-Htt gene. *Science, 301,* 386–389. Retrieved January 17, 2008, from http://www.sciencemag.org

Castano, E., & Giner-Sorolla, R. (2006). Not quite human: Infrahumanization in response to collective responsibility for intergroup killing. *Journal of Personality and Social Psychology, 90*(5), 804–818.

Castillo. R. J. (1997). *Culture and mental health: A client-centered approach.* Belmont, CA: Brooks/Cole.

Chen, S. X., Chan, W., Bond, M. H., Stewart, S. M. (2006). The effects of self-efficacy and relationship harmony on depression across cultures: Applying level-oriented and structure-oriented analyses. *Journal of Cross-Cultural Psychology, 37,* 643. Retrieved November 9, 2007, from http://sagepub.com

Chiao, J. Y., & Ambady, N. (2007). Cultural neuro-science: Parsing universality and diversity across levels of analysis. In S. Kitayama, & D. Cohen (Eds.), *Handbook of cultural psychology.* New York: The Guilford Press.

Chiavegatto, S., Demas, G. E., & Nelson, R. J. (2006). Nitric oxide and aggression. In R. J. Nelson (Ed.), *Biology of aggression.* Oxford: Oxford University Press.

Childress, A. R., Franklin, T. R., Listerud, J., Acton, P. D., & O'Brien, C. P. (2002). Neuroimaging of co-caine craving states: Cessation, stimulant administration, and drug cue paradigms. In K. L. Davis, D. Charney, J. T. Coyle, & C. Nemeroff (Eds.), *Neuropsychopharmacology: The fifth generation of progress.* American College of Neuropsychopharmacology.

Chinese Society of Psychiatry (2003). *CCMD-3.* Retrieved from http://www.cma-mh.org/English/

Chinese Society of Psychiatry (2005). *History of Chinese psychiatry.* Retrieved from http://www.cma-mh.org/English/

Chomsky, N. (1981). The case against B. F. Skinner. In E. B. Bolles (Ed.), *Galileo's commandment: 2500 years of great science writing.* New York: W. H. Freeman.

Christensen, L. (2001). The effect of food intake on mood. *Clinical Nutrition, 20*(Suppl. 1), 161–166.

Christensen, L. (2007). Cravings for sweet carbohydrate and fat-rich foods: Possible triggers and impact on nu-tritional intake. *Nutrition Bulletin, 32*(Suppl. 1), 43–51.

Christensen, L., & Burrows, R. (1990). Dietary treatment of depression. *Behavior Therapy, 21,* 183–193.

Cialdini, R. B., & Sagarin, B. J. (2005). Principles of interpersonal influence. In T. C. Brock, & M. C. Green (Eds.), *Persuasion: Psychological insights and perspectives* (2nd ed.). Thousand Oaks, CA: Sage Publications.

Cohen, D. (2007). Methods in cultural research. In S. Kitayama, & D. Cohen (Eds.), *Handbook of cultural psychology.* New York: The Guilford Press.

Cole, M. (1996). *Cultural psychology: A once and future discipline.* Cambridge, MA: The Belknap Press of Harvard University Press.

Cole, M. (2003). *Vygotsky and context: Where did the connection come from and what difference does it make?* Paper prepared for the biennial conferences of the International Society for Theoretical Psychology, Istanbul, Turkey, June 22–27, 2003. Retrieved March 7, 2006, from http://communication.ucsd.edu/lchc/People/MCole/lsvcontext.htm

Coolican, H. (2004). *Research methods and statistics in psychology* (4th ed.). London: Hodder & Stoughton.

Cosmides, L., & Tooby, J. (1997). *Evolutionary psychology: A primer.* Retrieved August 13, 2008, from http://www.psych.ucsb.edu/research/cep/

Curci, A., & Luminet, O. (2006). Follow-up of a cross-national comparison on flashbulb and event memory for the September 11th attacks. *Memory, 14*(3), 329–344.

Cutrona, C. E., Russell, D. W., Brown, P. A., Clark, L. A., Hessling, R. M., & Gardner, K. A. (2005, February). Neighborhood context, personality, and stressful life events as predictors of depression among African American women. *Journal of Abnormal Psychology, 114*(1), 3–15. Retrieved March 5, 2008, from http://www.pubmedcentral.nih.gov/picrender.fegi?artid=1913477+blobtype+pdf

Cutrona, C. E., Wallace, G., & Wesner, K. A. (2006). Neighborhood characteristics and depression: An examination of stress processes. *Current Directions in Psychological Science, 15*(4).

Davidson, P. S. R., Cook, S. P., Glisky, E. L., Verfaellie, M., & Rapcsak, S. (2005). Source memory in the real world: A neuropsychological study of flashbulb memory. *Journal of Clinical and Experimental Neuropsychology, 27,* 915–929.

Dawkins, R. (2006). *The selfish gene* (3rd ed.). Oxford: Oxford University Press.

Dement, W., & Vaughan, C. (1999). *The promise of sleep.* New York: Dell.

DeRubeis, R. J., Hollon, S. D., Amsterdam, J. D., Shelton, R. C., Young, P. R., Salomon, R. M., O'Reardon, J. P., Lovett, M. L., Gladis, M. M., Brown, L. L., & Gallop, R. (2005, April). Cognitive therapy vs. medications in the treatment of moderate to severe depression. *Archives of General Psychiatry, 62.* Retrieved March 12, 2008, from http://www.archgenpsychiatry.com

Dobbs, D. (2005, March 24). Fact or phrenology? The growing controversy over fMRI scans is forcing us to confront whether brain equals mind. *Scientific American Mind.* Retrieved August 2, 2008, from http://www.sciam.com

Dobbs, D. (2006, April/May). A revealing reflection. *Scientific American Mind, 17*(2).

Dusek, J. A., Chang, B., Zaki, J., Lazar, S., Deykin, A., Stefano, G.B., Wohlhueter, A. L., Hibberd, P. L., & Benson, H. (2006). Association between oxygen consumption and nitric oxide production during the relaxation response. *Medical Science Monitor, 12*(1), CR1–CR10. Retrieved November 10, 2008, from http://www.medsciencemonit.com

Ekman, P. (2003). *Emotions revealed.* New York: Henry Holt.

Ekman, P., Davidson, R. J., Ricard, M., & Wallace, B. A. (2005). Buddhist and psychological perspectives on emotions and well-being. *Current Directions in Psychological Science, 14*(2), 59–63.

Engel, S. (1995). *The stories children tell: Making sense of the narratives of childhood.* New York: W. H. Freeman.

Engler, B. (2007). *Personality theories: An introduction* (7th ed.). Boston: Houghton-Mifflin.

Fagan, G., Wilkinson, D. L., & Davies, G. (2007). Social contagion of violence. In D. J. Flannery, A. T. Vazsonyo, & I. D. Walkman (Eds.), *The Cambridge handbook of violent behavior and aggression.* Cambridge: Cambridge University Press.

Farah, M. J., Ed. (2008). *Neuroethics.* Retrieved March 9, 2008, from http://www.neuroethics.upenn.edu/

Finkenauer, C., Gisle, L., & Luminet, O. (1997). Flashbulb memory: A special case of memory as an individual and social faculty. In J. W. Pennebaker, D. Paez, & B. Rime (Eds.), *Collective memories of political events: Social and psychological perspectives* (pp. 191–208). Mahwah, NJ: Lawrence Erlbaum Associates.

Finkenauer, C., Luminet, O., Gisle, L., El-Ahmadi, A., van der Linder, M., & Philippot, P. (1998). *Flashbulb memories and the underlying mechanisms of their formation: Towards an emotional-integrative model.* Retrieved December 22, 2008, from http://www.esca.ucl.be/personnel/luminet/pdf/FBM_Baudouin.pdf.

Fiske, A. P., & Fiske, S. T. (2007). Social relationships in our species and cultures. In S. Kitayama, & D. Cohen (Eds.), *Handbook of cultural psychology.* New York: The Guilford Press.

Fiske, S. (2004). *Social beings: A core motives approach to social psychology.* Hoboken, NJ: John Wiley & Sons.

Fiske, S. T., & Taylor, S. E. (2008). *Social cognition: From brains to culture.* Boston: McGraw-Hill.

Flaws, B. (2003). A clinical audit of the treatment of depression with integrated Chinese-Western medicine. *Blue Poppy Press recent research report #335.* Retrieved October 31, 2008, from http://www.bluepoppy.com

Food, Drug, and Health Administration. (no date). *Cymbalta clinical trials.* Available from http://www.fda.org

Forest, G., & Godbout, R. (2004). Attention and memory changes. In C. A. Kushida & M. Dekker (Eds.), *Sleep deprivation: Basic science, physiology, and behavior.* New York: Informa Healthcare. Retrieved December 30, 2007, from http://www.questia.com

*Frontline* (Interviewer) & Carskadon M. (Interviewee). (1999). Inside the teenage brain: Interview with Mary Carskadon [Interview transcript]. Retrieved December 20, 2007, from http://www.pbs.org/wgbh/pages/frontline/shows/teenbrain/interviews/carskadon.html

*Frontline* (Interviewer) & Yurgelun-Todd, D. (Interviewee). (1999). Inside the teenage brain: Interview with Deborah Yurgelun-Todd [Interview transcript]. Retrieved December 30, 2007, from http://www.pbs.org/wgbh/pages/frontline/shows/teenbrain/interviews/todd.html

Gay, J., & Cole, M. (1967). *The new mathematics and an old culture: A study of learning among the Kpelle of Liberia.* New York: Holt, Reinhart, & Winston.

Gazzaniga, M. S., Ivry, R. B., & Mangun, G. R. (2002). *Cognitive neuroscience: The biology of the mind* (2nd ed.). New York: Norton & Norton.

Gazzaniga, M. S., Ivry, R. B., & Mangun, G. R. (2008). *Cognitive neuroscience: The biology of the mind* (3rd ed.). New York: Norton & Norton.

Goldapple, K., Segal, Z., Garson, C., Lau, M., Bieling, P., Kennedy, S., & Mayberg, H. (2004, January). Modulation of cortical-limbic pathways in major depression. *Archives of general psychiatry, 16.* Retrieved March 12, 2008, from http://www.archgenpsychiatry.com

Goodwin, C. J. (1998). *Research in psychology* (2nd ed.). New York: John Wiley.

Goodwin, C.J. (1999). *A history of modern psychology.* New York: John Wiley.

Gould, E., & Gross, C. G. (2002). Neurogenesis in adult mammals: Some progress and problems. *The Journal of Neuroscience, 22*(3), 619–623. Retrieved January 16, 2008, from http://www.jneurosci.org/egi/reprint/22/3/619.pdf

Grandin, T. (1999, February). *Social problems: Understanding emotions and developing talents.* Retrieved January 11, 2008, from http://www.autism.org/temple/social.html

Gray, P. (2007). *Psychology* (5th ed.). New York: Worth Publishers.

Grubin, D. (Executive Producer). (2001). The teenage brain: A world of their own. *The secret life of the brain* [PBS DVD Video]. California: Time Warner Company.

Gur, R. C., & Gur, R. E. (2007). Neural substrates for sex differences in cognition. In S. J. Ceci, & W. M. Williams (Eds.), *Why aren't more girls in science?* Washington, DC: American Psychological Association.

Haesler, S. (2007, June/July). Programmed for speech. *Scientific American Mind, 18*(3).

Halpern, D. F., Benbow, C. P., Geary, D. C., Gur, R. C., Hyde, J. S., & Gernsbacher, M. A. (2007). The science of sex differences in science and mathematics. *Psychological Science in the Public Interest, 8*(1).

Hammer, L. (2005). *Dragon rises, red bird flies: Psychology and Chinese medicine* (Revised ed.). Seattle, WA: Eastland Press.

Harvard Medical School. (2005, July). The adolescent brain: Beyond raging Hormones. *Harvard Mental Health Letter, 22*(1).

Harvard Medical School. (2006, January). Update on St. John's Wort. *Havard Mental Health Letter, 22*(7).

Hecker, J. E., & Thorpe, G.L. (2005). *Introduction to clinical psychology.* Boston: Pearson.

Heider, K. (2003). *Seeing anthropology: Cultural anthropology through film* (3rd ed.). Boston: Allyn & Bacon.

Herbert, J., & Stipek, D. (2005). The emergence of gender differences in children's perceptions of their academic performance. *Applied Developmental Psychology, 26,* 276–295.

Higgins, E. S. (2008). The new genetics of mental illness. *Scientific American Mind, 19*(3), 40–47.

Higgins, N. C., & Bhatt, G. (2001). Culture moderates the self-serving bias: Etic andemic features of causal attributions in India and Canada. *Social behavior and personality.* Retrieved April 2, 2008, from http://www.findarticles.com

Hofstede, G. (no date). *Dimensionalizing cultures: The Hofstede model in context.* Retrieved June 29, 2008, from http://www.ac.wwu.edu/~culture/hofstede.htm

Hofstede, G., & Hofstede, G. J. (2005). *Cultures and organizations: Software of the mind* (2nd ed.). New York: McGraw-Hill.

Hogg, M. A., Terry, D. J., & White, K. M. (1995). A tale of two theories: A critical comparison of identity theory with social identity theory. *Social Psychology Quarterly, 58*(4), 255–269. Retrieved June 6, 2008, from http://www.jstor.org

Horwitz, A. (2005). The age of depression. *Public Interest.* Retrieved December 8, 2008, from http://findarticles.com

Huesmann, L. R., & Kirwil, L. (2007). Why observing media violence increases the risk of violent behavior by the observer. In D. J. Flannery, A. T. Vazsonyi, & I. D. Waldman (Eds.), *The Cambridge handbook of violent behavior and aggression.* Cambridge: Cambridge University Press.

Hull, R., & Vaid, J. (2006). Laterality and language experience. *Laterality, 11*(5), 436–464.

Iacoboni, M., Molar-Szakacs, I., Gallese, V., Mazziotta, J. C., & Rizzolatti, G. (2005). Grasping the intentions of others with one's own mirror neuron system. *PLoS*

*Biology, 3*(3), e79. Retrieved May 9, 2008, from http://www.plosbiology.org

Jarvis, M., Russell, J., & Gorman, P. (2004). *Angles on psychology* (2nd ed.). Cheltenham, UK: Nelson Thomas.

Jeong, H., Sugiura, M., Sassa, Y., Haji, T., Usui, N., Taira, M., Horie, K., Sato, S., & Kawashima, R. (2007). Effect of syntactic similarity on cortical activation during second language processing: A comparison of English and Japanese among native Korean trilinguals. *Human Brain Mapping, 28,* 194–204.

Jones, J., & Brown, W. (2005). Any time is Trinidad time! Cultural variations in the value and function of time. In A. Strathman, & J. Joireman (Eds.), *Understanding behavior in the context of time.* Mahwah, NJ: Lawrence Erlbaum Associates.

Kagan, J. (2007). A trio of concerns. *Perspectives on Psychological Science, 2*(4), 361–376.

Kalat, J. (2007). *Biological psychology* (9th ed.). Belmont, CA: Wadsworth.

Kaptchuk, T. (1983). *The web that has no weaver: Understanding Chinese medicine.* Chicago: Congdon & Weed.

Keel, P. (2005). *Eating disorders.* Upper Saddle River, NJ: Pearson Prentice Hall.

Keller, M. B., McCullough, J. P., Klein, D. N., Arnow, B., Dunner, D. L., Gelenberg, A. J., Markowitz, J. C., Nemeroff, C. B., Russell, J. M., Thase, M. E., Trivedi, M. T., & Zajecka, J. (2008). A comparison of nefazodone, the cognitive behavioral-analysis system of psychotherapy, and their combination for the treatment of chronic depression. *The New England Journal of Medicine, 342,* 1462–1470. Retrieved October 28, 2008, from http://www.nejm.org

Kemmer, S. (2007, February/March). Sticking point. *Scientific American Mind, 18*(1), 65–69.

Kenny, M. C. (2006). An integrative approach to the treatment of a depressed American Indian client. *Clinical Case Studies, 5,* 37. Retrieved October 10, 2008, from http://www.sagepublications.com

Kim-Cohen, J., Caspi, A., Taylor, A., Williams, B., Newcombe, R., Craig, I. W., & Moffitt, T. E. (2006). MAOA, maltreatment, and gene-environment interaction predicting children's mental health: New evidence and a meta-analysis. *Molecular Psychiatry, 11,* 909–913.

Kimura. D. (1999). *Sex and cognition.* Cambridge, MA: The MIT Press.

Kimura, D. (2007). "Underrepresentation" or misrepresentation? In S. J. Ceci, & W. M. Williams (Eds.), *Why aren't more women in science?* Washington, DC: American Psychological Association.

Kimura, D., & Clarke, P. (2002). Women's advantage on verbal memory is not restricted to concrete words. *Psychological Record, 91,* 1137–1142. Retrieved March 16, 2005, from http://www.sfu.ca/~dkimura/

Kirmayer, L. J. (2002). Psychopharmacology in a globalizing world: The use of antidepressants in Japan. *Transcultural Psychiatry, 39,* 295. Retrieved October 10, 2008, from http://www.sagepub.com

Klein, D. N. (2008). Classification of depressive disorders in the DSM-V: Proposal for a two-dimensional system. *Journal of Abnormal Psychology, 117*(3), 552–560.

Kleinman, A. (2004, September 2). Culture and depression. *The New England Journal of Medicine, 31*(10). Retrieved March 11, 2008, from http://coe.stanford.edu/curriculum/courses/ethmedreadings06/em)601garcia1.pdf

Kolb, B. (1999). Toward an ecology of cortical organization: Experience and the changing brain. In J. Grafman, & Y. Christen (Eds.), *Neuronal plasticity: Building a bridge from the laboratory to the clinic.* New York: Springer.

Kolb, B., Gibb, R., & Robinson, T. E. (2004). Neuroplasticity and behavior. In J. Lerner, & A. E. Alberts (Eds.), *Current directions in developmental psychology.* Upper Saddle River, NJ: Pearson Prentice Hall.

Konner, M. (2007). Evolutionary foundations of cultural psychology. In S. Kitayama, & D. Cohen (Eds.), *Handbook of cultural psychology.* New York: The Guilford Press.

Kuhl, P. (2000). A new view of language acquisition. *PNAS, 97*(22). Retrieved May 1, 2008, from http://www.pnas.org

Lahey, B. (2008). *New developments in behavior genetics for introductory and developmental psychology.* Paper presented at the meeting of the National Institute for the Teaching of Psychology, St. Pete Beach, FL.

Lambert, C. (2000). Worse living through chemistry: The downsides of Prozac. *Harvard Magazine.* Retrieved October 23, 2008, from http://harvardmagazine.com/2000/p-the-downsides-of-prozac.html

Lambert, K. (2008). Depressingly easy. *Scientific American Mind, 19*(4), 31–37.

Lebow, J. L. (2003). Integrative approaches to couple and family therapy. In T. L. Sexton, G. R. Weeks, & M. S. Robbins (Eds.), *Handbook of family therapy.* New York: Routledge.

Lee, S. (2000). Eating disorders are becoming more common in the East too. *British Medical Journal, 321,* 10–23.

Lee, S., Ho, T. P., & Hsu, L. K. (1993). Fat phobia and non-fat phobic anorexia nervosa: A comparative study of 70 Chinese patients in Hong Kong. *Psychological Medicine, 23,* 999–1017.

Leuchter, A. F., Cook, I. A., Witte, E. A., Morgan, M., & Abrams, M. (2002). Changes in brain function of depressed subjects during treatment with placebo. *American Journal of Psychiatry, 159,* 122–129.

Leuchter, A. F., Morgan, M., Cook, I. A., Dunkin, J., Abrams, M., & Witte, E. (2004). Pretreatment neurophysiological and clinical characteristics of placebo responders in treatment trials for depression. *Psychopharmacology, 177,* 15–22.

Leventhal, T., & Brooks-Gunn, J. (2004). Children and youth in neighborhood contexts. In J. Lerner, & A. E. Alberts (Eds.), *Current directions in developmental psychology.* Upper Saddle River, NJ: Pearson Prentice Hall.

Lilienfeld, S. O., & Arkowitz, H. (2007, April/May). Autism: An epidemic? *Scientific American Mind, 18*(2), 82–83.

Lips, H. M. (2005). *Sex & gender: An introduction.* Boston: McGraw-Hill.

Lubinski, D. S., & Benbow, C. P. (2007). Sex differences in personal attributes for the development of scientific expertise. In S. J. Ceci, & W. M. Williams (Eds.), *Why aren't more women in science?* Washington, DC: American Psychological Association.

Ma, S. H., & Teasdale, J. D. (2004). Mindfulness-based cognitive therapy for depression: replication and exploration of differential relapse prevention effects. *Journal of Consulting and Clinical Psychology, 72*(1), 31–40. Retrieved January 20, 2009, from http://www.mbct.com

Makino, M., Tsuboi, K., & Dennerstein, L. (2004). Prevalence of eating disorders: A comparison of Western and non-Western countries. *MedGenMed: Medscape General Medicine, 6*(3). Retrieved 10/19/08 from http://www.pubmedcentral.nih.gov/articlerender.fcgi?artid=143625

Manuck, S. B., Kaplan, J. R., & Lotrich, F. E. (2006). Brain serotonin and aggressive disposition in humans and nonhuman primates. In R. J. Nelson (Ed.), *Biology of aggression.* Oxford: Oxford University Press.

Markus, H. R., & Kitayama, S. (1991). Culture and the self: Implications for cognition, emotion, and motivation. *Psychological Review, 98,* 224–253.

Marsella, A. J., & Yamada, A. M. (2007). Culture and psychopathology: Foundations, issues, and directions. In S. Kitayama, & D. Cohen (Eds.), *Handbook of cultural psychology.* New York: The Guilford Press.

Matsuda, N. (1985). Strong, quasi-, and weak conformity among Japanese in the modified Asch procedure. *Journal of Cross-Cultural Psychology, 16*(1), 83–97. Retrieved May 29, 2008, from http://jcc.sagepubs.com

Matsumoto, D. (1996). *Unmasking Japan: Myths and realities about the emotions of the Japanese.* Stanford, CA: Stanford University Press.

Matsumoto, D. (2002). *The new Japan: Debunking seven cultural stereotypes.* London: Intercultural Press, Nicholas Brealey Publishing.

Matsumoto, D. (2008). *Culture and the teaching of psychology.* Paper presented at the meeting of the National Institute for the Teaching of Psychology, St. Pete Beach, FL.

Matsumoto, D., & Juang, L. (2008). *Culture and psychology* (4th ed.). Belmont, CA: Wadsworth/Thomson Learning.

Maxson, S. C., & Canastar, A. (2006). Genetic aspects of aggressions in nonhuman animals. In R. J. Nelson (Ed.), *Biology of aggression.* Oxford: Oxford University Press.

Mazzeo, S. E., & Bulik, C. M. (2009). Environmental and genetic risk factors for eating disorders: What the clinician needs to know. *Child & Adolescent Psychiatric Clinics North America, 18*(1), 67–82.

McClure, S. M., Li, J., Tomlin, D., Cypert, K. S., Montegue, L. M., & Montegue, P. R. (2004). Neural correlates of behavioral preference for culturally familiar drinks. *Neuron, 44,* 379–387. Retrieved November 1, 2008, from http://www.commercialalert.org/neuromarketingcokepepsi.pdf

McSweeney, B. (2002). Hofstede's model of national cultural differences and their consequences: A triumph of faith—a failure of analysis. *Human Relations, 55*(1),

89–118. Retrieved March 9, 2007, from http://www.it .murdoch.edu.au/~sudweeks/b329/readings/ mcsweeney.doc

Miller, C. M. (2003, March). Are antidepressants placebos? *Harvard Mental Health Letter, 19*(9).

Miller, G. (2003, March). The cognitive revolution: A historical perspective. *Trends in Cognitive Sciences, 17*(3), 141–144.

Miller, P., Fung, H., & Koven, M. (2007). Narrative reverberations: how participation in narrative practices co-creates persons and cultures. In S. Kitayama, & D. Cohen (Eds.), *Handbook of cultural psychology.* New York: The Guilford Press.

Moll, H., & Tomasello, M. (2007). Cooperation and human cognition: The Vygotskian intelligence hypothesis. *Philosophical Transactions of the Royal Society.* Retrieved September 5, 2008, from http://email.eva .mpg.de/~tomas/pdf/Moll_PhilersTransact_07.pdf

Moran, M. (2005). Short-term psychodynamic therapy found effective in several disorders. *Psychiatric News, 40*(2), 53.

National Institute of Mental Health (2008a). *Depression.* Retrieved from http://www.nimh.nih.gov/

National Institute of Mental Health (2008b). *Men and depression.* Retrieved from http://www.nimh.nih.gov/

Neisser, U. (2000). Snapshots or benchmarks? In U. Neisser, & I. E. Hyman (Eds.), *Memory observed: Remembering in natural contexts* (2nd ed.). New York: Worth Publishers.

Neisser, U., & Harsch, N. (2000). Phantom flashbulbs. In U. Neisser, & I. E. Hyman (Eds.), *Memory observed: Remembering in natural contexts* (2nd ed.). New York: Worth Publishers.

Newsone, L., Richerson, P. J., & Boyd, R. (2007). Cultural evolution and the shaping of cultural diversity. In S. Kitayama, & D. Cohen (Eds.), *Handbook of cultural psychology.* New York: The Guilford Press.

Niemi, M. (2009). Cure in the mind. *Scientific American Mind, 20*(1), 42–49.

Nolan-Hoeksema, S. (2004). Gender differences in depression. In T. F. Oltmanns, & R. E. Emery (Eds.), *Current directions in abnormal psychology.* Upper Saddle River, NJ: Pearson Prentice Hall.

Okello, E. S., & Ekblad, S. (2006) Lay concepts of depression among the Baganda of Uganda: A pilot study.

*Transcultural Psychiatry, 43*(2), 287–313. Retrieved October 1, 2008, from http://www.sagepub.com

Parker, G., Gladstone, G., & Chee, Q. T. (2001). Depression in the planet's largest ethnic group: The Chinese. *American Journal of Psychiatry, 158,* 857–864. Retrieved September 30, 2008, from http://ajp.psychiatryonline/ cgi/content/reprint/158/6/857

Peele, S., & DeGrandpre, R. (1995, July). My genes made me do it. *Psychology Today, 28.* Retrieved February 4, 2005, from http://www.questia.com

Peterson, T. J. (2006). Enhancing the effects of antidepressants with psychotherapy. *Journal of Psychopharmacology, 20*(3), 19–28.

Petrova, P. K., Cialdini, R. B., & Sills, S. J. (2007). Consistency-based compliance across cultures. *Journal of Experimental Social Psychology, 43,* 104–111.

Phelps, E. A., O'Connor, K. J., Gatenby, C., Grillon, C., & Davis, M. (2001). Activation of the left amygdala to a cognitive representation of fear. *Neuroscience, 4*(4). Retrieved August 15, 2008, from http://neurosci.nature.com

Pinker, S. (1994). *The language instinct: How the mind creates language.* New York: HarperCollins.

Pinker, S. (2002). *The blank slate: The modern denial of human nature.* New York: Penguin Books.

Porvinelli, D. J., & O'Neill, D. K. (2000). Do chimpanzees use their gestures to instruct each other? In S. Baron-Cohen, H. Tager-Flushberg, & D. J. Cohen (Eds.), *Understanding other minds: Perspectives from developmental cognitive neuroscience* (2nd ed.). Oxford: Oxford University Press.

Price, D. D., Finniss, D. G, & Benedetti, F. (2008). A comprehensive review of the placebo effect: Recent advances and current thought. *Annual Review of Neuroscience, 59,* 2.1–2.6.

Raine, A. (2002). Biosocial studies of antisocial and violent behavior in children and adults: A review. *Journal of Abnormal Child Psychology, 30*(4), 311–326. Retrieved November 12, 2008, from http://findarticles.com/p/ articles/mi_0902/is_4_30?ai_89146368

Ramachandran V. S. (no date). *Mirror neurons and imitation learning as the driving force behind "the great leap forward" in human evolution.* Retrieved May 8, 2008, from http://www.edge.org/3rd_culture/ramachandran/ ramachandran_p1.html

Ramachandran, V. S. (1998). *Phantoms in the brain.* New York: HarperCollins.

Randazzo, A. C., Muehlbach, M. J., Schweitzer, P. K., & Walsh, J. K. (1998, December 15). Cognitive function following acute sleep restriction in children ages 10–14. *Sleep, 2*(8), 861–868. Retrieved December 30, 2007, from http://www.pubmed.com

Rappa, L. R., Larose-Pierre, M., Branch, E., Iglesias, A. J., Norwood, D. A., & Simon, W. A. (2001). Desperately seeking serendipity: The past, present, and future of antidepressant therapy. *Journal of Pharmacy Practice, 14,* 560. Retrieved October 10, 2008, from http://www.sagepub.com

Riggs, J. M., & Gumbrecht, L. B. (2005). Correspondence bias and American sentiment in the wake of September 11, 2001. *Journal of Applied Social Psychology, 35*(1), 15–28. Retrieved April 2, 2008, from http://www.ingentaconnect.com.

Rogers, C. (1961). *On becoming a person.* Boston: Houghton-Mifflin.

Sabbagh, L. (2006, August/September). The teenage brain hard at work: No, really. *Scientific American Mind, 17*(4), 20–25.

Sapolsky, R. M. (2004). *Why zebras don't get ulcers* (3rd ed.). New York: Henry Holt and Company.

Saxe, R., & Wexler, A. (2005). Making sense of another mind: The role of the right temporo-parietal junction. *Neuropsychologia.* Retrieved September 16, 2008, from http://www.elsevier.com/locate/neuropsychologia.com

Schnyer, R. N., & Flaws, B. (1998). *Curing depression naturally with Chinese medicine.* Boulder, CO: Blue Poppy Press.

Scorzelli, J. F. (2001). Cultural sensitivity and cognitive therapy in Thailand. *Journal of Mental Health Counseling, 23*(1), 85–92. Retrieved December 11, 2008, from http://findarticles.com

Sjoberg, R. L., Ducci, F., Barr, C. S., Newman, T. K., Dell'Osso, L., Virkkunen, M., & Goldman, D. (2008). A non-additive interaction of a functional MAO-AVNTR and testosterone predicts antisocial behavior. *Neuropsychopharmacology, 33,* 425–430.

Skinner, B. F. (1985). *A matter of consequences.* New York: New York University Press.

Skinner, B. F. (1989). *Recent issues in the analysis of behavior.* Columbus, OH: Merrill Publishing.

Slater, L. (1999). *Prozac diary.* New York: Penguin Books. Additional information retrieved from http://www.us.penguingroup.com/static/rguides/us/prozac_diary.html

Slobin, D. I. (1968). Imitation and Grammatical Development in Children. In A. Bandura (Ed.), *Psychological modeling: Conflicting theories* (1971). New Brunswick, NJ: Transaction Publishers. (Reprinted from Endler, N. S., Boulter, L. R., & Osser, H. (1968). *Contemporary issues in developmental psychology.* New York: Holt, Reinhart, & Winston.)

Small, G., & Vorgan, G. (2008). Meet your iBrain: How the technologies that have become part of our daily lives are changing the way we think. *Scientific American Mind, 19*(5), 42–49.

Somer, E. (1999). *Food & mood* (2nd ed.). New York: Henry Holt & Company.

Southgate, L., Tchanturia, K., & Treasure, J. (2008). Information processing bias in anorexia nervosa. *Psychiatry Research, 160,* 221–227.

Steinberg, L. (2008, January). *Inside the adolescent brain.* Paper presented at the meeting of the National Institute for the Teaching of Psychology, St. Pete Beach, FL.

Sternberg, R. (2006). *Cognitive psychology* (4th ed.). Belmont, CA: Wadsworth/Thomson Learning.

Tabassum, R., Macaskill, A., & Ahmad, I. (2000). Attitudes toward mental health in an urban Pakistani community in the United Kingdom. *International Journal of Social Psychiatry, 46*(3), 170–181. Retrieved November 9, 2007, from http://isp.sagepub.com

Takano, Y., & Sogon, S. (2008). Are Japanese more collectivist than Americans? Examining conformity in ingroups and the reference group effect. *Journal of Cross-Cultural Psychology, 30*(3), 237–250.

Tang, Y., Zhang, W., Chen, K., Feng, S., Shen, J., Reiman, E. M, & Liu, Y. (2006). Arithmetic processing in the brain shaped by cultures. *Proceedings of the National Academy of Sciences of the United States of America, 103*(28), 10775–10780. Retrieved May 5, 2006, from http://www.pnas.org

Tavris, C., & Wade, C. (2001). *Psychology in perspective* (3rd ed.). Upper Saddle River, NJ: Prentice Hall.

Teasdale, J. D., Segal, Z. V., Williams, J. M. G., Ridgeway, V. A., Soulsby, J. M., & Lau, M. A. (2000). Prevention of relapse/recurrence in major depression by mindfulness-based cognitive therapy. *Journal of Consulting and Clinical Psychology, 68*(4), 615–623. Retrieved January 20, 2009, from http://www.mbct.com

Tomasello, M. (2004). Culture and cognitive development. In J. Lerner, & A. Alberts (Eds.), *Current directions in developmental psychology.* Upper Saddle River, NJ: Pearson Prentice Hall.

Triandis, H. (1994). *Culture and social behavior.* New York: McGraw-Hill.

Triandis, H. (2007). Culture and psychology: a history of the study of their relationship. In S. Kitayama & D. Cohen (Eds.), *Handbook of cross-cultural psychology.* New York: The Guilford Press.

Triandis, H. C. (1995). *Individualism and collectivism.* Boulder, CO: Westview Press.

Triandis, H. C. (1999). Cross-cultural psychology. *Asian Journal of Social Psychology, 2,* 127–143. Retrieved August 15, 2005, from http://www.sinica.edu.tw/~kuoshu/people/Triandis/harry_triandis.htm

Triandis, H. C., & Suh, E. M. (2002). Cultural influences on personality. *Annual Review Psychology, 53,* 133–160.

Toman, W. (1976). *Family constellation: Its effects on personality and social behavior* (3rd ed.). New York: Springer.

Truax, P. (2001). Review: Group psychotherapy is effective for depression. *Evidence-Based Mental Health, 4*(82). Retrieved November 12, 2008, from http://ebmh.bmj.com/

Turner, E. H., Matthew, A. M., Linardatos, E., Tell, R. A., & Rosenthal, R. (2008, January 17). Selective publication of antidepressant trials and its influence on apparent efficacy. *The New England Journal of Medicine, 358,* 252–260.

Vernes, S. C., Newbury, D. F., Abrahams, B. S., Winchester, L., Nicod, J., Grozer, M., Alarcon, M., Oliver, P. L., Davies, K. E., Geschwind, D. H., Monaco, A. P., & Fisher, S. E. (2008). A functional genetic link between distinct developmental language disorders. *The New England Journal of Medicine, 359,* 2337–2345.

Vygotsky, L. (1934). *Thought and language.* Cambridge: The MIT Press.

Vygotsky, L. (1978). *Mind and society.* Cambridge: Harvard University Press.

Walker, E. (2001). *Stress, genes and the brain: What our students should know about psychology and neuroscience.* Paper presented at the meeting of the National Institute for the Teaching of Psychology, St. Pete Beach, FL.

Walker, E., & Tessner, K. (2008). Schizophrenia. *Perspectives on Psychological Science, 3*(1), 30–37.

Wang, Q. (2007). "Remember when you got the big, big bulldozer?" Mother-child reminiscing over time and across cultures. *Social Cognition, 25*(4), 455–471.

Wang, Q., & Aydin, C. (2009). Cultural issues in flashbulb memory. In O. Luminet, & A. Curci (Eds.), *Flashbulb memories: New issues and perspectives.* Hove and New York: Psychology Press.

Werner, E. E. (2005). Resilience in development. In C. L. Morf, & O. Ayduk (Eds.), *Current directions in personality psychology.* Upper Saddle River, NJ: Pearson Prentice Hall.

Weston, D., & Bradley, R. (2005). Empirically supported complexity: Rethinking evidence-based practice in psychotherapy. *Current Directions in Psychological Science, 14*(5).

Wilhelm, I., Diekelmann, S., & Born, J. (2008). Sleep in children improves memory performance on declarative but not procedural tasks. *Learning & Memory, 15,* 373–377.

Wolfe, H. L. (2005). *Acupuncture and depression.* Retrieved August 31, 2008, from http://www.bluepoppy.com

Wolfson, A. R., & Carskadon, M. A. (1998). Sleep schedules and daytime functioning in adolescents. *Child Development, 69*(4), 875–887. Retrieved from http://www.jstor.org, 12/30/2007

World Health Organization (2001). *World Health Report, 2001.* Retrieved from http://www.who.org

World Health Organization (2004). Prevalence, severity, and unmet need for treatment of mental disorders in the World Health Organization world mental health surveys. *Journal of the American Medical Association, 291*(21). Retrieved October 8, 2008, from http://www.jama.com

Wright, D. B., Boyd, C. E., & Tredoux, C. G. (2001). A field study of own-race bias in South Africa and England. *Psychology, Public Policy, and Law, 7*(1), 119–133. Retrieved May 12, 2008, from http://web.uct.ac.za/depts/psychology/plato/wright.pdf

Wrightsman, L. S., Greene, E., Nietzel, M. T., & Fortune, W. H. (2002). *Psychology and the legal system* (5th ed.). Belmont, CA: Wadsworth.

Yuki, M. (2003). Intergroup comparison versus intragroup relationships: a cross-cultural examination of social identity theory in North America and East Asian cultural contexts. *Social Psychology Quarterly, 66*(2), 166–183. Retrieved May 29, 2008, from http://www.jstor.org

Yuki, M., Maddux, W. W., Brewer, M. B., & Takemura, K. (2005). Cross-cultural differences in relationship- and group-based trust. *Personality and Social Psychology Bulletin, 31*(1), 48–62. Retrieved May 29, 2008, from http://psp.sagepub.org

Zimbardo, P. (2007). *The Lucifer effect.* New York: Random House.

Zinbarg, R. E., & Mineka, S. (2000, January). *Animal models of anxiety disorders.* Paper presented at the meeting of the National Institute for the Teaching of Psychology, St. Pete Beach, FL.

# Index